Human-Computer Interaction Series

T0142872

Human-Computer Interaction is a multidisciplinary field focused on human aspects of the development of computer technology. As computer-based technology becomes increasingly pervasive - not just in developed countries, but worldwide - the need to take a human-centered approach in the design and development of this technology becomes ever more important. For roughly 30 years now, researchers and practitioners in computational and behavioral sciences have worked to identify theory and practice that influences the direction of these technologies, and this diverse work makes up the field of human-computer interaction. Broadly speaking it includes the study of what technology might be able to do for people and how people might interact with the technology.

In this series we present work which advances the science and technology of developing systems which are both effective and satisfying for people in a wide variety of contexts. The human-computer interaction series will focus on theoretical perspectives (such as formal approaches drawn from a variety of behavioral sciences), practical approaches (such as the techniques for effectively integrating user needs in system development), and social issues (such as the determinants of utility, usability and acceptability).

Author guidelines: springer.com > Authors > Author Guidelines

Also in this series

Gill, S. (Ed.)
Cognition, Communication and Interaction –
Transdisciplinary Perspectives on Interactive
Technology
ISBN 978-1-84628-926-2, 2008

Law, E., Hvannberg, E., Cockton, G. (Eds.)
Maturing Usability – Quality in Software,
Interaction and Value
ISBN 978-1-84628-940-8, 2008

Lieberman, H., Paternò, F., Wulf, V. (Eds.)
End User Development
Vol. 9, ISBN 978-1-4020-4220-1, 2006

Lieberman, H., Paternò, F., Wulf, V. (Eds.)
End User Development
Vol. 9, ISBN 978-1-4020-5309-2, 2006 (softcover)

Seffah, A., Gulliksen, J., Desmarais, M.C. (Eds.)
Human-Centred Software Engineering –
Integrating Usability in the Software Development
Lifecycle
Vol. 8, ISBN 978-1-4020-4027-6, 2005

Ruttkay, Z., Pelachaud, C., (Eds.)
From Brows to Trust – Evaluating Embodied
Conservational Agents
Vol. 7, ISBN 978-1-4020-2729-1, 2004

Ardissono, L., Kobsa, A., Maybury, M.T. (Eds.)
Personalized Digital Television – Targeting
Programs to Individual Viewers
Vol. 6, ISBN 978-1-4020-2147-3, 2004

Karat, C.-M., Blom, J.O., Karat, J. (Eds.)
Designing Personalized User Experiences in
eCommerce
Vol. 5, ISBN 978-1-4020-2147-3, 2004

Ivory, M.Y.
Automating Web Site Evaluation – Researchers'
and Practitioners' Perspectives
Vol. 4, ISBN 978-1-4020-1672-1, 2004

Blythe, M.A., Overbeeke, K., Monk, A.F., (et al.)
(Eds.)
Funology – From Usability to Enjoyment
Vol. 3, ISBN 978-1-4020-2966-0, 2004 (softcover)

Blythe, M.A., Overbeeke, K., Monk, A.F., (et al.)
(Eds.)
Funology – From Usability to Enjoyment
Vol. 3, ISBN 978-1-4020-1252-5, 2003

Schreck, J.
Security and Privacy in User Modeling
Vol. 2, ISBN 978-1-4020-1130-6, 2003

Chi, E.H.
A Framework for Visualizing Information
Vol 1, ISBN 978-1-4020-0589-2, 2002

Gustavo Rossi • Oscar Pastor • Daniel Schwabe •
Luis Olsina
Editors

Web Engineering: Modelling and Implementing Web Applications

 Springer

Gustavo Rossi
Technical University of Valencia
Valencia, Spain

Daniel Schwabe
PUC-Rio
Brazil

Oscar Pastor
Technical University of Valencia
Valencia, Spain

Luis Olsina
National University of La Pampa
Argentina

British Library Cataloguing in Publication Data
A catalogue record for this book is available from the British Library

Human-Computer Interaction Series ISSN 1571-5035
ISBN: 978-1-84996-677-1   e-ISBN: 978-1-84628-923-1

Printed on acid-free paper

9 8 7 6 5 4 3 2 1

Springer Science+Business Media
springer.com

PREFACE

In this first part of the 21st century, a large portion of the global data infrastructure is built upon World Wide Web technology. This network of data users and providers has become as critical a part of our everyday lives as those networks that provide our electrical power and communications. We are informed, educated, and entertained by Web applications and services. The Web provides us with an international mall where we can shop for every imaginable item.

This infrastructure is held together by a complex interconnection of hardware, software, international standards, aesthetics, and accepted practices. Its intricacy is not unlike that found in the engineering and design of highway systems, buildings, and bridges. To address the growth of Web systems and to ensure their efficiency, reliability, and maintainability, the discipline of Web Engineering was defined. Web Engineering combines traditional project management and software development practices with a process that will evolve just as Web technology evolves into the future via such innovations as the Semantic Web and Web 2.0.

Modeling and Implementing Web Application is a definitive book on all of the crucial elements of Web Engineering by the international researchers and practitioners who are shaping the discipline. There is no other book available at this time that covers Web Engineering so comprehensively. As the field evolves, this book will certainly always be viewed as a fundamental reference. Its completeness illustrates the premise that Web Engineering is an important and critical engineering practice for designing, implementing, and maintaining Web services and applications. The book will provide a valuable resource for Web professionals, researchers, and students at the undergraduate and graduate levels.

Bebo White
Stanford Linear Accelerator Center (SLAC)
Stanford, California
April 2007

CONTENTS

Part III: Quality Evaluation and Experimental Web Engineering

LIST OF CONTRIBUTORS

Peter Barna
Technische Universiteit
Eindhoven, PO Box 513, 5600
MB Eindhoven, The Netherlands
Email: *p.barna@tue.nl*

Hubert Baumeister
Informatik og Matematisk
Modellering, Danmarks Tekniske
Universitet, Lyngby, Denmark
Email: *hub@imm.dtu.dk*

Davide Bolchini
TEC-Lab, Faculty of
Communication Sciences,
University of Lugano, Via G.
Buffi 13 6900 Lugano,
Switzerland
Email: *davide.bolchini@lu.unisi.ch*

Marco Brambilla
Dipartimento di Elettronica e
Informazione, Politecnico di
Milano, P.zza L. da Vinci 32,
20133, Milano, Italy
Email: *mbrambil@elet.polimi.it*

Jeen Broekstra
Technische Universiteit
Eindhoven, PO Box 513, 5600
MB Eindhoven, The Netherlands;
and Aduna, Prinses Julianaplein
14b, 3817 CS Amersfoort,
The Netherlands
Email: *j.broekstra@tue.nl*

Sven Casteleyn
Vrije Universiteit Brussel,
Pleinlaan 2, 1050 Brussels,
Belgium
Email: *Sven.Casteleyn@vub.ac.be*

Sara Comai
Dipartimento di Elettronica e
Informazione, Politecnico di
Milano, Piazza L. da Vinci 32,
20133, Milano, Italy
Email: *sara.comai@polimi.it*

Olga De Troyer
Research Group WISE,
Department of Computer Science,
Vrije Universiteit Brussel,
Pleinlaan 2, 1050 Brussel,
Belgium
Email: *Olga.DeTroyer@vub.ac.be*

Zoltán Fiala
Technische Universität Dresden,
Mommsenstr. 13, D-01062,
Dresden, Germany
Email: *zoltan.fiala@inf.
tu-dresden.de*

Joan Fons
Research Group OO-Method
Department of Information
Systems and Computation,
Valencia University of
Technology, Camí de Vera s/n,
E-46022, Valencia, Spain
Email: *jjfons@dsic.upv.es*

Flavius Frasincar
Erasmus Universiteit Rotterdam,
PO Box 1738, 3000 DR
Rotterdam, The Netherlands
Email: *frasincar@few.eur.nl*

Piero Fraternali
Dipartimento di Elettronica e
Informazione, Politecnico di
Milano, P.zza L. da Vinci 32,
20133, Milano, Italy
Email: *fraterna@elet.polimi.it*

Martin Gaedke
Chemnitz University of
Technology, Faculty of Computer
Science, Distributed and
Self-Organizing Systems Group,
Straße der Nationen 62,
09111 Chemnitz, Germany
Email: *martin.gaedke@informatik.
tu-chemnitz.de*

Franca Garzotto
HOC (Hypermedia Open Centre),
Department of Information and
Electronics, Politecnico di
Milano, Milan, Italy
Email: *garzotto@elet.polimi.it*

Geert-Jan Houben
Technische Universiteit Eindhoven,
PO Box 513, 5600 MB Eindhoven,
The Netherlands; and Vrije
Universiteit Brussel, Pleinlaan 2,
1050 Brussels, Belgium
Email: *Geert-
Jan.Houben@vub.ac.be*

Alexander Knapp
Institut für Informatik, Ludwig-
Maximilians-Universität
München, Munich, Germany
Email: *knapp@pst.ifi.lmu.de*

Nora Koch
Institut fur Informatik,
Ludwig-Maximilians-Universität
München, and F.A.S.T. GmbH,
Munich, Germany
Email: *kochn@pst.ifi.lmu.de*

Maristella Matera
Dipartimento di Elettronica e
Informazione, Politecnico di
Milano, Pizza L. da Vinci 32,
20133, Milano, Italy
Email: *matera@elet.polimi.it*

Johannes Meinecke
Chemnitz University of
Technology, Faculty of Computer
Science, Distributed and
Self-Organizing Systems Group,
Straße der Nationen 62,
09111 Chemnitz, Germany
Email: *johannes.meinecke@informatik
.tu-chemnitz.de*

Emilia Mendes
WETA Research Group,
Computer Science Department,
The University of Auckland,
Private Bag 92019, Auckland,
New Zealand
Email: *emilia@cs.auckland.ac.nz*

Hernán Molina
GIDIS_Web, Engineering School,
Universidad Nacional de La
Pampa, Calle 9 y 110, (6360)
General Pico, LP, Argentina
Email:
hmolina@ing.unlpam.edu.ar

Nathalie Moreno
Dept. Lenguajes y Ciencias de la
Computación, University of
Málaga, Málaga, Spain
Email: *vergara@lcc.uma.es*

San Murugesan
Southern Cross University, Coffs
Harbour NSW 2452, Australia
Email: *san.murugesan@scu.edu.au*

Luis Olsina
GIDIS_Web, Engineering School,
Universidad Nacional de La
Pampa, Calle 9 y 110, (6360)
General Pico, LP, Argentina
Email: *olsinal@ing.unlpam.edu.ar*

Fernanda Papa
GIDIS_Web, Engineering School,
Universidad Nacional de La
Pampa, Calle 9 y 110, (6360)
General Pico, LP, Argentina
Email: *pmfer@ing.unlpam.edu.ar*

Oscar Pastor
Research Group OO-Method,
Department of Information
Systems and Computation,
Valencia University of
Technology, Camí de Vera s/n,
E-46022, Valencia, Spain
Email: *opastor@dsic.upv.es*

Vicente Pelechano
Research Group OO-Method,
Department of Information
Systems and Computation.
Valencia University of
Technology, Camí de Vera s/n,
E-46022, Valencia, Spain
Email: *pele@dsic.upv.es*

Peter Plessers
Research Group WISE, Department
of Computer Science, Vrije
Universiteit Brussel, Pleinlaan 2,
1050 Brussel, Belgium
Email: *Peter.Plessers@vub.ac.be*

José Raúl Romero
Dept. Informática y Análisis
Numérico, University of Córdoba,
Cordoba, Spain
Email: *jrromero@uco.es*

Gustavo Rossi
LIFIA, Facultad de Informatica,
Universidad Nacional de La Plata,
Calle 5° y 115, La Plata,
Argentina and Conicet
Email:
gustavo@lifia.info.unlp.edu.ar

Daniel Schwabe
Departamento de Informática,
PUC-Rio, Rua Marquês de São
Vicente, 225 RDC
CEP 22453-900 Gávea Rio de
Janeiro, Brazil
Email: *dschwabe@inf.puc-rio.br*

Victoria Torres
Research Group OO-Method,
Department of Information
Systems and Computation,
Valencia University of
Technology, Camí de Vera s/n,
E-46022, Valencia, Spain
Email: *vtorres@dsic.upv.es*

Pedro Valderas
Research Group OO-Method,
Department of Information
Systems and Computation,
Valencia University of
Technology, Camí de Vera s/n,
E-46022, Valencia, Spain
Email: *pvalderas@dsic.upv.es*

Antonio Vallecillo
Dept. Lenguajes y Ciencias de la
Computación, University of
Málaga, Málaga, Spain
Email: *av@lcc.uma.es*

Kees van der Sluijs
Technische Universiteit
Eindhoven, PO Box 513, 5600
MB Eindhoven, The Netherlands
Email: *k.a.m.sluijs@tue.nl*

Gefei Zhang
Institut für Informatik,
Ludwig-Maximilians-Universität
München, Munich, Germany
Email: *zhangg@pst.ifi.lmu.de*

PART I

WEB ENGINEERING AND WEB APPLICATIONS DEVELOPMENT

Chapter 1

INTRODUCTION

Gustavo Rossi[1], Daniel Schwabe[2], Luis Olsina[3], Oscar Pastor[4]

[1]LIFIA, Facultad de Informatica, Universidad Nacional de La Plata (also at CONICET) Argentina, gustavo@lifia.info.unlp.edu.ar

[2]Departamento de Informática, PUC-Rio, Rio de Janeiro, Brazil, dschwabe@inf.puc-rio.br

[3]GIDIS_Web, Engineering School, Universidad Nacional de La Pampa, Calle 9 y 110, (6360) General Pico, LP, Argentina, olsina1@ing.unlpam.edu.ar

[4]DSIC, Valencia University of Technology, Valencia, Spain, opastor@dsic.upv.es

This book presents the major Web application design methods currently being developed and used in both academia and industry. The book is the main result of the IWWOST (International Workshop on Web-Oriented Software Technology) series, celebrated under the auspices of the WEST project, sponsored by CYTED (a Spanish organization supporting research and development in Ibero-America).

Since 2001, IWWOST has been an international forum for discussing state of-the-art modeling approaches, methods, and technologies for Web applications. The first workshop was held in Valencia, Spain, in 2001; the second in Malaga, Spain, together with the European Conference on Object-Oriented Programming (ECOOP) in 2002; the third in Oviedo, Spain; and the fourth in Munich, Germany [both co-located with the International Conference on Web Engineering (ICWE) in 2003 and 2004, respectively]. The fifth was organized in Porto, Portugal, in the context of the International Conference on Advanced Information Systems Engineering-CAiSE 2005. Finally, in 2007 IWWOST went back to ICWE, in Como, Italy.

At the same time, many of the authors of this book got involved in the Web Engineering Network of Excellence (WEE-NET), a project funded by the European Commission under the ALFA program, which provided invaluable support for research and students meetings following the spirit of IWWOST. The project itself was another source of inspiration for the book's contents.

These workshops and meetings were historically organized in order to stimulate a discussion and an exchange of ideas and experiences. They were conceived as a place for methodologists, designers, and developers to meet and exchange their experiences in the process of building complex Web applications. Usually, all participants received a problem statement of a typical, nontrivial, Web application and were asked to fully design and, if possible, implement this application using their proposed methods.

In the workshop each group presented its solution, which was compared with other solutions and discussed among all participants. During these discussions a large number of issues that must be addressed by design methods were raised. In this way, IWWOST attendees could compare their own approaches with other colleagues', and they could discuss strengths and weaknesses of each approach, following a very fruitful theoretical and practical approach.

In the same spirit, we have put this idea into this book, presenting a common problem, selecting the most widely known methods dealing with Web Engineering issues, and asking the authors to work on this same problem from their different points of view, each supported by their own methods or design approaches.

With this strategy in mind, our objective is to provide a practical book where both students and practitioners can find a precise view on how the different approaches work and provide their corresponding solutions. We do not intend to provide new cutting-edge technical solutions but rather mature, consolidated approaches to develop complex applications.

To make the book a complete handbook on Web Engineering issues and techniques, we have included a set of chapters that address different aspects of the engineering endeavor.

The book is divided into three parts and is organized as follows. The first part contains two chapters in addition to this one: Chapter 2 by San Murugesan describes the evolution of the Web and introduces the discipline of Web Engineering. Chapter 3 by Martin Gaedke and Johannes Meinecke discusses the Web as a platform for application development, focusing in particular on distributed applications.

Part II focuses on development approaches, emphasizing design methods: Chapter 4 by Gustavo Rossi, Daniel Schwabe, Luis Olsina, and Oscar Pastor presents the most important issues Web design methods must consider and introduces the common problem to be solved. Chapter 5 by Joan Fons, Vicente Pelechano, Oscar Pastor, Pedro Valderas and Victoria Torres presents the Object-Oriented Web Solutions Approach (OOWS). Chapter 6 by Gustavo Rossi and Daniel Schwabe focuses on the use of the Object-Oriented Hypermedia Design Model (OOHDM). Chapter 7 by Nora Koch, Alexander Knapp, Gefei Zhang and Hubert Baumeister discusses the

UML-based Web Engineering approach (UWE). Chapter 8 by Davide Bolchini and Franca Garzotto presents the Interactive Dialogue Model (IDM) approach. Chapter 9 by Marco Brambilla, Sara Comai, Piero Fraternali, and Maristella Matera presents WebML, the Web Modeling Language. Chapter 10 by Geert-Jan Houben, Kees van der Sluijs, Peter Barna, Jeen Broekstra, Sven Casteleyn, Zoltán Fiala, and Flavius Frasincar presents a solution to the problem using Hera. Chapter 11 by Olga De Troyer, Sven Casteleyn, and Peter Plessers introduces the Web Semantic Design Method (WSDM) Finally in Chapter 12, Nathalie Moreno, José Raúl Romero, and Antonio Vallecillo discuss the concept of model-driven Web Engineering.

Part III deals with quality evaluation and experimental Web Engineering and the book's conclusions. It contains three chapters: Chapter 13 by Luis Olsina, Fernanda Papa, and Hernán Molina analyzes the problem of measurement and evaluation of Web software. Chapter 14 by Emilia Mendes discusses empirical methods for Web Engineering. Finally, in Chapter 15, Oscar Pastor, Gustavo Rossi, Luis Olsina, and Daniel Schwabe summarize the book and present some conclusions.

We hope you will enjoy the reading of this book as much as we enjoyed the process of writing and editing it.

Chapter 2

WEB APPLICATION DEVELOPMENT: CHALLENGES AND THE ROLE OF WEB ENGINEERING

San Murugesan
University of Western Sydney, Sydney, Australia, `san1@internode.on.net`

2.1 INTRODUCTION

The World Wide Web, more commonly known as the Web, is increasingly pervading every aspect of our lives. In the 15 years since the Web came into existence, our lives and work have been inexorably changed. It has dramatically influenced us in several ways and has matured to become a very attractive and dominant platform for deploying business and social applications and organizational information systems. It has also become a universal user interface to business applications, information systems, databases, and legacy systems. It supports document and workflow management, cooperative work, and distributed knowledge and media (photo, audio, and video) sharing.

The growth of the Web has been exponential. A recent estimate put the size of the public Web at 40 billion pages, and the size of the "deep Web"—where the pages are assembled on the fly in response to users' request—between 400 and 750 billion pages. The interaction between a Web system and its back-end information systems, as well as with other Web systems, has become tighter and complex. Many organizations have extended, and still continue to extend, the scope and functionalities of their Web-based applications and are also beginning to provide mobile and wireless access to them. As a result, Web-based systems and applications now offer an array of content and functionality to a huge population of users and serve many different purposes. The Web has become a mainstay, and it is perhaps appropriate to say that our civilization "runs" on the Web as individuals, organizations, and nations rely on a multitude of Web-based systems.

The Web, and the Internet that supports it, has become one of the most important and most influential developments not only in computing history but in the history of mankind. For instance, Web sites such as google.com, yahoo.com, myspace.com, wikipedia.org, amazon.com, ebay.com, youtube.com, napster.com, blogger.com, and saloon.com are considered as the top 10 Web sites (in no particular order) that changed the world (Naughton, 2006). Some of these sites have over 100 million users (myspace.com, ebay.com, yahoo.com), about 1 billion visits a day (wikipedia.org), and over 1 billion searches per day (google.com).

Users expect Web applications to be more usable, more reliable, and more secure, personalized, and context-aware. As our dependence and reliance on Web-based applications have increased dramatically over the years, performance, reliability, quality, maintainability, and scalability of Web applications have become paramount importance. And most Web-based systems are tightly integrated with other, traditional information systems such as databases and transaction processing systems. Some of the newer applications are also linked with other Web applications/services that facilitate information exchange. As a result, the design, development, deployment, and maintenance of Web-based applications have become inherently complex and challenging. The complexity of Web-based systems is, however, not apparent, as the Web interface presents an illusion of simplicity by hiding the complexity.

But most Web developers don't recognize and take into consideration many multifaceted, unique requirements of Web applications. They also fail to recognize that characteristics and requirements of Web-based systems significantly differ from traditional software, and so does their development. They need to recognize these differences and take appropriate measures to fulfill the unique requirements of Web applications.

But many developers and their clients still continue to view Web development as just simple Web page creation using HTML or Web development software such as *Front Page* and *Dreamweaver*, embodying few images and hyperlinking documents and Web pages, or as Internet/Web programming (scripting). They overlook system-level requirements and key design considerations and don't make use of Web design and development methodologies and processes. Further, they also mistakenly carry out Web systems' development in the same manner as software development. Many Web development projects are carried out in ad hoc manner and fail to adopt sound design methodologies, resulting in poor design of Web systems. As a consequence, they fail to successfully and effectively develop Web-based systems that are complex and/or demand high performance.

Of course, there is more to Web application development than visual design and user interface. It involves planning, selection of an appropriate Web architecture, system design, page design, coding, content creation and its maintenance, testing, quality assurance, and performance evaluation. It also involves continual update and maintenance of the Web system as the requirements change, new functionalities are introduced, and usage grow, as well as post-launch operational review of the system.

To successfully build complex Web-based systems and applications, both large and small, Web developers need to adopt a disciplined development process and sound design methodologies and use better development tools.

The discipline of Web Engineering advocates a holistic, disciplined approach to successful Web development, taking into account the unique characteristics and requirements of Web-based systems. Web Engineering "uses scientific, engineering, and management principles and systematic approaches to successfully develop, deploy, and maintain high-quality Web systems and applications" (Murugesan et al., 1999). The essence of Web Engineering is to successfully manage the diversity and complexity of Web application development and, hence, avoid potential failures that could have serious implications.

Web Engineering is receiving greater interest and significance as Web-based systems become mainstream and we increasingly rely on them. While Web Engineering shares with software engineering some common objectives, goals, and general principles and, where appropriate, adopts soft engineering techniques, it is aimed at addressing characteristics and requirements that are unique to Web applications.

This book comprehensively deals with a key aspect of Web Engineering — design of Web systems and applications. It describes various Web design methodologies that developers could use, such as OOHDM and the OO method, and illustrates them using one common example.

This chapter outlines the role of Web Engineering in the design and development of Web applications. It traces the evolution of Web applications and discusses key challenges in developing Web applications as well as some of the key aspects that differentiate development of Web applications from other types of software or computer applications. It also examines the problems and limitations of current Web development practices and their implications and provides an overview of Web Engineering. It then briefly describes key elements of Web Engineering processes and discusses the role of Web design in successful Web application development.

2.2 EVOLUTION OF THE WEB
   ## AND WEB APPLICATIONS

The Web has evolved beyond anyone's imagination within a short span of 15 years, since Tim Berners-Lee conceived and publicized, on August 6, 1991, a system for turning the Internet into a publishing medium for sharing and dissemination of scientific data and information, which he called the "World Wide Web." It has become indispensable and essential to many people and organizations around the world.

The evolution of the Web has brought together some disparate disciplines such as media, information science, and information and communication technology, facilitating the easy creation, maintenance, sharing, and use of different types of information from anywhere, any time, and using a variety of devices such as desktop and notebook computers, pocket PCs, personal digital assistants (PDAs), and mobile phones.

The evolution of the Web could be traced and discussed along a few different dimensions and from a few different perspectives: the growth (number) of Web sites and Web pages; the number of Web users; the number of Web visits; the functionality and interactivity that Web applications offer; the technologies used for the creation of Web applications; the social and business impact of the Web; or a combination of these.

While the scope of this chapter is not to comprehensively discuss the evolution, in the context of Web design, it is helpful to classify Web systems and applications based on their key features and technology used for their creation as follows (see Figure 2.1):

1. the Shallow Web (Static Web)
2. the Deep Web (Dynamic Web)
3. the Wisdom Web (Web 2.0)
4. the Mobile Web
5. the Semantic Web

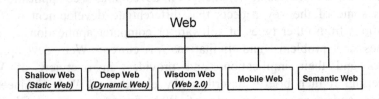

Figure 2.1. Classification of the Web.

2.2.1 Web 1.0

The Shallow Web, also known as the Static Web, is primarily a collection of static HTML Web pages providing information about products or services offered. To start with, most Web sites were just a collection of static Web pages. After a while, the Web became dynamic, delivering Web pages created on the fly. The ability to create Web pages from the content stored on databases enabled Web developers to provide customized information to visitors. These sites are known as the Deep Web, or the Dynamic Web. Though a visitor to such Web sites gets information tuned to his or her requirements, these sites provide primarily one-way interaction and limited user interactivity. The users have no role in content generation and no means to access content without visiting the sites concerned. The Shallow Web sites and Deep Web sites, which have no or very little user interaction, are now generally termed as Web 1.0.

2.2.2 Web 2.0: The New Face of the Web

In the last few years a new class of Web applications, known as Web 2.0 (or Service-Oriented Applications), has emerged. These applications let people collaborate and share information online in seemingly new ways—examples include social networking sites such as myspace.com, media sharing sites such as youtube.com, and collaborative authoring sites such as wikipedia.

The new- (second-) generation Web, also known as the *Wisdom Web* (Levy and Stone, 2006), the *People-Centric Web*, and the *Read/Write Web*, offers smart user interfaces and built-in facilities for users to generate and edit content presented on the Web and thereby enrich the content base. Besides leveraging the users' potential in generating content, Web 2.0 applications provide facilities to keep the content under the user's own categories (tagging feature) and access it easily (Web feed tool). These new breeds of Web applications are also able to integrate multiple services under a rich user interface.

With the incorporation of new Web technologies such as AJAX (Asynchronous JavaScript and XML), Ruby, blog, wiki, social bookmarking, and tagging, the Web is fast becoming more dynamic and highly interactive, where users can not only pick content from a site but can also contribute to it. The Web feed technology allows users to keep up with a site's latest content without having to visit it. Another feature of the new Web is the proliferation of Web sites with APIs (application programming interfaces). An API from a Web service facilitates Web developers in collecting data from the service and creating new online applications based on these data.

The Web 2.0 is a collection of technologies, business strategies, and social trends. The Web 2.0 is a highly interactive, dynamic application platform than its predecessor, Web 1.0, for fielding new kinds of applications. Recently, a wide array of Web 2.0 applications has been launched (for a list of these applications, refer to www.listible.com/list/complete-list-of-web-2-0-products-and-services; www.econsultant. com/web2/index.html; www. koolweb2.com).

For further information on Web 2.0, see Murugesan (2007a, b), O'Reilly (2005), and articles available at en.wikipedia.org/wiki/Web_2.0, www. whatsweb20.com, and www.readwriteweb. O'Reilly (2006) also defines four levels of Web 2.0 features.

2.2.3 Mobile Web

Advances in mobile computing and wireless communications and widespread worldwide adoption of mobile devices, such as smart mobile phones, PDAs, and Pocket PCs, are enabling a growing number of users to access the Web using handheld devices.

Mobile phones may soon challenge personal computers as the dominant platform for accessing the Web/Internet. According to a survey by Ipsos (2006), 28% of mobile phone owners worldwide browsed the Internet on a wireless handset in 2005, up from 25% in 2004. Almost all wireless device activities—information access and search, mobile commerce (i.e., purchasing a product or service via a mobile device), conducting financial transactions, mobile ticketing, etc.—experienced growth in 2005. Accessing the Internet on a wireless handheld device is becoming a common everyday occurrence for many people in some advanced and developing countries. This will become increasingly prevalent as high-end (smart) mobile phones and Pocket PCs become affordable, a higher number of people start using these more capable handheld devices, and more Web applications migrate to the wireless/mobile Web. Considering the adoption of mobile Web and its huge potential, the World Wide Web Consortium has established a new initiate called the Mobile Web.

Mobile Web applications could offer some additional features compared to traditional desktop Web applications such as location-aware services, context-aware capabilities, and personalization. Mobile Web applications have, however, some unique requirements and pose additional challenges, as outlined later in this chapter.

2.2.4 The Semantic Web

In current Web applications, information is presented in natural language, which humans can process easily. But computers can't manipulate natural language information on the Web meaningfully. The Semantic Web is aimed at overcoming this barrier.

The Semantic Web is an extension of the current Web in which information is given a well-defined meaning, better enabling computers and people to work in cooperation (Berners-Lee et al. 2001). It intends to create a universal medium for information exchange by putting documents with computer-processable meaning (semantics) on the Web. Adding semantics radically changes the nature of the Web—from a place where information is merely displayed to one where it is interpreted, exchanged, and processed. Associating meaning with content or establishing a layer of machine-understandable data enables a higher degree of automation and more intelligent applications and also facilitates interoperable services.

The ultimate goal of the Semantic Web is to support machine-facilitated global information exchange in a scalable, adaptable, extensible manner, so that information on the Web can be used for more effective discovery, automation, integration, and reuse across various applications. The three key ingredients that constitute the Semantic Web and help achieve its goals are semantic markup, ontology, and intelligent software agents. For further information on the Semantic Web, refer to Antoniou and Harmelen (2004), Berners-Lee (2001), and Shadbolt (2006).

2.2.5 Rich Internet Applications

Rich Internet applications (RIA) are Web-based applications that run in a Web browser and do not require software installation, but still have the features and functionality of traditional desktop applications. The term "RIA" was introduced in a Macromedia whitepaper in March 2002. RIA represents the evolution of the browser from a static request-response interface to a dynamic, asynchronous interface. Broadband proliferation, consumer demand, and enabling technologies, including the Web 2.0, are driving the proliferation of RIAs. RIAs promise a richer user experience and benefits—interactivity and usability that are lacking in many current applications. Some prime examples of RIA frameworks are Adobe's Flex and AJAX, and examples of RIA include Google's Earth, Mail, and Finance applications.

Enterprises are embracing the promises of RIAs by applying them to user tasks that demand interactivity, responsiveness, and richness. Predominant techniques such as HTML, forms, and CGI are being replaced by other programmer- or user-friendly approaches such as AJAX and Web services.

Building a Web application using fancy technology, however, doesn't ensure a better user experience. To add real value, developers must address users' real needs and implement structured testing techniques to understand and validate the appropriate use and design of RIAs.

2.3 UNIQUE ASPECTS OF WEB APPLICATIONS

The Web is different. Hence, a good understanding of the characteristics and demands placed on Web applications is essential for designing better Web systems and applications.

Web applications have certain unique intrinsic characteristics that make Web development different and perhaps more challenging compared to traditional software development. Web applications' operational environment and their development approach and the faster pace in which these applications are developed and deployed differentiate Web applications from those of traditional software. Further, greater emphasis is placed on the security of Web applications, which are more susceptible to security breaches than traditional computer applications. Key characteristics of Web applications are (Murugesan and Ginige, 2005)

- Most Web applications are evolutionary in their nature, requiring (frequent) changes of content, functionality, structure, navigation, presentation, or implementation. They particularly evolve in terms of their requirements and functionality (instability of requirements), especially after the system is put into use. In most Web applications, frequency and degree of change are much higher than in traditional software applications, and in many applications it is not possible to specify fully their entire requirements at the beginning. The frequency and degree of change of information content can be quite high. Thus, successfully managing the evolution, change, and newer requirements of Web applications is a major technical, organizational, and management challenge—more demanding than traditional software development.
- Web applications are meant to be used by a vast, diverse, remote community of users who have different requirements, expectations, and skill sets. Therefore, the user interface and usability features have to meet the needs of a diverse, anonymous user community. Furthermore, the number of users accessing a Web application at any time is unpredictable and could vary quite considerably, creating performance problems—there could be a "flash crowd" triggered by major events or promotions.
- Web-based applications demand presentation of a variety of content— text, graphics, images, audio, and/or video—and the content may also integrated with procedural processing. Hence, their development

includes the creation and management of the content and their presentation in an attractive manner, as well as a provision for subsequent content management (changes) on a continual basis after the initial development and deployment.

- Web-based systems, in general, demand good aesthetic appeal—"look and feel"—and easy navigation.
- Web applications, especially those meant for a global audience, need to adhere to many different social and cultural sentiments and national standards—including multiple languages and different systems of units.
- Security and privacy needs of Web-based systems are in general more demanding than those of traditional software. Hence, there is a greater demand on the security of Web applications.
- Web applications need to cope with a variety of display devices and formats and support hardware, software, and networks with vastly varying access speeds.
- Ramifications of failure or dissatisfaction of users of Web-based applications can be much worse than conventional IT systems. Also, Web applications could fail for many different reasons.
- Web applications' development timeframes are shorter, and this significantly influences the design and development methodology and process, if any, that are adopted for their development.
- Proliferation of new Web technologies and standards and competitive pressure to use them bring its own advantages and also additional challenges to development and maintenance of Web applications.
- The evolving nature of Web applications necessitates an incremental developmental process.

For a detailed and comprehensive discussion on differences between Web development and software development along 12 dimensions, see Mendes et al. (2006).

2.4 WEB SYSTEM DEVELOPMENT: CHALLENGES

Web system design and development is a complex and a challenging activity, as it needs to consider many different aspects and requirements, some of which may have conflicting needs (Cloyd, 2001; Ivory and Hearst, 2002; Siegel, 2003).

Scalability refers to how well a system copes with the new requirements and features, increases in content, increases in usage and the number of users, and higher security needs. Developing Web applications that scale well is a challenge. As Web sites grow and new functionalities are added, failures (reliability problems), usability problems, and security breaches could creep in. Today's Web-savvy consumers don't tolerate failures or slow responses.

Any system slowdown, failure, or security breach might result in loss of its customers—probably permanently. As Web applications are becoming mission-critical, there is a greater demand for their improved reliability, performance, and security.

On the Web there is virtually no control over visitor volumes and when and how visitors access a Web system. This makes developing Web applications that exhibit satisfactory performance even under a sudden surge in the number of users a nebulous and challenging task and calls for capacity planning.

Meeting the diverse expectations and needs of many different users with varying skills is hard. When users find a site unfriendly, confusing, or hard or that presents too much information or they are unable to find the information they need, they will leave that site feeling frustrated. The features that determine Web usability are (Becker and Berkemeyer, 2002) design layout, design consistency, accessibility, information content, navigation, personalization, performance, security, reliability, and design standards (naming conventions, formatting, and page organization). User feedback reveals features such as search functionality, consistent navigation structure throughout, site maps, and answers to frequently asked questions (FAQ) aid most sites' usability.

The need to making the majority of Web sites universally accessible—accessible by both the able and disabled users—places additional development challenges. However, very little has been done in practice to aid disabled Web users, such as the visually impaired (those who are blind or color blind), and there is a growing number of retired surfers who seek design features such as color contrasts, text-to-speech, and resizable text. Though there have been standards and technologies to support disabled Web users, their adoption is slow. There have been lawsuits against enterprises and Web developers for not providing Web access to the visually impaired. Several countries have legal requirements to make most public Web sites accessible to the visually impaired. Web developers need to meet the legal requirements in terms of Web accessibility.

Localization of Web applications is the process of adapting Web pages/applications (often written in English and targeted for users in a particular country) for use in other countries, considering their culture, standards, regulations, and technological conditions. It is more than just language translation and Web applications that need to be specifically designed to accomplish this multifaceted requirement.

Terms like scalability, reliability, availability, maintainability, usability, and security are used to describe how well the system meets current and future needs and service-level expectations. These *ilities* characterize (Williams, 2000) a Web system's architectural qualities. In the face of increasingly complex systems, these system qualities are often more daunting to understand and to incorporate.

Web systems should be up and running 24 hours a day, 7 days a week, and each day of the year—24/7/365. Furthermore, Web applications should function properly when accessed from diverse browsers. This necessitates that Web sites must adopt their presentation and code to work with all major browsers and client computers.

Design and development of Web applications for mobile and device-independent operations is very complex and challenging, as it needs to address many additional aspects compared to traditional Web applications. Testing and validation of Web applications for access by mobile devices is a challenge, as there are many types of devices with varying shapes and sizes. We need to make sure that applications work as intended on many different makes and models of mobile devices and evaluate their usability. Design guidelines and usability methods that work for desktop systems do not necessarily work for mobile systems. New approaches might be required to test and validate mobile Web applications. For a detailed discussion on the challenges of mobile Web application development, see Murugesan and Venkatakrishnan (2005).

Thus, the challenge is to design and develop sustainable Web systems for better

- usability, interface design, and navigation
- comprehension
- performance (responsiveness)
- security and integrity
- evolution, growth, and maintainability
- testability
- mobility

A Web-based system also has to satisfy many different stakeholders besides the diverse range of the system's users: persons who maintain the system, the organization that needs the system, and also those who fund the system development. These may pose some additional challenges to Web-based system design and development.

2.4.1 Web System Complexity

Complexity is an omnipresent phenomenon in many Web systems. A Web application fits the general characteristics of a complex system—consists of a large number of heterogeneous, highly interacting components, interactions among the components result in nonlinear behavior, and the systems often evolve. Many factors contribute to the complexity of Web systems, as shown in Figure 2.2.

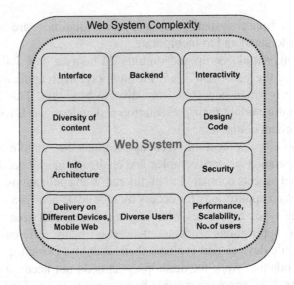

Figure 2.2. Landscape of Web systems.

Web applications become more complex as they deal not only with technological issues but also with organizational issues largely beyond a Web project team's control. Developers need to understand the dimensions of Web project complexity and how they affect project outcome. Complexity could be addressed by taking a holistic, engineering approach. Web developers need to simplify the system, meeting the given requirements rather than increasing its complexity.

2.5 STATE OF PRACTICE OF WEB DEVELOPMENT: CONCERNS

Web development has a very short history, compared to software development, information system development, or other computer application development. But within a period of a few years, a large number of Web systems and applications have been developed and put into widespread use. The complexity of Web applications has also grown significantly—from information dissemination [consisting of simple text and images to image maps, forms, common gateway interface (CGI), applets, scripts, and style sheets] to online transactions, enterprise-wide planning and scheduling systems, Web-based collaborative work environments, and now multilingual Web sites, Web services, and mobile Web applications.

Nevertheless, many pursue Web development primarily as an authoring work (content/page creation and presentation) rather than an application development requiring planning, system/architecture design, coding, Web page creation, navigation design, and testing and evaluation. They often get carried away by the myth that Web development primarily deals with "media manipulation and presentation". Sure, Web development has an important artistic side, but Web developers need to follow a disciplined and systematic process during the entire life cycle of a Web project, rather than simply "hacking" together a few Web pages.

Several attributes of quality Web-based systems such as usability, navigation, accessibility, scalability, maintainability, compatibility and interoperability, security, and reliability are not given the due consideration they deserve during development. Many Web applications also fail to address cultural and regional considerations and privacy, moral, and legal obligations and requirements. Most Web systems also lack proper testing and evaluation and design documentation.

Many developers, while designing and developing a Web application, fail to acknowledge that Web systems' requirements change and evolve, and hence don't take this into consideration while developing Web systems. Web-based systems development is not a one-off event as perceived and practiced by many; it is a process with an iterative life cycle.

Another problem is that most Web application development activities heavily rely on the knowledge and experience of individual (or a small group of) developers and their individual development practices rather than standard practices.

Poorly developed Web-based applications have a high probability of low performance and/or failure. In enterprise applications, a system failure can propagate broad-based problems across many functions, causing a major Web disaster. Bad design, shabby development, poor performance, and/or poor content management for Web-based applications could have serious implications.

Thus, there are concerns about the manner in which complex Web-based systems are created as well as the level of performance, quality, and integrity of these systems.

The primary causes of these failures are a lack of vision, short-sighted goals, a flawed design and development process, and poor management of development efforts—not technology (Ginige and Murugesan, 2001a). The way we address these concerns is key to successful deployment and maintenance of Web applications.

2.6 WEB FAILURES

Web failure is defined as the inability of a Web application to correctly function or deliver information or documents required by the users. While the success of a Web application hinges on whether or not it is usable and serves the intended purpose, Web failures could arise due to many different reasons. They include

- not meeting functionality and the users' needs
- poor usability
- poor performance
- security breaches
- not functioning properly, including errors and crashes
- poor maintainability
- poor scalability
- schedule and cost over-runs
- abandoned projects—poor project management

The Web system/application failures could also be caused by failure of a supporting infrastructure such as host hardware or software, network, and browser, or Web software/application failure such as information source failure or individual page failures.

There is a need for a better way of doing things, a Web design and development methodology—an established way of delivering projects that meet the client's needs on time and on budget. Performance problems could be caused by any number of things: a poorly designed Web architecture, poorly designed Web software or Web page, an underpowered CPU, limited network bandwidth, or a combination of several factors. A higher load can easily overwhelm a system's resources and cause performance problems. For instance, in September 2006, when news of the "crocodile hunter" Steve Irwin's sudden and bizarre death broke, too many people logged on to news Web sites, these sites showed signs of strain, and some, including the CNN and Australian ABC Web sites, had to switch to a "lite" mode, in which bandwidth-hungry elements on the home page were removed in order to cope with the surge in usage. However, a higher volume is not always required to cause performance problems. Poorly designed software that does not handle resource allocation and contention properly can easily cause deadlocks that eventually lead to performance problems even at a normal load.

Although performance problems can have many causes, the outcome is always the same—slow response. To resolve such problems, a holistic approach—also known as an all-out systems approach—is needed where the application software, the network, and the underlying computing hardware are all considered and evaluated.

Web project failures are often attributed to projects running overtime, budgets blowing up, and applications not meeting the intended purpose and failing to meet the business needs. There could be many reasons for failure, including developers interpreting a client's requirements differently from the client's own interpretation, underestimation of work required to do the project, poor project management, poor staffing, ad hoc development strategy, underdeveloped or non-existent design paradigm, and poor or no code reuse within a project or between projects.

Many Web sites have suffered site crashes, performance failures, security breaches, and outages—resulting in irate customers, lost revenue, devalued stocks, a tarnished reputation (bad publicity, lack of customer confidence), permanent loss of customers, and lawsuits (Williams, 2000). Stock prices have become inextricably linked to the reliability of a company's e-commerce site. There are also legal implications when Web applications go bad; refer to Verdon (2006) for details.

2.7 WEB ENGINEERING

Ad hoc methods are no longer capable of delivering high-quality complex Web applications, which are becoming more and more important and mission-critical. Complex interdependencies of Web systems challenge our ability to comprehend, create, maintain, and control these systems. Also, as failure of a Web application could be costly, there is a growing demand for methodologies, models, and tools that can improve Web design and the Web quality and reliability. There is also a pressing need for better methodologies, techniques, and tools for testing Web applications.

In the absence of a disciplined approach to Web-based systems development, we will find sooner or later that:

- Web-based applications are not delivering required functionality and desired performance and quality.
- The Web application development process becomes increasingly complex and difficult to manage and also expensive and grossly behind schedule.

Can adding engineering rigor to Web development address the challenges facing developers in developing and deploying complex Web systems and applications? We and many other researchers and practitioners believe it will, and practical experience and evidence support this claim.

Web Engineering seeks to address the problem of Web application development by building a foundation for the systematic creation of Web-based systems. This foundation will consist of a body of theoretical and empirical knowledge for development, deployment, and support of continual evolution of Web applications.

Web Engineering is the application of scientific, engineering, and management principles and disciplined and systematic approaches to the successful development, deployment, and maintenance of Web-based systems and applications (Murugesan et al., 1999; Kappel et al., 2006). It is a systematic way of managing the complexity and diversity of Web applications. It is also concerned with the development and organization of new knowledge about Web application development and application of that knowledge to develop Web applications and to address new requirements and challenges facing Web developers.

A Web-based system is a *living* system—it grows, evolves, and changes. An appropriate infrastructure is necessary to support the growth of a Web-based system in a flexible and controlled manner. Web Engineering helps to create an infrastructure that will allow evolution and maintenance of a Web system and also support creativity.

Web Engineering could also be viewed as a holistic and proactive approach to the development of complex Web-based systems. In a holistic approach, all aspects of the development processes, functional requirements, the application's operational environment, the supporting IT and other infrastructure, and the linkages and interactions among them are identified, analyzed, prioritized, implemented, and evaluated. It is important for developers to understand "the wider context in which a Web-based system or application will be used, and design an architecture that will support the development, operation and maintenance as well as evolution of the Web application in that context, addressing the key issues and considerations" (Murugesan and Ginige, 2005).

Web development is a process, not simply a one-time event. Thus, Web Engineering deals with all aspects of Web-based systems development, starting from conception and development to implementation, performance evaluation, and continual maintenance. Web Engineering, therefore, covers a range of areas: requirements elicitation and analysis; Web system modeling; Web architecture; Web system design; Web page design; scripting/coding; interface with databases, ERP systems, and other Web-based systems; Web quality; Web usability; Web security; Web system performance evaluation; Web testing; Web development methodologies; Web development process; Web metrics; and Web project management.

"Contrary to the perception of some professionals, Web Engineering is not a clone of software engineering although both involve programming and software development" (Ginige and Murugesan, 2001a). While Web Engineering uses software engineering principles, it encompasses new approaches, methodologies, tools and techniques, and guidelines to meet the unique requirements of Web-based systems. In many respects, development of Web-based systems is much more than traditional software development. As highlighted in previous sections, there are subtle differences in the nature and life cycle of Web-based systems and traditional software systems and the way in which they are developed and maintained.

The nature and characteristics of Web-based applications and their development demand Web Engineering to be multidisciplinary, encompassing inputs from diverse areas such as systems analysis and design, software engineering, hypermedia/hypertext engineering, requirements engineering, human-computer interaction, user interface, information engineering, information indexing and retrieval, testing, modeling and simulation, project management, and graphic design and presentation (Deshpande et al., 2002).

A well-engineered Web system (Murugesan and Ginige, 2005)

- is functionally complete and correct
- is usable
- is robust and reliable
- is maintainable
- is secure
- performs reasonably even under flash and peak loads
- is scalable
- is portable, where required (perform across different common platforms), compatible with multiple browsers
- is reusable
- is interoperable with other systems
- has universal accessibility (access by people with different kinds of disabilities)
- is well-documented

Since its origin and promotion as a new discipline in 1998, Web Engineering has been receiving growing interest among researchers, developers, academics, and clients.

2.8 WEB DEVELOPMENT

Development of high-quality Web applications is not an accident; it calls for a systematic plan for development and implementation as well as architectural design, testing, and evaluation, incorporation of security safeguards, and adoption of sound implementation polices. The design and analysis of Web systems, however, presents a significant challenge: Systems need to be understood at many different levels of abstraction and examined from many different perspectives. Web systems modeling and architecture play an important role in the development of today's complex Web systems.

2.8.1 Web Architecture

Following the IEEE Standard 1471-2000 definition of software architecture, Web architecture may be defined as "the fundamental organization of a system, embodied in its components, their relationships to each other and the environment, and the principles governing its design and evolution." It uses abstractions and models to simplify and communicate complex structures.

Architecture presents a framework, describes the structure, and makes the system understandable. It helps in making the transition from analysis to implementation (Eichinger, 2006). Architecture of some high-volume Web sites is presented by Dantzing (2002).

In Web system architecture design, various components of the system and how they are linked are decided.

Web subsystem architecture is composed of the following:

- an overall system architecture that describes how the network and the various servers such as Web servers, application servers, and database servers interact
- an application architecture that depicts various information modules and the functions available
- a software architecture that identifies various software and database modules required to implement the application architecture

Several factors influence the choice of a Web architecture, including the following:

- functional requirements
- quality, security, and performance considerations
- technical aspects
- experience

2.8.2 Web Design

Design plays an important role in the development of high-performance, high-quality Web applications. Web design has to cater to many different requirements, some of which might pose conflicting demands:

- design for usability—interface design, navigation
- design for comprehension
- design for performance—responsiveness
- design for security and integrity
- design for evolution, growth, and maintainability
- design for testability

- design for universal accessibility
- design for localization
- graphics and multimedia design
- Web page design

Design methodologies and models described later in this book are aimed at helping developers tackle the complexity of Web application development and achieve the above multifaceted goals.

2.8.3 Web Security

As more and more applications—everything from email and buying and selling to banking and business-to-business interactions and their associated data—are now running on the Web, hackers and criminals are increasingly targeting Web applications. Hence, Web security is under the spotlight. Information is one of the very important assets in almost all organizations. Once the internal networks of those organizations are connected to the Internet and Web, it becomes a potential target for cyber attacks. The number of Web-based vulnerabilities keeps increasing; in the first half of 2005, for the first time, reported Web-based vulnerabilities (61% of vulnerabilities) outpaced those of all other platforms (www.symantec.com/enterprise/threat report).

Data and information have to be protected from unauthorized access as well as from malicious corruption. A recent article (Meier, 2006) looks at the Web from an empirical perspective and, using a direct "do's and don'ts" approach, identifies security-specific activities that developers can integrate throughout the Web development life cycle. It also presents basic concepts to focus on while developing Web applications.

Programming flaws top the list of Web application security problems (Mimoso, 2003). No matter how good your process or design is, bugs will slip into the code—it's up to quality assurance (QA) and testing to weed them out. For a good survey of Web application security assessment tools, see Curphey and Araujo (2006).

A wide range of legal and regulatory issues surrounds Web development, including the need to protect sensitive business and consumer information. A good set of security policies and practices will limit Web security breaches and unintended exposure of information. A good review of several real-world security incidents, of how the law and regulations view such incidents, and how the right kind of policies and best practices can provide legal coverage for a company if (or when?) someone breaches its Web application is provided by Verdon (2006). For a discussion on who is liable for bugs and security flaws in the Web, refer to Cusumano (2004).

Glisson (2006) supports the need to establish a comprehensive security improvement approach (SIA) for Web applications and identifies six security criteria for Web application development based on empirical evidence:

1. active organizational support for security in the Web development process
2. proper controls in the development environment
3. security visibility throughout all areas of the development process
4. delivery of a cohesive system, integrating business requirements, software, and security
5. prompt, rigorous testing and evaluation
6. trust and accountability

2.8.4 Web Testing and Evaluation

Testing plays a crucial role in the overall Web development process. However, more often than not, testing and evaluation is a neglected aspect of Web development. Many developers test the system only after the system meets with failures or after limitations have become apparent, resorting to what may be called *retroactive testing*, whereas what is desired in the first place is *proactive testing* at various stages of the Web development life cycle. Benefits of proactive testing include assurance of proper functioning and guaranteed performance levels, avoidance of costly retroactive fixes, optimal performance, and lower risk.

Testing and validating a large complex Web system is a difficult and expensive task. Testing shouldn't be done only near the end of the development process. Developers and their managers need to take a broader view and follow a more holistic approach to testing—from design all the way to deployment and maintenance and continual refinement.

The test planning needs to be carried out early in the project's life cycle. A test plan provides a road map so that the Web site can be evaluated through requirements or design statements. It also helps to estimate the time and effort needed for testing, establishing a test environment, getting test personnel, and writing test procedures before any testing can actually start.

Lam (2001) groups Web testing into the following broad categories and provides helpful practical guidelines on how to test Web systems:

1. browser compatibility
2. page display
3. session management
4. usability
5. content analysis
6. availability

7. backup and recovery
8. transactions
9. shopping, order processing
10. internalization
11. operational business procedures
12. system integration
13. performance
14. login and security

Experience shows that there are many common pitfalls in Web testing (Lam, 2001), and attempts should be made overcome them. Testing and evaluation of a Web application may be expensive, but the impact of failures resulting from a lack of testing could be more costly or even disastrous. A chapter in this book is devoted to a framework for measurement and evaluation of the quality of Web applications.

While rich Internet applications (RIAs) promise improved experiences for users, they are newer and more complex than their HTML counterparts, making them vulnerable to well-known—and potentially undiscovered—usability flaws. To ensure that RIAs don't frustrate users with problems that could have been avoided, designers should look for common pitfalls and test their applications—in the context of the full site experience—throughout the design and implementation phases of an RIA.

2.9 KNOWLEDGE COLLABORATION

The creation of large Web systems requires knowledge from a wide range of domains such as Web programming, Web architecture, Web design, multimedia, Web security, and Web performance and usability. Since hardly a few Web developers may have all the required knowledge, the development of Web-based systems is no longer confined to an individual but has to rely on a group of people who can collaboratively work on developing and implementing a Web system or a Web application. Knowledge collaboration has thus become an important aspect of Web development.

Development of a Web application requires a team of people with diverse skills and backgrounds: programmers, graphic designers, Web page designers, usability experts, content developers, database designers and administrators, data communication and networking experts, and Web server administrators. A Web development team is multidisciplinary and must be more versatile than a traditional software development team.

2.10 WEB PROJECT MANAGEMENT

The purpose of project management is to ensure that all the key processes and activities work in harmony. Building successful Web-based applications requires close coordination among various efforts involved in the Web development cycle. Successfully managing a large, complex Web development is a challenging task requiring multidisciplinary skills and is, in some ways, different from managing traditional IT/software projects.

Various aspects of Web project management and how Web project management differs from software/IT project management are outlined in Mayr (2006).

2.11 WHY DO WEB PROJECTS FAIL?

Many studies reveal that poor project management is the major cause of Web failures both during development and subsequently in the operational phase. Poor project management will defeat good engineering; good project management is a recipe for success. The 10 most common factors that contribute to Web project failure, in no particular order, are (adopted from Charette, 2005)

1. unrealistic, unarticulated, poorly articulated project goals and requirements
2. inaccurate estimate of time, effort, and resources needed for development of Web applications
3. sloppy development practices and lack of development methodology (a road map from conception to deployment)
4. poor communication among developers and between developers and clients
5. inability to handle the project's complexity
6. poor project management
7. use of immature technology
8. stakeholder politics
9. commercial pressures
10. poor reporting and monitoring of project progress

Project managers need to address these project management problems.

2.12 STEPS TO SUCCESSFUL DEVELOPMENT

Ten key steps for successful development and deployment of Web applications are (Ginige and Murugesan, 2001c)

1. Understand the system's overall function and operational environment, including the business objectives and requirements, organization culture, and information management policy.
2. Clearly identify the stakeholders—that is, the system's main users and their typical profiles, the organization that needs the system, and who funds the development.
3. Elicit or specify the (initial) functional, technical, and nontechnical requirements of the stakeholders and the overall system. Recognize that these requirements may not remain the same; rather, they are bound to change and evolve over time during the system development.
4. Develop an overall system architecture of the Web-based system that meets the technical and nontechnical requirements.
5. Identify subprojects or subprocesses to implement the system architecture. If the subprojects are too complex to manage, further divide them until they become a set of manageable tasks.
6. Develop and implement the subprojects.
7. Incorporate effective mechanisms to manage the Web system's evolution, change, and maintenance. As the system evolves, repeat the overall process or some parts of it, as required.
8. Address the nontechnical issues such as revised business processes, organizational and management policies, human resources development, and legal, cultural, and social aspects.
9. Perform periodic post-implementation audit. Measure and evaluate the system's performance, analyze the usage of the Web application from Web logs, and review and address users' feedback and suggestions.
10. Refine and update the system.

2.13 CONCLUSIONS

As Web applications continue to grow in importance and extend into new territories, a disciplined approach to their development becomes mandatory. With advances in various aspects of Web Engineering, we know now how to do Web applications well. It is time to act on what we know. This book and other publications in Web Engineering would help Web developers in this important endeavor.

To successfully develop and implement a large, complex Web application:

- Adopt a sound strategy and follow a suitable methodology to successfully manage the development and maintenance of Web systems.
- Recognize that, in most cases, development of a Web application is not an event, but a process, since the application's requirements evolve. It will have a start, but it will not have a predictable end as in traditional IT/software projects.
- Within the continuous process, identify, plan, and schedule various development activities such that they have a defined start and finish.
- Remember that planning and scheduling of the activities are very important to successfully manage the overall development, allocate resources, and monitor progress.
- Consider the big picture during context analysis and planning and designing of the Web application. If you do not, you may end up redesigning the entire system and repeating the process all over. If you address the changing nature of requirements early on, you can build into the design cost-effective ways of managing change and dealing with new requirements.
- Recognize that the development of a large Web application calls for teamwork and shared responsibility among the team members, and motivate a team culture.

REFERENCES

Antoniou, G.F., and Harmelen, F., 2004, *A Semantic Web Primer*. The MIT Press, Cambridge, MA.

Becker, A.S., and Berkemeyer, A., 2002, Rapid application design and testing for usability. *IEEE Multimedia*, October–December, pp. 38–46.

Berners-Lee, T. et al., 2001, The semantic Web. *Scientific American*, May, pp. 34–43.

Charette, R.N., 2005, Why software fails. *IEEE Spectrum*, September, pp. 36–43. http://www.spectrum.ieee.org/print/1685.

Cloyd, M.H., 2001, Designing user-centered Web applications in Web time. *IEEE Software*, January, pp. 62–69.

Curphey, M., and Araujo, R., 2006, Web application security assessment tools, *IEEE Security & Privacy*, July–August, pp. 32–41.

Cusumano, M.A., 2004, Who is liable for bugs and security flaws in software? *Communications of the ACM*, March, **47**(3): 25–27.

Dantzing, P., 2002, Architecture and design of high volume Web sites. *Proceedings of International Conference on Software and Knowledge Engineering*, 2002, Ischia, Italy.

Deshpande, Y. et al., 2002, Web Engineering. *Journal of Web Engineering*, **1**(1): 3–17.

Eichinger, C., 2006, Web application architecture. In *Web Engineering: The Discipline of Systematic Development of Web Applications*, Kappel, G. et al. (eds.)., John Wiley and Sons, New York, pp. 65–84.

Ginige, A., and Murugesan, S., 2001a, Web Engineering: An introduction. *IEEE Multimedia,* January–March, **8**(1): 14–18.

Ginige, A., and Murugesan, S., 2001b, The essence of Web Engineering: Managing the diversity and complexity of Web application development, *IEEE Multimedia,* April–June, **8**(2): 22–25.

Ginige, A., and Murugesan, S., 2001c, Web Engineering: A methodology for developing scalable, maintainable Web applications. *Cutter IT Journal,* July, **14**(7): 24–35.

Glisson, W.B., 2006, Web Engineering security: A practitioner's perspective, *Proceedings of the International Conference on Web Engineering,* pp. 257–264.

Ipsos, 2006, Mobile phones could soon rival the PC as world's dominant Internet platform. Online version: www.ipsosna.com/news/pressrelease.cfm?id=3049.

Ivory, M.Y., and Hearst, M.A., 2002, Improving Web site design. *IEEE Internet Computing,* March–April 2002, pp. 56–63.

Kappel, G. et al. (eds.), 2006, *Web Engineering: The Discipline of Systematic Development of Web Applications.* John Wiley and Sons, New York.

Lam, W., 2001, Testing e-commerce systems: A practical guide. *IT Professional,* March, pp. 19–27.

Mayr, H., 2006, Web project management. In *Web Engineering: The Discipline of Systematic Development of Web Applications,* Kappel, G. et al. (eds.), John Wiley and Sons, New York, pp. 171–195.

Meier, J.D., 2006, Web application security engineering. *IEEE Security & Privacy,* July–August, pp. 16–24.

Mendes, W. et al., 2006, The need for Web Engineering: An introduction. In *Web Engineering,* E. Mendes and N. Mosley (eds.), Springer, Berlin, pp. 1–27.

Mimoso, M.S., 2003, Top Web application security problems identified. Online version: searchsecurity.techtarget.com/originalContent/0,289142,sid14_gci873823,00.html?NewsEL=9.25.

Murugesan S. et al., 1999, Web Engineering: A new discipline for development of Web-based systems. *Proceedings of the First ICSE Workshop on Web Engineering,* Los Angeles, pp. 1–9.

Murugesan, S., and Ginige, A., 2005, Web Engineering: Introduction and perspectives. In *Web Engineering: Principles and Techniques,* W. Suh (ed.). Idea Group Publishing, Hershey, PA.

Murugesan, S., and Venkatakrishnan, B.A., 2005, Addressing the challenges of Web applications on mobile handheld devices. *Proceedings of International Conference on Mobile Business,* pp. 199–205.

Murugesan, S., 2007a, Business uses of Web 2.0: Potential and prospects. Cutter Business-IT Strategies Executive Report, **10**(1), January.

Murugesan, S., 2007b, Understanding Web 2.0, *IEEE IT Professional,* July–Aug., **9**(4).

Naughton, J., 2006, 10 Web sites that changed the world. Good weekend. *The Sydney Morning Herald,* September 9, p. 38.

O'Reilly, T., 2006, Levels of the game: The hierarchy of Web 2.0 applications. Online version: radar.oreilly.com/archives/2006/07/levels_of_the_game.html.

O'Reilly, T., 2005, What is Web 2.0? Design patterns and business models for the next generation of software. Online version: www.oreillynet.com/pub/a/oreilly/tim/news/2005/09/30/what-is-web-20.html.

Shadbolt, N., 2006, The Semantic Web revisited. *IEEE Intelligent Systems,* May–June, **21**(3): 96–101.

Siegel, D.A., 2003, The business case for user-centred design: Increasing your power. *Software,* **18**(1): 62–69.

Verdon, D, 2006, Security policies for the software developer. *IEEE Security & Privacy,* July–August, pp. 42–49.

Wikipedia-1, Web 2.0, http://en.wikipedia.org/wiki/Web_2.0.

Wikipedia-2, Rich Internet applications, http://en.wikipedia.org/wiki/Rich_Internet_application.

Williams, J., 2000, Correctly assessing the "ilities" requires more than marketing hype. *IT Professional,* November, **2**(6): 65–67.

Williams, J., 2001, Avoiding the CNN moment. *IT Professional,* Nov–Mar., **3**(2): 72, 68:70.

Chapter 3

THE WEB AS AN APPLICATION PLATFORM

Martin Gaedke and Johannes Meinecke
Chemnitz University of Technology, Faculty of Computer Science, Distributed and Self-Organizing Systems Group, Straße der Nationen 62, 09111 Chemnitz, Germany

3.1 PARADIGM SHIFT IN WEB HISTORY

When Tim Berners-Lee invented the Web in 1990 at the European Particle Physics Laboratory (CERN) (Berners-Lee, 1990), he did so in the context of a development that had started long before. One idea that considerably influenced the nature and intended purpose of the early Web had its roots in the concept of *hypertext*, which had come up about half a decade before. Coined by Ted Nelson, the term "hypertext" can be understood as "nonlinear writing," i.e., creating documents that can be read not only from the beginning to the end, but rather in an order that is preferred and controlled by the reader, who navigates through the text by following associative links. On Web pages, the associative link is reflected by the concept of the anchor tag <a> used in HTML. As a precondition for realizing a large-scale hypertext system, Tim Berners-Lee first proposed a unique addressing scheme for all documents at CERN to be linked universally, the Universal Document Identifier (UDI). With this concept, he created the predecessor of the Web's Uniform Resource Identifiers (URI) and their prominent subset, the Uniform Resource Locators (URL), which provide a means of locating resources by describing their primary access mechanisms (Berners-Lee et al., 2005). As a result of the hypertext roots, everything about the early Web was characterized by a focus on documents, including HTML and the first Web browser prototype. More precisely, the intension was to support the publication and exchange of documents by scientists, who initially were the main audience.

What followed during the next 10 years was a period of continuous growth. As the scope of application quickly exceeded CERN, its popularity contributed greatly to the advance of the Internet as a whole, of which it became the major driving application. Along with the increase in available sites and servers, more and more end users started to join the Web with an Internet-capable computer. The content, which was originally published by scientists, was now also coming from professional enterprises as well as private individuals, who established their Web presence in the form of homepages, covering a wide variety of topics. Consequently, Web technology advanced to meet the requirements of the new emerging scenarios, which included, in particular, commercial applications. As a means for reaching vast numbers of consumers with comparatively low investments, the Web partially changed its focus from a forum for the publication of information toward an electronic marketplace. While overrated expectations and lack of concentration on business values during the new economy boom of the late 1990s resulted in disillusion and crashing stock prices, market consolidation followed and the Web has now returned to its period of growth.

Due to the described evolution of the Web and its manifold applications, its shape has been influenced by different, partially competing perspectives on how it is or should be used. In 1995, Guay distinguished between several *publishing paradigms* present in the early Web. The print paradigm, for example, is reflected in sites that do not make use of hypertext concepts at all and instead present their linear content in ways similar to how it is traditionally presented in print media. This approach, which was partially a result of a transitional phase toward the Web as a new medium, is gradually being replaced by the mentioned hypermedia paradigm. Another development impacting the Web is the multimedia paradigm, which took advantage of the increase in bandwidth as well as improving hardware capabilities to deliver not only text, but all sorts of media, including images, audio, and video. Ted Nelson's docuverse (Nelson, 1987) can be seen as a paradigm for the Web, describing the idea of a global library of interconnected documents. Finally, the interactive paradigm recognizes the potential of users influencing the sites they visit beyond merely deciding upon where to navigate next. Whereas formerly the author supplied information and the reader controlled the flow of information, now the author provides application logic and the reader controls the program flow.

As the interaction paradigm began to spread and the Web technology adjusted to the new requirements, new forms of Web sites evolved, which resembled applications more than documents. While many aspects of these applications can be compared to conventional software programs, there are also a number of characteristics typical for the Web platform that distinguish them from other platforms (Deshpande et al., 2002). These characteristics are challenging for the process of developing applications, but also offer innovative opportunities for business and society as a whole that were impossible to realize before. An important factor is the potential audience of the software, which, once deployed, can be accessed by millions of users from whole different regions, countries, or cultures. At the same time, this also applies for the competition, making user satisfaction a vital success factor. Unlike on other platforms, software on the Web is always operating and does not depend on time-consuming processes of rolling out new releases. Hence, scenarios can be supported that require constantly up-to-date information. In addition, there is an evolving set of technologies and standards that opens new advantages to applications that adopt them, including many specifications recommended by the World Wide Web Consortium (W3C). In contrast to common applications, the Web is also repeatedly influenced by emerging trends that encourage (if not enforce) a large number of sites to follow them. Together, these factors, among many others, have led to the emergence of a huge variety of different applications and as such contribute to the still ongoing growth of the Web.

3.2 WEB APPLICATION CONCERNS

In order to develop software for the Web platform with respect to its specific nature, a number of engineering issues have to be addressed every time an application is constructed. For the sake of clarity, such problems can be allocated to multiple concerns (Dijkstra, 1982) that may then be treated separately in design and implementation. In the following sections we distinguish between concerns related to the data being processed (Data), the interface experienced by the user (Presentation, Navigation, Dialogue), and the distributed system acting in between (Process, Communication) (Gaedke, 2000). The concerns reappear in the Web Engineering methods presented in this book that comprise approaches to deal with them in a systematic, disciplined, and quantifiable way.

3.2.1 Data

From the viewpoint of the early Web's paradigms, the data are the content of the documents to be published. Although content can be embedded in the Web documents together with other concerns like presentation or navigation, the evolution of Web applications often demands a separation, using data sources such as XML files, databases, or Web services. Traditional issues include, for example, the structure of the information space as well as the definition of structural linking. In the context of the dynamic nature of Web applications, additional dimensions have to be considered. For instance, one can distinguish between static information that remains stable over time and dynamic information that is subject to changes. Depending on the media type being delivered, either data can be persistent, i.e., accessible independently of time, or it can be transient, i.e., accessible as a flow, as in the case of a video stream. Moreover, *metadata* can also describe other data, e.g., following the de facto standard of the Dublin Core Metadata Initiative (Andresen, 2003). Such descriptions facilitate the usefulness of the data within the global information space established by the Web. The machine-based processing of information is further supported by Semantic Web approaches that apply technologies like the Resource Description Framework (RDF) to make metadata statements (e.g., about Web page content) and express the semantics about associations between arbitrary resources worldwide.

3.2.2 Presentation

Besides the question of what to publish, an import matter is also how to present it, especially in the context of the large number of competing information sources on the Internet. The task of communicating content in an appropriate way combines artistic visual design with engineering disciplines. Usually, there are numerous factors to be considered, many of them related to the assumed audience of the Web site. For example, in the international case, cultural differences may have to be accounted for, affecting not only languages but also, for example, the perception of color schemes. Further restrictions may originate from the publishing organizations themselves that aim at reflecting the company's brand with a corresponding corporate design or legal obligations with respect to accessibility [The World Wide Web Consortium (W3C), 1997]. Although presentation technologies have advanced over time, such as in terms of multimedia capabilities, the core technology of the Web application platform, the Hypertext Markup Language (HTML), has remained relatively stable. Consequently, application user interfaces have to be mapped to document-oriented markup code, causing a gap between design and implementation.

3.2.3 Navigation

Given the data and the presentation methods to communicate it, an additional challenge lies in the task of making the information easily accessible to the user. Because of the potential complexity of arbitrarily linked resources on the Web, a lack of systematic design may result in what it referred to as the "lost in hyperspace" syndrome. This holds true even though the Web makes use of only a subset of the rich capabilities of hypertext concepts, e.g., allowing only unidirectional links. Over time, a set of common patterns has evolved [cf. repositories like Lowe (1999)] that, being familiar to many users, aids them in navigating through new Web sites they have not visited before. Applied to Web application development, navigation concepts can be extended for accessing not only static document content, but also application functionality. Today, there are several Web Engineering approaches with a hypermedia background that cover navigational aspects with dedicated models and methodologies.

3.2.4 Dialogue

As expressed within the interaction paradigm, the execution of a Web application is usually characterized by a degree of user control that goes beyond the free choice of navigation. Interactive elements in Web applications often appear in the shape of forms that allow users to enter data that are used as input for further processing. More generally, the dialogue concern covers not only interaction between humans and the application, but rather between arbitrary actors (including other programs) and the manipulated information space. The flow of information is governed by the Web's interaction model, which, due to its distributed nature, differs considerably from other platforms. The interaction model is subject to variations, as in the context of recent tendencies toward more client-sided application logic and asynchronous communication between client and server, for example. This trend, based on technologies referred to as *AJAX* (Asleson and Schutta, 2006), focuses on user interfaces that provide a look and feel that resembles desktop applications.

3.2.5 Process

Beneath the user interface of a Web application lies the implementation of the actual application logic, for which the Web acts as a platform to make it available to the affected stakeholders. The *process* concern relates to the operations performed on the information space that are generally triggered by the user via the Web interface and whose execution is governed by the business policy. Particular challenges arise from scenarios with frequently changing policies, demanding agile approaches with preferably dynamic wiring between loosely coupled components. In case the application is not distributed, the process concern is hardly affected by Web-specific factors, allowing for standard non-Web approaches to be applied, such as

Component-Based Software Engineering (CBSE) (Heineman and Councill, 2001). Otherwise, service-oriented approaches account for cases where the wiring extends over components that reside in different locations on the Web, as covered by the next section.

3.2.6 Communication

Due to the Web's foundation on the Internet with its distributed and heterogeneous architecture of clients and servers, communication is obviously the underlying success factor for the Web as well as a major source of complexity challenging Web application development. To begin with, this applies to the message exchange between user agents (e.g., browsers) and server-sided applications. In this context, issues to be addressed are closely related to the dialogue concern and include, for example, caching strategies as well as session handling to overcome the stateless nature of the underlying communication protocols. More complexity arises when applications are involved that go beyond isolated monolithic sites, connected only on the surface via HTML links. Such application-to-application communication scenarios allow multiple distributed autonomous and loosely coupled services to interact with each other within the scope of a *service-oriented architecture* (SOA) (Booth et al., 2003). Together with the means to describe, publish, and find services, this architecture paves the way for extending the application idea on a global scale.

3.3 PLATFORM FOR DISTRIBUTED APPLICATIONS

As mentioned before, the Web is still growing in size and simultaneously changing in terms of how it is put to use. In order to highlight some recent paradigm shifts, this section elaborates solely on the communication aspect to show how the Web is increasingly turning into a platform for distributed applications, whereas the following chapters mainly focus on the remaining five aspects.

3.3.1 Technological Trends

Many concepts found in the state of the art of distributed Web applications are not completely new, but can also be found in earlier approaches. Pre-Web communication standards like message-oriented mechanisms or remote procedure call (RPC) have been applied by technologies such as CORBA or (D)COM. As an equivalent specification for the Web, the

Simple Object Access Protocol (SOAP) (Box et al., 2000) emerged, governing the invocation of *Web services*. Being an application of the XML, this protocol is independent of platform technology and transport mechanism, as required by the heterogeneous environment of the Web. A diversity of transport alternatives, including HTTP over port 80, mail, or even fax, makes it suitable for innovative end-to-end communication scenarios involving the invocation of services worldwide. As such, SOAP, together with WSDL as a specification to define service interfaces, and UDDI as a specification of a registry service for advertising these, provide a basic infrastructure for distributed applications on the Web. To account for additional messaging needs, further specifications have been developed as protocol extensions, covering issues such as message security, reliability, and transactions.

The first fields of application for the Web service concept were mostly restricted to the intranet of individual companies. Seen as a means for integrating legacy systems that may be distributed over multiple platforms and company sites, this technology can be applied to rigidly connect applications that may not be related to the Web at all. From the perspective of the Web as a platform, more interesting scenarios involve a larger number of services that are as publicly available as Internet Web sites and that are combined to create additional value. Today, tendencies in the Web to this end, together with many other emerging concepts, can collectively be referred to as Web 2.0 (O'Reilly, 2005). As a simple form of service, the XML-based RSS feed has already become relatively popular, often in the shape of Weblogs (short form: blog). The resulting kinds of applications are characterized by a new style of collaborative development, e.g., Wikipedia or interorganizational business applications. In this context, a growing number of Web services are published that give access to massive data stores or process logic as a new business concept, such as the functionality belonging to Amazon or Google. The sum of available services, also referred to as the API-Cloud, has the potential to add value to other Web applications that could not provided by locally deployed components.

3.3.2 Selected Aspects of Distributed Web Applications

Returning to the matter of Web application development with special emphasis on distribution and the mentioned technological advances, this section presents some problem aspects of corresponding applications. For the purpose of visualization, architecture illustrations are given for each case, using the notations of the WebComposition Architecture Model (WAM) (Meinecke and Gaedke, 2005). WAM is specialized on the description of distributed interorganizational Web applications and comprises an easy-to-communicate

Figure 3.1. WAM symbol for a single Web application.

"pen & paper" graphical notation. Figure 3.1 contains, as the most basic case of a Web application model, the symbol for a single Web portal that is not distributed in any way.

In the subsequent sections, this abstract example is gradually extended to outline a selection of possibilities that arise from the integration of distributed artifacts over the Web. More specifically, the presented subjects of integration are services, access policies, federation partners, and devices.

3.3.3 Service Integration

As a first alternative of distribution, a Web portal can invoke Web services that either offer functionality formerly included in the monolithic Web application or serve as access points to external data sources and systems. Hence, the service-oriented approach offers a way of decomposing functionality into reusable parts with defined interfaces. The invoked services may in turn invoke others to perform the requested operation and afterwards combine the obtained results. This is also the case in the scenario in Figure 3.2, in which a composite Web service aggregates the functionality of three atomic services.

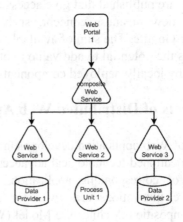

Figure 3.2. Example involving the integration of legacy data sources and process units.

Depending on the concrete realization, service composition may vary from a hardwired approach up to a completely loosely coupled binding of exchangeable services. On a higher detail level, one can distinguish between the service and the component that provides the actual functionality to be integrated. In the example, there are two data providers that, from the model's point of view, only act as components for storing and retrieving data, as well as a process unit that, when triggered by the wrapping Web service, performs additional operations.

3.3.4 Identity and Access Management

The need for identity and access management arises in situations where the offered services and applications are not intended to be publicly available in an uncontrolled manner. For example, payment might be charged for the usage of a service, up to the point where a company's business model depends exclusively on rendering services over the Web. Other reasons include the necessity of confidentiality due to legal obligations or the need for an established identity to enable service personalization. Unlike, for example, an operation system platform, the Web does not include the concept of a uniform user identity (Cameron, 2005). Hence, to overcome the diversity of proprietary approaches built into individual applications and services, additional security- and identity-related protocols have to be applied (Scavo and Cantor, 2005). In the example in Figure 3.3, a common security zone has been established (defining a uniform access control policy for *Company A*), surrounding all services and applications of the company.

User identities are managed with the help of an identity provider that facilitates a central login form and account database, allowing for single sign-on (SSO) across multiple portals. This concept can also be extended for

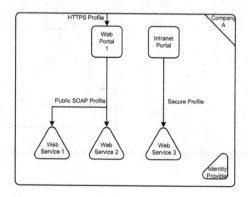

Figure 3.3. Example involving a uniform access control context (realm).

controlling accesses on Web services by obliging requestors to include security tokens (obtained from the identity provider) into their SOAP messages. Further security-related design decisions include the distinction between different access profiles that specify the allowed protocols and scope of visibility for individual services and applications.

3.3.5 Federation

Situations in which the necessity for the integration of external services (as in Section 3.3.3) coincides with requirements for established identities and access control (as in Section 3.3.4) raise a set of new problems. Among these problems, many are related to identities that have multiple accounts for accessing resources from multiple realms, causing security vulnerabilities and unnecessary administration efforts. In contrast, identity federation approaches assume only one account per identity, accepting requestors with external accounts based on explicit trust relationships between the federation partners. As one of several issues related to "portal federation," this topic is receiving growing attention in science and industry (Gootzit and Phifer, 2003). Figure 3.4 depicts the architecture of an application that extends across two companies.

Here, the two partners agreed upon a unidirectional trust relationship, allowing users at *Company A* to sign on at *Web Portal 2* with their native account as a form of interorganizational single sign-on. Furthermore, *Web Service 4*, which is otherwise not accessible to the general public, is made available. In both cases, the authorization is governed by predefined rules that map the foreign identities to locally meaningful access control decisions.

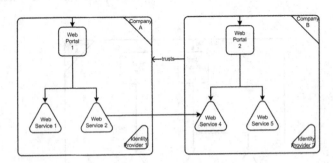

Figure 3.4. Example involving the sharing of resources from autonomous partners.

3.3.6 Device-Spanning Applications

Regarding distribution from a more hardware-oriented point of view, Web applications can be enriched by the use of nontraditional platforms other than the personal computer. To this end, the vision of the *Embedded Web* is to extend the common use of the Web by integrating Web server technology into all sorts of equipment to improve their overall intelligence, functional capability, and interactivity (Lee et al., 1997). This can take the form of Web user interfaces, integrated into car radios, for example, or Web service interfaces that expose device functionality to be integrated into device-spanning Web applications. A challenging question in this context is how the concepts and technologies targeted at the common Web can be applied to Web applications enriched with devices. As an example, Figure 3.5 describes a federated scenario in which sensors and actuators belonging to multiple organizations are being integrated as physical components into the distributed Web application, allowing for innovative kinds of business concepts.

Like in the scenario in Section 3.3.5, a foreign Web service is made available, only in this case to provide control over an underlying air-conditioning system. This allows *Company A*, which possesses a network of meteorological stations and temperature sensors providing accurate weather forecasts, to regulate the indoor climate at *Company B* very efficiently. The involved Web services are either integrated into the devices themselves or deployed on computers that are connected to the devices with non-Web technologies—allowing for these new kinds of service provider solutions.

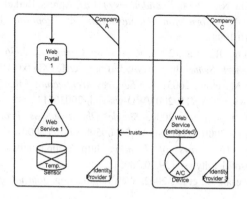

Figure 3.5. Example involving a device-spanning federation.

3.4 SUMMARY

This chapter gave an overview of the development of the Web, seen as a platform for delivering applications to users worldwide. Originally focused on the publications of documents, the Web has been used in different ways, reflected by changing paradigms such as the print paradigm, the hypertext paradigm, the multimedia paradigm, the docuverse paradigm, and the interactive paradigm. During this development, the Web application has emerged as a new form of interaction between humans and machines. For the disciplined construction of such Web applications, one can distinguish between different concerns, i.e., Web-specific aspects of the design and implementation: data, presentation, navigation, interaction, process, and communication. As the Web continues to grow, new types of applications evolve. Among the current tendencies that are often referred to as Web 2.0, one is the trend toward applications that compose functionality from distributed sources using Web service technology. Resulting from this new paradigm, applications can integrate data and software systems via service interfaces, share access policies, extend safely across organizational boundaries, and include the functionality of devices as integral parts.

REFERENCES

Andresen, L., 2003, *Dublin Core Metadata Element Set, Version 1.1: Reference Description.* http://dublincore.org/documents/dces/.

Asleson, R., and Schutta, N.T., 2006, *Foundations of Ajax.* Apress, Berkeley, CA.

Berners-Lee, T., 1990, *Information Management: A Proposal.* http://www.w3.org/Proposal.html (10.10.1998).

Berners-Lee, T., Fielding, R., et al., 2005, *Request for Comments: 3986, Uniform Resource Identifier (URI): Generic Syntax.* http://www.ietf.org/rfc/rfc3986.txt (10.05.2006).

Booth, D., Champion, M., et al., 2003, *Web Services Architecture - W3C Working Draft 14 May 2003.* http://www.w3.org/TR/2003/WD-ws-arch-20030514/.

Box, D., Ehnebuske, D., et al., 2000, *Simple Object Access Protocol (SOAP) 1.1.* http://www.w3.org/TR/2000/NOTE-SOAP-20000508/ (12.05.2000).

Cameron, K., 2005, *The Laws of Identity.* http://msdn.microsoft.com/library/en-us/dnwebsrv/html/lawsofidentity.asp (29.10.2005).

Deshpande, Y., Murugesan, S., et al., 2002, Web Engineering, *Journal of Web Engineering,* **1**(1): 3–17.

Dijkstra, E.W., 1982, How do we tell truths that might hurt? *SIGPLAN Notices,* **17**(5): 13–15.

Gaedke, M., 2000, *Komponententechnik für Entwicklung und Evolution von Anwendungen im World Wide Web.* Shaker Verlag, Aachen, Germany.

Gootzit, D., and Phifer, G., 2003, *Gen-4 Portal Functionality: From Unification to Federation.* Stamford, CT.

Guay, T., 1995, *WEB Publishing Paradigms.* http://www.faced.ufba.br/~edc708/biblioteca/interatividade/web%20paradigma/Paradigm.html (06.02.2006).

Heineman, G.T., and Councill, W.T. 2001, *Component-Based Software Engineering—Putting the Pieces Together.* Addison-Wesley, Boston.

Lee, B., Houtchens, S., et al., 1997, *WWW6 Workshop on Embedded Web Technologies.*

Lowe, D., 1999. *Hypermedia Patterns Repository (HPR).* Version 1.0, http://www.designpattern.lu.unisi.ch (23/03/99).

Meinecke, J., and Gaedke, M., 2005, Modeling federations of Web applications with WAM. *Third Latin American Web Congress (LA-WEB 2005),* Buenos Aires, Argentina, IEEE Computer Society.

Nelson, T., 1987, All for one and one for all. *Hypertext '87 Proceedings,* The Association for Computing Machinery, Chapel Hill, NC.

O'Reilly, T., 2005, *What Is Web 2.0—Design Patterns and Business Models for the Next Generation of Software.* http://www.oreillynet.com/pub/a/oreilly/tim/news/2005/09/30/what-is-web-20.html (18.10.2005).

Scavo, T., and Cantor, S., 2005, *Shibboleth Architecture—Technical Overview Working Draft 02, 8 June 2005.* http://shibboleth.internet2.edu/shibboleth-documents.html (02.11.2005).

The World Wide Web Consortium (W3C), 1997, *Web Accessibility Initiative (WAI).* http://www.w3.org/WAI/ (10.05.2006).

PART II

WEB DESIGN METHODS

Chapter 4

OVERVIEW OF DESIGN ISSUES FOR WEB APPLICATIONS DEVELOPMENT

Gustavo Rossi,[1] Daniel Schwabe,[2] Luis Olsina,[3] Oscar Pastor[4]

[1]*LIFIA, Facultad de Informatica, Universidad Nacional de La Plata (also at CONICET) Argentina,* gustavo@lifia.info.unlp.edu.ar

[2]*Departamento de Informática, PUC-Rio, Rio de Janeiro, Brazil,* dschwabe@inf.pucrio.br

[3]*GIDIS_Web, Engineering School, Universidad Nacional de La Pampa, Calle 9 y 110, (6360) General Pico, LP, Argentina,* olsina1@ing.unlpam.edu.ar

[4]*DSIC, Valencia University of Technology, Valencia, Spain,* opastor@dsic.upv.es

4.1 INTRODUCTION

In this part of the book we will focus on design issues in Web applications development. To make the book useful both for practitioners and for researchers, we decided (following the successful style of the IWWOST series) to use a common example throughout the rest of the chapters in which each design method is presented. In the following two sections we summarize the most important aspects that development approaches should consider, and then we briefly present the example that will be solved subsequently in each chapter. The aspects we introduce in Sections 4.2 and 4.3 will be refined in each subsequent chapter of the book.

4.2 ISSUES FOR DESIGN METHODS

For discussion purposes, we have grouped the issues under four headings; in Section 4.7 we discuss some additional issues.

1. data/information, with issues relating to data representation
2. navigation, with issues relating to navigation structure and behavior

3. functionality, with issues relating to application functionality beyond navigation
4. presentation/interface, with issues relating to interface and presentation design

This order reflects to some extent the historical evolution of Web applications over time—from simple "read-only" applications to full-fledged information systems—and also reflects the nature of the methods themselves.

This is in contrast with a more software engineering-centered view, which might place "functionality" first, since it is an aspect of applications that all traditional software design methods have taken into account, followed by navigation, which was the "new" abstraction introduced by hypermedia and the Web.

The issues presented here address different aspects of Web applications, which exist to a greater or lesser extent in any such application. Any method purporting to help design Web applications should, therefore, address a significant number of such issues, if not all.

4.3 DATA/INFORMATION/CONTENT—WHAT IS THE SUBJECT MATTER OF THE APPLICATION?

Web applications, like any application, must deal with information items that constitute the problem domain, i.e., the subject matter of the application. The first aspect that a method must define is how to characterize such information items, providing a data model.

This is not a new problem; it has been dealt with in software development as well as in database design methods. Among the most popular are the entity–relationship (E/R) model and the relational model, which are clear examples of widely used extended data models. Also, the data counterparts of popular object-oriented (OO) models, such as UML and ORM, address this same problem. Although differing in details, they all provide for the definition of information items as composed of attributes, which characterize individual properties of such items. Most methods provide means to describe sets of items with the same attributes, usually through concepts such as "classes" or "entities." In addition, generalization and specialization hierarchies can typically be defined among classes or entities.

While Web-based applications do not present additional requirements for the expressiveness of such models, some methods offer additional abstraction mechanisms that allow one to deal with specific issues of the contents of Web applications, such as multimedia data types, or with multiple representations for the same information item.

Besides the information items, relations must also be represented. While some methods allow a single relation type, others provide specialized types such as aggregation and composition relations. In addition, cardinality constraints must also be expressed.

When applications must deal with extensive domains, model specification may become very large. Some methods provide modularization primitives that allow the specification to be broken into smaller parts.

The application itself may be represented in many ways. In some models, it is the union of all items; in others, there is a special element that stands for the application itself. For example, in object-oriented methods, it is sometimes called an "application singleton" since it is a single object instance of its class.

4.4 NAVIGATION

Although it might seem obvious, given the widespread experience people have using the Web, many authors do not distinguish navigation from other application functionalities or, frequently, equate it with any event that causes changes in the interface. It is clear that navigation is a salient feature of Web applications, but such authors don't consider it worthy of particular attention during application design; it is simply "another application functionality," and the notion of linking is simply ignored.

On the other hand, most current Web application design methods recognize navigation as an outstanding feature of Web applications and provide models and notations to specify it. Briefly stated, characterizing navigation aspects of a Web application entails defining the "things" being navigated and specifying how the navigation space is structured—what items are reachable from any given item. Since the semantics of navigation is better understood, it justifies providing specialized notations that help users describe this functionality on an appropriate level of abstraction.

Much in the same tradition as in the database world, design method proposers have realized that the items being navigated (variously called *nodes, objects,* etc.) are different from the conceptual items that make up the problem domain. Whereas conceptual items represent the information in a task- and user-independent way, navigation items are defined taking into account user requirements, providing a view over conceptual items. The idea is that this abstraction mechanism allows the hiding of unwanted details as well as the grouping of interrelated items, with respect to the user profile and the task being supported. This is analogous to the "external views" as related to "conceptual views" in traditional database design, where users actually manipulate (external) views over the conceptual objects.

Once navigation items have been characterized, methods must also allow the definition of the navigation space. For any reasonably sized application, defining the navigation space topology directly in terms of only "nodes-and-links" is too restrictive, since the amount of information quickly overwhelms both designers and users. Furthermore, descriptions at this low level miss the opportunity to exploit typically occurring regularities in the navigation space topology.

Many methods introduce higher-level abstractions that allow the navigation space to be defined in a more concise way, such as sets or (indexed, ordered) lists, navigation chains, etc. Such abstractions play an analogous role with respect to navigation topology as classes do with respect to object instances—they allow one to refer to the navigation properties of a large number of nodes (respectively, the structure and behavior properties of objects) with a single primitive (respectively, classes).

Such specifications will, in most cases, translate straightforwardly into implementation mechanisms for dynamic Web sites, where pages are not stored explicitly but are generated dynamically, on demand, combining HTML or XML templates with the appropriate data directly retrieved or computed from application data stored in databases.

The initial focus of most novice designers is on the navigation items that will be made available to users. More experienced designers have realized that equally important are the access structures that will lead users to the desired information items—there is no point in having elaborate, detailed information if the user can't reach it!

Consequently, defining the navigation space of Web applications necessarily entails defining its access structures. Once again, higher-level abstractions are necessary, such as (ordered) lists, guided tours, etc. For example, in our exemplar application described at the end of the chapter, we find indexes for accessing films by each of its specific features, such as genres or actors, or film directors, etc. More opportunistic indexes such as top-selling DVDs or today's recommendations are increasingly being used as well. Additionally, some methods also provide the means to specify items that are always accessible, i.e., items that can be reached from anywhere in the navigation space. For example, easy access to each key functionality is usually provided, for example, television movies, DVDs, access to the user's account or shopping cart, and so on.

4.5 FUNCTIONALITY (BEYOND NAVIGATION) AND TASKS

When the first applications were deployed in the WWW, they were mostly "read-only," meaning they allowed users to browse information (hence the name "Web browsers"!), but not to create or change information items. With the increased sophistication of the run-time environments of Web servers, applications have become increasingly more complex, reaching the current stage where browsers are really interfaces to full-fledged applications allowing the creation and modification of information items, often in a distributed, asynchronous fashion.

Since navigation is recognized as a special kind of functionality, most methods must allow the characterization of navigation states, i.e., the dynamic behavior of the application as the user navigates from node to node. The original browse-only applications had, therefore, only navigation states.

As additional functionality was added, the need arose to deal with its associated states and state changes. Stateful applications were already the norm outside the Web, and design methods proposed a variety of mechanisms to specify them. Web application design methods must allow the specification of such applications and integrate the application states with the navigation states. For example, the check-out operation in electronic stores represents a task that the user must fulfill; it is represented as a set of subtasks, although finally it consists of filling in a set of forms accessed as a sequence of nodes.

The added complexity arises from the combination of this functionality with navigation operations and the sometimes subtle interplay between them. For example, some application functions may only be accessed in certain navigation states, or, more generally, accessible functions may change depending on the navigation state. Conversely, certain navigation alternatives may only be available in certain functionality states; for example, personal data may only be accessed after the user has logged in.

The inclusion of states, coupled with the distributed nature of the WWW, naturally leads to the notion of non-atomic processes and transactions. Many applications allow functionality to be accessed as a sequence of steps, which may sometimes be interspersed with navigation operations. Conversely, some applications have the notion of transactions, which must be implemented over an essentially stateless run-time environment. Design methods must allow the specification of both types of run-time behavior, preferably independently of the run-time environment.

Another source of complexity is the inclusion of multimedia data, which are often combined with elaborate timing and synchronization requirements that must be integrated with the other functionalities.

To deal with these aspects, some methods propose new mechanisms, but many rely on integrating with or extending existing methods that have already been successfully applied to such aspects of application design.

4.6 INTERFACE AND PRESENTATION

Web applications are, obviously, interactive applications. Users access the application functionality, including navigation, through the interface. For some authors, the interface directly presents the conceptual information items and exposes the application functionality. In fact, applications typically react to some interface event (such as a link or button being clicked), triggering the corresponding functions, which in turn cause the interface elements to change in some way. Even for non-Web environments, many design methods already decouple interface design from functionality design as a way to modularize and reduce the complexity of the design task.

In contrast, for many design methods, a distinction should be made between interface transformations and navigation operations in Web applications. In other words, some interface events that trigger application functionality do not correspond to any navigation operation, even if the interface changes in some way. This is true even if there is access to the server as a result of the interface operation. A simple example is an update operation to an order being made, changing, for instance, the quantity of some item in the order. Even though this causes an access to the server, which triggers some script that updates the internal data structure representing the order (and possibly reflecting it in a database), there is no associated navigation—the item being "navigated" is still the same order.

Consequently, Web design methods must provide a way for the designer to specify the interface—which elements compose it and how it reacts to all possible events. The interface behavior must necessarily be tied to the application functionality, including navigation.

Web application interface design must deal with another dimension, namely graphic design. In contrast with non-Web applications, where the complete design is carried out by software engineers, the interface appearance of Web applications is mostly defined by graphic (or, in current parlance, user experience) designers, who determine the actual "look and feel" of the application. Design methods must allow the clear separation between the so-called abstract interface design, where interface functionality is defined, and the concrete design, where layout and graphical appearance are defined.

In addition, the existence of an abstract interface design is also useful because of the rapidly evolving technological platforms upon which Web applications are implemented. New standards are issued and new versions of Web browsers are released almost every six months. Having an abstract interface design allows a more stable part of the design that remains unchanged by such technological evolution to be encapsulated. Besides this type of evolution, market reasons tend to pressure many Web applications to periodically completely change their graphical appearance; the abstract interface designs also help to cope with this requirement.

The rapid introduction of new devices used to access the Web, such as palmtops and cell phones, presents yet another dimension of requirements. Since such devices provide radically different run-time environments, with more limited display and interaction capabilities, some design methods strive to identify a "device-independent" portion of the interface design that remains unchanged regardless of the device being used to access it.

4.7 FURTHER ISSUES

4.7.1 Design Process

The discussion so far has focused mostly on the representational needs of Web application design methods. Beyond that, methods must also address the design process itself. The Web environment presents additional demands on the development process, caused by factors such as

1. the specific target environment, which is a hypermedia, distributed client-server environment
2. the rapid evolution and constant change in the implementation environment
3. the accelerated design cycle
4. the broader and sometimes harder-to-characterize audience (or intended target user categories)
5. the multidisciplinary nature of the development team, involving other professional skills such as communicators, content experts, graphics designers, etc.

Some methods provide additional tools to capture or model requirements that are better suited for this environment; typically, they are also more focused on user (or stakeholder) needs, as opposed to focusing on the designer or contractor alone.

Although a very large number of applications are available on the WWW (basically, most moderately sized Web sites can be considered Web applications of some sort), it is also true that several of their characteristics can be found repeatedly across many applications. In other words, many subproblems recur, thereby presenting an opportunity for design reuse. After all, if a certain subproblem has been faced and resolved, why not reuse its solution, perhaps adapting it to the situation at hand?

There are several approaches to deal with this, some directly incorporated into the design methods themselves, others complementary to them. In this latter category, mechanisms such as design patterns are employed, allowing known problems and their solutions to be characterized in an easily used format.

On a higher abstraction level, it is also possible to recognize that certain types of applications, in given domains, also exhibit recurring structures. For example, most institutional Web sites are similar, as are many online stores. Some methods can be extended to allow the characterization of families of similar applications, effectively forming Web application design frameworks. Starting with such frameworks, it is possible to rapidly instantiate specific applications in the given domain, by appropriately instantiating the framework's hotspots.

As the number of different applications being deployed on the WWW increases, software engineers have identified a number of recurring functionalities. In addition to the various forms mentioned above, another approach to leverage this accumulated experience is to encapsulate these functionalities in components that can be composed to form a more complex application. More generally, complex applications can eventually be defined as the composition of simpler ones. In some methods, the notion of a component is available as a primitive, together with language specifying how a component can be composed.

4.7.2 Model Representation

An integral part of any method is the definition of the notation used to describe its models. Such a notation has many uses, as it must support the communication between

1. customers and designers
2. designers and end users
3. designers and other designers
4. designers and implementor
5. implementor and end users

and so on. Each of these communications poses different requirements on the notation. For example, the client–designer communication must allow the client to express himself as closely as possible to his own world and vocabulary; the designer–implementor communication must be precise and unambiguous to ensure that the implementation adheres to the specified application. Notations may be graphical, textual, or both.

Most methods propose a new notation, extend some existing notation, or use existing notation directly. The advantages of directly using or extending existing notation are that, in most cases, users do not have to relearn entirely new conventions, and existing tools may be used directly or extended as needed. On the other hand, if the existing notation is too limited in its expressive power, extending it may require so much that the additions offset these advantages, and it may be more effective to use an entirely new notation.

Since many methods propose different models for describing different aspects of the application, different notations are used, and the relations between the models must also be represented.

Other considerations for notations regard their adequacy for automated tool support and legibility in printed form.

4.7.3 Implementation

Designing and implementing applications using methods produces several documents and, as with any larger software development, is best supported by computer-aided software engineering (CASE) tools. Such tools may support only the specification and help manage the documentation but may also include the generation of the final running implementation. This may be achieved in a completely automatic fashion or may be semi-automated, requiring the designer to manually fill in implementation details that cannot be automatically determined by the CASE environment.

Most complex Web applications involve dynamic processing of information, which in turn requires extensions to the server. The CASE environment may only generate the application targeted at a specific run-time environment, for example, Apache server with PhP scripting, or may be configured to generate the application for various such environments. In some cases, run-time environments are part of a larger framework, such as J2EE.

In addition, it may be further customized to also take into account the various access devices possible, such as cellular phones or handhelds, and provide environment information to support ubiquitous applications.

Dynamic Web applications rely heavily on databases to store and manage their data. An important part of the generated application is its interface to the DBMS. Typically, this involves establishing a mapping between the information items in the application and the data items stored in the database. Once more, this interface may be automatically generated and managed by the CASE environment, or it may require the manual intervention of the designer. In some cases, the CASE environment may also provide support for performance tuning and for maintenance and evolution of the application.

However, the task of implementing Web applications is increasing in complexity day by day due to the continuous emergence of new platforms and technologies. Specific needs are also arising for the development of several kinds of Web applications: Web data systems, interactive systems, transactional systems, workflow-based systems, collaborative systems, site-oriented systems, social systems, ubiquitous systems, or Semantic Web applications.

In this context, Web Engineering methods are evolving to be properly adapted to the continuous evolution of Web system requirements and technology. Web Engineering is a domain where model-driven software development (MDSD) principles can be used to address the evolution and adaptation of Web software to new platforms and technologies in order to achieve technological independence.

The Model-Driven Architecture (MDA®) initiative from the Object Management Group (OMG™) proposes defining the software building process based on a set of models. Depending on the level of abstraction, these models are dependent or independent of technological issues. One of the major benefits that introduce this separation of concerns is that system definitions can be reused for generating the system implementation in different technologies. On the other camp, Software Factories promote the systematic reuse, the application of the product lines philosophy, the model-driven development, the definition and use of domain-specific languages, the development of frameworks, and the generation of incremental code.

Recent Web Engineering approaches have made real advances in the prospects that are offered by model-driven software development (MDSD). This becomes more evident if we consider that some Web Engineering methods have successfully adopted the MDSD principles. They address different concerns using separate models (navigation, presentation, data, etc.) and are supported by model compilers that produce most of the application's Web pages (using PHP, JSP, ASP.NET, etc.). Moreover, they also take into account the possibility of accessing these systems via different devices, such as cellular phones or handhelds, and business logic (using COM+, EJB, J2EE, Web services) based on the models. This may be achieved either completely automatically or semi-automatically, requiring the designer to manually fill in implementation details that the tool cannot automatically determine.

Several signs point out that the use of the MDSD approach is going to rapidly increase. First, MDSD has received significant support from both the

MDA and the Software Factories. Second, the proliferation of CASE tools that support MDSD-based approaches that claim to be "MDA-compliant" is widespread. Third, technologies and tools for developing "your own" DSDM tools (graphical editors, model transformers, code generators, etc.) have also become abundant. In this category of tools we can find a set of projects developed under the Eclipse Modeling Project (EMF, GMF, GMT, etc.) and the DSL tools that are integrated with the MS Visual Studio 2005 Team System Edition. In this context, companies and research groups are considering the development of their own CASE tool for supporting their own Web Engineering method (following the MDA, Software Factories, Product Lines, Generative Programming of whatever other, more specific proposal) using one of these tools.

Although current Web Engineering methods still present some limitations when it comes to modeling further concerns, such as architectural styles or distribution, the adoption of MDSD principles can help achieve a real technological independence. In this way, methods are ready to be adapted to the second (Web 2.0) or third (Web 3.0) generation of Web applications, giving support to AJAX-based (Asynchronous Javascript and XML) Rich Client applications, Mashups, folksonomies, REST or XML Web Services to integrate current Web applications with third-party services, portals, as well as legacy systems.

4.7.4 Evolution and Maintenance

The dynamic nature of the current Web environment, and of the Internet in general, means that applications evolve very rapidly, as does the environment in which they run. Some methods provide direct support for the evolution of Web applications or provide support for tracing design decisions at various levels, easing the maintenance problem.

The resilience of applications designed with such methods with respect to changes is in good part determined by the abstraction levels supported by the method. If the adequate abstraction levels have been provided, the magnitude of changes in the application should be directly proportional to the magnitude of the changes in their requirements or of their run-time environments.

4.7.5 Role of Standards

Perhaps the main reason for the success of the Web was its establishment and adherence to standards. Following this tradition, some methods adopt some of the more recent standard notations such as UML at the design level or XML at the data level, some with direct support from CASE tools. In such cases, adopting such standards may also affect the target run-time environments, since several of them already provide direct support for these standards. The adoption of these standards may also facilitate model interchange between tools supporting different methods, such as XMI for UML-based notations.

Although standards such as XML address the syntactical aspect of model specifications, it may also be possible to use other standards that advance further into the semantic realm, such as RDF, RDFS, or OWL.

4.7.6 Personalization and Adaptation

Personalization has become a very important issue in the Internet, as a consequence of the increasing sophistication of Web sites, driven by the unabated competition between sites to attract viewers. Even though almost from the beginning browsers allowed personalization of presentation features, the current ubiquity of the World Wide Web, together with the myriad of platforms that support some kind of browsing, has reshaped this problem toward building applications customized to the individual.

Designing personalized Internet applications may mean building different interfaces, customized to a particular device; providing different navigation topologies to different persons; recommending specific products according to the user's preferences; implementing different pricing policies, and so on. All these facets of personalization share the need of modeling the user and his preferences, building profiles, finding algorithms for best linking options, etc., and integrating them in a cohesive design.

Several types of personalization must be accommodated:

1. role-based personalization, where the user sees different items and has different options depending on his role
2. link personalization, where the actual navigation topology depends on the individual and her access rights
3. content personalization, where actual contents of information items change depending on the person accessing the content
4. behavior or functionality personalization, where the functions the user can activate, and their behavior, change depending on the user
5. structure personalization, where the entire application may be customized according to the user's preferences or profile
6. presentation personalization, where the appearance (look and feel) of the content is adapted to the user, not the content itself

Many methods provide primitives that directly support personalization design, whereas others provide only guidelines.

Personalization can be seen as a special case of a more general behavior, adaptation. This behavior allows Web applications to alter some of their own characteristics as a function of various possible parameters. Personalization is really adaptation in which the input parameter is the user's identity and role. Other possible parameters are geographic location, available bandwidth, input device, past browsing history, etc.

Adaptation is paramount in the case of ubiquitous Web applications, i.e., applications that can be accessed anywhere, anytime. This means that they must be context-aware, in the broadest sense—not only must the logical context be taken into account, but also the physical and geographical environments as well. Such awareness may be directly expressible by some primitives in certain methods or implemented by lower-level primitives in others.

4.7.7 Quality Assurance Issues

Current Web applications can be very complex products and critical assets for an organization, so their quality can, to some extent, determine the organization's success or failure.

Quality assurance is a key support process and strategy mainly at the organization's software project level, in order to assure high-quality products and services by providing the main project stakeholders with the appropriate visibility, control, and feedback on resources, processes, and associated products throughout the software and Web life cycle.

Quality assurance applies to evaluation not only of products, processes, and services but also of resources as development methods, development teams, among others. To be effective, the quality assurance strategy should be planned and integrated to the main processes in the early phases of a project: That is, plans, activities, and procedures that will add value to the project and satisfy functional and nonfunctional requirements should be established from the very beginning. Quality assurance as a support process deals ultimately with preventive, evaluative, and corrective actions.

To measure, evaluate, verify, and validate functional and nonfunctional requirements from the quality assurance standpoint, different classes of methods can be categorized, including, for example, testing, inspection, simulation, and surveys, among others. In turn, for each category, particular methods and techniques can be applied (e.g., feature analysis method, heuristic guidelines inspection, Web usage analyses, white box testing, and user testing, among many possibilities) regarding the specific evaluation objectives and information needs.

Functional requirements actually represent what the Web application must do and provide (i.e., the scope) in terms of functions, contents, and services for the intended users. Nonfunctional requirements actually specify the capabilities, properties, and constraints that those functions, contents, and services should satisfy under certain conditions, for the intended users and contexts of use. The former are supported by different Web development methods by providing constructors and models at the conceptual, navigational, or presentational level, etc., as introduced in earlier sections here (and illustrated throughout this book). These models usually serve as input to many evaluation, verification, and validation activities, in addition to particular models for functional testing as test cases models, among others. The latter are currently supported to some extent by a couple of Web development methods; moreover, very often methods are not well integrated with quality assurance activities.

For instance, in order to measure and evaluate the external quality or quality in use of a Web application (or its components), models for quality, or quality in use, or subcharacteristics such as usability, security, reliability, etc. should be specified. These models, which represent nonfunctional requirements, can be performed by means of characteristics and attributes, or by means of heuristic guidelines, or by categories and questionnaire items.

Therefore, as the reader can surmise, conceptual frameworks for evaluation (as we will discuss in Chapter 13) that allow specifying nonfunctional requirements at different stages, in addition to the measurement (e.g., based on metrics) and the evaluation (e.g., based on indicators) components, might be necessary in order to support the analyses and recommended actions. In fact, some of the measurement, evaluation, and verification activities may be integrated and even automated in software and Web development methods in a sounder way.

4.8 THE PROBLEM STATEMENT

We deliberately kept the specification of the example for this book simple to make it more understandable for a broad audience. The requirements of the proposed application case are just described textually to leave place for each author to express it using the corresponding method's primitives.

The goal is to model an Internet site like www.imdb.com (the Internet Movies Database). The site allows users to explore movies and television programs, their actors, directors, and producers. Movies descriptions contain director, actors, genre(s), user comments, user ratings, country of origin, qualification, etc. Information about soundtracks can also be obtained. Relationships with related movies can be explored. External links (such as the official movie Web site) are also provided. Actors and directors are described by a short bio, a photograph, and his/her filmography (as actors, producers, writers, directors, and other related roles). For example, for each actor one can explore all the movies he participated in. Photo galleries of the actor/director can also be explored. The filmography can be explored according to different criteria: awards, user's votes, genre, etc.

The site provides daily information on new movies, biographies of selected actors, and news on the world of movies. Regarding nonnavigational behaviors, it is possible to add comments to films (in the style of sites such as www.amazon.com). It is also possible to explore show times and to buy tickets in selected cinemas. In this regard it is possible to select a city and a movie (currently on exhibition) and get the list of cinemas in that city that are showing the film. It is possible to select one show time of a given cinema and buy a ticket to see the chosen movie. The site maintains a list of films currently playing, giving a short description, together with access to user comments.

In a similar sense, the site maintains a list of upcoming movies, information on festivals, awards (like Emmy, Oscar, etc.), and miscellaneous news. It is also possible to buy DVDs for some movies online, with the usual functionality for online stores. Search facilities are also provided for movies, actors, companies, etc.

Chapter 5

APPLYING THE OOWS MODEL-DRIVEN APPROACH FOR DEVELOPING WEB APPLICATIONS. THE INTERNET MOVIE DATABASE CASE STUDY

Joan Fons, Vicente Pelechano, Oscar Pastor, Pedro Valderas, Victoria Torres
Research Group OO-Method. Department of Information Systems and Computation. Valencia University of Technology. Camí de Vera s/n, E-46022, Spain, jjfons@dsic.upr.es

5.1 INTRODUCTION

A decade after the emergence of the Web Engineering (Murugesan and Desphande, 2001) discipline, the development of complex Web applications is still a relevant research topic. For many years, Web Engineering approaches have done an excellent job adapting software engineering (Pressman) methods that were initially conceived to support traditional (non-Web) software development to provide solutions for the development of Web applications.

All of these Web Engineering methods were based on a similar principle: Web applications must be developed by starting with a sound, precise, and non-ambiguous description of an information system in the form of a conceptual schema (CS). Then, the CS must be properly transformed into its corresponding software product by defining the mappings between conceptual primitives and software representations. To achieve this, traditional conceptual schemas, which were mainly focused on capturing the static structure and the system behavior, were extended with new models and abstraction mechanisms to capture the new aspects introduced by Web applications. There are basically two aspects: navigation aspects and presentation aspects. Some representative efforts to introduce these aspects into traditional conceptual modeling approaches are the Object-Oriented

Hypermedia Design Model (OOHDM) (Rossi and Schwabe, 2001), WebML (Ceri et al., 2002), UML-base Web Engineering (UWE) (Knapp et al., 2004), and Web Site Design Method (WSDM) (De Troyer, 2001).

In this context, recent Web Engineering approaches have made real advances in the prospects that are offered by the model-driven strategy (Mellor et al., 2003). This becomes more evident if we consider that some Web Engineering methods have successfully adopted the Model-Driven Architecture (MDA) proposed by OMG (MDA, 2004). In accordance with the MDA approach, CSs are compared to Platform-Independent Models (PIM). Then, these PIMs are transformed into Platform-Specific Models (PSM) by the application of model-to-model transformations.

Our proposal provides a very specific contribution within this context. We have adapted the Web Engineering method, Object-Oriented Web Solutions (OOWS), to be compliant with MDA. OOWS proposes a PIM that allows us to fully describe the different aspects that define Web applications. This PIM extends the conceptual schema of a traditional object-oriented development method called OO-Method (Pastor et al., 2001) by introducing new models for describing the navigational and presentational aspects that characterize Web applications.

The PIM proposed by the OOWS method provides all the information needed to perform what MDA calls an "automatic transformation." This transformation is made using a tool to transform a PIM directly into deployable code. This can be done since the PIM is computationally complete. To achieve this transformation, we extend the OO-Method code generation strategy by presenting a precise transformational process for obtaining code from the new models introduced by OOWS. This process introduces a set of correspondences between the PIM abstractions and the final software components. We have also extended the commercial tool that supports OO-Method in the code generation process (OlivaNova Model Execution, CARE Technologies) by integrating mechanisms that allow us to incorporate the transformational process into the automatic code generation process.

We also explain how the transformational process proposed to obtain code from the PIM has been defined taking into account the unique characteristics of Web applications that have not been dealt with in the past by the software engineering community. In particular, we focus on the increased emphasis on user interfaces that has emerged in the development of Web applications. In a world where success is measured in terms of number of visits, Web applications need to provide attractive user interfaces in order to engage users. Therefore, development companies need to involve not only software engineers [as occurs in traditional development projects (Reifer, 2000)] but also graphic designers who are able to design more attractive interfaces. We explain how our approach allows software engineers and graphic designers to work in a collaborative way through the entire development process.

The structure of this work is the following: Section 5.2 introduces an MDA-based view of the OOWS approach. It also describes the OO-Method foundations on which the OOWS is based. The new models that OOWS introduces in the PIM model are of special relevance. Section 5.3 presents a discussion of the model transformation strategy used to obtain code from these models. This section also presents an implementation framework that helps in the development of the final solution. Section 5.4 presents the Internet Movie Database case study in which all of these ideas are put into practice.

5.2 OOWS: AN MDA-BASED WEB ENGINEERING METHOD

OOWS is a Web Engineering method that provides methodological support for Web application development. OOWS is the extension of an object-oriented software production method called OO-Method. Nowadays, the OO-Method approach has an industry-oriented implementation named OlivaNova (OlivaNova Model Execution, CARE Technologies) that has been developed by CARE Technologies S.A.

Section 5.2.1 presents the OO-Method approach that deals with "classic" software development using model-driven techniques for software development. Section 5.2.2 presents OOWS, introducing the diagrams that are needed to capture Web-based applications requirements.

5.2.1 OO-Method Conceptual Modeling

OO-Method (Pastor et al., 2001) (see left side in Figure 5.1) is an OO software production method that provides model-based code generation capabilities and integrates formal specification techniques with conventional OO modeling notations.

OO-Method provides a PIM where a system's static and dynamic aspects are captured by means of three complementary views, which are defined by the following models:

- a **Structural Model** that defines the system structure (its classes, operations, and attributes) and relationships between classes (specialization, association, and aggregation) by means of a *class diagram*
- a **Dynamic Model** that describes the valid object-life sequences for each class of the system using *state-transition diagrams*. Object interactions

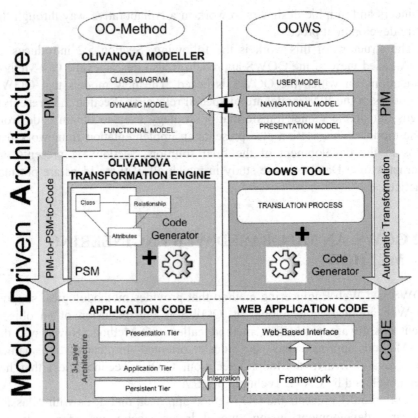

Figure 5.1. The MDA-based OO-Method/OOWS process development.

(communications between objects) are also represented by *sequence diagrams* in this model

- a **Functional Model** that captures the semantics of state changes to define service effects using a textual formal specification

OlivaNova, a commercial product, provides an operational, MDA-compliant framework, where a Model Compiler transforms a PIM into its corresponding Software Product. On one hand, the OlivaNova Modeller (OlivaNova Modeller, CARE Technologies) allows us to graphically define the different views that describe a system (the structural, dynamic and functional models). On the other hand, a set of OlivaNova Transformation Engines (OlivaNova Transformation Engines, CARE Technologies) compile these views in order to translate the conceptual primitives defined in the PIM into a specific implementation language. According to MDA, each OlivaNova Transformation Engine is a tool that automatically performs PIM-to-PSM transformations and PSM-to-Code transformations.

A three-tier architectural style has been selected to generate software applications:

- **Presentation tier:** It includes the graphical user interface components for interacting with the user.
- **Application tier:** This tier is divided into the Business façade, which publicizes the interfaces provided by the Business Logic, which implements the structure and the functionality of the classes in the conceptual schema.
- **Persistence tier:** It implements the persistence and the access to persistent data to hide the details of data repositories from the upper tiers.

As stated in Murugesan and Desphande (2001), Web applications introduce additional properties that are not addressed by software methods during the development process. In this sense, OO-Method is not an exception and requires some extensions in order to cope with them. These new properties refer to aspects such as navigation, presentation, and other advanced features such as user personalization. To achieve this, OOWS (see right side in Figure 5.1) introduces three new models into the PIM supported by the OlivaNova Modeller: the **user model**, the **navigational model,** and the **presentation model**.

These three new models allow one to fully describe Web applications at the PIM level. The code generation process implemented by the OlivaNova Transformation Engines must also be extended in order to automatically generate code from the OOWS models. However, this extension must be performed in a conservative way with respect to the transformation engines to assure compatibility with already developed software.

In order to achieve this conservative extension, we have defined a parallel translation process that generates code from the OOWS models. Then, the integration of both translation processes (OO-Method and OOWS) are performed at the implementation level.

The parallel translation process is supported by a tool that generates Web-based interfaces from the OOWS models. These interfaces are directly implemented from the OOWS models since these models contain all the necessary information to generate code. In accordance with MDA, we perform an automatic transformation.

The Web-based interface constitutes the presentation tier of the Web applications. To obtain full Web applications, this tier must be integrated with the application and persistent tiers generated by the OlivaNova Transformation Engine (the two tiers that implement the functionality of the system from the static and dynamic aspects described in the OO-Method models). To achieve this integration, we have developed a framework that allows us to implement Web-based interfaces and connect them with the services provided by the application tier generated by the OlivaNova Transformation Engine.

The following sections explain in detail the set of models introduced by the OOWS extension.

5.2.2 OOWS: Extending Conceptual Modeling to Web Environments

In order to fill the gap left by conventional software methods, the OOWS (Fons et al., 2003) approach defines the three new models mentioned above. The first model (the *User Model*) allows us to specify a categorization about the kind of users that can interact with the system as well as the inheritance relationships among these kinds of users. The second model (*the Navigation Model*) allows us to specify the system visibility (in terms of data and functionality) and the valid paths to traverse the system structure (navigational semantics) for each type of user. Finally, the third model (*the Presentation Model*) is introduced to specify presentation requirements for the elements defined in the Navigation Model.

5.2.3 User Model: User Identification and Categorization

A user diagram allows us to specify the types of users that can interact with the system. Types of users are organized in a hierarchical way by means of inheritance relationships, which allow us to specify navigation specialization (MDA, 2004). Child types of users can inherit the navigational semantics associated to their parent, which allows us to reuse navigational descriptions. This model categorizes types of users into three groups:

- *Anonymous users* (depicted with the '?' symbol). They represent users who are not logged into the system.
- *Registered users* (depicted with a pad-lock symbol). They represent users who are identified (logged) in the system as valid users.
- *Generic users* (depicted with a cross symbol). They are used to represent abstract users (users who cannot be instantiated).

An example of a graphical representation of this model is depicted in Figure 5.2. As this figure shows, the *Management Personnel* user has been defined as a *generic* user. This means that this kind of user will have an associated navigational model that will be enriched by the models defined by their inherited types of users. This inheritance mechanism allows different users to reuse navigational models.

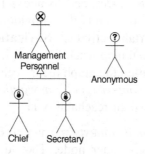

Figure 5.2. User diagram.

5.2.4 Navigational Model: Representing Navigation

The Navigational model was introduced in the OOWS approach to specify the view over the system in terms of classes, class attributes, and operations and relationships between classes for each kind of user defined in the *User Model*. This model is built in two phases. The first phase defines a global view over the navigation. This global representation is called "Authoring-in-the-large." The second phase makes a detailed description of the elements defined in the previous phase. This detailed view is called "Authoring-in-the-small."

5.2.5 The "Authoring-in-the-Large" Phase

The "Authoring-in-the-large" phase involves describing the navigation allowed for each kind of user by means a **Navigational Map.** Figure 5.3 depicts this map graphically by means of a directed graph whose nodes represent *navigational contexts* or *navigational subsystems* and whose arcs represent *navigational links* that define the valid navigational paths over the system.

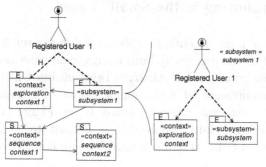

Figure 5.3. Navigational map and navigational subsystem.

Navigational contexts correspond to nodes from the navigational map and represent user interaction units that provide a set of cohesive data and operations to perform certain activities. **Navigational subsystems** are used to structure the navigational map when these get highly complex. They allow us to define subgraphs within the graph recursively.

Both *Navigational contexts* and *navigational subsystems* can be categorized depending on their reachability in

- *Exploration navigational contexts/subsystems* (depicted with an "E" label) are reachable from any other node. They define implicit navigational links. which are represented as dashed arrows pointing to these contexts.
- *Sequence navigational contexts/subsystems* (depicted with an "S" label) are nodes that can only be accessed following a predefined path. These paths are defined by linking different nodes using *sequence links*.

The *home* context (the context displayed by default when the user logs into the system) is defined as an exploration context whose implicit link is labeled with an "H."

Navigational links correspond to arcs from the navigational map and are used to define reachability paths among different nodes. There are two types of navigational links:

- *Sequence links* or *"contextual links"* (represented using solid arrows) involve a semantic navigation between two contexts and understand semantic navigation as the activity of carrying some information from a source context to a target context.
- *Exploration links* or *"noncontextual links"* (represented using dashed arrows) represent valid navigation paths through different contexts. In contrast to the navigation defined by sequence links, this navigation does not involve carrying information between contexts. These links are implicitly defined by exploration contexts or exploration subsystems.

5.2.6 The "Authoring-in-the-Small" Phase

Once navigational maps are built, the *"Authoring-in-the-small"* phase details the specification of the previously built navigational contexts. Navigational contexts are made up of a set of **Abstract Information Units** (AIU), which represent the requirement of retrieving a chunk of related information. *Contextual AIUs* (labeled with a circled C in Figure 5.4) filter this information using the information that is related to a sequence link. *Noncontextual AIUs* (labeled with a circled NC) do not depend on sequence links.

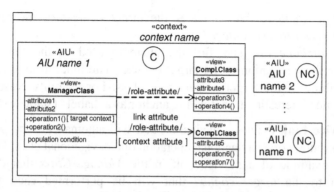

Figure 5.4. Navigational context.

AIUs are made up of **navigational classes**, which represent views over the classes defined in the Class Diagram (see Figure 5.4). These views are represented graphically as UML classes that are stereotyped with the *«view»* keyword and that contain the set of attributes and operations that will be available to the user.

Each AIU must include one navigational class (called the **manager class**) and can optionally include a set of complementary class views (called **complementary classes**) to complete the information retrieved by the manager class.

Navigational classes are related by unidirectional binary relationships called **navigational relationships**. These relationships are defined over existing association or inheritance relationships defined in the Class Diagram. To eliminate any possible ambiguity in the case of multiple relationships between two classes, navigational relationships must include the role name of the relationship (depicted graphically as /role-attribute/) as well as the attribute used as an anchor to move between navigational contexts. Moreover, depending on the navigational capability of the navigational relationship, these can be of two types:

1. A **context dependency relationship** (graphically represented using dashed arrows) represents a basic information retrieval by crossing a structural relationship between classes. When a context dependency relationship is defined, all the object instances related to the origin class object are retrieved.

2. A **context relationship** (graphically represented using solid arrows) represents the same information recovery as a context dependency relationship does plus a navigation capability to a target navigational context, creating a sequence link in the navigational map. Context relationships have the following properties:

- a *context attribute* that indicates the target context of the navigation
  (depicted as *[target context]*).
- a *link attribute* that specifies the attribute used as the *"anchor"* to
  activate the navigation to the target context. The link attribute is usually
  an attribute of the target navigational class. For usability reasons, it is
  sometimes interesting to define the anchor as a "label" (static text).

A **Service Link** defines a navigation that will automatically be performed
after the execution of a navigational operation of a navigational class. Figure 5.4
shows an example of a service link in the *ManagerClass* that defines a
navigation to the *target context* that will be performed each time the
"operation1()" is executed inside this context.

Apart from attributes and operations, navigational classes can also define
conditions to filter the retrieved objects. These filters are called **population
condition filters** and are specified by means of OCL formulas at the bottom
section of the class view primitive.

These are the core primitives for navigational specifications. However,
this specification can be enriched by introducing mechanisms to help the
user explore and filter the huge amount of information inside a context. The
following section explains how to introduce advanced navigational features
to the OOWS navigational model.

5.2.6.1 Advanced Navigational Features

Navigational contexts retrieve the population of classes defined in the
conceptual schema. We define the cardinality of a navigational context as
the number of instances that should be retrieved. Sometimes, the retrieved
information is difficult to manage mainly due to its size. To help users
browse through that amount of information, we have defined mechanisms
for browsing and filtering in a navigational context. There are two main
search mechanisms: **indexes** and **filters**. Those features are described in a
dashed-line box at the bottom of each AIU.

An **index** is a structure that provides an *indexed access* to the population
of the manager class. Indexes create a list of summarized information by
using an attribute or a set of attributes. If the indexed property belongs to the
manager class, it is defined as an **attribute index**. If the indexed property
belongs to any complementary class, the index is defined as a **relationship
index**, and the relationship must be specified. When an index is activated, a
list of all possible values for the indexed attribute(s) is created. By choosing
one of these values, all objects that have the same value for this property will
be shown in a search view. This search view describes the information that
will be available to the user to aid him in selecting an instance. This selected
instance will be activated in the navigational context.

A **filter** defines a *population condition* to restrict the object instances to be retrieved. If the filter condition is applied to attributes of the manager class, it is defined as an **attribute filter**. If the filter condition is applied to attributes of complementary classes, it is defined as a **relationship filter**. There are three types of filters:

- *exact filters*, which take one attribute value and return all the instances that match it exactly.
- *approximate filters*, which take one attribute value and return all the instances whose attribute values include this value as a substring.
- *range filters*, which take two values (a maximum and a minimum) and return all the instances whose attribute values fit within the range. If we specify only one value, it is only bounded on that side (upper or lower bounded).

Moreover, it is possible to predefine the values of the filter conditions at the modeling stage. This sort of filter is called a *static population condition*. The main difference between a *population condition filter* and a *static population condition* is that the former is always active while the latter has to be activated by the user. When a static filter is activated, the instances that fulfill the condition are displayed in a search view that behaves the same way as the *exact* filter defined above.

5.2.7 Presentational Modeling

Once the navigational model is built, we must specify presentational requirements of Web applications using a **Presentation Model** (see Figure 5.1). This model is strongly dependent on the navigational model since it uses navigational contexts (system–user interaction units) to define the presentation properties.

Presentation requirements are specified by means of patterns that are associated to the primitives of the navigational context (navigational classes, navigational links, searching mechanisms, etc.). The basic presentation patterns are as follows:

Information Paging. This pattern allows us to specify information "scrolling." All the retrieved instances are broken into logical blocks so that only one block is visible at a time. Mechanisms to move forward or backward are provided. This pattern can be applied to the *manager class*, to a *navigational relationship*, or to an *index* or a *filter*. The required information is

- *Cardinality*, which represents the number of instances that make a block.
- *Access mode*, which can be defined as *Sequential*, providing mechanisms to go to the next, previous, first, and last logical block or *Random*, where the user can directly access any block.

- *Circularity.* When this property is active, the set of blocks behaves as a circular buffer.

Ordering Criteria. This pattern defines a class population ordering (*ASC*endant or *DESC*endant) using the value of one or more attributes. It can be applied to either navigational classes or access structures, specifying how the retrieved instances will be ordered.

Information Layout. We provide three basic layout patterns and one layout operator. The three patterns are: *register*, *tabular (vertical and horizontal)*, and *tree*. The operator pattern (*master-detail*) is applied to many-to-many relationships using one of these basic layout patterns to show the detail portion. Any of these layout patterns can be applied either to the *manager class* or to a *navigation relationship*.

These presentation patterns, together with the specified navigation features, capture the essential requirements for the construction of Web interfaces.

5.3 DEVELOPING THE WEB SOLUTION

This section presents the development strategy defined in OOWS to implement Web application interfaces extending and using the OO-Method approach. The development strategy is based on the following principles:

- *Integrating OOWS code generation with the OO-Method software solution.* Web application interfaces developed with the OOWS approach must be integrated within the OO-Method implemented applications architectural style. Section 5.3.1 explains in more detail this requirement and the software artifacts offered by the OO-Method implemented applications for integration purposes.
- *Building Web-based user interfaces.* We defined a taxonomy of Web pages and contents by analyzing many implemented Web pages. This taxonomy allows us to build Web pages using "contents" as page components. Section 5.3.2 provides more details about this approach.
- *Implementation strategy.* We implemented a framework that provides us with a more abstract interface to develop Web pages. This framework produces HTML pages that use OO-Method implemented applications. The most relevant primitives of this framework are presented in Section 5.3.6.
- *Dealing with graphical design.* To cope with the look and feel of the implemented Web interfaces, we have defined a strategy that allows us to define visualization rules to improve Web page aesthetics. These rules

are categorized within two groups of rules: domain-dependent and domain-independent. Section 5.3.9 provides detailed information about this strategy and how it is applied by the framework.

5.3.1 Integrating OOWS Code Generation with the OO-Method Software Solution

As explained in Section 5.2.1, OO-Method uses a three-tier architectural style to generate software applications: a *presentation tier*, an *application tier*, and a *persistence tier*.

The information (*persistence tier*) and functionality (*application tier*) of the Web application are generated by the OlivaNova Model Transformation Engines taking as basis the OO-Method's structural and behavioral models.

Taking into account the navigational and presentation features introduced by the OOWS models, the generation process is enriched by providing a new translation process to generate the *presentation tier* for Web applications.

Applications generated with the OlivaNova Transformation Engines provide the following two integration mechanisms:

1. *Components.* The code generated by the ONME[1] is accompanied by two types of components for each domain class: *querying* and *business logic* components. *Querying components* provide operations for querying class population (retrieving instances by their identifiers or by filtering conditions, etc.) and operations for retrieving the population of related classes. *Business logic components* provide the functional operations for each class. Depending on the target technologies, those components are COM+ (VisualBasic), .NET components (C#), and EJB3.0 (Java).
2. *Web services.* The generated Web services encapsulate the previous components. These Web services decouple integrating applications from the ONME code technology. OlivaNova generates the following Web services: (1) a Web service for each domain class, which provides an interface for querying and for accessing business logic functionality, and (2) a generic Web service (*XML_Listener*) in an SOA architectural style; the port type of this Web service is implemented using the inversion of control pattern that provides an operation for each querying and business logic domain operation (see Figure 5.5).

---

[1] Acronym for OlivaNova Model Execution strategy

```
<?xml version="1.0" encoding="UTF-8"?>
<definitions name="XML_Listener">

    <message name="XML_Listener.XMLRequestInput">
        <part name="xmlRequest" type="xsd:string"/>
    </message>
    <message name="XML_Listener.XMLRequestOutput">
        <part name="return" type="xsd:string"/>
    </message>

    <portType name="XML_ListenerPortType">
        <operation name="XMLRequest" parameterOrder="xmlRequest">
            <input name="XMLRequestRequest" message="tns:XML_Listener.XMLRequestInput"/>
            <output name="XMLRequestResponse" message="tns:XML_Listener.XMLRequestOutput"/>
        </operation>
    </portType>

    <binding name="XML_ListenerBinding" type="tns:XML_ListenerPortType">
        <soap:binding style="rpc" transport="http://schemas.xmlsoap.org/soap/http"/>
        <suds:class type="ns0:XML_Listener" rootType="ServicedComponent">
        </suds:class>
        <operation name="XMLRequest">
            <soap:operation/>
            <suds:method attributes="public"/>
            <input name="XMLRequestRequest">
                <soap:body use="encoded" encodingStyle="http://schemas.xmlsoap.org/soap/encoding/"/>
            </input>
            <output name="XMLRequestResponse">
                <soap:body use="encoded" encodingStyle="http://schemas.xmlsoap.org/soap/encoding/"/>
            </output>
        </operation>
    </binding>

    <service name="XML_ListenerService">
        <port name="XML_ListenerPort" binding="tns:XML_ListenerBinding">
            <soap:address location="http://ascalon.dsic.upv.es:80/WSIMDb/IMDbWebSpace.XML.XML_Listener.soap"/>
        </port>
    </service>
</definitions>
```

Figure 5.5. XML_Listener Web service definition provided by OlivaNova.

5.3.2 Building Web-Based User Interfaces

Before defining Web page implementation, we started by analyzing many implemented Web pages. Our objective was to define what types of Web pages are commonly implemented as well as the contents that these should include. The idea was to try to define a strategy to decompose Web pages into different types of contents and, then, to try to map conceptual modeling primitives into these different contents.

This strategy also allows us to define different types of Web pages depending on the objective of each Web page. As an example, the following subsections show that there are Web pages whose purpose is to structure navigation, such as the "*home*" Web page.

Section 5.3.3 analyzes the different types of Web pages used to implement Web applications by defining the main objectives or goals of each one. Next, Section 5.3.4 defines the different types of contents that are used to define a Web page. Finally, Section 5.3.5 relates the Web page taxonomy with Web contents by defining which types of contents should or must appear in each type of Web page.

5.3.3 Web Page Taxonomy

After analyzing many implemented Web pages, we have categorized them into three basic types of Web pages: navigation structuring, informational, and data input. Each one of these types has a different objective within the Web application.

- *Navigation structuring Web pages.* This type defines some kind of navigation organization. When a user reaches a Web page of this type, the page provides the user with a set of links to the natural navigational links that she can follow. Web pages of this type should appear when there are a lot of navigation capabilities.
- *Informational Web pages.* This type provides the user with information and functionality related to an instance or group of instances of the system. With these Web pages, the system provides the user with information about the system state and the operations that are available in that state. Also, these Web pages can define navigation capabilities to other Web pages by "clicking" on some of their contents. These Web pages are the most common pages within a Web application.
- *Data input Web pages.* Web pages of this type are related to an operation execution (whenever the system needs some data from the user). When a user invokes an operation, if this operation requires additional arguments, the system displays a Web page of this type to the user. This Web page basically contains a form that includes an input mechanism for each argument that must be introduced.

A final consideration must be made with regard to this taxonomy. As the following section shows, each Web page can provide different types of contents, for instance, navigation content. This might lead to a misconception such as the following: All Web pages that have navigation contents are *navigation structuring Web pages*. However, this is not always true. We consider that a Web page has only one main objective and may have other objectives, but those are secondary. This reasoning is explained in more detail in Section 5.3.5.

5.3.4 Web Page Contents

At first glance, the types of Web pages described above appear to include totally different contents. However, a more careful analysis shows that this is not really true; in most cases, there exist different "pieces" of Web pages that are basically the same within many other Web pages, and other "pieces" that appear in all Web pages. For instance, most Web pages have a zone[2] where a navigational menu (made of navigational links) is provided.

After defining the different types of Web pages, we analyze the different types of contents of those Web pages. Following the same approach, we encountered the following zone contents:

- *Navigation zone*. It provides the user with a set of navigable links that can be activated within the Web page.
- *Location zone*. It provides the user information about where the user is and the navigation path (sequence of navigational pages) that he has followed to reach that location.
- *Information zone*. It provides information about the system (usually in a database).
- *Services zone*. It provides access to the operations that can be activated. This zone is contained inside an information zone, and all the operations are related to that information.
- *User information zone*. It shows identification information about the logged user. This zone only appears for registered users.
- *Institutional zone*. It contains information about the institution (company, entity, organization, etc.) that is responsible for the Web application. It usually shows information regarding the name of the institution, the logo, etc.
- *Data entry zone*. It is responsible for providing the user with a form to input data to execute certain operations. Then, a submit-like button links the input data with the associated functionality.
- *Application links zone*. It contains some common Web functionalities such as Login, Logout, and Home.
- *Access structures zone*. It contains search mechanisms to help in browsing data. In fact, this zone is always related to one *information zone*. For this reason, this zone always appears inside an information zone.
- *Custom zone*. It contains information regarding other types of contents that cannot be catalogued in the other zones. This zone is normally used for domain-independent content, such as advertisements, other related Web applications, external applications, etc.

To complete the approach, these content zones should be joined to compose Web pages. The next section discusses how these contents can be appropriately combined to build Web pages.

---

[2] We refer to "Web page zone" or simply "Web zone" as a cohesive data and functionality that has a meaning of its own.

5.3.5 Relating Web Page Taxonomy to Web Page Contents

Once Web page types and content zones have been defined, a relationship between them must be established by indicating which type of contents should or must appear in each type of Web page and how many times these contents can appear. We can mark a content zone as being *mandatory, recommended, optional,* and *not recommended.* We have followed a quality strategy to define what content zones appear to ensure that this particular type of Web page provides the user with the minimum information needed to accomplish the objective of that Web page type.

Moreover, there is a basic rule that is applied: A Web page must *always* provide the user with information regarding *where the user is, how the user arrived there* (navigational path), and *the places where the user can move from there.* This rule implies that any Web page must contain navigation and location zones.

Taking into account these basic principles, we have defined Table 5.1, which combines Web pages with content zones, indicating the suitability of including each content zone within each Web page category.

Table 5.1. Web Page Taxonomy Related to Web Page Contents

✓- Mandatory   ✗- Not recommended
♦ - Recommended   ?- Optional
✳- It can appear more than once

	Information Web Page	Navigation Web Page	Data Entry Web Page
Navigation zone	✓, ✳	✓, ✳	✓, ✳
Location zone	✓	✓	✓
Information zone	✓, ✳	✗	✗
Services zone	?, ✳	✗	?, ✳
User info. zone	♦	♦	♦
Institution zone	?, ✳	?, ✳	?, ✳
Link app. zone	♦	♦	♦
Data entry zone	✗	✗	✓
Access struct. zone	?	?	?
Custom zone	?, ✳	?, ✳	?, ✳

The *not recommended* tag is intended to mark contents that can overload a type of Web page with different objectives, possibly causing the user to get confused about or deviate from the main objective of that type of Web page. For instance, in a navigation Web page, content zones regarding information or data entry are *not recommended,* so that the main objective of this Web page is only to structure navigation.

Finally, note that this table has been used to define the types of Web pages that must be implemented as well as the types of contents that these pages should have. We have built an HTML framework that implements this table (see Section 5.3.6).

5.3.6 Implementation Strategy

The OOWS Tool provides a code generator that takes two PIM models (the OO-Method model and the OOWS models) and translates them into Web application code. This code defines the interface tier for Web application environments (see Figure 5.1). The generation process is only possible by having a set of predefined transformation rules that represents abstract concepts of the PIM model into specific code.

The following subsections explain the implementation strategy based on an implementation framework in detail. This framework raises the level of abstraction of the HTML code to a set of implementation patterns that define correspondences between conceptual modeling primitives and the implementation framework components. This framework also provides facilities to integrate with the OlivaNova generated code.

5.3.7 Implementation Framework

By following a pure MDA approach, we have defined a PSM model of the HTML language, which we implemented using PHP, creating an implementation framework that allows us to implement Web pages at a more abstract level of abstraction. We have implemented this Web page definition and implementation framework applying the taxonomy of Web pages and content zones presented in Section 5.3.2. This framework basically provides us with a set of primitives for defining two types of objects: a Web application and Web pages.

The *Application* object contains all the information about the application. It needs a name and the reference to the component that implements the functionality interface (provided by OlivaNova). This object provides the following operations:

- *AddRol(User, UserAlias, ValidationMethod, inheritsFrom)*. This operation defines the different types of users that can interact with the Web application. If a validation method is specified (by means of the OlivaNova generated user validation primitive), the user is registered. The final argument is used to specify user inheritance.
- *AddPageGroup(GroupName, GroupAlias, Group, User, Visibility)*. This operation defines a group of pages that will only be visible when navigating inside the group. The third (optional) argument specifies the group that this group is in. The fourth argument refers to the user who owns the page. The last argument can take the following values: "always" (a Web page that is always accessible) and "fromPage" (a Web page that is only accessible through another Web page).
- *AddPage(PageName, PageAlias, Group, User, Visibility)*. This operation defines a Web page (that can be inside a group) for a user. The last argument has the same meaning as in the *AddPageGroup* operation.
- *SetDefaultStyle(StyleName)*. This operation specifies the default style that will be used. If no style is defined, no style will be applied. More information about Web page visualizations is included in Section 5.3.9.
- *SetHomePage(PageName, User)*. This operation allows specifying the page that will be used as the user's home page.

These application primitives define the properties of the entire Web application. These primitives also implicitly define other properties. For instance, the navigational menu of every Web page is automatically created by using the *AddPage* and *AddPageGroup* operations (by using the visibility argument) and with the *AddRol* operation (for inheritance specification).

Figure 5.6 shows an excerpt of the code that implements a Web application using the proposed implementation framework. Both *AnonymousUser* and *RegisteredUser* are allowed to access the Web site (*AddRol*), and registered users also have access to the Web pages of the

```php
<?php
include_once "../Framework/ApplicationBegin.php";

$Application = new Application("OrderThingsDemo", "SimpleOrders");

$Application->AddRol("Anonymous","","","");
$Application->AddRol("RegisteredUser","RegisteredUser",
                     "RegisteredUser_MVAgentValidation","AnonymousUser");

$Application->AddFirstLevelPage("MembersList","Clients","AnonymousUser");
$Application->AddFirstLevelPage("ItemsList","Products","AnonymousUser");
$Application->AddFirstLevelPage("OrdersList","Client's Orders","AnonymousUser");
...
$Application->AddFirstLevelPage("MembersList","Clients","RegisteredUser");
$Application->AddPage("memberDetail","Detailed Information","RegisteredUser");

$Application->SetDefaultStyle("UPV-like");

$Application->SetHomePage("MembersList","AnonymousUser");
...

include_once "../Framework/ApplicationEnd.php";
?>
```

Figure 5.6. Example of an excerpt of a Web application definition.

AnonymousUser (through inheritance). There are five Web pages, three of which are separate and two of which are in a group. The three separate Web pages belong to the *AnonymousUser* (*MemberList*, *ItemsList*, and *OrdersList*), and the remaining two (*MemberPersonalInfo* and *memberDetail*) belong to the *RegisteredUser*. All of these Web pages are always accessible through the navigational menu. However, the *memberDetail* for the *RegisteredUser* isn't visible from the navigational menu. It can only be reached by navigating from another Web page. The *UPV-like* visualization style (*SetDefaultStyle*) has been selected. Finally, the home Web pages for the *AnonymousUser* and *RegisteredUser* are specified (*SetHomePage*).

Once each Web page has been defined, it must be described. The framework provides primitives to describe the content zones of these Web pages. Following the conclusions obtained in Section 5.3.5, the navigation and location zones must appear in every Web page. As the links in the navigation zone are derived from the Web application configuration and the location zone is derived from the user navigation path, the framework does not provide explicit primitives to define these zones. It calculates them automatically.

The framework provides a primitive to introduce the other type of content. Some examples are *AddInformationZone*, *AddInstitutionZone*, *AddUserInfoZone*, etc. The information zone is based on a manager class and provides operations for adding fields (*AddField*, class attributes), linking to other pages using a field as the anchor (*AddInternalLink*), and sorting by using a field (*SetSorted*) in "ascendant" or "descendant" mode, etc. The *AddDetailedRelationship* retrieves related data from a related class. Each one of these zones is implemented using HTML DIV containers.

Figure 5.7 presents an excerpt of the MemberList Web page definition for the *RegisteredUser*. It is made up of the following zones: (1) the navigation zone (implicit); (2) the location zone (implicit); (3) a user zone

```php
<?php
include_once "../Framework/PageBegin.php";

    $Page = new Page("MemberList","RegisteredUser");

    $UserZone = $Page->AddUserInfoZone();

    $InfoZone = $Page->AddInformationZone("MembersList","Member");
    $InfoZone->AddField("Username","Name");
    $InfoZone->Username->AddInternLinkTo("memberDetail");
    $InfoZone->Username->AddDynamicFilter("Approach");
    $InfoZone->Username->SetSorted("Ascendant");
    $InfoZone->AddField("Adress","Adress");
    $InfoZone->AddField("City","City");
    ...

    $ServicesZone = $InfoZone->AddServicesZone("MemberServices","Operations for Registered Users");
    $ServicesZone->AddServiceReference("RegisteredUser_create_instance","New");
    $ServicesZone->AddServiceReference("RegisteredUser_MVChangePassword","Change password");
    ...

include_once "../Framework/PageEnd.php";
?>
```

Figure 5.7. Example of an excerpt of a Web page definition using the framework.

(*AddUserInfoZone*) in which information about the user is displayed; (4) an information zone called *MemberList* that provides information about the *Member* class and its *Username, Address,* and *City* attributes (sorted by *Username* "ascendant"). The username has been defined as an anchor to navigate to the *memberDetail* Web page (*Username->AddInternalLinkTo*). Finally, (5) the service zone has been included inside this information zone (*InfoZone->AddServicesZone*) to allow *RegisteredUser*s to execute the *RegisteredUser_create_instance* and *RegisteredUser_MVChangePassword* operations. These operations come from the OlivaNova specification (see Section 5.3.1 for more details about integration with OlivaNova).

5.3.8 Implementation Patterns Using the Framework

Finally, correspondences between the OOWS conceptual modeling primitives with the implementation framework primitives must be defined. This step is automatically applied by a model-to-code generator. The first rule always creates a Web application project by defining the application (name) and the default visualization style (see the Figure 5.6 primitive *new Application*). Then several groups of transformation rules are applied to complete this transformation process, taking the OOWS models as input.

(1) Transformation rules referring to the user diagram:

(1.1) *User rule*: For each user defined in the navigational map, an *AddRol* operation is created in the Web application definition file. If it is an anonymous type of user, the validation operation is not specified. If a user is a specialization of another user, it is specified using this *AddRol* operation.

(2) Transformation rules referring to the navigational map:

(2.1) *Page group rule*: For each navigational subsystem that appears in the navigational map, an *AddPageGroup* operation with the "always" *visibility* argument is created. It is specified to belong to the user of the navigational map in which it is defined. If it is inside a subsystem, the group that is related to that subsystem is specified.

(2.2) *Page rule*: For each exploration navigational context that appears in the navigational map, an *AddPage* operation with the "always" *visibility* argument is created. For each sequence navigational context, an *AddPage* instruction with the "fromPage" *visibility* argument is created. All these pages are specified to belong to the user of the navigational map in which they are defined. When these nodes are inside a subsystem, the group that is related to that subsystem is specified.

(2.3) *Home page rule*: A home navigational node can be defined in a navigational map. The generation process establishes this page as the home page with the *SetHomePage* operation. If no node has been defined as the home page, a new page is created using *AddFirstLevelPage* and marking *SetHomePage*. Each navigational subsystem must have a home page. The same algorithm is applied recursively, treating each navigational subsystem as if it were a navigational map.

(3) Transformation rules from the navigational node specifications

Each navigational node has been specified as a Web page by the (2.1) rule in the Web application definition file. In this step, the transformation process creates a Web page definition file for each one of these specified Web pages. Depending on the type of the navigational node, one of the following rules is applied:

(3.1) *Navigational context rule*: An informational web page (see taxonomy in Section 5.3.3) file is created. A new information zone is created for each AIU. Then an *AddField* is invoked for each navigational attribute of the manager class. A (sub)zone is created using the *AddServicesZone* if the manager class has at least one operation. This (sub)zone includes a service reference (*AddReference*) for each operation of the manager class. Finally, an *AddDetailedRelationship* operation is created for each navigation relationship. Each attribute, operation, or relationship is also defined.

(3.2) *Navigational subsystem rule*: A navigation structuring Web page file is created. As the pages inside this subsystem have already been created with the (2.1) rule, the framework automatically creates a navigation zone containing the links to all these related Web pages.

The transformation process has more rules than the ones just mentioned (for instance, it includes rules regarding the presentation model). However, for reasons of brevity, these transformation rules are not presented.

5.3.9 Dealing with the Graphical Design of Web Interfaces

The graphical design, or "look and feel," of a Web application is a requirement that must be properly managed when building Web applications. Nowadays, Web application graphical design is usually built by means of *visual styling rules* defined in specific languages such as the CSS language (cascade style sheet), which is standardized by the W3C.

The OOWS implementation strategy objective is to deal with a few basic principles with regard to graphical design:

- *Separation of concerns*. System designers should not take graphical design into account when designing the system. Only graphical designers should deal with these graphical designs.
- *Reusability*. Graphical designs should be reusable for any application.

- *Adaptability*. Graphical designs should be easily adapted for specific applications so that specific visualization rules can be defined.
- *Visualization patterns*. On the World Wide Web, visualization patterns are used now and then in Web applications. Those visualization patterns that are widely used must facilitate the graphical design description. These visualization patterns should be used.

OOWS follows this strategy to apply these principles to define Web interfaces:

1. Use specific languages for the definition of the visualization rules (CSS) and do it in separate files: None of the implemented Web pages should include visualization rules (we use XHTML to define Web pages).
2. Define a markup of Web pages based upon conceptual terms and not on implementation terms.
3. Create two files for defining visualization rules: a domain-dependent file that includes rules that can only be used in Web pages of the same domain, and a domain-independent file that includes generic rules that can be applied to any Web page, independently of the application domain.
4. Publicize a repository of graphical designs and visualization patterns. This repository should be used by the implemented Web pages to obtain the visualization rules.

The implementation framework is responsible for marking up the Web pages and linking to the two graphical design files (domain-dependent and domain-independent files). Section 5.3.10 discusses the markup strategy that must be undertaken in each implemented Web page. Section 5.3.11 explains how to define domain-independent and domain-dependent visualization rules.

5.3.10 Web Page Markup

The framework implements a Web page markup strategy that divides the tags into two groups: domain-dependent tags and domain-independent tags.

The **domain-independent tags** are based upon the OO-Method/OOWS primitives and terms that come from the Web page and content taxonomy discussed in Section 5.3.2. Each specific content zone has its own tags. This group of tags defines generic visualization rules that can be applied to every Web application implemented with the framework since the concepts they use are domain- and platform-independent.

The **domain-dependent tags** are based upon domain-specific terms. These group of tags can appear anywhere in the Web page where the term related to the tag is used. This markup defines visualization rules for that specific application. However, as the following section discusses, the visualization rules that use these tags won't be reusable.

The following list shows the most representative Web zones as well as the domain-independent (DI) and domain-dependent (DD) tags that are used within those zones. This markup is shown in Figure 5.8.

- **Web page body.** The following tags can be applied to the HTML BODY construct:
  DI tags: *Context, Subsystem*
  DD tags: the name of the context or the subsystem
- **Location zone**
  DI tags: *LocationZone, Path, PathStep, PathStepSeparator*
  DD tags: the name of the contexts or subsystems related to each *PathStep*
- **Navigation zone**
  DI tags: *NavigationZone, NavigationLink, NavigationGroup*
  DD tags: the name of the contexts or subsystems related to each *NavigationLink*
- **Information zone.** This is the most complex zone. The tags are structured into the different DIVs that define this zone.
  DI tags: *InformationZone, AIU, ManagerClass, ComplementaryClass, AttributeName, AttributeValue, Operation,* etc.
  DD tags: the *AIU* name, the name of the OOWS navigational classes related to the *ManagerClass* and *ComplementaryClass* tags, etc.

CSS provides two types of tags that can be used for marking up the HTML code: *class* and *id*. Domain-independent tags are defined using the *class* construct. Domain-dependent tags are defined with the *id* construct.

Figure 5.8 shows an example of a Web page excerpt that has been implemented using this markup strategy. This Web page has been generated using the OOWS implementation framework for the *Movie.Overview. MainDetails* Web page that appears in Section 5.4.5 (Figure 5.20).

5.3.11 Visualization Rules

The visualization rules define how elements of the Web page must be visualized, referring to their location, size, color (background, text, etc.), type, etc. depending on the element type and tag used. These rules are defined in separate files from the HTML content using CSS as its definition language.

```
<?xml version="1.0" encoding="iso-8859-1"?>
<!DOCTYPE html PUBLIC "-//W3C//DTD XHTML 1.0 Strict//EN" "http://www.w3.org/TR/xhtml1/DTD/xhtml1-strict.dtd">
<html xmlns="http://www.w3.org/1999/xhtml" lang="en-US">
<head>
<title></title>
<link rel="stylesheet" type="text/css" href="style/dd-IMDb.css" />
<link rel="stylesheet" type="text/css" href="http://ascalon.dsic.upv.es/Styles/IMDb/di-IMDb.css" />
</head>

<body class="Context" id="NC_Movie_Overview_MainDetails">

<div class="LocationZone">
 <div class="Path">
  <div class="PathStep"><a class="PathStep" id="Movie_Overview_MainDetails" href="MainDetails.php"><span
                        class="PathStep" id="NS_Movie">Movie</span></a></div>
   <div class="PathStepSeparator"><span class="PathStepSeparator"></span></div>
   <div class="PathStep"><a class="PathStep" id="Movie_Overview_MainDetails" href="MainDetails.php"><span
                        class="PathStep" id="NS_Overview">Overview</span></a></div>
    <div class="PathStepSeparator"><span class="PathStepSeparator"></span></div>
    <div class="PathStep"><a class="PathStep" id="Movie_Overview_MainDetails" href="MainDetails.php"><span
                        class="PathStep" id="NC_MainDetails">main details</span></a></div>
 </div>
</div>

<div class="NavigationZone">

<div class="NavigationGroup">
 <div class="NavigationLink" id="NC_NowPlaying"><a class="NavigationLink" id="NC_NowPlaying"
        href="NowPlaying.php"><span class="NavigationLink" id="NC_NowPlaying">NOW PLAYING</span></a></div>
<div class="NavigationLink" id="NC_MovieNews"><a class="NavigationLink" id="NC_MovieNews"
        href="MovieNews.php"><span class="NavigationLink" id="NC_MovieNews">MOVIE/TV NEWS</a></div>
<div class="NavigationLink" id="NC_MyMovies"><a class="NavigationLink" id="NC_MyMovie"
        href="MY_Movies.php"><span class="NavigationLink" id="NC_MyMovies">MY MOVIES</a></div>
...
</div>

<div class="InformationZone">

<div class="AIU" id="AIU_Movie_Main_Details">
<table class="ManagerClass" id="Class_Movie">
 <tr><th class="AttributeName" id="Class_Movie_Title"><span class="AttributeName"
                                id="Class_Movie_Title">Title</span></th>
     <td class="AttributeValue" id="Class_Movie_Title"><span class="AttributeName"
                                id="Class_Movie_Title">The Godfather</span></td></tr>
 <tr><th class="AttributeName" id="Class_Movie_Year"><span class="AttributeName"
                                id="Class_Movie_Year">Year</span></th>
     <td class="AttributeValue" id="Class_Movie_Year"><span class="AttributeName"
                                id="Class_Movie_Year">1972</span></td></tr>
...
</table>
</div>

<div class="AIU" id="AIU_User_Comments">
...
</div>

...

</div>

</body>
</html>
```

Figure 5.8. Web page with both domain-dependent and domain-independent tags.

As discussed in Section 5.3.10, we define two types of visualization rules: domain-independent and domain-dependent rules, so there are two files with two groups of rules.

By combining those ideas with the markup strategy, we can define really complex visualization rules, even those that involve both domain-dependent and domain-independent tags (in this case, the rule must be considered domain-dependent).

Graphical designers focus their efforts on defining these files. There is no need to interact with system developers because the graphical designers know a priori which tags will be used to implement the Web application. In addition, it is more effective to define the visualization rules based on conceptual terms rather than defining or converting these rules into solution-dependent terms (HTML, etc.).

Here we present two examples of visualization rules:

- "Put the navigation zone of each Web page at the top of the page. Put a vertical bar between each navigational link. All IMDb Web pages must show the IMDb logo." These are three examples of domain-independent visualization rules.
- "Movie titles must appear in large-sized, bold type." This is an example of a domain-dependent visualization rule.

Figure 5.9 shows the representation of these visualization rules using CSS markup language. These visualization rules come from the IMDb visualization rules used in the implementation discussed in Section 5.4.

```
...
.Context {
      background-image: url("logo.jpg");
}

.NavigationZone {
            z-index:1;
            position: absolute; top:35px; left: 170px;      ...
            font-weight: bold;                               #Class_Movie_Title {
            font-size: 9px;                                        font-weight: bold;
}                                                                  font-size: 15px;
                                                          }
.NavigationGroup div.NavigationLink + div.NavigationLink {
            border-left-style: solid;                        ...
            border-width: thin;
            padding-left: 5px;
}

...
```

Figure 5.9. Example of domain-independent (left panel; di-IMDb.css) and domain-dependent visualization rules (right panel; dd-IMDb.css), respectively.

5.4 CASE STUDY: THE IMDB INTERNET MOVIE DATABASE

The IMDb Internet Movie Database (IMDb) is an online repository of information related to the movie world. As stated in its official Web site (www.imdb.org), it is "the Earth's Biggest Movie Database." Any kind of information regarding a specific movie can be found in the IMDb: movie details (production notes, duration, format, trailers, photo galleries, soundtracks, memorable quotes, etc.); movie participants (credited cast, directors, writers, and producers, etc.); and information about current showtimes (where those movies are being played). Moreover, registered users are allowed to introduce movie reviews and ratings, and they can also introduce their votes in the daily poll. Anonymous users can also interact with this Web application to search and browse through the movie catalogue, but they cannot introduce their opinions, votes, etc. However, they can register at any time to access this functionality.

The purpose of this section is to describe the conceptual model that leads to the implementation at www.imdb.org. Following the OO-Method approach, Section 5.4.1 describes the conceptual model of the IMDb Web application by defining (1) the structural and behavioral parts of the system and (2) the system navigational and presentation properties using the OOWS approach. Those (PIM) models are taken as the input for the development process to apply a Model-Driven Development strategy. An MDA-based code generator produces the final application by implementing a set of predefined model-to-code transformation rules. The results of this step are presented in Section 5.4.2.

Due to the size of the application, it is not possible to present all the concepts in detail. Therefore, we have selected a representative part of this system to present in depth.

5.4.1 The IMDb Conceptual Model

Following the OO-Method/OOWS approach described in Figure 5.1, the first step is to describe the structural and behavioral aspects of the Web application. These requirements are gathered by means of a class diagram, state-transition diagrams, and a functional model, which are presented in Section 5.4.2.

Section 5.4.3 presents the navigational properties of the IMDb Web system by means of a user diagram, which describes the different types of users who can use the application. This section also presents the navigational model, which is related to each kind of user and describes its accessibility through the system. Finally, Section 5.4.4 introduces some abstract presentation requirements, which are related to the specified navigational model to complete the Web interface specification.

5.4.2 The IMDb OO-Method Conceptual Model

The first step in building an OO-Method conceptual model is to describe its structural model (by means of a class diagram) and its behavioral model (using a dynamic and functional model). According to the main objectives of the IMDb Web application, the structural model must capture information about the movies, their main participants, showtimes, user reviews, ratings, and daily polls. Figure 5.10 presents the IMDb class diagram.

This figure focuses on the portion of the system that is related to movie information. As the figure shows, *Movie* is the central main class. The system provides a lot of information about a movie: its title and production year, a brief general description, the official URL Web site, its production state ("filming," "post-production," etc.), a main photo, languages, color,

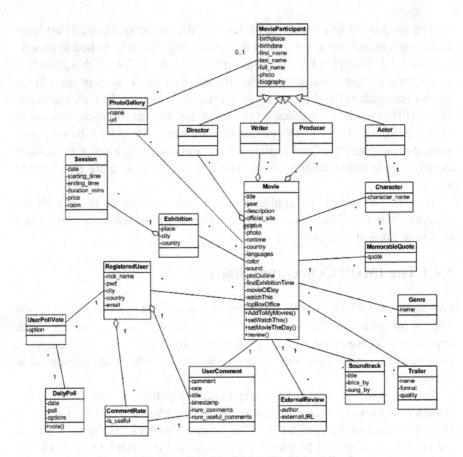

Figure 5.10. Class diagram of the IMDb Web application.

sound, etc. Also, a movie can be checked with different flags to indicate that it is the "movie of the day" or a "watch this" recommendation. By using the "firstExhibitionTime" property, the system can also dynamically derive the "coming soon" movies. Multimedia contents (soundtracks, trailers, and photoGallery) are also collected for each movie. The system organizes the movies within a set of *Genres* and lists the different places where the movies are being shown (*Exhibition*).

A movie has many participants (*MovieParticipant*), and they can play different roles in different movies. These participant roles include *Directors*, *Writers, Producers,* and *Actors*. For instance, Harrison Ford appears in the IMDb system as an actor, a producer, and a writer. Each time an actor/actress participates in a movie, he or she interprets a specific *Character*. This character can have a set of memorable quotes (interesting dialogue) within the movie.

The IMDb also has *RegisteredUsers*. These users are allowed to introduce comments (*UserComment*) about the movies they have seen and to rate the comments (*CommentRate*) provided by other users. With this information, IMDb provides an easy way of sharing the "non-expert" opinions of the users. Moreover, the IMDb publicizes a *DailyPoll* asking for user opinions on a certain topic, and registered users can introduce their own opinions for that specific question.

5.4.3 The IMDb Navigational Model

Once the structural and functional requirements have been determined, the next step is to specify the navigational capabilities of the system. Following the OOWS approach, the following diagrams must be specified: (1) a user diagram; (2) a navigational map; and (3) a presentation model.

There are two visible types of users: *AnonymousUser*s and *RegisteredUser*s. Both types can explore the movie database, but only *RegisteredUser*s are allowed to introduce their opinions and votes.

Figure 5.11 shows the User diagram. The *AnonymousUser*s are labeled with a "?" mark to specify that they do not need identification to access the system. *RegisteredUser*s have been specialized from *AnonymousUser*s to inherit their navigational maps (Fons et al., 2003). These *RegisteredUser*s are labeled with a padlock symbol to represent the fact that they need to be identified to enter the system. Following the OO-Method point of view, the *RegisteredUser*s are directly related to one class (*RegisteredUser* class) of the class diagram (Figure 5.10).

The next step involves the definition of a *navigational map* for each type of user. This navigational map defines the user accessibility within the system. Figure 5.12 presents the navigational map for the *RegisteredUser*s. The navigational map for the *RegisteredUser*s is made up of 18 navigational contexts and 1 navigational subsystem. Each of these navigational contexts provides a different view over the class diagram. The *"Now Playing"* navigational context shows information about the movies that are currently being shown, and the *"Showtime & Tickets"* navigational context shows where these movies are being exhibited. The figure shows a link (solid

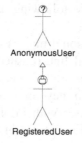

Figure 5.11. The IMDb user diagram.

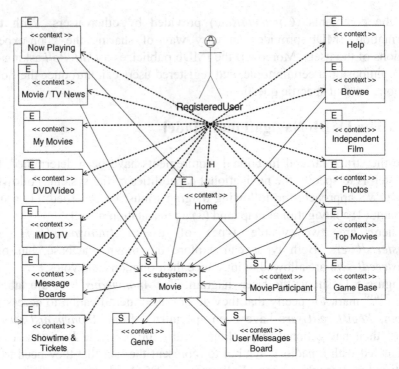

Figure 5.12. RegisteredUser navigational map.

arrow) from the "*Now Playing*" context to the "*Showtime & Tickets*" context. This link represents the capability of navigating from the "*Now Playing*" context to the "*Showtime & Tickets*" to obtain the current showtimes and ticket information.

Another example is the "*My Movies*" navigational context, which allows *RegisteredUsers* to mark their preferred movies.

Fourteen of these navigational nodes are labeled with an "E" (exploration). This means that these nodes are always accessible for *RegisteredUsers*. They appear in the navigational map as the target of a dashed arrow. The other nodes are labeled with an "S" (sequence), meaning that they are only reachable by following a predefined navigational path (solid arrows).

At the center of the navigational map is a navigational context (named *Home*) that has its explorational link (dashed-arrow) labeled with an "H." That means that this context will be the *default* node that the *RegisteredUsers* will reach when they connect to the system. This context is responsible for providing the user with information about: current movies (trailers and more), daily poll, the movies of the day, top at the box office, "opening this week," and "coming soon" movies. Figure 5.13 shows the *Home* navigational context. Due to the amount of information that this

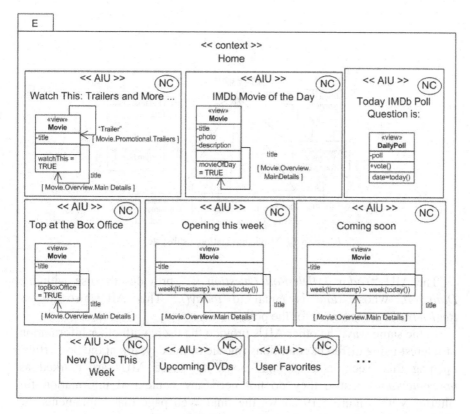

Figure 5.13. Home navigational content.

context provides, it has been defined as having a set of AIUs, each of which provides a part of the information.

The AIU *"Watch This: Trailers and More ..."* provides the users with the titles of the movies that are marked as being *"watchThis"* (see class diagram in Section 5.4.1). This requirement has been defined by specifying the Movie class view with the title attribute and a population filter condition *"watchThis = TRUE."* Two navigational capabilities are defined within this AIU by means of two context relationships (solid arrows). The first context relationship defines a navigation capability to the *Trailer* navigational context, which is inside the *Promotional* subsystem, which is inside the *Movie* subsystem (see Figure 5.14). This capability allows users to select a specific movie to see its available trailer. The second context relationship defines a navigation capability to the *Main Details* context, which is inside the *Overview* subsystem, which is inside the *Movie* subsystem. This capability allows users to obtain more detailed information about a movie by clicking on its title (anchor).

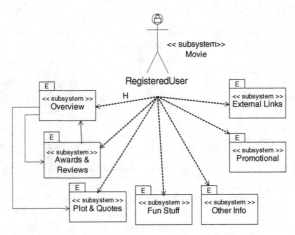

Figure 5.14. Movie navigational subsystem.

The AIU *"Today IMDb Poll Question is:"* provides the use with the *DailyPoll,* whose *date* is equal to *today()*.[3] This AIU also allows *RegisteredUser*s to *vote()* for the poll.

In the same way, the other AIUs provide the users with other information of interest using different conditions (movie of the day, top at the box office, opening this week, and coming soon). All these AIUs are marked as *noncontextual* because they do not need any contextual information for filtering with. Figure 5.19 shows the final Web page that implements the *Home* context.

Since there is so much information about a movie, it has been organized inside the *Movie* subsystem of the navigational map. This subsystem is responsible for providing different views for the same movie. This subsystem has also been organized using different subsystems: *Overview, Awards & Reviews, Plot & Quotes, Fun Stuff, Other Info, Promotional,* and *External Links* subsystems (see Figure 5,15). For example, the Overview subsystem is labeled with an "H," which converts it to the default node.

An expanded view of the *Promotional* and *Overview* subsystems, which are inside the *Movie* subsystem, are shown in Figure 5.15. The *Movie.Promotional* subsystem allows users to navigate through the *Taglines, Trailers, Posters,* and *Photo Gallery* of a specific *movie* (for instance, the *Trailer* context inside the Promotional subsystem can be accessed from the *Home* context using the *"Watch This: Trailers and More..."* AIU; see Figure 5.13). The *Movie.Overview* subsystem provides the main information about a movie (it can be considered as the main part of the IMDb movie database): *Main Details, Full Cast & Crew, Combined Details,* and *Company Credits.*

---

[3] *Today()* is an environment operation that returns the current system date.

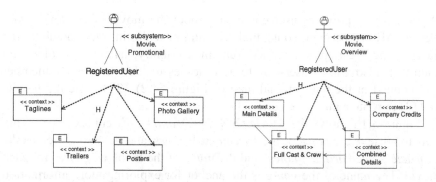

Figure 5.15. Promotional and *Overview* navigational subsystems
inside the *Movie* subsystem.

Within the *Movie.Overview* subsystem is the *Main Details* context, which
is responsible for retrieving the main information about a movie: *title*,
plotOutline, runtime, country, languages, etc. It also provides information
about the *Directors, Writers,* and *Producers*. It presents the characters and
memorable quotes for each actor and actress in the movie (Figure 5.16).

This *Main Details* context is made up of four contextual AIUs
(depending on the selected movie) and one noncontextual AIU (*Message*

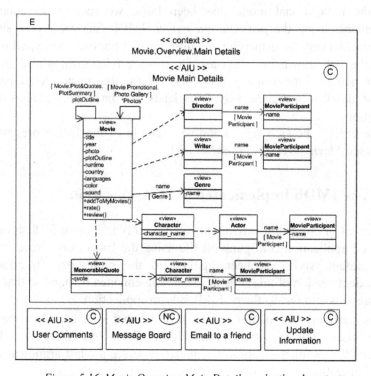

Figure 5.16. Movie.Overview.Main Details navigational content.

Board), which provides user comments about the movie. The *Movie Main Details* AIU is the main contextual AIU and provides information about the movie (title, year, plotSummary, run time, country, languages, color, and sound). It also allows users (1) to add movies to "*My Movies*" (remember that context at the navigational map of Figure 5.12), (2) to rate the movie, and (3) to write a movie review.

Figure 5.16 shows the *Movie.Overview.MainDetails* context, specifying how to retrieve the *name* of the *Directors, Writers,* and *Actors*, as well as the *characters, memorable quotes,* and the *name* of the involved *genres* for each movie. The name of the *genre* is the anchor for exploring more information about that genre within the *Genre* navigational context. This is the case because there is a context relationship between the *Movie* and the *Genre* view classes. In the same way, the *plotOutline* value is the anchor for exploring more details of that plot summary in the *Movie.Plot&Quotes.PlotSummary* context, and the static text "*Photos*" leads to the *Movie.Promotional.PhotoGallery* context.

5.4.4 The IMDb Presentation Model

Once the navigational model has been built, we specify presentational requirements using the *presentation model*. IMDb follows a very simple, homogeneous way for displaying the information: For each entity, all related subentities are shown in a register. One-to-one relationships also use the register pattern. One-to-many relationships use the master-detail pattern, with the detail in a register way. This leads to a basic presentation model description.

Figure 5.17 shows a representative example of the IMDb presentation model (see *Movie.Overview.MainDetails*).

5.4.5 The IMDb Implemented Web Application

This section presents the IMDb generated prototype. Figure 5.18 shows the generated application configuration file using the framework. Note that the IMDb default style has been applied in the prototype. The domain-independent version of this style has been implemented by hand so that it has the same look and feel as the real IMDb Web application.

This configuration file defines the two different roles (*AddRol*) specified in the user diagram shown in Figure 5.11. As this file shows, *RegisteredUser*s inherit from *AnonymousUser*s (see the last argument of the *AddRol* operation).

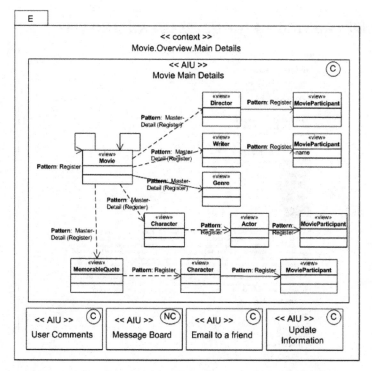

Figure 5.17. Movie.Overview.Main Details presentation context.

```php
<?php
include_once "../Framework/ApplicationBegin.php";

    $Application= new Application("IMDB","IMDB");

    $Application->AddRol("AnonymousUser","","","");
    $Application-
>AddRol("RegisteredUser","RegisteredUser","RegisteredUser_MVAgentValidation","AnonymousUser");

    $Application->AddPage("NowPlaying","NOW PLAYING","","AnonymousUser","always");
    $Application->AddPage("MovieTVNews","MOVIE/TV NEWS","","AnonymousUser","always");
    $Application->AddPage("MyMovies","MY MOVIES","","AnonymousUser","always");
    $Application->AddPage("DVD/Video","DVD/VIDEO","","AnonymousUser","always");
    $Application->AddPage("IMDbTV","IMDb TV","","AnonymousUser","always");
    $Application->AddPage("MessageBoards","MESSAGE BOARDS","","AnonymousUser","always");
    $Application->AddPage("Showtime&Tickets","SHOWTIME&TICKETS","","AnonymousUser","always");
    $Application->AddPage("GameBase","GAME BASE","","AnonymousUser","always");

    $Application->AddPage("Home","Home","","AnonymousUser","always");
    ...

    $Application->AddPageGroup("PG_BrowseMovie","Movie","","AnonymousUser","always",);

    $Application->AddPageGroup("PG_Overview","Overview","Movie","AnonymousUser","always",);
    $Application->AddPage("MainDetails","main details","PG_Overview","AnonymousUser","always");
    $Application->AddPage("CombinedDetails","combined details","PG_Overview","AnonymousUser","always");
    $Application->AddPage("FullCastAndCrew","full cast and crew","PG_Overview","AnonymousUser","always");
    $Application->AddPage("CompanyCredits","company credits","PG_Overview","AnonymousUser","always");

    $Application->AddPageGroup("PG_Awards&Reviews","Awards & Reviews","Movie","AnonymousUser","always",);
    $Application->AddPage("UserComments","user comments","PG_Awards&Reviews","AnonymousUser","always");
    ...

    $Application->SetDefaultStyle("IMDB")

    $Application->SetHomePage("Home","AnonymousUser");

include_once "../Framework/ApplicationEnd.php";
?>
```

Figure 5.18. Generated IMDb Web Application configuration file.

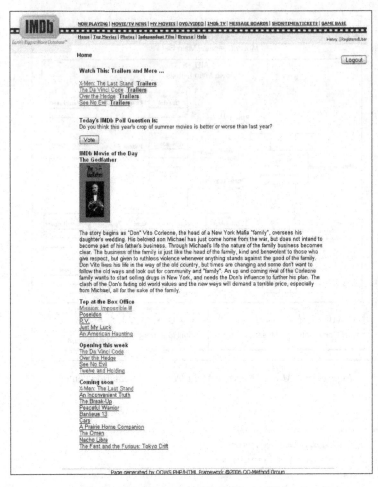

Figure 5.19. Implemented IMDb home Web page.

A Web page is created (*AddPage*) for each navigational context defined in the navigational map (Figure 5.12). A Web page group (*AddPageGroup*) is also created for each navigational subsystem. All these Web pages belong to the *AnonymousUser*. Since *RegisteredUser*s are a specialization of *AnonymousUser*s, they can also access these Web pages. The *Home* navigational context has been defined as the *Home* Web page.

As specified in its definition context (see Figure 5.13), this Web page retrieves six different types of information, each of which comes from a different AIU: Watch this, Today's poll, IMDb movie of the day, Top box office, Opening this week, and Coming soon. Following its definition, the Watch this (AIU) portion of the Web page shows the title of movies that are marked as watch this. The title is the anchor to navigate to the *Movie.Overview.MainDetails* Web page. A link named "Trailers" is attached to each title (as specified in the AIU) to navigate to the *Movie.Promotional.Trailers* navigational context.

The IMDb *Movie of the day* AIU shows the title, photo, and description of the movie with its *movieOfDay* set to true. The photo has been defined as the anchor for navigating to the *Movie.Overview.MainDetails*. If that photo is clicked on, the *MainDetails* Web page is shown.

The *MainDetails* Web page comes from the *MainDetails* navigational context, which is inside the *Overview* subsystem, which is inside the *Movie* subsystem. This requirement can be seen in the Web application configuration file (Figure 5.18). This page has been generated by the OOWS tool as shown in Figure 5.20.

```php
<?php
include_once "../../Framework/PageBegin.php";

    $Page=new Page("Movie Overview Main Details","RegisteredUser");
    $Page->AddUserInfoZone();

    $InfoZone = $Page->AddInformationZone("AIU-1","Movie Main Details.","Movie");
    $InfoZone->AddField ("title","Title");
    $InfoZone->AddField("year","Year");
    $InfoZone->AddImageField ("photo","Photo");
    $InfoZone->AddField("plotOutline","Plot");
    $InfoZone->AddField("country","Country");
    $InfoZone->AddField("languages","Languages");
    $InfoZone->AddField("runtime","Runtime");
    $InfoZone->AddField("color","Color");
    $InfoZone->AddField("sound","Sound");
    $InfoZone->plotOutline->AddInternLinkTo("Movie_Plot&Quotes_PlotSummary");
    $InfoZone->photo->AddInternLinkTo("Movie_Promotions_PhotoGallery");

    $ServiceZone = $InfoZone->AddServicesZone("movieServices","");
    $ServiceZone->AddServiceReference("Movie_AddToMyMovies","Add to my Movies");
    $ServiceZone->AddServiceReference("Movie_rate","Rate it");
    $ServiceZone->AddServiceReference("Movie_review","Add a Review");

    $InfoZone->AddDetailRelationship("Director");
    $InfoZone->RelatedDirector->AddRelatedField("name","Name","MovieParticipant");
    $InfoZone->RelatedDirector->MovieParticipant_name->AddInternLinkTo("Movie_Participant");

    $InfoZone->AddDetailRelationship("Writer");
    $InfoZone->RelatedWriter->AddRelatedField("name","Name","MovieParticipant");
    $InfoZone->RelatedWriter->MovieParticipant_writer->AddInternLinkTo("Movie_Participant");

    $InfoZone->AddDetailRelationship("Genre");
    $InfoZone->RelatedGenre->AddField("name","");
    $InfoZone->RelatedGenre->name->AddInternLinkTo("Genres");

    $InfoZone->AddDetailRelationship("Character");
    $InfoZone->RelatedActorParticipant->AddField("character_name","Character");
    $InfoZone->RelatedActorParticipant->AddRelatedField("name","Name","Actor.Character");
    $InfoZone->RelatedActorParticipant->Actor_Character_name->AddInternLinkTo("Movie_Participant");

    $InfoZone->AddDetailRelationship("MemorableQuote");
    $InfoZone->RelatedMemorableQuote->AddField("quote","Quote");
    $InfoZone->RelatedMemorableQuote->AddRelatedField("character_name","Character","Character");
    $InfoZone->RelatedMemorableQuote->AddRelatedField("name","Name","Character.MovieParticipant");
    $InfoZone->RelatedMemorableQuote->Character_MovieParticipant_name->AddInternLinkTo("Movie_Participant");

            $InfoZone = $Page->AddInformationZone("AIU-2","User Comments.","User");
            ...

include_once "../../Framework/PageEnd.php";
?>
```

Figure 5.20. Generated code for the Movie.Overview.MainDetails
with the implementation framework.

This Web page, *Movie.Overview.MainDetails*, retrieves all the information specified in its related context for the selected movie (title, year, photo, plotOutline, etc.). This is represented by the *AddField* operator to the manager class of the AIU (AIU-1). The *plotOutline* attribute is used as the anchor for navigating to the *Movie.Plot&Quotes.PlotSummary* page (*plotOutline->AddInternalLinkTo*). This page finally leads to the implemented Web page shown in Figure 5.21.

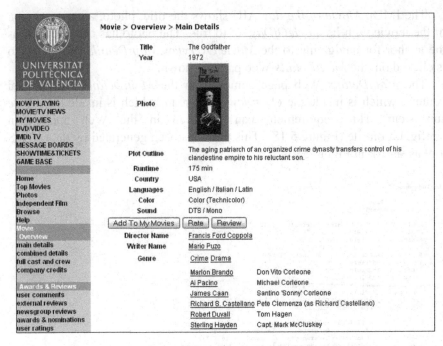

Figure 5.21. Implemented *Movie.Overview.MainDetails* Web page.

As stated in Section 5.3.11, we have manually implemented the visualization rules to recreate the IMDb look and feel (see Figure 5.9).

To demonstrate the reusability of the graphical designs, we have applied a graphical design that we had previously used in another Web application. This design implements the visualization of the UPV Web site (www.upv.es). The visualization view can be changed by simply changing the *SetDefaultStyle* in the Web application definition file to

$Application->**SetDefaultStyle**("UPV-like");

and a visualization like the one in Figure 5.22 will be obtained.

5.5 METHOD EXTENSIONS

During the last few years, the OOWS approach has evolved by including features to support some new extensions. These extensions cope with the following topics: *Web requirements modeling, adaptive systems modeling, business process modeling, applications of the semantic Web technologies,* and *service-oriented architectures.*

Figure 5.22. IMDb using the UPV graphical design.

5.5.1 Web Requirements Modeling

This extension proposes the use of a requirements model for Web applications development (Valderas et al., 2006). This model is based on the concept of a task that has been reoriented to capture not only structural and behavioral requirements (as happens in non-Web applications) but also navigational requirements.

This OOWS requirements model is created in three main stages:

1. In the first stage, a *task taxonomy* is created. This task taxonomy hierarchically specifies the tasks that users should achieve when interacting with the Web application. There are general and specific tasks. Structural and temporal decompositions are proposed to perform the task refinement.

2. In the second stage, each leaf task is described by analyzing the interaction that users require from the Web application. A strategy based on *activity diagrams* is used. Each activity diagram is defined using system actions and interaction points that represent the moments during a task where the system and the user exchange information (this information allows us to capture navigational semantics at the requirements level).

3. In the third stage, a set of *information templates* is described. These templates describe the information that is exchanged in each interaction point.

Then, a strategy to specify and to apply model-to-model transformations to obtain partial navigational models from the requirements model has been defined. The code generation process allows us to obtain prototypes in a multidisciplinary environment by defining the different roles (graphical designers, usability experts, etc.) and responsibilities. Model-to-model and model-to-code transformations provide us with a high level of traceability between code and requirements. This characteristic facilitates the management of volatile requirements and application evolution.

5.5.2 Adaptive Systems Modeling

Most of the research efforts in the field of adaptive hypermedia have focused on implementing adaptivity concepts to solve specific problems and on developing and improving adaptation strategies and algorithms, which are introduced at later stages of the software development process.

Providing a higher level (more general and domain-independent) perspective of adaptive hypermedia applications development, different model-driven approaches have been proposed. However, important problems are still related to the poor conceptual support to multiple adaptive techniques and to the lack of a complete methodological support.

The approach that OOWS proposes for the development of adaptive Web applications provides conceptual tools to describe different adaptive techniques, at a high abstraction level. To provide methodological support, the main parts of this OOWS extension are the following:

1. A user modeling strategy based on the description of the intended users of the application as a domain concept, considering their personal characteristics, their relationships with the application domain, and the description of their interaction with the application (Rojas and Pelechano, 2006).

2. A set of conceptual structures and properties, incorporated into the OOWS navigational model, that give support to well-known adaptive

techniques, such as link-hiding, link-ordering, or conditional fragments (Rojas et al., 2005).

3. A requirements specification approach including capabilities to define the requirements relative to the distinct users of the application (user classification, information, and functionality requirements). Furthermore, it provides us with tools to describe the set of adaptivity requirements of the application, in terms of the adaptive characteristics of the system tasks (discussed in Section 5.5.1). In this way, the decisions about adaptivity that are taken in the conceptual modeling phase are supported by their corresponding user-related and adaptivity requirements (Rojas et al., 2006).

4. A systematic approach to derive conceptual specifications of adaptivity characteristics from their corresponding requirements specifications, through the definition of mapping rules to the structures of the OOWS conceptual models (Rojas et al., 2006).

5.5.3 Business Process Modeling

The increasing widespread use of the Web service technology makes the Internet the most adequate platform for the development of business applications (many companies are already providing services to third parties by means of this technology).

Some of the challenges that arise with these kind of applications are the following: (1) Sometimes the description of these business applications is highly related to a business process (BP) definition, where the objective of these applications is not only *information management* but also *process management*; (2) real BPs do not only include automated activities and system participants; in fact, they can also include human participants (participants who require a user interface to interact with the process) and manual activities (activities that are not automated at all; for instance, "to make a phone call" or "to review a document").

From the OOWS approach, we propose the automatic generation of Web applications that give full support to the execution of BPs (Torres and Pelechano, 2006). To achieve this goal, we propose to generate from a BP definition (1) the required graphical user interface to launch and complete process activities, as well as (2) the equivalent executable definition of the process. However, this approach enforces us to revise the OOWS approach not only from the modeling point of view but also from the architectural one (in some cases the execution of the process is going to be performed by a process engine). This proposal allows us to obtain BP implementations that are totally integrated within the Web application. This integration is achieved at three levels: *data/content, functionality,* and *graphical user interface.* For this purpose we have defined an extension to the OOWS navigational model that allows us to model the graphical interfaces that are necessary to allow interaction between human participants and the business process.

5.5.4 Application of the Semantic Web Technology

In order to turn the vision of the Semantic Web into reality (Berners-Lee et al., 2006), it is necessary to provide developers with guides, methods, and tools that encourage them to make use of semantic technologies for the development of real-world applications. The development of the Semantic Web involves not only the generation of semantic content (defining specific domains using ontologies) but also the semantics of some functionality that allows external users and software agents to discover, invoke, compose, and monitor this functionality with a high degree of automation.

In this sense, Web Engineering methods should now be prepared to provide solutions that tackle the modeling of this new dimension, which refers to the view over the system from the Semantic Web point of view. This new dimension allow us to generate applications intended not only for humans, but also for automated software agents, which can understand the application contents (data and functionality) because they are expressed in a language that provides a vocabulary along with a formal semantics.

We propose generating part of the system specification that is going to be accessible through the use of the Semantic Web technology (Torres et al., 2006). This generation can be performed since the OO-Method/OOWS approach includes a set of models that specify in a sound and precise way the system structure and behavior in the form of a conceptual schema. The OO-Method/OOWS approach has been enriched with a mechanism to define—at the modeling level—the system in terms of the Semantic Web point of view. This new dimension specifies the view/access over the system for external agents by defining two models: The first model specifies the system domain (tourism, health, news, education, etc.), and the second model describes how external entities/agents should use the system functionality exposed in business settings.

5.5.5 Service-Oriented Architectures

A main objective of Service-Oriented Architectures (SOA) is to solve integration problems between heterogeneous applications in a distributed environment. Architectures of this kind provide appropriate scenarios to integrate Web applications. Web Engineering methods should provide mechanisms to apply SOA architectures to support the use of external Web services to develop new services.

In accordance with SOA, a methodological guidance to automatically design and implement fully operative Web services from OO-Method/OOWS models has been defined. In order to design and implement these Web services, the OO-Method/OOWS models are used as the key point. In this strategy, we have first determined which models are useful to identify Web services operations, and then we have proposed a guidance to design these operations (Ruiz et al., 2005, 2006).

This extension is supported by an additional tool that takes the conceptual model as input and applies the guide to obtain Web services operation descriptions. This tool finally generates the code for this Web services operation automatically (Ruiz et al., 2006).

REFERENCES

Berners-Lee, T., Hendler, J., and Lassila, O., 2001, The Semantic Web. *Scientific American*, May.

CARE Technologies. *OlivaNova Model Execution*. http://www.care-t.com, accessed 2007.

CARE Technologies. *OlivaNova Modeller*. http://www.care-t.com/products/modeler.html, accessed 2007.

CARE Technologies. *OlivaNova Transformation Engines*. http://www.care-t.com/products/transengine.html, accessed 2007.

Ceri, S., Fraternali, P., and Matera, M., 2002, Conceptual modeling of data-intensive Web applications. *IEEE Internet Computing*, 6(4): 20–30.

De Troyer, O., 2001, Audience-driven Web design. In *Information Modeling in the New Millennium*, Eds. Matt Rossi and Keng Siau, Publ. IDEA Group Publishing, Hershey, USA, ISBN: 1-878289-77-2, pp. 442–462.

Fons, J., Pelechano, V., Albert, M., and Pastor, O., 2003, Development of Web applications from Web enhanced *conceptual schemas*. ER'2003, Springer *Lecture Notes in Computer Science*, 2813: 232–245.

Knapp, A., Koch, N., Zhang, G., and Hassler, H.M., 2004, Modeling business processes in Web applications with ArgoUWE. UML 2004, Springer *Lecture Notes in Computer Science*, 3273: 69–83.

Mellor, S.J., Clark, A.N., and Futagami, T., 2003, Model-driven development—Guest editor's introduction. *IEEE Software*, Sept.–Oct., 20(5): 14–18.

Murugesan, S., and Desphande, Y., 2001, *Web Engineering. Software Engineering and Web Application Development*. Lecture Notes in Computer Science—Hot Topics, Springer, New York.

Object Management Group, 2004, Model Driven Architecture (MDA). www.omg.org/mda.

Pastor, O., Gomez, J., Insfran, E., and Pelechano, V., 2001, The OO-Method approach for information systems modeling: From object-oriented conceptual modeling to automated programming. *Information Systems*, 26: 507–534.

Pressman, R.S., 2005, *Software Engineering: A Practitioner's Approach*. MacGraw-Hill, New York, ISBN: 0-07-285318-2.

Reifer, D.J., 2000, Web development: Estimating quick-to-market software. *IEEE Software*, Nov.–Dec., 17(6): 57–64.

Rojas, G., and Pelechano, V., 2005, A methodological approach for incorporating adaptive navigation techniques into Web applications. *Proceedings Sixth International Conference on Web Information Systems Engineering* (WISE 2005), New York.

Rojas, G., Pelechano, V., and Fons, J., 2005, A model-driven approach to include adaptive navigational techniques in Web applications. *Proceedings Fifth International Workshop on Web-Oriented Software Technologies* (IWWOST'05) [within The 17th Conference on Advanced Information Systems Engineering (CAiSE'05)], Porto, Portugal.

Rojas, G., Valderas, P., and Pelechano, V., 2006, Describing adaptive navigation requirements of Web applications. *Proceedings Fourth International Conference on Adaptive Hypermedia and Adaptive Web-Based Systems* (AH2006), Dublin, Ireland.

Rossi, G., and Schwabe, D., 2001, Object-oriented Web applications modeling. In *Information Modeling in the New Millennium*, IGI Publishing, USA, ISBN: 1-878289-77-2, pp. 463–484.

Ruiz, M., Valderas, P., and Pelechano, V., 2005, *Applying a Web engineering method to design Web services. Proceedings Third International Conference on Service-Oriented Computing* (ICSOC), pp. 576–581.

Ruiz, M., Pelechano, V., and Pastor, O., 2006a, Designing Web services for supporting user tasks: A model driven approach. *Proceedings of Conceptual Modeling of Service-Oriented Software Systems* (CoSS).

Ruiz, M., Valverde, F., and Pelechano, V., 2006b, Desarrollo de servicios Web en un método de generación de código dirigido por modelos. *II Jornadas Científico-Técnicas en Servicios Web* (JSWEB) [in Spanish].

Torres, V., and Pelechano, V., 2006, Building business process driven Web applications. *Proceedings Fourth International Conference on Business Process Management* (BPM 2006),.Vienna, Austria, pp. 322–337.

Torres, V., Pelechano, V., and Pastor, O., 2006, Building Semantic Web services based on a model driven Web engineering method. Workshop on Conceptual Modeling of Service-Oriented Software Systems (CoSS2006), Tucson, Arizona.

Valderas, P., Pelechano, V., and Pastor, O., 2006, A transformational approach to produce Web application prototypes from a Web requirements model. Submitted to *International Journal on Web Engineering and Technology* (IJWET).

Chapter 6

MODELING AND IMPLEMENTING WEB APPLICATIONS WITH OOHDM

Gustavo Rossi[1] and Daniel Schwabe[2]

[1]*LIFIA, Facultad de Informatica,Universidad Nacional de La Plata, (also at CONICET), Argentina,* `gustavo@lifia.info.unlp.edu.ar`
[2]*Departamento de Informática, PUC-Rio, Rio de Janeiro, Brazil,* `dschwabe@inf.puc-rio.br`

6.1 INTRODUCTION

The Object-Oriented Hypermedia Design Method (OOHDM) (Schwabe and Rossi, 1998) is a model-based approach to develop Web applications. It allows the designer to specify a Web application, seen as an instance of a hypermedia model, through the use of several specialized meta-models. Each model focuses on different aspects of the application. Once these models have been specified for a given application, it is possible to generate runtime code that implements the application. The examples shown in this chapter use the HyperDE environment (Nunes and Schwabe, 2006) for this.

OOHDM uses different abstraction and composition mechanisms in an object-oriented framework to allow, on the one hand, a concise description of complex information items and, on the other hand, the specification of complex navigation patterns and interface transformations. The principles of OOHDM have also been applied in another version of the method, SHDM (Schwabe et al., 2004), in which the data model used is based on RDF and RDFS (Brickley and Guha, 2004).

In OOHDM a Web application is built in a five-step process supporting an incremental or prototype process model. Each step focuses on a particular design concern, and an appropriate model is built. Classification and generalization/specialization are used throughout the process to enhance abstraction power and reuse opportunities. We next summarize the five activities.

6.1.1 Requirements Gathering

The first step is to gather the stakeholder requirements. To achieve this, it is necessary to first identify the actors (stakeholders) and the tasks they must perform. Next, scenarios are collected (or drafted) for each task and type of actor. The scenarios are then collected to form use cases, which are represented using User Interaction Diagrams (UIDs). These diagrams provide a concise graphical representation of the information flow between the user and the application during the execution of a task. The UIDs are validated with the actors, and redesigned if necessary. In sequence, a set of guidelines is applied to the UIDs to extract a basic conceptual model.

6.1.2 Conceptual Design

In this step a conceptual model of the application domain is built using well-known object-oriented modeling principles. There is no concern for the types of users and tasks, only for the application domain semantics. A conceptual schema is built out of subsystems, classes, and relationships. OOHDM uses UML (Fowler, 1997), with slight extensions, to express the conceptual design.

6.1.3 Navigational Design

In OOHDM, an application is seen as a navigational view over the conceptual model. This reflects a major innovation of OOHDM [also adopted by other methods such as UWE (Koch and Kraus, 2002)] and WebML (Ceri et al., 2002), which recognizes that the objects (items) the user navigates are *not* the conceptual objects, but other kinds of objects that are "built" from one or more conceptual objects, to suit the users and tasks that must be supported.

   In other words, for each user profile we can define a different navigational structure that reflects the objects and relationships in the conceptual schema according to the tasks this kind of user must perform. The navigational class structure of a Web application is defined by a schema containing navigational classes. In OOHDM there is a set of predefined basic types of navigational classes: nodes, links, anchors, and access structures. The semantics of nodes, links, and anchors are the usual in hypermedia applications. Nodes in OOHDM represent logical "windows" (or views) over conceptual classes defined during conceptual design. Links are the hypermedia realization of conceptual relationships as well as task-related associations. Access structures, such as indexes, represent possible ways for starting navigation.

Different applications (in the same domain) may contain different linking topologies according to the various users' profile. For example, in the Internet Movie Database (IMDB) application, a rental store view of a certain DVD may indicate for each available copy when it is due to be returned, whereas the customer view may omit this information.

The navigational structure of a Web application is described in terms of navigational contexts, which are sets of related nodes that possess similar navigation alternatives (options) and are meaningful for a certain step in some task the user is pursuing. Navigation contexts play an analogous role with respect to navigation that classes play with respect to the structure and behavior of objects—they provide a way to talk about the navigation alternatives for sets of nodes without requiring talking about individuals, the same way as classes allow talking about the structure and behavior of objects without requiring talking about individuals objects. For example, we can model the set of actors in a film, the set of films directed by a director, the set of DVD copies of a film, and so on.

6.1.4 Abstract Interface Design

The abstract interface model is built by defining perceptible objects—also called widgets—that contain information (e.g., a picture, a city map, etc.) in terms of interface classes. Interfaces are defined as recursive aggregations of primitives classes (such as exhibitors or capturers) or of other interface classes. Interface objects map to navigational objects, providing them with a perceptible appearance, or to input values. Interface behavior is defined by specifying how to handle external and user-generated events and how communication takes place between interface and navigational objects.

6.1.5 Implementation

Implementation maps interface and navigation objects to run-time objects and may involve elaborate architectures, e.g., client–server, in which applications are clients to a shared database server containing the conceptual objects. A number of DVD-ROM–based applications, as well as Web–sites, have been developed using OOHDM, employing various technologies such as Java (J2EE), .NET (aspx), Windows (asp), Lua (CGILua), ColdFusion, and Ruby (Ruby on Rails). In this chapter, we will illustrate the implementation using HyperDE, an environment based on Ruby on Rails that is freely available on the Internet (see http://server2.tecweb.inf.puc-rio.br:8000/hyperde).

In the following sections we show some details of the OOHDM notation using an example that can be considered a simplified version of the Internet Movie Database (www.imdb.com) together with an associated site such as www.amazon.com where one can buy a DVD. For the sake of simplicity, we will focus mainly on the process of finding movies, i.e., in the store catalogue; less emphasis is put in the buying and check-out process (see Schmid and Rossi, 2004). This example is somewhat archetypical as many different Web applications can be modeled using the ideas we will show next.

6.2 REQUIREMENTS GATHERING AND SPECIFICATION

6.2.1 Identifying Actors

In OOHDM we build a different navigational model for each user profile; in this application we clearly have at least two different user profiles: the customer, who is looking for a movie to buy or just for information about the movie, and the administrator, who maintains the movies database. We will mostly discuss the application for the customer profile. Once we have identified the actors, we must identify the tasks the user will accomplish using the application, in order to obtain usage scenarios.

Clearly, there are many tasks to be supported in our application scenario. Some of the typical tasks for the customer user profile are

- Find a movie given its title.
- Find a movie given an actor's name.
- Find information about an actor or actress.
- Find movies of a particular genre.
- Find recently released movies.
- Choose movies to buy given one of the above criteria.

6.2.2 Use Case Specification

We next describe the usage scenarios. A scenario represents the set of subtasks the user has to perform to complete a task. Scenarios are specified textually using the point of view of the final user, in our case a customer. Whenever possible, the user scenarios should be obtained from a sample of real users who are representative of the intended audience. When this is not possible, this role can be played by members of the design team or by other stakeholders. More than one scenario can be defined for the same task.

As an example of the first task ("Find a movie given its title"), a possible scenario would be

> "I enter the movie title or part of it, and I see a list of matching movie titles. For each movie matching the title, I get some information such as a picture of the DVD cover, the year the movie was released, and its main actors. I can get additional information such as all the actors, director, soundtrack information, user comments, etc. For some films, I can also see a short trailer."
>
> "After reading the information, I can decide to buy it or to quit."

After collecting several such scenarios, a generalization is captured in a use case, defined next. We use the following heuristics:

1. Identify those scenarios related with the task at hand. In our case we will use the previous scenario.
2. For each scenario, identify information items that are exchanged by the user and the application during their interaction.
3. For each scenario, identify which data items are associated among themselves; they typically appear together in the text of the use case.
4. For each scenario, identify those data items organized as sets. Usually, the use case text refers to them explicitly as sets.
5. The sequences of actions appearing in scenarios should also appear in the use case.
6. All operations on data items that appear on scenarios should be included in the use case.

After defining the data involved in the interaction, the sequence of actions, and the operations, we can specify the use case. A use case will be constructed based on the sequence of actions, detailed with the information about the data items and operations involved. Use cases can also be enriched with information from other use cases or provided by the designer. The resulting use case for the previous scenario is the following:

Use case: Find a movie given its title.

1. The user enters the movie title (or part of it).
2. The application returns a list of movies matching the data entered or the information about the movie (if only one movie matches, see step 4). For each movie, the title, main actor, and cover art are shown.
3. In case the user wants to see more information on the movie, he selects it.

4. The system returns detailed information for the movie: title, cover, availability, actors' names, director, and other technical information. If the user wants to buy the movie, he can include it in the shopping cart to buy later (use case: Buy a DVD given its title). If he wants, he can watch a trailer of the movie.

5. If the user wants to know information about an actor who had a role in the movie, he can select the actor and the application will return his name, date of birth, a photograph, and a list of movies in which he participated.

The specification of other use cases follows a similar process.

6.2.3 User Interaction Diagrams

Use cases are described using a graphical notation called a User Interaction Diagram (UID) (Vila et al., 2000), which captures the flow of information and helps detail the information items and choices made by the user.

The specification of UIDs from use cases can be done following the guidelines described below. For illustration purposes, we detail the process of building the UID for the use case "Find a movie given its title," as described above.

1. Initially, the use case is analyzed to identify the information exchanged between the user and the application. Information provided by the user and information returned by the system are tagged accordingly. Next, the same information is identified and made evident in the use case.

2. Items that are exchanged during the interaction are shown in UID states. Information provided by the user and that provided by the system are always in separate states. Information that is produced from computations should be in separate states from the information used as input to this computation. The ordering of states depends on the dependencies between data provided by the user and returned by the application. In Figure 6.1, we show the first draft of the UID where parts of the use case are transcribed; information exchanged is shown in italics.

3. After identifying the data items exchanged, they must be clearly indicated in the UID. Data entered by the user (for example, the movie title) are specified using a rectangle; if it is mandatory, the border is a solid line; if it is optional, the border is a dashed line, as shown in Figure 6.2. Ellipsis (…) in front of a label indicates a list (e.g., …*Movie* indicates a list of *Movies*). The notation *Movie (Title, Actor(Name), Cover)* is called a *structure*. A shaded ellipsis represents a separate UID.

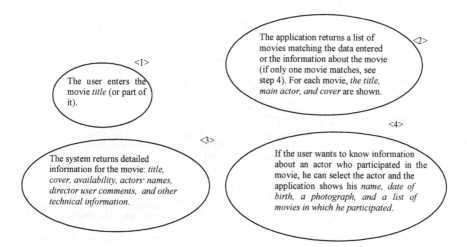

<1>
The user enters the movie *title* (or part of it).

<2>
The application returns a list of movies matching the data entered or the information about the movie (if only one movie matches, see step 4). For each movie, *the title, main actor, and cover* are shown.

<3>
The system returns detailed information for the movie: *title, cover, availability, actors' names, director user comments, and other technical information.*

<4>
If the user wants to know information about an actor who participated in the movie, he can select the actor and the application shows his *name, date of birth, a photograph, and a list of movies in which he participated.*

Figure 6.1. Defining the UID.

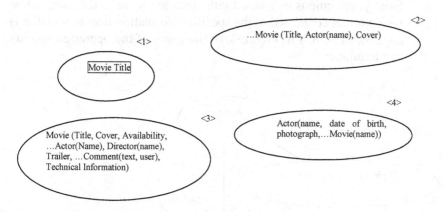

<1>
Movie Title

<2>
...Movie (Title, Actor(name), Cover)

<3>
Movie (Title, Cover, Availability, ...Actor(Name), Director(name), Trailer, ...Comment(text, user), Technical Information)

<4>
Actor(name, date of birth, photograph,...Movie(name))

Figure 6.2. Refining interaction states in UIDs.

4. Transitions between interaction states must be indicated using arrows. Multiple paths as indicated in the use cases might arise as shown in Figure 6.3. Labels between brackets indicate conditions (e.g., [2..N] indicates more than one result); a label indicating cardinality represents a choice. (In the example, "1" indicates only one option may be chosen. For any choice, the source of the arrow is the list from which the option is selected, or the whole state if it is not ambiguous.)

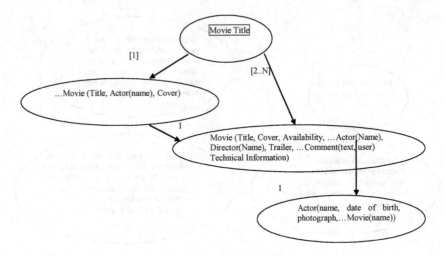

Figure 6.3. Transitions between interaction states in UIDs.

5.   Finally, operations executed by the user are represented using a line
      with a bullet connected to the specific information item to which it is
      applied, as shown in Figure 6.4. The name of the operation appears
      in parentheses.

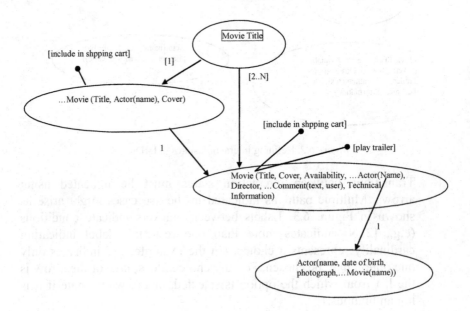

Figure 6.4. Complete specification of the UID for the use case "Find movie given its title
(including the buying operation)."

6.3 CONCEPTUAL MODELING

The conceptual model in OOHDM comprises a set of classes (their attributes and behaviors) and their relationships using UML. To develop a conceptual model, the information gathered from use cases and UIDs can help to identify core information classes that can later be refined. We next describe a set of guidelines to derive classes from UIDs, and we illustrate them using the UID in Figure 6.4 ("Find movie"). These guidelines are especially useful in aiding less experienced designers.

1. **Class definition.** For each data structure in the UID, we define a class. In the example: *Movie, Actor, Director.*
2. **Attribute definitions.** For each information item (provided by the user or returned by the system) appearing in the UID, an attribute is defined according to the following validations:
   (a) If, given an instance of the class X, it is possible to obtain the value of attribute A, then A can be an attribute of X (provided X is the only class fulfilling this condition).
   (b) If, given classes X and Y, it is possible to obtain the value of attribute A, then A will be an attribute of an association between X and Y.
   (c) If the attribute corresponding to a data item does not depend on an existing class, or combination of classes, this indicates the need to create a new one.
   The following attributes were identified from the information returned by the system as shown in the UID in Figure 6.4:
   > *Movie: title, cover, availability, trailer, user comments, technical information.*
   > *Actor: name, date of birth, photograph, list of movies*
   > *Director: name*
3. **Definition of associations.** For each UID, for attributes appearing in a structure that does not correspond to their class, include the association if there is a relationship between its class and the class representing the structure.
4. **Definition of associations.** For each UID, for each structure s1 containing another structure s2, create an association between the classes corresponding to structures s1 and s2.
5. **Definition of associations.** For each transition of interaction states in each UID, if different classes represent the source interaction state and the target interaction state, define an association between corresponding classes.

The following associations were identified by applying guidelines 3, 4, and 5 to the UID in Figure 6.4:

> *Movie-Actor*
> *Movie-Director*

6. **Operation definition.** For each option attached to a state transition in each UID, verify if there is an operation that must be created for any of the classes that correspond to the interaction states.

The following operations were identified from this last guideline:

> *Movie: includeInShoppingCart*
> *Movie: PlayTrailer*

In Figure 6.5, we show an initial conceptual model derived from the UID "Find movie given its title."

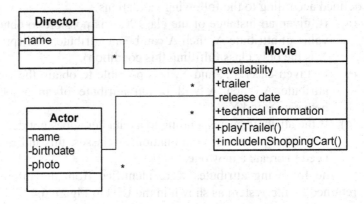

Figure 6.5. Initial conceptual model.

While the process and guidelines described above can help in defining a preliminary model, several refinements have to be made by hand, incorporating the designer's understanding of the domain. Among other concepts, the designer must identify

- Generalization and specialization hierarchies—for example, Actor and Director can be recognized as subclasses of Person.
- Association classes—for example, Role of an Actor in a Movie.
- Hidden classes—for example, Order. In fact, the Shopping Cart is not really a class by itself, but rather the set of Items that are part of an Order. Similarly, there is a User class, who is the buyer and also makes comments.
- Redundant classes.
- The arity of relations.

Besides these adjustments, it is worth noticing that this conceptual model might need further improvements as the application evolves, since these classes are "just" the ones we derive from the requirements gathering activity. However, this evolution belongs more to the general field of object-oriented design and is not as relevant for the current discussion.

After analyzing the complete set of UIDs and performing needed adjustments, we can obtain the conceptual model of Figure 6.6. Notice that we have included a Series class to stand for TV Series, and a generalization class Feature, abstracting both Series and Movies.

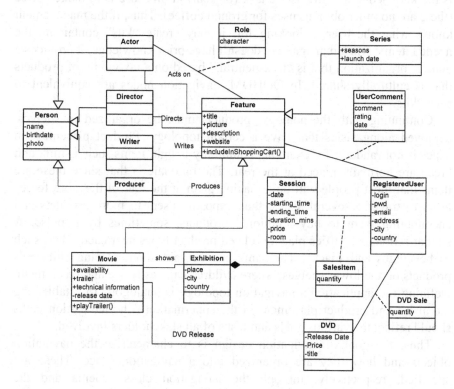

Figure 6.6. Conceptual model for the Movies Web site.

6.4 NAVIGATION DESIGN

To help understand the OOHDM approach to navigation design, we draw an analogy with supermarkets. Let's suppose you want to get some ground coffee, and you go to a supermarket you've never been to before. Not knowing where each type of merchandise is kept, you look up at the signs hanging from the ceiling, where the various categories of products are listed.

The signs establish a simple taxonomy of product types which is widely understandable, at least in Western society. Following the signs, you go to the aisle and section where ground coffee is kept.

However, looking at the shelves around the section, you notice that there are also coffee filters, jars, mugs, etc. Clearly, these items are not of the same category as ground coffee. The supermarket management put them here because they know that the user needs them to make coffee—just the grounds are not enough. One may regard the ground coffee, filters, jars, etc. as a "virtual" product, a "coffee making kit." What enables defining this kit is the knowledge that the user's task (or goal) in this case is to make coffee (there are no other obvious uses for ground coffee). Thus, if the management knows what the user is looking for, it may create "kits" containing the needed items; when management doesn't have prior knowledge, it provides a generic organization that is "task-neutral," based on a taxonomy of products that is culturally shared. In OOHDM, navigation nodes are equivalent to such "kits."

Continuing with the analogy, products must be organized in shelves, deployed along aisles that have a certain topology. Product placement in aisles is not random; for example, commonly bought items such as milk and bread are normally placed at the rear. The rationale is that since these are items that most people will buy, placing them at the rear of the store forces users to traverse several aisles, thus exposing users to more products and encouraging them to buy additional products, sometimes by impulse. A similar rationale justifies placing related product types near each other, such as beverages and snacks. The same can be said about placing children's products on the lower shelves, where children can easily see and reach them. Defining the application's navigation topology is analogous to establishing the aisles and product placement in the supermarket—the navigation paths should reflect the various goals and tasks of all stakeholders involved.

Thus, the goal of navigation design is to characterize the navigation objects and how they are organized into a navigation space. These are specified, respectively, through the navigation class schema and the navigation context schema. The latter indicates possible navigation sequences to help the user complete her task, and the former specifies the navigation objects (nodes and links) being processed. Whereas designers may create both schemas from different sources, User Interaction Diagrams, use cases, and the conceptual model are the natural sources from which to derive a sound navigational model. In addition to these, designers use their own experience or that from other designers, for example, using navigation patterns, as described in Section 6.7.

6.4.1 From Conceptual Modeling to Navigation Design

One of the cornerstones of the OOHDM approach is the fact that navigational objects—nodes and links—are explicitly defined as views on conceptual objects, according to each different user profile. These views are built using an object-oriented definition language that allows one to "copy and paste" or to filter attributes of different related conceptual classes into the same node class and to create link classes by selecting the appropriate relationships.

6.4.2 Navigational Schema

For each set of user profiles, we define a different navigational class schema and context schema. The navigational schema contains the nodes and links of the application. Nodes contain perceivable information (attributes) and anchors for links. Anchors are objects that allow triggering links. Links, meanwhile, are the hypermedia realization of conceptual relationships.

6.4.2.1 Nodes and Anchors

Nodes are derived from conceptual classes by selecting those classes we want that the user to perceive; attributes are defined in an opportunistic way according to usage needs. Sometimes it is necessary to combine attributes from different objects to describe a node.

In the example we may want nodes representing Movies to contain an attribute with the names of all the actors that participated in the movie, eventually using the names as anchors to each Actor's page.

As shown in the conceptual model of Figure 6.6, the name of the actor is an attribute of Class Actor and should not be included in Class Movie. Meanwhile, in a different application (for example, the application for administrators), we may want to filter out some attributes (such as detailed data of the movie) or include new relationships as links.

Node classes are defined using a query language similar to the one in Kim (1994). Nodes possess single-typed attributes, link anchors, and may be atomic or composite. Anchors are instances of Class Anchor (or one of its subclasses) and are parameterized with the type of link they host. In fact, since navigation always occurs within some context, as will be explained later, the Anchor specification must also include the destination context.

From an object-oriented point of view, nodes implement a variant of the Observer design pattern (Gamma et al., 1995) as they express a particular view on application objects. Changes in conceptual objects are broadcast to existing observers, while nodes may communicate with conceptual objects to forward events generated in the interface to them.

As an example we define the Node class Movie, including as one of its attributes the name of the director and an anchor for the link that connects both nodes. We say that the conceptual class Movie is the subject of Node class Movie. In OOHDM we defer the definition of how objects will be perceived until the interface design activity.

> NODE Movie [FROM Movie:m]
> director: String [SELECT Name] [FROM Director:d WHERE D
>   Directs m]
> .... (other attributes "preserved" from the conceptual class Movie}
> directedBy: Anchor [DirectedBy, Directors in Alphabetical order]

In the definition above, we express that attribute Director contains the name of the instance of the Director class corresponding to the director of the actual movie. Similarly, directedBy is a link to the Director node, in the context Directors in Alphabetical order. The notation above can be easily mapped into a query to a relational database of the implementation. We may combine both in case we want to have an anchor whose label is the Director's name, which would be expressed as

> NODE Movie [FROM Movie:m]
> directedBy: Anchor [DirectedBy, Director in Alphabetical order] label
>   [SELECT Name]
>   [FROM Director:d WHERE d Directs m]
> .... (other attributes "preserved" from the conceptual class Movie}

Nodes may also possess attributes that are used to trigger operations in their object counterparts in the conceptual model.

6.4.2.2 Links

Links connect navigational objects. The result of traversing a link is expressed either by defining the navigational semantics procedurally as a result of the link's behavior or by using an object-oriented state-transition machine similar to Statecharts (Turine et al., 1997). Since Web applications usually implement simple navigation semantics (closing the source page and opening the target), we do not discuss this issue further.

The syntax for defining Link classes also allows one to express queries on relationships as shown in the example below in which, for the sake of simplicity, we omit link attributes.

```
LINK DirectedBy
SOURCE: Movie: M
TARGET: Director: D
WHERE S.D directs S.M
END
```

Notice that in a running implementation, links may not exist as full-fledged objects. For example, they may be just the result of selecting an anchor (that in fact might be simply a URL). However, expressing the navigational diagram considering nodes and links as object classes allows us to express the intended navigation semantics in a better way.

In Figure 6.7 we show the navigational class diagram of the Movie site, using a UML-like syntax. (Notice that the semantics of links are different from the semantics of UML associations.)

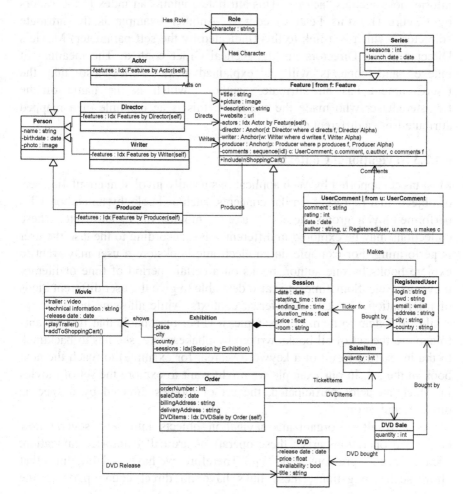

Figure 6.7. Navigational class diagram of the Movies Web site.

It is important to stress the similarities and differences among the conceptual and navigational schema. They are similar because both are abstract and implementation-independent and they represent concepts of the underlying application domain using objects. However, while the former should be neutral with respect to navigation, the latter expresses a particular user's view (in the navigation sense) that is strongly influenced by the tasks he is supposed to perform. OOHDM enforces a clear separation between the specification of navigation and other application behavior. However, in complex Web applications it may be necessary to integrate both kinds of behaviors, such as the process of buying the DVD of a movie.

This difference between navigation classes and conceptual classes can be seen in the diagram, where we can see that, while similar to the conceptual classes, navigation classes contain additional information. For instance, the navigation class Feature has several attributes that contain navigation information, such as "actors." This attribute contains an index to the Actors by Feature (for this Feature) context. Another example is the attribute "director," which is a link to this (indicated by the self parameter) Movie's Director in the Directors in Alphabetical Order context. The meaning of indexes and contexts will be explained next. Notice also that the UserComment has an attribute, "author," which is the name of the RegisteredUser who made the comment; this is an example of a mapped attribute from a different class.

6.4.2.3 Navigational Contexts

Most tasks supported by Web applications usually involve manipulating sets of objects that represent similar concepts, such as books by an author, CDs performed by a group, hotels in a city, movies of a genre, etc. These collections may be explored in different ways, according to the task the user is performing. For example, in an electronic bookstore a user may want to explore books by one author, books on a certain period of time or literary movement, etc. Sometimes it is also desirable to give the user different kinds of information or detail in different contexts, while allowing her to move easily from item to item. For example, it is not reasonable that if she wants to explore the set of all books written by Shakespeare, she has to backtrack to the index (the result of a keyword search, for example) to reach the next book in the set. In our example we might want to explore the set of movies in which an actor participated, the set of movies directed by a specific director, and so on.

As a result of organizing navigation objects into sets, several new navigation operations arise; these operations are called intraset navigation, such as "next," "previous," and "up." Therefore, we have to define links that allow such navigations; these links have no direct counterparts in the conceptual model. In other words, there is no conceptual relationship that directly translates into intraset navigation links.

Unfortunately, most modeling approaches (for example, the UML) ignore sets as first-class citizens, and therefore operations such as "next" and "previous" are not common while traversing sets. To complicate matters, the same node may appear in different sets: For instance, a movie directed by Spielberg may appear in the set of Comedies or in the set of movies acted by Tom Hanks. We may intend to include some comments about the movie in the corresponding context, such as when accessed as a comedy or some comments about comedies.

OOHDM structures the navigational space into sets, called navigational contexts, represented in a context schema. Each navigational context is a set of nodes, and it is described by specifying its elements, indicating its internal navigational structure (e.g., if it can be accessed sequentially) and associated indexes. Generally speaking, contexts are defined by properties of its elements, which may be based on their attributes or on their relations, or both. Navigational contexts usually induce associated access structures called indexes, which are collections of links pointing to each of the context's elements.

Another way to understand contexts is that they provide an abstraction mechanism that allows us to specify the navigation opportunities available to sets of objects all at the same time, without having to do so for each individual element within the context. In this respect, contexts play a role with respect to navigation that is analogous to the role classes play with respect to object structure and behavior—they allow us to specify navigation properties that are common to all its elements without requiring individual specification.

Consider a movie directed by Peter Jackson. While looking at its details, the user may want to see details of its actors or details of one of the songs in the soundtrack. In fact, these navigation alternatives are true not only for that particular movie, but also for the set of all movies directed by Peter Jackson. It is possible then to specify the navigation alternatives for any movie in the set in a more abstract way using navigational contexts. In this case, the navigational context would be "Movies by Peter Jackson." Additional reflection about this problem shows that one could generalize even further, since there is nothing particular about Peter Jackson in these alternatives — they are the same for any director. Therefore, we can define a group of navigational contexts as "Movies by director," where the particular director is a parameter, and all movies in any navigational context in this group share the alternatives of seeing the details of its actors or of songs in its soundtrack.

Figure 6.8 contains a portion of the navigational context diagram for our example; we will use it to explain the notation.

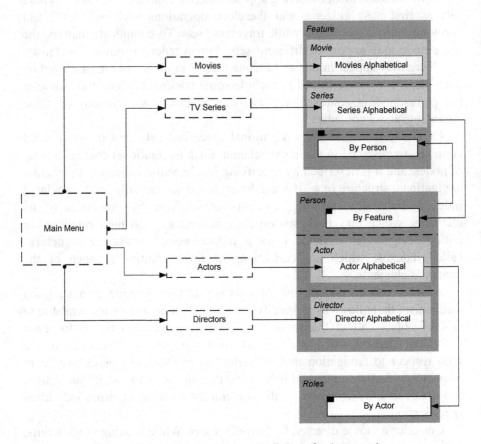

Figure 6.8. Partial navigation context diagram for the example.

The small black boxes within some contexts in Figure 6.8 indicate that these contexts have associated indexes. Instead of drawing them as dashed rectangles, this notation is used to prevent cluttering the diagram, making it graphically evident that these indexes are associated with the enclosed context.

The arrows with solid circles in the origin indicate landmarks, or places in the navigation space that are accessible from every other place. Typically, these landmarks are implemented as options included in a global navigation bar that is present on all pages of the application.

The details of each context and access structure are described by a context (respectively, access structure) specification card as shown in Figures 6.9 and 6.10.

Context: Feature by Person
Type: static
Parameters: p: Person
Elements: f: Feature WHERE a ActsIn m
In context Classes:
Ordering: by name, ascending
Internal navigation: by index (**Feature by Actor**)
Operations:
Users: Client   **Permissions:** read
Comments:

Figure 6.9. The context specification card.

Access structure : Feature by Actor		
Type: simple		
Parameters: a: Actor		
Elements: m: Movie WHERE a *ActsIn* m		
Attributes **Target** title: m.name................Ctx Feature by Artist (self) role: r.character, WHERE a HasRole r and m HasCharacter r cover: m.cover "Play Trailer"............... play_trailer() "Buy DVD"................ buy()		
Ordering: by name, Ascending		
Users: Client **Permission:** read		
Comments:		

Figure 6.10. The access structure specification card.

Consider the access structure specification for Movie by Artist. Since this is an index induced by a context (Movies by Artist), it will contain one entry for each element in the context. Each entry has four attributes—the (movie) title, which is an anchor to the Movie by Artist context (for the movie corresponding to this entry); the artist's role in this movie; an activation that allows one to play the movie's trailer; and an activation that allows one to buy the movie's DVD. The former two attributes are calls to methods which will have to be mapped to active interface elements that can trigger the associated operations when activated by the user. This also illustrates how we separate application functionality from its interface rendering.

The reader will notice that both the context and the access structure specification cards also include information on access restrictions. Although we will not elaborate on this here, it is possible to restrict access to navigation objects by specifying the conditions in the corresponding specification cards.

6.4.3 Deriving Navigational Contexts

Navigation design is, to a large extent, the definition of the various navigational contexts that the user will be traversing while performing the various tasks the applications purports to support. Therefore, the natural place to look for them is in the task descriptions, as described in the UIDs.

For each task, we define a partial navigational context representing a possible navigational structure to support the task. As an example, we detail the derivation of the navigational contexts corresponding to the use case "Find Movie given its title," whose UID we repeat in Figure 6.11 for convenience.

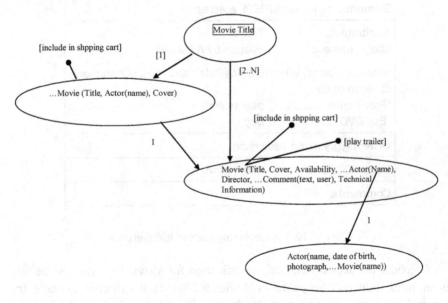

Figure 6.11. Complete specification of the UID for use case "Find Movie given its title" (including the buying operation)."

First, each structure that has been represented in the UID (and the corresponding class in the conceptual model) is analyzed to determine the type of primitive that it will give raise to, e.g., an access structure, a navigational context, or a list. The following guidelines can be used to derive a navigational context:

1. When the task associated with the UID requires that the user inspects a set of elements to select one, we map the set of structures into an access structure. An access structure is a set of elements, each of which contains a link, and is represented by a rectangle with a dashed border. In Figure 6.12 we show the partial diagram for access structures Movies and Artists.

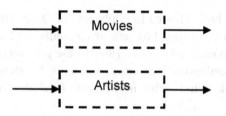

Figure 6.12. Access structures.

2. When the task does not require such inspection but requires the elements to be accessed simultaneously, map the set into a list, e.g., the list of Songs in the soundtrack of a DVD (see Figure 6.13).

```
Movie

title, cover, availability, director, technical information,
 Actors: Idx Artists by Movie (self),
Comments: c: UserComment, c.comment WHERE
               u makes c and c about self
  includeShoppingCart ()
```

Figure 6.13. List for DVD soundtrack.

3. After mapping the different sets of structures, we analyze singular structures in the UID using the following guideline: When the task requires that the information about an element be accessed by the user, we map the structure into a navigational context, represented

by a rectangle with solid borders. In Figure 6.14 we show the partial context diagram from this example.

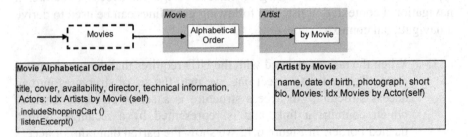

Figure 6.14. Partial context for the UID "Find Movie given its title."

In the example, both Movies in Alphabetical Order and Artist by Movie are contexts, which correspond to sets of elements. The elements and their attributes making up each set are described in the gray boxes.

Following an analogous reasoning, Figure 6.15 shows the navigation diagram for the task "Find Actor information (including movies) given the Actor name."

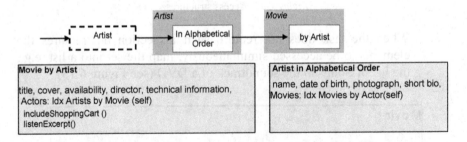

Figure 6.15. Partial context for the UID "Find Actor information (including movies) given the Artist name."

This process is repeated for each collected UID, resulting in a set of partial navigation diagrams supporting all intended tasks. The next step is to integrate these partial diagrams by unifying them, to arrive at a single diagram for the whole application. The unification process identifies contexts and indexes that are composed of either the same kind of elements or elements that could be substituted by elements of a more abstract (super) class. In addition, each time a partial diagram is integrated into the evolving final diagram, navigation between the various contexts in each partial diagram must also be considered and included when relevant.

Considering the diagrams in Figures 6.14 and 6.15, one would obtain the unified diagram shown in Figure 6.16.

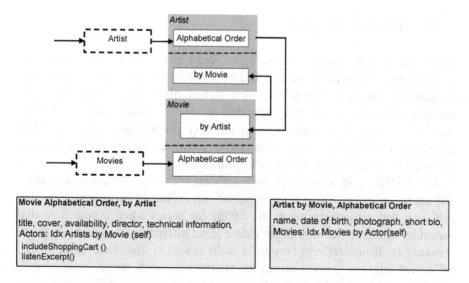

Figure 6.16. Unification of diagrams in Figures 6.14 and 6.15.

Notice that the navigation from the context "Artist in Alphabetical Order" to the "Movie by Artist" has been generalized to the "Artist by Movie" context—hence the arrow leaving the gray box "Artist," the Artist scope. The same reasoning applies to the contexts within the "Movies" scope.

The dashed lines within each scope in Figure 6.16 indicate that it is not possible to move freely between contexts separated by the lines. In other words, if one is looking at an Artist in the "Alphabetical Order" context, it is not possible to navigate to the next "Artist by Movie." If there was another context such as "Artist by Nationality," it could make sense to allow the user to navigate to the next artist of the same nationality, instead of the next artist in alphabetical order, so that these two contexts would not be separated by a dashed line in the corresponding diagram.

Another result from the unification process is the identification of generalizations. Consider the diagram in Figure 6.15. The reasoning that leads to the creation of the "Movie by Artist" context also applies to directors; similarly, for all contexts for TV series with respect to contexts with movies. The generalization becomes the "Feature by Person" context. Notice that scopes may be nested, as in Figure 6.8, to represent the subclass hierarchy of the classes for the corresponding elements (e.g., Movie and TV Series within Feature, and Artist and Director within Person).

6.4.4 InContext Classes

When the same node (e.g., Movie, Actor, etc.) may appear in more than one set (context), we need to express the peculiarities of this node within each particular context. We may take as a default that "next" and "previous" anchors and links are automatically defined for traversing each set; but we may also want that some context-sensitive information appears when accessing a Movie by genre context (for example, giving access to some comments on movies on that specific genre).

In OOHDM this is achieved with InContext classes; for each node class and each context in which it appears, we can define an InContext class that acts as a decorator (Gamma et al., 1995) for nodes when accessed in that particular context. Decorators provide a good alternative to subclassing and prevent us from defining multiple subclasses of the base node class. InContext classes are organized in hierarchies with some base classes already provided by the design framework; for example, InContext classes defined as subclasses of InContextSequential inherit anchors for sequential navigation and for backtracking to the context index. When we do not define InContext classes, a default one is assumed according to the type of context defined.

Notice that the navigational contexts schema complements the navigational schema by showing the way in which nodes are grouped into navigable sets. Additional nodes' behavior can be implemented in InContext classes; in amazon.com, for example, when we access a book in the context of a query, we have an option to move it to the shopping basket. When we access the same book in the context of the shopping basket, we should have other, different, operations to perform.

6.5 INTERFACE DESIGN

Any hypermedia (Web) application must exchange information with its environment in order to fulfill its tasks. The functions implemented by the application all receive some information, process it, and trigger changes in the interface, restarting the cycle. Very often the cycle is triggered by user actions at the interface, but sometimes the cycle is started by some other event, such as a timeout.

From this point of view, the role of the interface is to make the navigation objects and application functionality perceptible to the user, which is the goal of the interface design. From the application business logic's point of view, all that is needed regarding the interface is the definition of the information exchange between the application and the user, including activation of functionalities. In particular, from the standpoint of the interface, navigation is just another (albeit distinguished) application functionality.

Since the information exchange is driven by the tasks, it is reasonable to expect that it will be less sensitive to run-time environment aspects, such as particular standards and devices being used. The design of this task-related aspect of the interface can be carried out by interaction designers or software engineers and is almost totally independent of the particular hardware and software run-time environment. The concrete appearance of the interface, defining the actual look and feel of the application, including layout, font, color, and graphical appearance, is typically carried out by graphics designers. The result of this separation of concerns, specifying the information exchange at the interface separately from its look and feel, leads to isolating the essence of the interaction design from inevitable technological platform evolution, as well as from the need to support users in a multitude of hardware and software run-time environments.

The most abstract level is called the abstract interface and focuses on the various types of functionality that can be played by interface elements with respect to the information exchange between the user and the application. The vocabulary used to define the abstract interface is established by an abstract widget ontology (Moura and Schwabe, 1994), shown in Figure 6.17, which specifies that an abstract interface widget can be any of the following:

- SimpleActivator, a widget capable of reacting to external events, such as mouse clicks.
- ElementExhibitor, a widget able to exhibit some type of content, such as text or images.
- VariableCapturer, a widget able to receive (capture) the value of one or more variables. Examples are input text fields, selection widgets such as pull-down menus and checkboxes, etc. It generalizes two distinct (sub-) concepts.

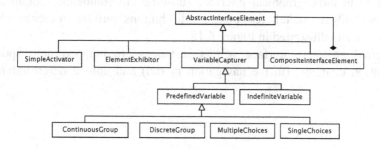

Figure 6.17. Abstract widget ontology.

- IndefiniteVariable, a widget allowing one to enter hitherto unknown values, such as a text string typed by the user.
- PredefinedVariable, a widget that allows the selection of a subset of values from a predefined set of possibilities; quite often this selection must be a singleton. Specializations of this concept are ContinousGroup, DiscreteGroup, MultipleChoices, and SingleChoice. The first allows one to select a single value from an infinite range of values; the second is analogous, but for a finite set; the remainder are self-evident.
- CompositeInterfaceElement, a widget composed of any of the above.

It becomes evident from this ontology the essential roles that interface elements play with respect to the interaction—they exhibit information, or they react to external events, or they accept information. Composite elements allow us to build more complex interfaces out of simpler building blocks. The abstract interface design should be carried out by the software designer, who understands the application logic and the kinds of information exchanges that must be supported to carry out the operations. This software designer does not have to worry about usability issues, or look and feel, which will be dealt with during the concrete interface design, typically carried out by a graphics (or "experience") designer.

Each element of the abstract interface must be mapped onto both a navigation element, which will provide or receive its contents, and a concrete interface widget, which will actually implement it in a given run-time environment. Figure 6.18 shows an example of an interface showing the information about an artist in the Artist in Alphabetical Order context, and Figure 6.19 shows an abstract representation of this interface as a composition of widgets from the vocabulary defined above.

Before proceeding to show how this is achieved, we must first define the concrete widget ontology, which characterizes the actual widgets available in concrete run-time environments.

The concrete interface is specified in terms of actual widgets commonly available in most graphical interface run-time environments. Examples of concrete widgets include text boxes, radio buttons, pull-down menus, check boxes, etc., as illustrated in Figure 6.18.

Actual abstract interface widget instances are mapped onto specific navigation elements (in the navigation model) and onto concrete interface

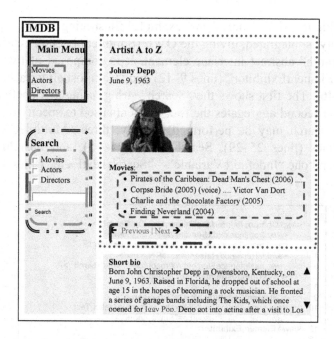

Figure 6.18. An example concrete interface.

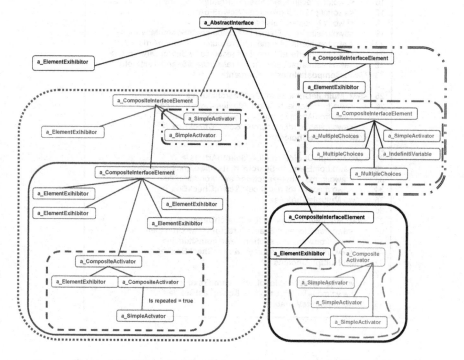

Figure 6.19. Abstract widget instance for the example in Figure 6.18.

widgets. Figure 6.20 shows an example illustrating how application functionality is integrated, giving the OWL (Smith et al., 2002) specification of the "Search" abstract interface element. It is composed of two abstract widgets, "ElementExhibitor" (lines 9–12) and "CompositeInterfaceElement" (lines 14–46). The first shows the "Search" string, using a "Label" concrete widget. The second aggregates the four elements used to specify the field in which the search may be performed, namely, three "MultipleChoices"— SearchMovies (lines 25–29), SearchArtists (31–35), and SearchDirectors (37–41)—and one "IndefiniteVariable"—"SearchTextField" (lines 43–45).

```
     ...
1    <awo:CompositeInterfaceElement rdf:ID="Search">
2        <awo:fromIndex>idxSearch</awo:fromIndex>
3        <awo:mapsTo rdf:resource="&cwo;Composition"/>
4        <awo:isRepeated>false</awo:isRepeated>
5        <awo:hasInterfaceElement rdf:resource="#TitleSearch"/>
6    </awo:CompositeInterfaceElement>
8
9    <awo:ElementExihibitor rdf:ID="TitleSearch">
10       <awo:visualizationText>Search</awo:visualizationText>
11       <awo:mapsTo rdf:resource="&cwo;Label"/>
12   </awo:ElementExihibitor>
13
14   <awo:CompositeInterfaceElement rdf:ID="SearchElements">
15       <awo:fromIndex>idxSearch</awo:fromIndex>
16       <awo:abstractInterface>SearchResult</awo:abstractInterface>
17       <awo:mapsTo rdf:resource="&cwo;Form"/>
18       <awo:isRepeated>false</awo:isRepeated>
19       <awo:hasInterfaceElement rdf:resource="#SearchMovies"/>
20       <awo:hasInterfaceElement rdf:resource="#SearchArtists"/>
21       <awo:hasInterfaceElement rdf:resource="#SearchDirectors"/>
22       <awo:hasInterfaceElement rdf:resource="#SearchTextField"/>
23   </awo:CompositeInterfaceElement>
24
25   <awo:MultipleChoices rdf:ID="SearchMovies">
26       <awo:fromElement>SearchMovies</awo:fromElement>
27       <awo:fromAttribute>section</awo:fromAttribute>
28       <awo:mapsTo rdf:resource="&cwo;CheckBox"/>
29   </awo:MultipleChoices>
30
31   <awo:MultipleChoices rdf:ID="SearchArtists">
32       <awo:fromElement>SearchArtists</awo:fromElement>
33        <awo:fromAttribute>section</awo:fromAttribute>
34       <awo:mapsTo rdf:resource="&cwo;CheckBox"/>
35   </awo:MultipleChoices>
36
37   <awo:MultipleChoices rdf:ID="SearchDirectors">
38       <awo:fromElement>SearchDirectors</awo:fromElement>
39       <awo:fromAttribute>section</awo:fromAttribute>
40       <awo:mapsTo rdf:resource="&cwo;CheckBox"/>
41   </awo:MultipleChoices>
42
43   <awo:IndefiniteVariable rdf:ID="SearchTextField">
44       <awo:mapsTo rdf:resource="&cwo;TextBox"/>
45   </awo:IndefiniteVariable>
```

Figure 6.20. Example of the OWL specification of the "Search" part of Figure 6.19.

The *CompositeInterfaceElement* element, in this case, has the properties *fromIndex, isRepeated, mapsTo, abstractInterface,* and *hasInterfaceElement.* The *fromIndex* property in line 2 indicates to which navigational index this element belongs. This property is mandatory if no antecessor element of type *CompositeInterfaceElement* has declared it. The association with the "idxSearch" navigation element in line 2 enables the generation of the link to the actual code that will run the search. Even though this example shows an association with a navigation element, it could just as well be associated with a call to application functionality such as "buy."

The *isRepeated* property indicates if the components of this element are repetitions of a single type (false in this case). The *mapsTo* property indicates which concrete element corresponds to this abstract interface element. The *abtractInterface* property specifies the abstract interface that will be activated when this element is triggered. The *hasInterfaceElement* indicates which elements belong to this element.

The *ElementExhibitor* element has the *visualizationText* and *mapsTo* properties. The former represents the concrete object to be exhibited, in this case the string "Search."

The *MultipleChoices* element has the *fromElement, fromAttribute,* and *mapsTo* properties. The *fromElement* and *fromAttribute* properties indicate the corresponding element and navigational attribute in the navigational model, respectively. The *IndefiniteVariable* element has the *mapsTo* property.

6.6 FROM DESIGN TO IMPLEMENTATION

Mapping design documents into implementation artifacts is usually time-consuming, and, in spite of the general acceptance about the importance of software engineering approaches, implementers tend to overlook the advantages of good modeling practices.

A model here can be seen as a simplified, textual, or graphical description of the artifact being designed. Preferably, a model should have precise, non-ambiguous semantics that enables understanding of the artifact being modeled. Software development, according to the model-driven design approach (MDD), is a process whereby a high-level abstract model is successively translated into increasingly more detailed models, in such a way that eventually one of the models can be directly executed by some platform. The model that is directly executed by a platform that satisfies all the requirements, including the nonfunctional ones, is also called "code" and is usually the last model in the refinement chain.

Although this approach has been used for a number of years, its adoption is not completely widespread, at least not in its pure form. A major stumbling block has been the problem that the mapping between models, especially into actually executing code, has had little or no support from tools. Therefore, designers may use the models mostly as thinking tools, and at some stage they are forced to manually map these models into code. This process is error-prone, and once the code has been generated, changes or updates to the application are directly implemented in the code, instead of adjusting the models and re-generating the code.

On the other hand, several more recent proposals have attempted to alleviate this problem by having automated translations (or transformations) between models, supported by appropriate tools. Among the most prominent are MDA (Miller and Mukerji, 2003) and Software Factories (Greenfield and Short, 2004).

Following the MDD approach, we have developed the HyperDE environment (freely available at http://server2.tecweb.inf.puc-rio.br:8000/HyperDe), based on the MNVC framework, which extends the MVC framework with navigation primitives. It allows the designer to input OOHDM navigational models (the "model" in the MVC framework) and interface definitions (the "view" in the MVC framework), and it generates complete applications adherent to the specification. It also provides an interface to create and edit instance data, although, strictly speaking, this should actually be part of the generated application. Figure 6.21 shows the architecture of HyperDE. The actual version of OOHDM used in HyperDE is SHDM (Schwabe et al., 2002), which uses an object model derived from the RDF data model (Brickley and Guha, 2004) that has been proposed for describing data and meta-data on the Semantic Web.

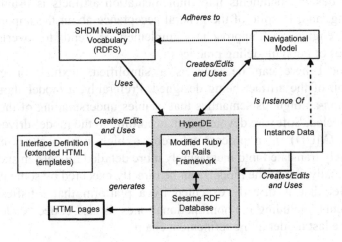

Figure 6.21. The architecture of the HyperDE environment.

HyperDE is implemented as a modification of the Ruby on Rails framework (http://www.rubyonrails.com), where the persistence layer (ActiveRecord) has been replaced by another one based on the Sesame RDF database. The SHDM meta-models, the user-defined navigation models, as well as the application instance data are all stored as RDF data.

Applying the MDD approach, designing a Web application using OOHDM (or SHDM) corresponds to instantiating its meta-model, which is supported by the HyperDE environment. Before giving an example, we briefly outline the meta-model used by HyperDE, so it will be clear from the example how it is being instantiated during a particular design.

6.6.1 SHDM Meta-Model

Figure 6.22 shows the SHDM meta-model, with the main classes highlighted. The class NavClass models the navigation nodes, and the class Link models the links between them. Each NavClass has NavAttributes, NavOperations, and links and can be a specialization of a BaseClass. Contexts are sets of objects belonging to a NavClass. This set is defined through a query whose expression is specified in one of the context attributes; this query may have a parameter. Indexes are made out of IndexEntries, which contain either anchors to other indexes or anchors to elements within a context. Landmarks are anchors to either Indexes or to Context elements. Views allow one to exhibit the contents of NavClass instances within some context or to exhibit Indexes.

All HyperDE functions can be accessed via Web interfaces. In addition, HyperDE also generates a domain-specific language (DSL) as an extension of Ruby, allowing direct manipulation within Ruby scripts of both the model and SHDM's meta-model.

To give an idea of HyperDE functionalities, we give a brief description of the example application. First, we show a couple of screen dumps of the generated application, and then we show how some of the model elements that generated this application are specified. It should be noted that HyperDE generates a default simple interface for models whose interface has not yet been fully specified; the examples below use this default interface. Evidently, the designer has all the freedom to override this default and define sophisticated interfaces with complex layouts.

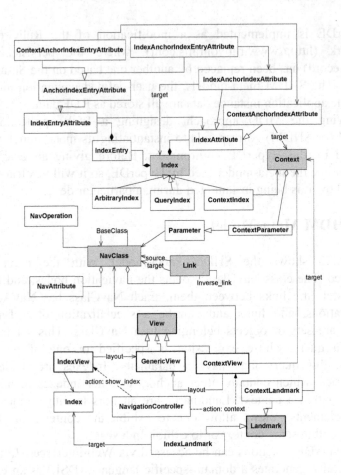

Figure 6.22. The SHDM meta-model.

Figure 6.23 shows the interface for a node "Movie" in the "Movies in Alphabetical Order" context. Notice the index for the context on the left and the contextual navigation (in this case, only the "previous" link, to "The Da Vinci Code," is defined, since it is the last node in the context). Suppose the user clicks on "Ian McKellen," leading to the interface shown in Figure 6.24. Notice that the link followed carries a parameter (the "Feature"), shown in the detail of the context, right beneath the Actor's name.

This particular actor has played roles in other movies, e.g., "The Da Vinci Code" (the "Sir Leigh Teabing" role). Following the link to this movie brings the user to the interface shown in Figure 6.25. Notice that this instance has more data defined than the one in Figure 6.23; HyperDE handles this because it is supported by the underlying RDF data model, which is more flexible than strict object-oriented models. Notice also that the context index that appears in the column on the left, automatically generated by HyperDE, is different in this case since the context is different.

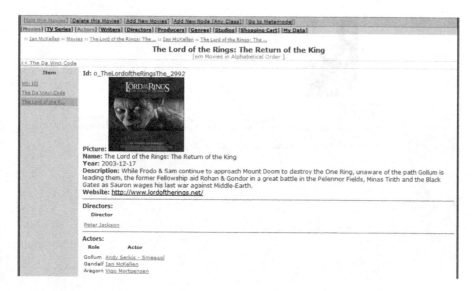

Figure 6.23. An interface showing a movie in the "Movies in Alphabetical Order" context.

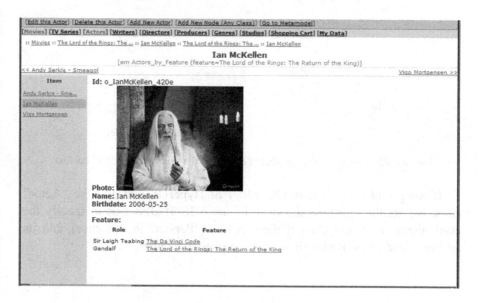

Figure 6.24. An interface for a node of type "Actor" in the "Actor by Feature" context.

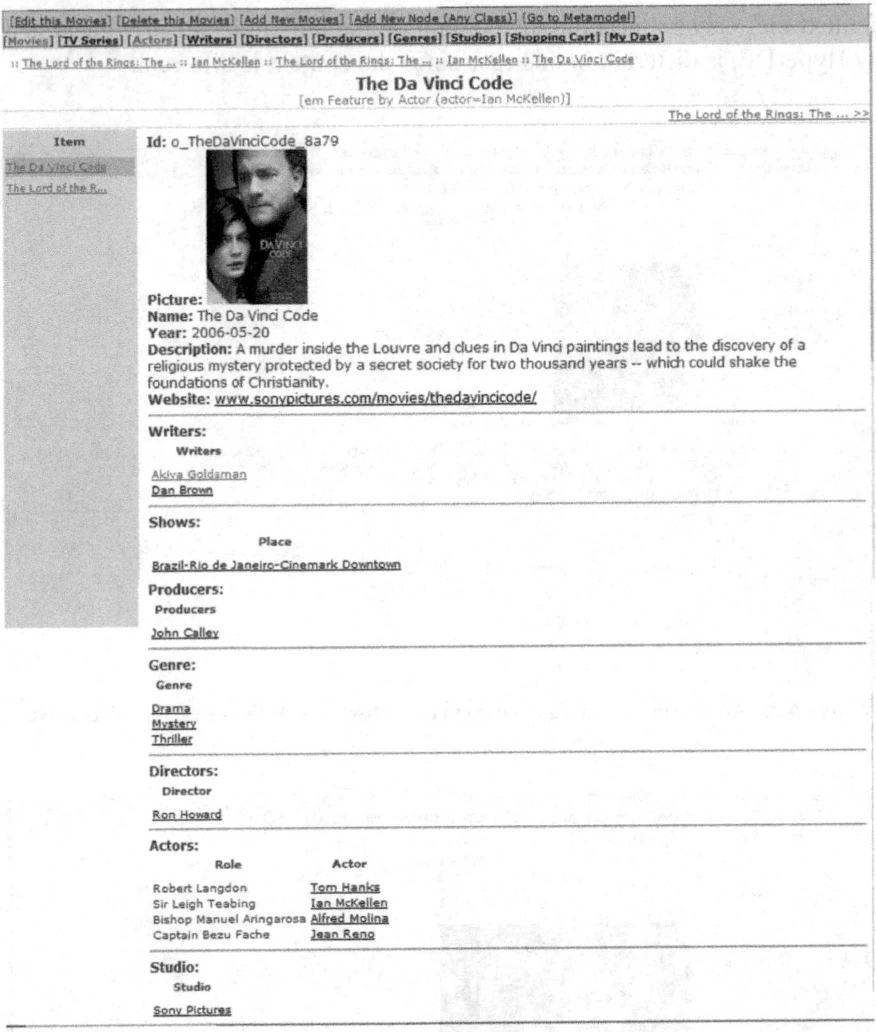

Figure 6.25. An interface for another "Feature" in the "Feature by Actor" context.

If we go into the meta-model editor of HyperDE and edit the "Actor" class, we get the interface shown in Figure 6.26. It allows us to specify the class name, its parent class if there is one ("Person" in this case), and its attributes and links. It also shows the inherited attributes.

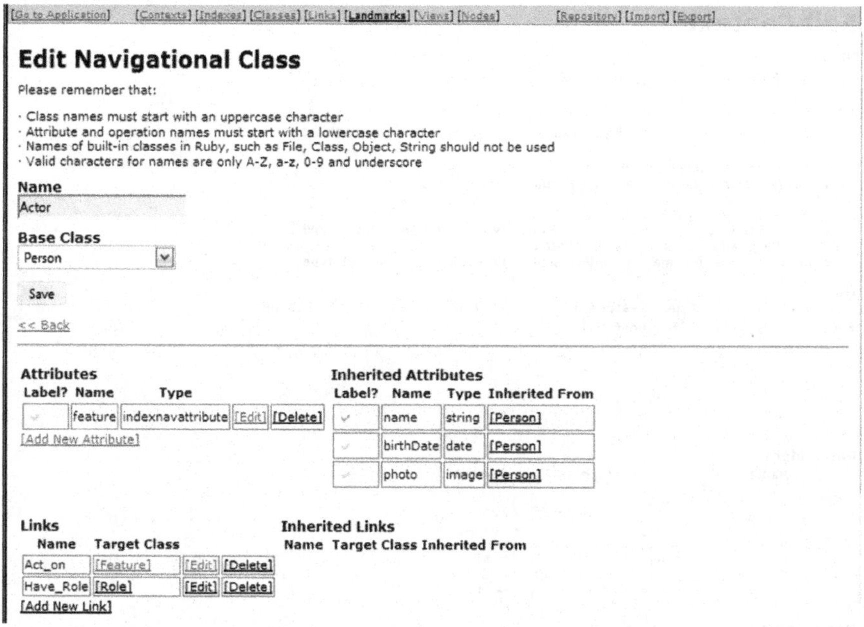

Figure 6.26. HyperDE interface to edit a navigational class.

As explained earlier, a navigational class may have attributes that are derived from other classes, and attributes that contain navigation information. An example here is the "feature" attribute of an actor, which is an index to the "Features by Actor" context (thus allowing navigation from an actor to one of the features he has acted in). Figure 6.27 shows the interface for defining the "Features by Actor" context.

There are two related aspects worth observing in this definition. The first is the use of a simplified query language to express the context selection. Since the vast majority of contexts found in practice fall into the "x by y" pattern—e.g., "Actor by Feature," "Feature by Director," etc., HyperDE uses a simple notation allowing the specification of the source class, the destination class, the relation (link) name, and the ordering. If desired, it is possible to specify a full query in the RQL query language, or to specify a Ruby expression using the generated domain-specific language that HyperDE provides. The second aspect to be noted is that this context is actually a group of contexts, since it is parameterized—there is one context for each actor, which is passed as a parameter.

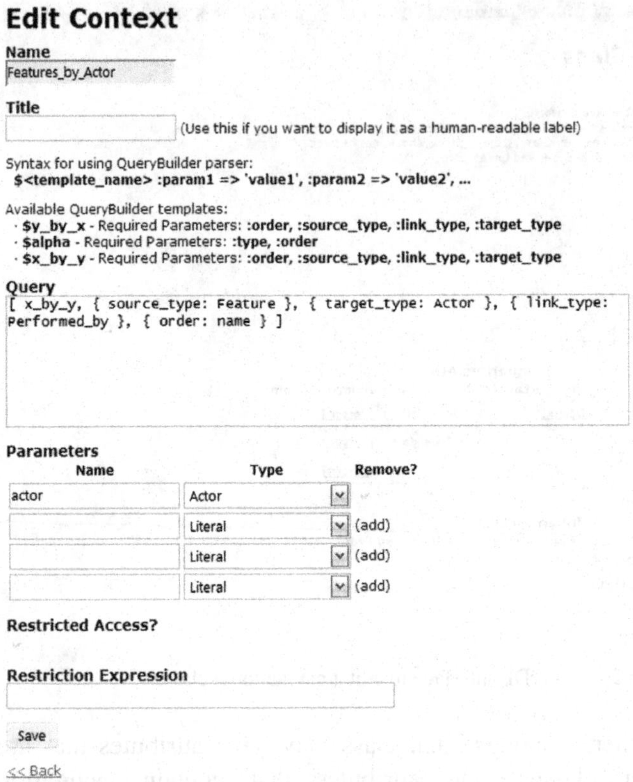

Edit Context

Name

Features_by_Actor

Title

_____ (Use this if you want to display it as a human-readable label)

Syntax for using QueryBuilder parser:
  $<template_name> :param1 => 'value1', :param2 => 'value2', ...

Available QueryBuilder templates:
  · **$y_by_x** - Required Parameters: **:order, :source_type, :link_type, :target_type**
  · **$alpha** - Required Parameters: **:type, :order**
  · **$x_by_y** - Required Parameters: **:order, :source_type, :link_type, :target_type**

Query

[x_by_y, { source_type: Feature }, { target_type: Actor }, { link_type:
Performed_by }, { order: name }]

Parameters

Name	Type	Remove?
actor	Actor ⌄	
	Literal ⌄	(add)
	Literal ⌄	(add)
	Literal ⌄	(add)

Restricted Access?

Restriction Expression

_____

Save

<< Back

Figure 6.27. HyperDE interface to edit a context definition.

It should be recalled that the "feature" attribute of an "actor" is an index into the context defined in Figure 6.27; entries in this index will have links to the actual nodes in the context.

Figure 6.28 shows the interface for defining the "Features by Actor" index.

The query definition for the index specified in this figure uses the generated DSL to compute the elements of the index. In this case, the expression first finds the Actor object whose id was passed as a parameter. Then it takes the list of features this actor has acted on ("aa.act_on"), and, for each feature in it, it generates a hash table of three keys: "feature," "role," and "actor." The value for the key "feature" is the feature itself; the value for the "role" key is the intersection between the list of roles the actor has played and the list of characters of the feature; and the value for the "actor" key is the actor that was passed as a parameter to the context. This hash table is used by HyperDE to generate the index entries, each of which will have two attributes: a role and a feature. This generates the list of "role, feature" pairs seen in the "Feature" attribute of an actor illustrated at the bottom of Figure 6.24. A similar definition is used to generate the list of "role, actor" pairs seen in the "Actors" attribute of a feature, illustrated in Figures 6.23 and 6.25.

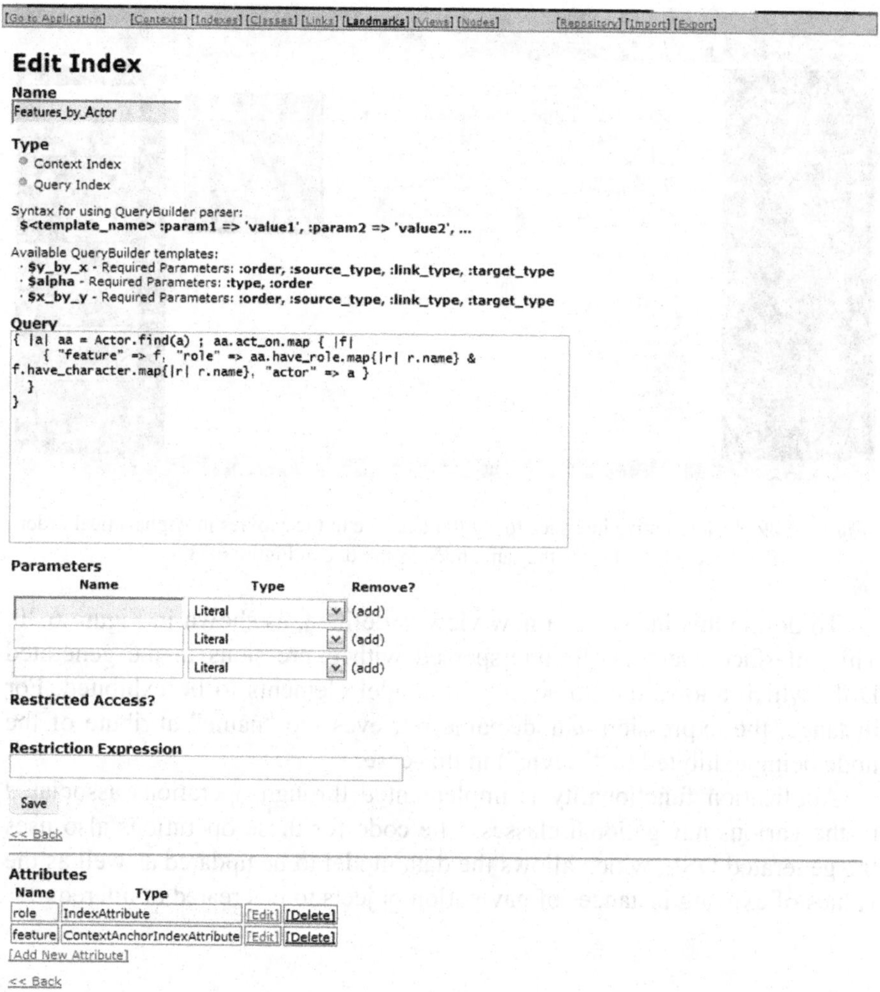
[Go to Application] [Contexts] [Indexes] [Classes] [Links] [Landmarks] [Views] [Nodes] [Repository] [Import] [Export]
Edit Index
Name
Features_by_Actor
Type
Context Index
Query Index
Syntax for using QueryBuilder parser:
$<template_name> :param1 => 'value1', :param2 => 'value2', ...
Available QueryBuilder templates:
· $y_by_x - Required Parameters: :order, :source_type, :link_type, :target_type
· $alpha - Required Parameters: :type, :order
· $x_by_y - Required Parameters: :order, :source_type, :link_type, :target_type
Query
{ |a| aa = Actor.find(a) ; aa.act_on.map { |f|
{ "feature" => f, "role" => aa.have_role.map{|r| r.name} &
f.have_character.map{|r| r.name}, "actor" => a }
}
}
Parameters
Name
Type
Remove?
Literal
(add)
Literal
(add)
Literal
(add)
Restricted Access?
Restriction Expression
Save
<< Back
Attributes
Name
Type
role
IndexAttribute
[Edit]
[Delete]
feature
ContextAnchorIndexAttribute
[Edit]
[Delete]
[Add New Attribute]
<< Back

Figure 6.28. HyperDE interface to define an index.

HyperDE allows easy customization of interfaces. For example, it is possible to define a different layout to be used to exhibit nodes of a given class in a certain context, such as a movie in the Movies in Alphabetical Order context. Figure 6.29 shows an alternative layout for the interface shown in Figure 6.23.

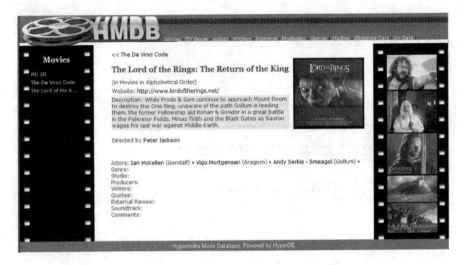

Figure 6.29. An alternative interface to exhibit a movie in the Movies in Alphabetical order context. This is the same node as the one in Figure 6.23.

To define this interface, a new view is defined, as shown in Figure 6.30. This interface uses HTML interspersed with expressions in the generated DSL, which allows one to access the model elements to be exhibited. For instance, the expression @node.name retrieves the "name" attribute of the node being exhibited (a "Movie") in this case.

Application functionality is implemented through operations associated to the various navigational classes. The code for these operations also uses the generated DSL, which allows the data model to be updated as well as the values of existing instances of navigation objects to be created or altered.

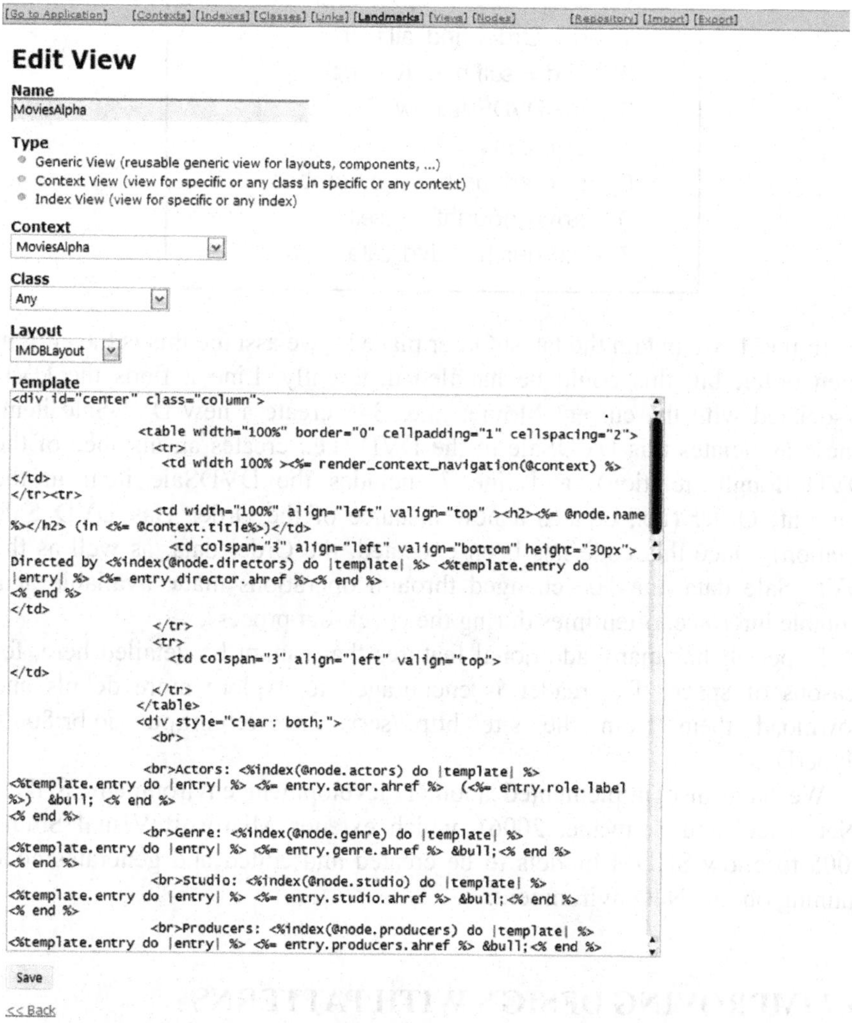

[Go to Application]   [Contexts] [Indexes] [Classes] [Links] [**Landmarks**] [Views] [Nodes]   [Repository] [Import] [Export]

Edit View

Name
MoviesAlpha

Type
- Generic View (reusable generic view for layouts, components, ...)
- Context View (view for specific or any class in specific or any context)
- Index View (view for specific or any index)

Context
MoviesAlpha

Class
Any

Layout
IMDBLayout

Template
```
<div id="center" class="column">

                <table width="100%" border="0" cellpadding="1" cellspacing="2">
                    <tr>
                    <td width 100% ><%= render_context_navigation(@context) %>
</td>
</tr><tr>
                        <td width="100%" align="left" valign="top" ><h2><%= @node.name
%></h2> (in <%= @context.title%>)</td>
                        <td colspan="3" align="left" valign="bottom" height="30px">
Directed by <%index(@node.directors) do |template| %> <%template.entry do
|entry| %> <%= entry.director.ahref %><% end %>
<% end %>
</td>
                    </tr>
                    <tr>
                        <td colspan="3" align="left" valign="top">
</td>
                    </tr>
                </table>
                <div style="clear: both;">
                    <br>

                    <br>Actors: <%index(@node.actors) do |template| %>
<%template.entry do |entry| %> <%= entry.actor.ahref %> (<%= entry.role.label
%>) &bull; <% end %>
<% end %>
                    <br>Genre: <%index(@node.genre) do |template| %>
<%template.entry do |entry| %> <%= entry.genre.ahref %> &bull;<% end %>
<% end %>
                    <br>Studio: <%index(@node.studio) do |template| %>
<%template.entry do |entry| %> <%= entry.studio.ahref %> &bull;<% end %>
<% end %>
                    <br>Producers: <%index(@node.producers) do |template| %>
<%template.entry do |entry| %> <%= entry.producers.ahref %> &bull;<% end %>
```

Save

<< Back

Figure 6.30. The interface definition for the layout shown in Figure 6.29.

Let us briefly consider what happens when, while navigating in a "Movie" object, the user invokes the addToShoppingCart operation, which has the following (simplified) code:

```
1    o = Order.find_all.first
2    dvd = self.has_dvd.first
3    s = DVDSale.new
4    s.quantity = 1
5    s.orderNumber = o.number
6    s.dvd_bought << self
7    o.order_has_dvd_sale << s
```

In line 1, we obtain the latest Order placed—we assume this is the current open order, but this could be handled differently. Line 2 finds the DVD associated with the current Movie; lines 3–5 create a new DVDSale item; line 6 associates this DVDSale to the DVD (i.e., creates an instance of the DVD_Bought relation); and line 7 includes the DVDSale item in the (current) Order (i.e., creates a new instance of the Order_Has_DVD_Sale relation). Once this code has been executed, the Order data, as well as the DVD_Sale data, may be changed through operations made available at a suitable interface, oftentimes during the check-out process.

HyperDE has many additional features that cannot be detailed here, for reasons of space. The reader is encouraged to explore more details and download them from the site http://server2.tecweb.inf.puc-rio.br:8000/HyperDe.

We have also implemented another development environment, SHDM .Net (Ricci and Schwabe, 2006), which extends Microsoft Visual Studio 2005 to allow SHDM models to be created and edited and generates code running on the .Net environment.

6.7 IMPROVING DESIGN WITH PATTERNS

Web applications are usually built from scratch, which is not surprising given the relative youth of the Web Engineering discipline. However, the key reason why Web components are not systematically reused is that most design approaches are not completely effective in helping the designer to reason about the composition of existing structures. While reuse can be obtained at the application model level, less has been achieved in the domain of navigation structures. In this section we argue in favor of a high-level kind of reuse: the reuse of design experience.

Expert Web application designers typically do not solve every problem from scratch. Most of the time, they reuse solutions that they have used previously. It is common, however, that critical design decisions made while defining, for example, the interaction and navigational styles of an application usually remain hidden in code or are poorly documented. It is widely accepted that reusability of either design experience or design structures is the most valuable kind of reuse (Gamma et al., 1995). From the expert's point of view, it helps communicate the decisions made or discuss the different alternatives with the rest of the working team in a simple and accurate way.

Consider the question of how a Web designer can guarantee (in the context of our Movies site) that the user always knows that there are new films in the site. A good solution for this general problem would be to devote a space in the home page to inform users about novelties, including a link to new movies.

Note that in the simple example above we are not using any particular design notation though such a notation may be useful for expressing in a non-ambiguous way the relationships among objects in the solution. In this section we motivate the use of patterns to record design solutions in the Web applications domain. Reasoning about abstract design structures in terms of Web patterns is a key step toward reuse of Web applications design experience.

6.7.1 A Brief Summary of Design Patterns

Design patterns are being increasingly used in software design. They systematically name, explain, and evaluate important and recurrent designs in software systems. They describe problems that occur repeatedly, and describe the core of the solution to that problem, in such a way that we can use this solution many times in different contexts and applications.

A design pattern is described by stating the context in which the pattern may be applied, the problem and interacting forces that bring it to life, and the collaborating elements that make up the reusable solution. These elements are described in an abstract way because patterns are like templates that can be applied in many different situations. Patterns allow communication to be improved within and across software development teams, by providing a shared vocabulary. They help to capture explicitly the knowledge that designers use implicitly.

The patterns movement began in the area of architectural design 30 years ago with the work of Christopher Alexander (Alexander et al., 1977). In the 1990s, the object-oriented community started using patterns to capture and convey object-oriented micro-architectures. Hypermedia patterns were introduced in Rossi et al. (1997), and an interesting corpus of hypermedia (The Hypermedia Patterns, 2002) and Web patterns (van Duyne et al., 2002) already exists.

There is no fixed format to describe patterns, although the essential elements must always appear: name, problem, solution, consequences. We next give a framework to describe and discuss patterns, and then we present some examples of Web patterns, exemplifying them in the context of our exemplary application.

6.7.2 A Pattern Taxonomy

In our research we have identified different categories in which patterns can be classified and organized. As a direct consequence of the activities in the OOHDM design space (similar to other methods), we can classify patterns in

- Conceptual or design patterns. These patterns appear during conceptual design and, as a consequence, are similar to traditional design patterns such as those in Gamma et al. (1995) or Fowler (2004).
- Navigation patterns. These patterns address the problem of organizing the navigational space of an application.
- User interface patterns. These deal with recurrent decisions in the layout and interaction styles of Web software. See, for example, Rossi et al. (2000).
- Implementation patterns. These patterns tend to be specific to a concrete run-time environment, such as J2EE, Struts, .Net, Ajax, XML, etc. See, for example, Ajax Patterns (2004) and XML Patterns (2004).

Patterns can be general or domain-specific. General-purpose patterns can be used in any application, while domain-specific patterns arise in a particular domain and are usual in that domain, such as e-commerce [see Lyardet et al. (2000)]. In other specific domains such as e-learning, other patterns may arise.

6.7.3 Examples

To illustrate the subject, we will next describe some of the patterns we discovered in the past, by mining design structures in successful Web applications. For each one, we indicate the kind of pattern and the intended domain. Patterns are described using a simple template that indicates the intent of the pattern, the problem being addressed, and the solution including examples. Complete descriptions of these patterns can be found in Rossi et al. (1999).

Landmark (Navigational, Generic)
  Intent:
  Provide easy access to different though unrelated items or sets of items in a hypermedia or Web application.

Problem:

Suppose we are building a Web Information System for a complex electronic shopping store such as www.amazon.com. By entering the site, we can build many different products such as videos, books, or CDs. We can explore the products and provide links to recommendations, comments on the products, news, etc. When we build the navigational schema, we try to follow closely those relationships existing in the underlying object model; for example, we can navigate from an author to his books, from a DVD to the list of songs it includes. We can go from a book to some comments previous readers made, read about related books, etc. However, we may want the reader to be able, at any moment, to jump to the music or book (sub-) stores or to her shopping basket.

Solution:

Define a set of landmarks and make them accessible from every node in the network. Make the interface of links to a landmark look uniform, so that users have a consistent visual cue about the landmark. We may have different levels of landmarking according to the hypertext area we are visiting. In Figure 6.31 we can see an example of landmarks in www.imdb.com, where we have landmarks to Showtime and tickets, DVD/Video, TV Movies, etc.

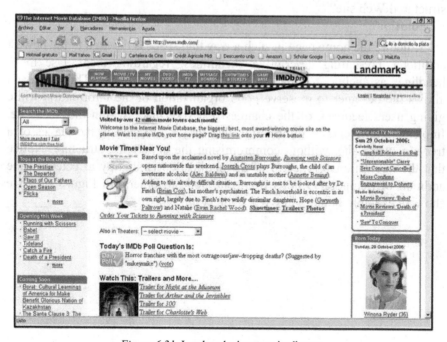

Figure 6.31. Landmarks in www.imdb.com.

News (Navigational, Generic)

Intent:

Given a large and dynamic Web application, provide the users with information about new items that have been added.

Problem:

Most large Web sites are tree-structured, which, though not perfect, offers a simple mechanism to organize considerable amounts of information. These information spaces tend to be large and are hardly ever completely navigated by a single user. In our example, each new movie is added in the corresponding branch of a huge tree (according, for example, to film genre taxonomies). However, the user has no way to know that there is a novelty. In e-commerce sites, for example, there is a need to make the user aware of the addition of new products. This problem poses a design challenge for Web designers, who must balance between a well-structured Web site where information is organized in items with subitems, etc. and a structure-less, star-shaped navigational structure where all information is reachable from the home page. The latter approach is clearly not desirable because the site's usability is greatly reduced and it may become unmanageable as it grows. Therefore, how is the user provided with instant feedback of any recent changes or additions to the information available while maintaining a well-structured Web site?

Solution:

Structure the home page in such a way that space is devoted to the newest additions, presenting descriptive "headlines" regarding them. Use those headlines as anchors to link them with their related pages. This approach allows the designer to preserve good organization of the information while giving users feedback of the changes that take place within the Web site. Implement shortcuts to information that may be located in the leaves of a tree-structured site, without compromising the underlying structure. Notice that the navigational structure of the application is slightly affected by the addition of (temporary) links from one node to others. In Figure 6.32 we show an example of news in www.imdb.com.

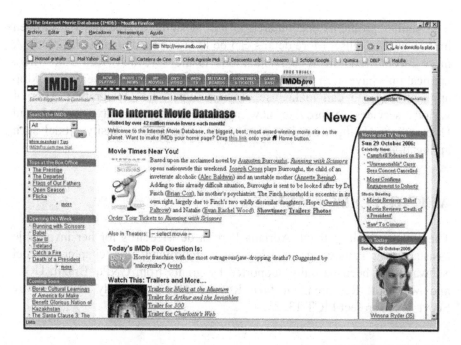

Figure 6.32. News pattern in www.imdb.com.

6.8 CONCLUSIONS

Work on OOHDM and SHDM has been taking place since 1995. OOHDM was one of the first methods to identify the currently common separation of concerns into contents, navigation, presentation, and (business) functionality. It has been extensively used in industry and academia, in applications that are running to this day.

Based on this continuous experimentation and evaluation in practice, it is an evolving method, and several new aspects are being constantly added, and improvements and refinements of earlier versions are being made.

One of the first improvements of OOHDM was in the area of personalization (see Schwabe et al., 2002). More recent work has generalized these concepts, extending SHDM to include user modeling and adaptivity, and HyperDE has also been extended accordingly (Assis et al., 2006).

This work also integrates with the original OOHDM primitives in allowing specification of access restrictions to navigation objects and contexts.

Another important aspect dealing with reuse is the study of design rationale, which allows one to capture entire reasoning structures behind a given design. Once this rationale has been recorded, it is possible to reapply it to similar problems encountered in new designs, thus achieving an even higher level of reuse. More details can be found in Medeiros et al. (2005). A more recent trend in Web applications is the so-called Web 2.0, where applications have rich interfaces (closer in interaction power to desktop applications) and can make use of "mash-ups," i.e., integrating APIs of various services to provide new application functionality. SHDM and HyperDE are being extended once again to be able to easily model such applications.

ACKNOWLEDGEMENTS

The authors wish to thank Adriana Pereira de Medeiros for her invaluable assistance in reviewing, revising, and improving this chapter. Daniel Schwabe has been partially supported by grants from CNPq–Brazil, UOL, and Microsoft Research. Gustavo Rossi has been partially supported by Secyt under project PICT 13623.

REFERENCES

Ajax Patterns, 2004. http://www.ajaxpatterns.org.
Alexander, C., Ishikawa, S., Silverstein, M., Jacobson, M., Fiksdahl-King, I., and Angel, S., 1977, *A Pattern Language*, Oxford University Press, New York.
Assis, P.A., Schwabe, D., and Nunes, D.A., 2006, ASHDM—Model-driven adaptation and meta-adaptation. *Proceedings Fourth International Conference on Adaptive Hypermedia and Adaptive Web-Based Systems*, Dublin, Ireland, June 21-23, pp. 213–222.
Brickley, D., and Guha, R.V., 2004, RDF Vocabulary Description Language 1.0, RDF Schema, W3C Recommendation, February 10. http://www.w3.org/TR/2004/REC-rdf-schema-20040210/.
Ceri, S., Fraternali, P., Bongio, A., Brambilla, M., Comai, S., and Matera, M., 2002, *Designing Data-Intensive Web Applications*, Morgan Kaufmann, San Francisco.
Fowler, M., 1997, *UML Distilled*, Addison-Wesley, Reading, MA.
Fowler, M., 2006, Analysis Patterns. http://www.martinfowler.com/articles.html.
Gamma, E., Helm, R., Johnson, R., and Vlissides, J., 1995, *Design Patterns, Elements of Reusable Object-Oriented Software*, Addison-Wesley, Reading, MA.
Greenfield, J., and Short, K. 2004, *Software Factories, Assembling Applications with Patterns, Frameworks, Models & Tools*, Wiley, New York.
Hypermedia patterns repository. http://www.designpattern.lu.unisi.ch/.
Kim, W., 1994, *Advanced Database Systems*, ACM Press, New York.
Koch, N., and Kraus, A., 2002, The expressive power of UMLbased Web engineering. *Proceedings Second International Workshop on Web-Oriented Software Technology* (IWWOST02), Málaga, Spain, June.
Lyardet, F., Rossi, G., and Schwabe, D., 2000, Patterns for E-commerce applications. *Proceedings of EuroPLoP*.
Medeiros, A.P., Schwabe, D., and Feijó, B., 2005, Kuaba ontology, design rationale representation and reuse in model-based designs. *Proceedings 24th International Conference on Conceptual Modeling* (ER 2005), Klagenfurt, Austria, pp. 241–255.

Miller, J., and Mukerji, J., 2003, The MDA Guide. Draft version 2, OMG doc. ab/2003-01-03.

Moura, S.S., and Schwabe, D., 2004, Interface development for hypermedia applications in the Semantic Web. *Proceedings LA Web 2004*, Ribeirão Preto, Brazil, pp. 106–113.

Nunes, D.A., and Schwabe, D., 2006, Rapid prototyping of Web applications combining domain-specific languages and model-driven design. *Proceedings Sixth International Conference on Web Engineering* (ICWE'06), pp. 153–160.

Ricci, L., and Schwabe, D., 2006, An authoring environment for model-driven Web applications. XII Simpósio Brasileiro de Sistemas Multimídia e Web—Webmedia 2006, Sociedade Brasileira de Computação, pp. 11–19.

Rossi, G., Schwabe, D., and Garrido, A., 1997, Design reuse in hypermedia applications development. *Proceedings of Hypertext 1997*, pp. 57–66.

Rossi, G., Schwabe, D., and Lyardet, F., 1999, Patterns for designing navigable information spaces. In *Pattern Languages of Programs IV*, Addison-Wesley, Reading, MA.

Rossi, G., Schwabe, D., and Lyardet, F., 2000, User interface patterns for hypermedia applications. *Proceedings of AVI00, Advanced Visual Interfaces*, Palermo, Italy.

Schmid, H., and Rossi, G., 2004, Modeling and designing processes in e-commerce applications. *IEEE Internet Computing*, January–February.

Schwabe, D., and Rossi, G., 1998, *An Object Oriented Approach to Web-Based Application Design. Theory and Practice of Object Systems*, **4**(4). Wiley and Sons, New York.

Schwabe, D., Guimarães, R., and Rossi, G., 2002, Cohesive design of personalized Web applications. *IEEE Internet Computing*, March.

Schwabe, D., Szundy, G., de Moura, S.S., and Lima, F., 2004, Design and implementation of Semantic Web applications. *Proceedings of the Workshop on Application Design, Development and Implementation Issues in the Semantic Web* (WWW 2004), CEUR Workshop Proceedings, **105**, May.

Smith, M., McGuiness, D., Volz, R., and Welty, C., 2002, Web Ontology Language (OWL) Guide Version 1.0. W3C working draft, November 4. http://www.w3.org/TR/owl-guide/.

Turine, M.A.S., de Oliveira, M.C.F., and Masiero. P.C., 1997, A navigation-oriented hypertext model based on statecharts. *Proceedings Eighth ACM International Hypertext Conference*, Southampton, UK.

van Duyne, D.K., Landay, J.A., and Hong, J.I., 2002, *The Design of Sites, Patterns, Principles, and Processes for Crafting a Customer-Centered Web Experience*, Addison-Wesley, Reading, MA.

Vilain, P., Schwabe, D., and de Souza, C.S., 2000, A diagrammatic tool for representing user interaction in UML. *Proceedings UML 2000*. York, UK, pp. 133–147.

XML Patterns Web page, 2004. www.xmlpatterns.com.

Chapter 7

UML-BASED WEB ENGINEERING
An Approach Based on Standards

Nora Koch,[1,2] Alexander Knapp,[1] Gefei Zhang,[1] Hubert Baumeister[3]

[1]*Institut für Informatik, Ludwig-Maximilians-Universität München, Germany,*
{kochn, knapp, zhangg}@pst.ifi.lmu.de

[2]*F.A.S.T. GmbH, Germany, koch@fast.de*

[3]*Informatik og Matematisk Modellering, Danmarks Tekniske Universitet, Lyngby, Denmark,*
hub@imm.dtu.dk

7.1 OVERVIEW

UML-based Web Engineering (UWE; www.pst.ifi.lmu.de/projekte/uwe) came up at the end of the 1990s (Baumeister et al., 1999; Wirsing et al., 1999) with the idea to find a standard way for building analysis and design models of Web systems based on the then-current methods of OOHDM (Schwabe and Rossi, 1995), RMM (Isakowitz et al., 1995), and WSDM (de Troyer and Leune, 1998). The aim, which is still being pursued, was to use a common language or at least to define meta-model-based mappings among the existing approaches (Koch and Kraus, 2003; Escalona and Koch, 2006).

At that time the Unified Modeling Language (UML), which evolved from the integration of the three different modeling techniques of Booch, OOSE, and OMT, seemed to be a promising approach for system modeling. Since those early integration efforts, UML became the "lingua franca" of (object-oriented) software engineering (Object Management Group, 2005). A prominent feature of UML is that it provides a set of aids for the definition of domain-specific modeling languages (DSL)—so-called extension mechanisms. Moreover, the newly defined DSLs remain UML-compliant, which allows the use of all UML features supplemented, e.g., with Web-specific extensions.

Both the acceptance of the UML as a standard in the development of software systems and the flexibility provided by the extension mechanisms are the reasons for the choice of the Unified Modeling Language instead of the use of proprietary modeling techniques. The idea followed by UWE to adhere to standards is not limited to UML. UWE also uses XMI as a model exchange format (in the hopes of future tool interoperability enabled by a truly portable XMI), MOF for meta-modeling, the model-driven principles given by OMG's Model-Driven Architecture (MDA) approach, the transformation language QVT, and XML.

UWE is continuously adapting, on the one hand, to new features of Web systems, such as more transaction-based, personalized, context-dependent, and asynchronous applications. On the other hand, UWE evolves to incorporate the state of the art of software engineering techniques, such as aspect-oriented modeling, integration of model checking using Hugo/RT (Knapp et al., 2002; www.pst.ifi.lmu.de/projekte/hugo), and new model transformation languages to improve design quality.

The remainder of this chapter is structured as follows: The features distinguishing UWE's development process, visual notation, and tool support are briefly outlined below. UWE's modeling techniques are discussed step by step in Section 7.2 by means of the online movie data-base case study. The UWE extensions of the UML meta-model are outlined in Section 7.3. UWE's model-driven process and, in particular, the model transformations integrated into the process are described in Section 7.4. The CASE tool ArgoUWE, which supports the UWE notation and method, is described in Section 7.5. Finally, we give an outlook on future steps in the development of UWE.

7.1.1 Characteristics of the Process

The development of Web systems is subject to continuous changes in user and technology requirements. Models built so far in any stage of the development process have to be easily adaptable to these changes. To cope efficiently with the required flexibility, UWE advocates a strict separation of concerns in the early phases of the development and implements a model-driven development process, i.e., a process based on the construction of models and model transformations. The ultimate challenge is to support a development process that allows fully automated generation of Web systems.

7.1.1.1 Separation of Concerns

Similarly to other Web Engineering methods, the UWE process is driven by the separate modeling of concerns describing a Web system. Models are built at the different stages of requirements engineering, analysis, design, and implementation of the development process and are used to represent different views of the same Web application corresponding to the different concerns (content, navigation structure, and presentation). The content model is used to specify the concepts that are relevant to the application domain and the relationships between these concepts. The hypertext or navigation structure is modeled separately from the content, although it is derived from the content model. The navigation model represents the navigation paths of the Web system being modeled. The presentation model takes into account representation and user–machine communication tasks.

UWE proposes at least one type of UML diagram for the visualization of each model to represent the structural aspects of the different views. However, in addition, very often UML interaction diagrams or state machines are used to represent behavioral aspects of the Web system. Figure 7.1 shows how the scope of modeling spans these three orthogonal dimensions: development stages, systems' views, and aspects.

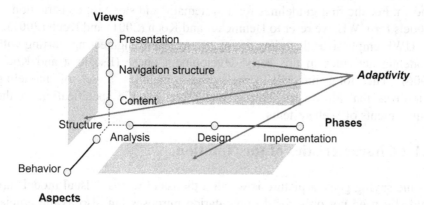

Figure 7.1. Modeling aspects in UWE (from Schwinger and Koch, 2006).

Another concern also handled separately is adaptivity. Personalized and context-dependent Web systems provide the user with more appropriate information, links, or pages by being aware of user or contextual features. We propose to view adaptivity as a cross-cutting concern and thus use aspect-oriented techniques to model adaptive Web systems. It can be seen as a fourth dimension influencing all other Web modeling dimensions: views, aspects, and phases. Requirements models and architecture models focusing on specific Web aspects complete the specification of the Web system. Separation of concerns offers advantages in the maintenance and re-engineering of a Web system as well as for the generation of Web systems for different contexts and platforms.

7.1.1.2 Development Driven by Models

The model-driven development (MDD) approach not only advocates the use of models (as those described above) for the development of software, but also emphasizes the need of transformations in all phases of the development, from requirements specification to designs and from design models to implementations. Transformations between models provide a chain that enables the automated implementation of a system in successive steps from the different models.

The development of Web systems is a field that lends itself to applying MDD due to the Web-specific separation of concerns and continuous changes in technologies in the Web domain.

Meta-model-based methods such as OO-H (Gómez et al., 2001) and UWE constitute a good basis for the implementation of a model-driven process for the development of Web systems. They included semiautomated model-based transformations even before MDD concepts became well-known. For the first guidelines for a systematic and stepwise construction of models for UWE, we refer to Hennicker and Koch (2001) and Koch (2001).

UWE emphasizes the relevance of requirements engineering starting with modeling activities in this early development phase (Escalona and Koch, 2006). Therefore, the UWE meta-model includes a set of modeling primitives that allows for simpler and more specific specification of the requirements of Web systems.

7.1.2 Characteristics of the Notation

As the saying goes, a picture is worth a thousand words. Visual models are naturally used not only for documentation purposes but also as the crucial chain link in the software development process. The trend is the production of domain-specific visual models. Conversely, the importance of the selection of the modeling language is not self-evident.

From our point of view, a modeling language has to

1. provide powerful primitives to construct expressive, yet intuitive models
2. offer wide CASE tool support
3. facilitate extension
4. provide a formal or at least a semiformal semantics
5. be easy to learn

Although UML fulfills only the first three requirements, it seems that UML is currently the best approach. UML and various UML extensions are successfully used in many different application domains. However, there is no formal semantics covering the whole UML, and the fifth requirement can only be satisfied if we restrict ourselves to a subset of the modeling constructs of UML.

7.1.2.1 Modeling with UML

The distinguishing feature of UWE is its UML compliance since the model elements of UWE are defined in terms of a UML profile and as an extension of the UML meta-model (Koch and Kraus, 2002, 2003).

Although the UML is expressive enough to model all requirements that arise in modeling Web systems, it does not offer Web domain-specific elements. To ease the modeling of special aspects of Web applications, we define in UWE special views—using UML's extension mechanisms—graphically represented by UML diagrams, such as the navigation model and the presentation model (Koch, 2001; Koch et al., 2001).

UML modeling techniques comprise the construction of static and dynamic views of software systems by object and class diagrams, component and deployment diagrams, use case diagrams, state and activity diagrams, sequence and communication diagrams. The UML extension mechanisms are used to define stereotypes that we utilize for the representation of Web constructs, such as nodes and links. In addition, tag definitions and constraints written in OCL (Object Constraint Language) can be used. This way we obtain a UML-compliant notation—a so-called UML lightweight extension or better known as a UML profile. UWE notation is defined as such a UML profile.

The advantage of using UML diagrams is the common understanding of these diagrams. Furthermore, the notation and the semantics of the modeling elements of "pure" UML, i.e., those modeling elements that comprise the UML meta-model, are widely described in the OMG documentation (Object Management Group, 2005). For any software designer with a UML background, it is easy to understand a model based on a UML profile, such as the extension that UWE suggests. We observe that UML extensions "inherit" the problems of UML, e.g., the lack of a complete formal semantics covering all modeling elements.

UWE focuses on visual modeling together with systematic design and automatic generation. The aim is to cover the entire development life cycle of Web systems, providing techniques and notations to start with requirements models, moving through design models, as well as including architecture and aspect models. All these models are visualized using UML diagrammatic techniques.

7.1.2.2 Meta-Modeling

Meta-modeling plays a fundamental role in CASE tool construction and is as well the core of the model-driven process. A meta-model is a precise definition of the elements of a modeling language, their relationships, and the well-formedness rules needed for creating syntactically correct models.

Tool-supported design and model-based system generation are becoming essential in the development process of Web systems due to the need for rapid production of new Web presences and Web applications. CASE tools have to be built on a precisely specified meta-model of the modeling constructs used in the design activities, providing more flexibility if modeling requirements change. Meta-models are essential for the definition of model transformations and automatic code generation.

The UWE meta-model is defined as a conservative extension of the UML meta-model (Koch and Kraus, 2003). It is the basis for the UWE notation and UWE tool support. "Conservative" means that the modeling elements of the UML meta-model are not modified, e.g., by adding additional features or associations to the UML modeling element Class. OCL constraints are used to specify additional static semantics (analogous to the well-formedness rules in the UML specification). By staying thereby compatible with the MOF interchange meta-model, we can take advantage of meta-modeling tools based on the corresponding XML interchange format (XMI).

In addition, the UWE meta-model is "profileable" (Baresi et al., 2002), which means that it is possible to map the meta-model to a UML profile. A UML profile consists of a hierarchy of stereotypes and a set of constraints. Stereotypes are used for representing instances of metaclasses and are written in guillemets, like «menu» or «anchor». The definition of a UML profile has the advantage that it is supported by nearly every UML CASE tool either automatically, by a tool plug-in, or passively when the model is saved and then checked by an external tool. The UWE meta-model could also be used as the basis for building a common meta-model (or ontology) of the concepts needed for the design in the Web domain (cf. Koch and Kraus, 2003; Escalona and Koch, 2006). Using for this purpose the standardized OMG meta-modeling architecture would facilitate the construction of meta-CASE tools.

7.1.3 Characteristics of the Tool Environment

The UML compliance of UWE has an important advantage: All CASE tools that support the Unified Modeling Language can be used to build UWE models. For this purpose it is sufficient to name stereotypes after the names of the UWE modeling concepts. Many tools offer additional support with an import functionality of predefined UML profiles. In such a case, the profile model elements can be used in the same way as the built-in UML model elements.

7.1.3.1 CASE Tool Support

A wider developer support is achieved by the open source plug-in ArgoUWE (www.pst.ifi.lmu.de/projekte/uwe) for the open source CASE tool ArgoUML (www.argouml.org). In addition to providing an editor for the UWE notation, ArgoUWE checks the consistency of models and supports the systematic transformation techniques of the UWE method. Using the UWE profile, models designed with other UML CASE tools can be exchanged with ArgoUWE. The use of tools that support not only the modeling itself but also a model-driven approach shortens development cycles and facilitates re-engineering of Web systems.

7.1.3.2 Model Consistency Check

ArgoUWE also checks the consistency of models according to the OCL constraints specified for the UWE meta-model. Consistency checking is embedded into the cognitive design critiques feature of ArgoUML and runs in a background thread. Thus, model deficiencies and inconsistencies are gathered during the modeling process, but the designer is not interrupted. The designer obtains feedback at any time by taking a look at this continuously updated list of design critiques, which is shown in the to-do pane of the tool.

In the following, we exemplify how UWE's model-driven process, notation, and tool support are used to develop Web applications.

7.2 METHOD BY CASE STUDY

We use a simple online movie database example that allows users to explore information about movies and persons related to the production of the movies. This example is inspired by www.imdb.org and named the "Movie UWE Case Study" (MUC). Movies are characterized, among other things, by their genre, the cast, memorable quotes, trailers, and a soundtrack. Persons related to the movie production include the director, producer, composer, and the actors. The user interested in watching a movie can access information on theaters that show the movie. Registered users—identified by an email address and a password—can provide comments, rate comments, vote movies, manage "their movies," and buy tickets in theaters of their preference. The MUC online movie database personalizes the application, giving some recommendations about movies and providing personalized news to the user.

The focus in the following is on the models built for the different views of the analysis and design phases (see Figure 7.1). Model transformations are described as part of the model-driven process in Section 7.4.

7.2.1 Starting with Requirements Specification

The first step toward developing a Web system is the identification of the requirements for such an application that are specified in UWE with a *requirements model*. Requirements can be documented at different levels of detail. UWE proposes two levels of granularity when modeling Web system requirements. First, a rough description of the functionalities is produced, which are modeled with UML use cases. In a second step, a more detailed description of the use cases is developed, e.g., by UML activity diagrams that depict the responsibilities and actions of the stakeholders.

7.2.1.1 Overview of Use Cases

Use case diagrams are built with the UML elements Actor and UseCase. Actors are used to model the users of the Web system. Typical users of Web systems are the anonymous user (called User) in the MUC case study, the registered user (RegisteredUser), and the Web system administrator. Use cases are used to visualize the functionalities that the system will provide. The use case diagram depicts use cases, actors, and associations among them, showing the roles the actors play in the interaction with the system, e.g., triggering some use cases.

In addition to the UML features, UWE distinguishes among three types of use cases: navigation, process, and personalized use cases. Navigation use cases are used to model typical user behavior when interacting with a Web application, such as browsing through the Web application content or searching information by keywords. The use case model of Figure 7.2, for example, includes the «navigation» (□) use cases ViewMovie, Search, and GoToExternalSite. Process use cases are used to describe business tasks that end users will perform with the system; they are modeled in the same way as it is done for traditional software. These business tasks normally imply transactional actions on the underlying database. We use "pure" UML notation for their graphical representation. Typical examples for business use cases are Register, CommentMovie, and BuyTicket. A third group of use cases are those that imply personalization of a Web system, such as ViewRecommendations and ViewLatestNews. They are denoted by a stereotype «personalized» (☆). Personalization is triggered by user behavior.

All UML elements for modeling use case diagrams are available, such as system boundary box, package, generalization relationship, stereotyped dependencies «extend» and «include» among use cases. Figure 7.2 illustrates the use case diagram for the MUC case study restricted to the functional requirements from the User and RegisteredUser viewpoint.

7.2.1.2 Detailed View of Use Cases

The level of detail and formality of requirements specifications depends on project risks and the complexity of the Web application to be built. But very often a specification based only on use cases is not enough (Vilain et al., 2000). Analysts use different kinds of refinement techniques to obtain a more detailed specification of the functional requirements, such as workflows, formatted specifications, or prototypes. These representations usually include actors, pre- and postconditions, a workflow description, exceptions and error situations, information sources, sample results, and references to other documents. In particular, for the development of Web

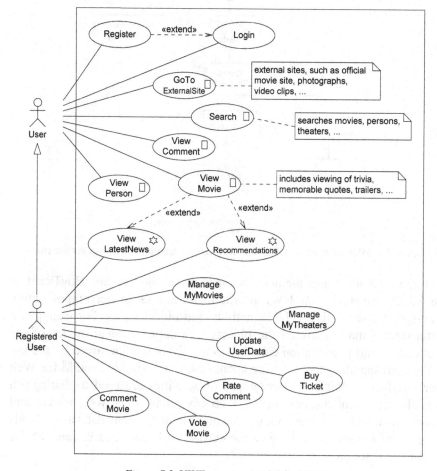

Figure 7.2. UWE use case model for MUC.

systems, the informational, navigational, and process goals have to be gathered and specified. Informational goals indicate content requirements. Navigational goals point toward the kind of access to content, and process goals specify the ability of the user to perform some tasks within the Web system (Pressman, 2005).

Following the principle of using UML whenever possible for the specification, we refine requirements with UML activity diagrams. For each nontrivial business use case, we build at least one activity diagram for the main stream of tasks to be performed in order to provide the functionality indicated by the corresponding use case. Optionally, additional diagrams can be depicted for exceptions and variants. Activity diagrams include activities, shareholders responsible for these activities (optional), and control flow elements. They can be enriched with object flows showing relevant objects for the input or output of those activities.

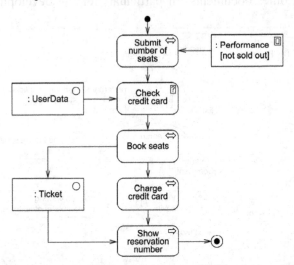

Figure 7.3. MUC case study: UWE activity diagram detailing the buy-ticket use case.

Figure 7.3 illustrates the activity diagram for the use case BuyTicket of our MUC case study. The UWE profile includes a set of stereotypes adding Web-specific semantics to UML activity and object nodes. For example, a distinction is made between the objects that define content, nodes of the application, and presentation elements. Visualization is improved by the use of the corresponding icons: O for «content», □ for «node», and ▣ for Web user interface («WebUI»). Stereotypes of activities are used to distinguish possible actions of the user in the Web environment: browse, search, and transactional activities that comprise changes in at least one database. To this category of stereotypes belong ⇨ for «browse», ⍰ for «query», and ⇔ for transactional actions.

7.2.2 Defining the Content

Analysis models provide the basis for the design models, in particular the *content model* of a Web system. The aim of the content model is to provide a visual specification of the domain-relevant information for the Web system that mainly comprises the content of the Web application. However, very often it also includes entities of the domain required for customized Web applications. These entities constitute the so-called user profile or user model.

Customization deals not only with adaptation to the properties of users or user groups, but also with adaptation to features of the environment. A so-called context profile or context model is built in such a case. The objects occurring in the detailed view of the use cases provide natural candidates of domain entities for the content and user model.

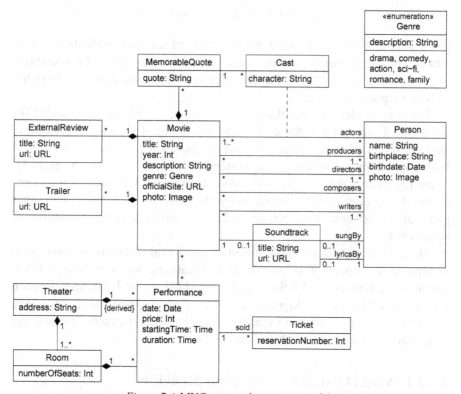

Figure 7.4. MUC case study: content model.

The separation of content and user model (or context model) has proven its value in practice. Both are graphically represented as UML class diagrams. The content model of MUC is depicted in Figure 7.4; the user model is shown in Figure 7.5. The entities representing content and user or context properties respectively, are modeled by classes, i.e., instances of the UML metaclass Class. Relationships between content and user properties are modeled by UML associations. In particular, movies are modeled by a class Movie with a set of properties, such as title and genre forming the attributes of the class Movie, or as classes associated to Movie

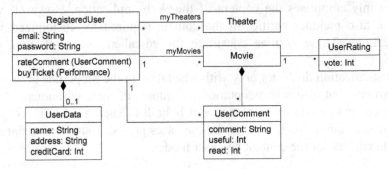

Figure 7.5. MUC case study: user model.

like Trailer and ExternalReview. Stakeholders of the film production, e.g., a movie's producer, composer, and cast, are modeled as roles of associations to the class Person. Note that Performance and Ticket were inferred from the activity diagram in Figure 7.3.

The user model contains the user data (again see Figure 7.3) needed for the login of the user and the comments and rating of the movies. All these data are provided by the users themselves during registration or use of the Web application. In addition, the system collects information on users by observing their behavior. The collected data are used for adaptation and are modeled as a cross-cutting aspect and woven into the user model and other parts of the system (see Section 7.2.6 on aspect-oriented modeling of adaptivity).

There is no need for the definition of additional elements as there is no distinction to modeling of non-Web applications. We use "pure" UML notation and semantics. All the features provided by the UML specification for constructing class diagrams can be used, in particular, packages, enumerations (e.g., Genre in Figure 7.4), generalizations, compositions, and association classes (e.g., Cast in Figure 7.4).

7.2.3 Laying Down the Navigation Structure

Based on the requirements analysis and the content modeling, the *navigation structure* of a Web application is modeled. Navigation classes (visualized as □) represent navigable nodes of the hypertext structure; navigation links show direct links between navigation classes. Alternative navigation paths are handled by «menu» (⊟). Access primitives are used to reach multiple instances of a navigation class («index» ≡, or «guided tour» ⇥) or to select items («query» ⍰). In Web applications that contain business logic, the business processes must be integrated into the navigation structure. The entry and exit points of the business processes are modeled by process classes (∑) in the navigation model, the linkage between each other and to the navigation classes is modeled by process links. Each process class is associated with a use case that models a business process. Navigation

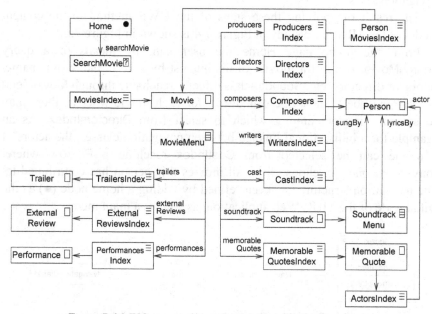

Figure 7.6. MUC case study: navigation from **Movie** (fragment).

structures are laid down in stereotyped UML class diagrams with navigation and process classes, menus, and access primitives extending the UML metaclass **Class**, and navigation and process links extending the UML metaclass **Association**.

7.2.3.1 Initial Navigation Structure

UWE provides methodological guidelines for developing an initial sketch of the navigation structure from the content model of a Web application (see also Koch and Kraus, 2002; Knapp et al., 2003): Content classes deemed to be relevant for navigation are selected from the content model, and these classes as well as their associations are put into a navigation model as navigation classes and navigation links, respectively. Navigation links represent possible steps to be followed by the user, and thus these links have to be directed; if navigation back and forth between two navigation classes is desired, an association is split into two. Menus are added to every navigation class that has more than one outgoing association. Finally, access primitives (index, guided tours, and queries) allow for selecting a single information entity, as represented by a navigation class. An index, a guided tour, or a query should be added between two navigation classes whenever the multiplicity of the end target of their linking association is greater than 1. The properties of the content class corresponding to the navigation class over which the index or the query runs are added as navigation attributes to the navigation class.

The result of applying these steps of the UWE method to the content model of the MUC case study in Figure 7.4 is shown in Figure 7.6.

From the home page Home the user can, by means of a query SearchMovie, search for movies of his interest by criteria like movie name, actors, or directors, etc. Soundtrack is directly reachable through MovieMenu as there may be at most one soundtrack for each movie whereas there may be several directors among which to select from DirectorsIndex. As an example for a bidirectional linkage between navigation classes, the actors of a movie can be selected from CastIndex reaching a Person, where, conversely, one can choose from all movies this person has contributed to. The navigation structure has been refined by adding a home node (●) as the initial node of the MUC Web application, as well as a main menu.

Figure 7.7. "Pure" UML (left) and shorthand notation (right) for index.

The UWE profile notation for menus and access primitives provides a compact representation of patterns frequently used in the Web domain. Figure 7.7 (right) shows the shorthand notation for indexes. Using "pure" UML for modeling an index would instead require an additional model element: an index item as depicted in Figure 7.7 (left). The result would be an overloaded model if it contains many such indexes.

7.2.3.2 Adding Business Processes

In a next step, the navigation structure can now be extended by process classes that represent the entry and exit points to business processes. These process classes are derived from the nonnavigational use cases. In Figure 7.8 the business processes Register (linked to the use case Register) and Login (linked to the use case Login) have been added. The integration of these classes in the navigation model requires an additional menu (MainMenu), which provides links to Register, Login, and SearchMovies. A user may only manage her movies if she has logged in previously. Finally, a user can buy tickets for a selected movie and a selected performance by navigating to BuyTicket.

A single navigation structure diagram for a whole Web application would inevitably lead to cognitive overload. Different views to the navigation structure should be produced from the content model focusing on different aspects of the application, like navigation to particular content or integration of related business processes.

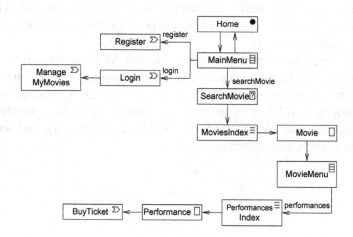

Figure 7.8. MUC case study: integration of business processes into navigation (fragment).

7.2.4 Refining the Processes

Each process class included in the navigation model is refined into a process model consisting of a process flow model and optionally of a process structure model. The control and data flow is modeled in the process flow model in the form of a UML activity diagram. It is the result of a refinement process that starts from the workflow in the requirements model.

Figure 7.9 illustrates the result of the refinement process applied to Figure 7.3. This process mainly consists of the integration of the main stream of the actions with alternatives, such as Enter new credit card info in case of invalid card numbers or exception handling (not included in this example). Control elements are added with the purpose of providing the business logic. Activities and objects can be added to the activity diagram. A process structure model has the form of a class diagram and describes the relationship between a process class and other classes whose instances are used to support the business process.

7.2.5 Sketching the Presentation

The presentation model provides an abstract view of the user interface (UI) of a Web application. It is based on the navigation model and abstracts from concrete aspects of the UI, like the use of colors, fonts, and the location of UI elements on the Web page; instead, the presentation model describes the basic structure of the user interface, i.e., which UI elements (e.g., text, images, anchors, forms) are used to present the navigation nodes. The advantage of the presentation model is that it is independent of the actual techniques used to implement the Web site, thus allowing the stakeholders to discuss the appropriateness of the presentation before actually implementing it.

The basic elements of a presentation model are the presentation classes, which are directly based on nodes from the navigation model, i.e., navigation classes, menus, access primitives, and process classes. A presentation class (◻) is composed of UI elements, like text («text» ≈), anchor («anchor» ▬), button («button» ●), image («image» ▣), form («form» 吕), and anchored collection («anchored collection» ≡).

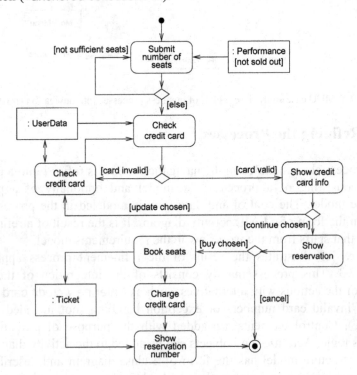

Figure 7.9. MUC case study: UWE process flow model for the buy-ticket process.

Figure 7.10 shows an example of a presentation class for the navigation class Movie. Note that to ease the identification of which navigation node is presented by a presentation class, the presentation class uses by default the same name as the corresponding navigation node. Each attribute of a navigation class is presented with an appropriate UI element. For example, a text element is used for the title attribute, and an image element is used for the photo attribute. The relationship between presentation classes and UI elements is that of composition. For presentation models, composition is pictured by drawing the component, i.e., the UI element, inside the composite, i.e., the presentation class; note, however, that this notation is not supported by all CASE tools.

Figure 7.10. MUC case study: presentation class Movie.

Usually, the information from several navigation nodes is presented on one Web page, which is modeled by pages («page») in UWE. Pages can contain, among other things, presentation classes and presentation groups («presentation group»). A presentation group can itself contain presentation groups and presentation classes. An excerpt of the presentation model of the movie page is shown in Figure 7.11. It contains a presentation class for the main menu, which in turn contains a link (represented by the anchor UI element) to home, a presentation class for the SearchMovie query, and button UI elements to start the login and registration processes. The SearchMovie query also provides an example of the form UI element to enter the movie name to search for. The presentation class for MovieMenu contains links to the presentation classes of the corresponding indexes—based on the navigation model in Figure 7.6—providing additional information on the movie.

The presentation classes of these indexes plus the presentation classes for movie are assembled in a presentation group. The use of the stereotypes «default» and «alternative» for the associations from Movie, ProducersIndex, etc. to MovieMenu indicates that the elements of the presentation groups are alternatives, i.e., only one of them is shown depending on which link was followed from the movie menu, with the presentation class Movie being shown by default. For example, when the user follows the producers link in the MovieMenu, the ProducersIndex is shown, containing the list of the producers of that film.

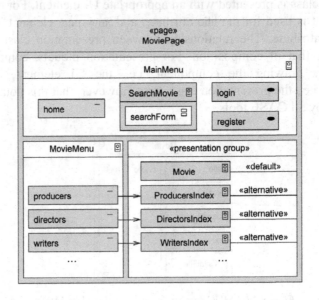

Figure 7.11. MUC case study: the presentation model of the movie page.

7.2.6 Aspect-Oriented Modeling of Adaptivity

Adaptivity is an increasingly important feature of Web applications. Adaptive Web applications provide more appropriate pages to the user by being aware of user or context properties. An example of adaptivity is recommendations based on user behavior, like movie of favorite actors in our MUC case study. In general, adaptivity is orthogonal to three views: content, navigation structure, and presentation (see Figure 7.1). In order to model adaptive features of Web applications non-invasively, we use techniques of aspect-oriented modeling (AOM; cf. Filman et al., 2004) in UWE.

We introduce a new model element named *aspect*. An aspect is composed of a *pointcut* part and an *advice* part. It is a (graphical) statement expressing that, in addition to the features specified in the principal model, each model element selected by the pointcut also has features specified by the advice. In other words, a complete description, including both general system functionality and additional, cross-cutting features of the quantified model elements, is given by the composition of the principal model and the aspect. The process of composition is called *weaving*.

UWE defines several kinds of aspects for modeling different static and run-time adaptivity (Baumeister et al., 2005). In order to model the recommendation feature modularly, we use on the one hand a model aspect and a run-time aspect for keeping track of the number of visits to movie pages. On the other hand, another run-time aspect integrates the recommendation feature into the login process: A list of movies is presented ranked according to the appearing actors, who in turn are ranked according to their relevance in the visited movies.

The static model aspect for extending the user model (see Figure 7.5) by an operation that returns the number of visits of a registered user to a movie page is shown in Figure 7.12 (left). The pointcut is a pattern containing a special element, the *formal parameter*, which is annotated by a question mark. The pointcut selects all model elements in the base model that match the pattern, thereby instantiating the formal parameter. In our case the formal parameter is a class in which only the name RegisteredUser is specified. The pointcut therefore selects all classes (actually, there is exactly one such class) in the navigation model with the name RegisteredUser. The advice defines the change to the selected model elements. After weaving, our RegisteredUser class is thus extended by the operation visited (see Figure 7.12, right); no other elements are affected by this aspect.

Model aspects are a special case of aspect-oriented class diagrams (AOCDs), which are also defined in a lightweight UML extension and are therefore UML-compatible; see Zhang (2005). Since a model aspect specifies a static modification of the base model, other, standardized model transformation languages such as the Atlas Transformation Language (ATL; Jouault and Kurtev, 2005), QVT-P (QVT-Partners, 2003), or QVT (QVT-Merge Group, 2004) may also be used. The advantage of AOCD compared with these languages is, however, that it does not require the modeler to have expert knowledge of the UML meta-model, which may make AOCD easier to use (cf. Section 7.4).

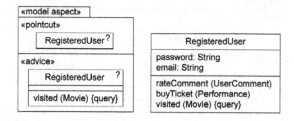

Figure 7.12. MUC case study: model aspect (left) and the weaving result (right).

The dynamic behavior of our MUC system is extended by two run-time aspects. Figure 7.13 shows a link traversal aspect, used to ensure that visited returns the correct result: The pointcut selects all links from any object—note that neither the name nor the type of the object to the left is specified and thus it matches any object—to some Movie object. The advice defines with an OCL constraint the result of the action fired when such a link is visited: If the current user is logged in, the system increases his respective record by 1. After weaving, the system's behavior is thus enriched by counting user visits to the movie pages.

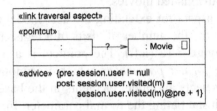

Figure 7.13. MUC case study: link traversal aspect for counting movie visits.

Figure 7.14 shows how the business process Login is extended by a flow aspect. The base model depicted in Figure 7.14 (top) defines the normal workflow without considering adaptivity: The user is asked to input her email address and password, and then the system verifies the input and responds accordingly.

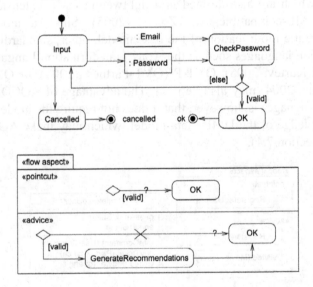

Figure 7.14. MUC case study: flow aspect (bottom) extending business process Login (top).

The adaptive feature of generating recommendations for the user is added by the aspect shown in Figure 7.14 (bottom). The pointcut selects every (in this concrete example, exactly one) control flow edge from a decision point to the OK action, which is guarded by the condition valid. The advice deletes this edge by crossing it out and adds an action for recommendation generation and two new control flow edges to bind it into the process.

7.3 UWE META-MODEL

The UWE meta-model is defined as a conservative extension of the UML 2.0 meta-model. "Conservative" means that the model elements of the UML meta-model are not modified. Instead, all new model elements of the UWE meta-model are related by inheritance to at least one model element of the UML meta-model. We define additional features and relationships for the new elements. Analogous to the well-formedness rules in the UML specification, we use OCL constraints to specify the additional static semantics of these new elements. The resulting UWE meta-model is profileable, which means that it is possible to map the meta-model to a UML profile (Koch and Kraus, 2003). In particular, UWE stays compatible with the MOF interchange meta-model and therefore with tools that are based on the corresponding XML interchange format XMI. The advantage is that all standard UML CASE tools that support UML profiles or UML extension mechanisms can be used to create UWE models of Web applications. If technically possible, these CASE tools can further be extended to support the UWE method. ArgoUWE (see Section 7.5) presents an instance of such CASE tool support for UWE based on the UWE meta-model.

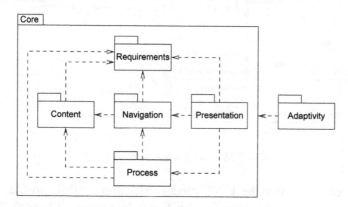

Figure 7.15. Overview of the UWE meta-model.

The UWE extension of the UML meta-model consists of adding two top-level packages, Core and Adaptivity, to the UML (cf. Figure 7.15). The separation of concerns of Web applications is reflected by the package structure of Core and the cross-cutting of adaptation by the dependency of Adaptivity on Core (see Figure 7.1). The package Requirements comprises the UWE extensions on UseCase for discerning navigational from business process and personalized use cases and the different markings for ActivityNode («browse», «query», and «transaction») and ObjectNode («content», «node», and «WebUI») (see Escalona and Koch, 2006).

The navigation and presentation packages bundle UWE's extensions for the corresponding models. Figure 7.16 details a part of the meta-model for Navigation with the connection between Node and Link and their various subclasses. NavigationClass and ProcessClass with the related NavigationLink and ProcessLink as well as Menu and the access primitives Index, GuidedTour, and Query provide the Web domain-specific metaclasses for building the navigation model. The packages Contents and Process are currently only used as a stub, reflecting the fact that UWE allows the designer to develop content and process models using all UML features. Finally, Adaptation contains UWE's aspect facilities by representing Aspect as a UML Package with two subpackages, Pointcut and Advice.

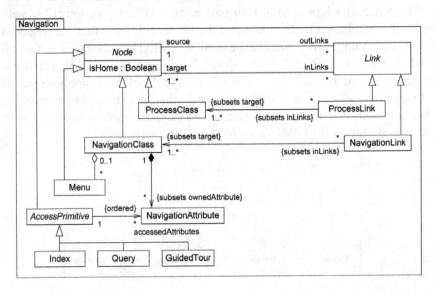

Figure 7.16. UWE navigation meta-model.

In order to transfer the UWE meta-model into a UML profile, we use UML's extension mechanisms (see Section 7.1). Figure 7.17 shows how the metaclasses of the UWE navigation meta-model are rendered as a stereotype hierarchy, forming the UWE navigation profile: Node becomes a stereotype of Class, NavigationAttribute a stereotype of Property, and Link a stereotype of Association.

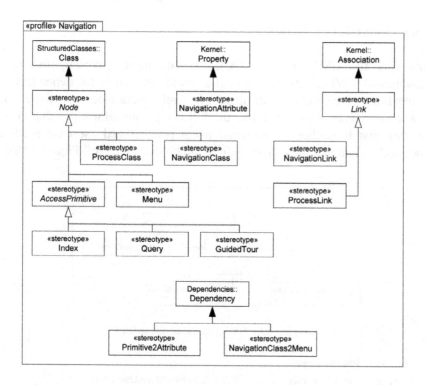

Figure 7.17. UWE navigation profile.

The associations of the UWE navigation meta-model, e.g., connecting Link to Node, cannot be represented by meta-associations (see Object Management Group, 2005) and have to be added either by stereotyping the UML metaclass Dependency or by using the association from the UML meta-model from which the association is derived. The latter approach is used for representing the composition between NavigationClass and NavigationAttribute using the association ownedAttributes; for the association between AccessPrimitive and NavigationAttribute and the association between NavigationClass and Menu, we stereotype Dependency, leading, e.g., to the following constraint:

```
context Dependency
inv: self.stereotypes->
             includes("Primitive2Attribute") implies
        (self.client.stereotypes->
                 includes("AccessPrimitive") and
          self.supplier.stereotypes->
                 includes("NavigationAttribute"))
```

where client and supplier denote the ends of the Dependency relationship.

7.3.1 Consistency Rules

Following the UML, we use OCL to state more precisely the static semantics of UWE's new meta-model elements as well as the dependencies of meta-model elements both inside a single meta-model package and between packages. As an example, the following constraint states that every use case that is neither a navigation nor a personalized use case needs a process class and that the converse direction holds as well (cf. Figure 7.18):

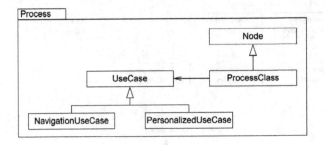

Figure 7.18. UWE process meta-model.

```
context ProcessClass
inv: not self.useCase.oclIsKindOf(NavigationUseCase) and
         not self.useCase.oclIsKindOf(PersonalizedUseCase)


context UseCase
inv: (not self.oclIsKindOf(NavigationUseCase) and
         not self.oclIsKindOf(PersonalizedUseCase)) implies
      ProcessClass.allInstances()->
         exists(pn | pn.useCase = self)
```

7.4 MODEL-DRIVEN DEVELOPMENT IN UWE

The UWE approach includes the specification of a process for the development of Web systems in addition to the UML profile and the UWE meta-model. The UWE process is model-driven following the MDA principles and using several other OMG standards, like MOF, UML, OCL, and XMI, and forthcoming standards, like QVT (QVT-Merge Group, 2004). The process relies on modeling and model transformations, and its main characteristic is the systematic and semiautomatic development of Web systems, as detailed in Chapter 12 by Moreno et al. on model-driven Web Engineering. The aim of such an MDD process is automatic model transformation, which, in each step, is based on transformation rules.

Focusing on model transformations, the UWE process is depicted in Figure 7.19 as a stereotyped UML activity diagram (Meliá et al., 2005). Models are shown as objects, and transformations are represented with stereotyped activities (special circular icon).

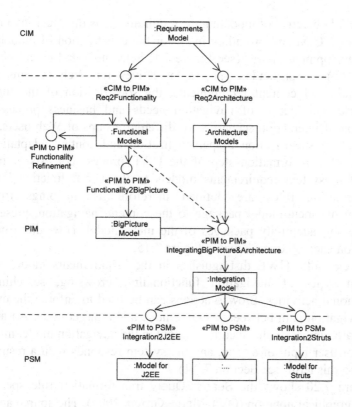

Figure 7.19. Overview of model transformations in the UWE process.

The process starts with the business model, which MDA calls the computational independent model (CIM), used to specify the requirements. Platform-independent models (PIMs) are derived from these requirement models. The set of design models represents the different concerns of the Web applications, comprising the content, the navigation, the business processes, the presentation, and the adaptation of the Web system (summarized as FunctionalModels in Figure 7.19). In a next step, the different views are integrated into a "big picture" model of the Web systems, which can be used for validation (Knapp and Zhang, 2006) and also for generation of platform-dependent models (see below). A merge with architectural modeling features, either of the "big picture model" or of the design models directly, results in an integrated PIM covering functional and architectural aspects. Finally, the platform-specific models (PSMs) derived from the integration model are the starting point for code generation.

7.4.1 Transformations from Requirements to Functional Models

The overall objective of modeling the requirements is the specification of the system as a CIM and providing input for the construction of models in the other development phases (see Figure 7.1, Schwinger and Koch, 2006, and Section 7.2). In particular, specific objectives for Web systems are the specification of content requirements, the specification of the functional requirements in terms of navigation needs and business processes, the definition of interaction scenarios for different groups of Web users, and, if required, the specification of personalization and context adaptation. The first model transformation step of the UWE process consists of mapping these Web system requirements models to the UWE functional models. Transformation rules are defined therefore as mappings from the requirements meta-model package to the content, navigation, presentation, process, and adaptivity packages of the meta-model. How these packages depend on each other is shown in Figure 7.15.

For example, UWE distinguishes in the requirements model between different types of navigation functionality: browsing, searching, and transactional activities. Browse actions can be used to enforce the existence of a navigation path between a source node and a target node. An action of type search indicates the need for a query in the navigation model in order to allow for user input of a term, and the system responds with a resulting set matching this term (see Section 7.2.1).

Figure 7.20 shows the Search2Query transformation rule specified in QVT's graphical notation (QVT-Merge Group, 2004). The source and target of the transformation are the UWE meta-model defined as *checkonly* and *enforce*, respectively (identified with a "c" and "e" in Figure 7.20). For each search with content p2 in the requirements model, a query in the navigation model is generated with an associated navigation attribute p2. For the associated node object in the requirements model, an index and objects of a navigation class, as well as corresponding links, will be generated.

For more details about the UWE meta-model for Web requirements, we refer the reader to Escalona and Koch (2006). A detailed description of the transformation rules between CIMs and PIMs for the functional aspects of Web applications has been presented in Koch et al. (2006). A meta-model of the nonfunctional requirements for Web applications and mappings of nonfunctional requirements to architectural model elements are subject to future work.

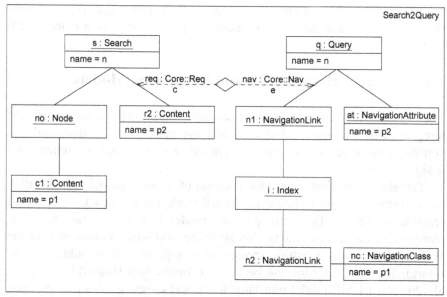

Figure 7.20. Transformation rule **Search2Query**.

7.4.2 Refinement of Functional Models

The transformations for refining the functional models comprise mappings from content to navigation model, refinements of the navigation model, and from the navigation into the presentation model. In UWE, an initial navigation model is generated based on classes of the content model marked as navigation-relevant (see Section 7.2.3). This generation step can be rendered as a transformation Content2Navigation. From a single content model, different navigation views can be obtained, e.g., for different stakeholders of the Web system like anonymous user, registered user, and administrator. The generation of each navigation view requires a set of marks on elements of the content model that form a so-called marking model kept separately from the content model. The development process cannot be completed in an entirely automatic way, as the designer has to make the decision about the "navigation relevance" marks; the Content2Navigation transformation is applied once the marks have been set.

Conversely, the remaining transformation steps for navigation models mentioned in Section 7.2.3 are turned into transformation rules that can be applied fully automatically. These rules include, for example, the insertion of indexes and menus. Presentation elements are generated from navigation elements. For example, for each link in the navigation model, an appropriate anchor is required in the presentation model. The main difficulty is the introduction of the "look and feel" aspects.

All these transformations are defined as OCL constraints (by preconditions and postconditions) in UWE and are implemented in Java in the CASE tool ArgoUWE.

7.4.3 Creation of Validation and Integration Models

The UWE MDD process comprises two main integration steps: the integration of all functional models and the integration of functional and nonfunctional aspects; the latter integration step is related to architectural design decisions.

The aim of the first step is the creation of a single model for validating the correctness of the different functional models and that allows seamless creation of PSMs. This "big picture" model is a UML state machine, representing the content, navigation structure, and business processes of the Web application as a whole (presentation aspects will be added in the future). The state machine can be checked by the tool Hugo/RT (Knapp et al., 2002)—a UML model translator for model checking, theorem proving, and code generation.

The transformation rules Functional2BigPicture are defined based on a meta-model graph transformation system. For the implementation of the graph transformation rules, any (non-Web-specific) tool for graph transformations can be used. An example of the graph transformation of a navigation node to a state of the validation model is sketched in Figure 7.21. The aim of the second step is the merge of the validation model elements with information on architectural styles. Following the WebSA approach (Meliá et al., 2005), we propose merging functional design models and architecture models at the PIM level. For example, the elements of the WebSA models provide a layer view and a component view of the architecture, which are also specified as PIMs. Transformation rules are defined based on the UWE and WebSA meta-models.

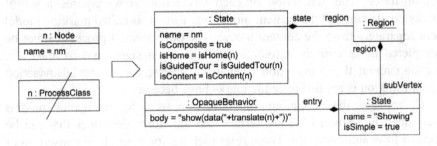

Figure 7.21. Transformation rule Node2State.

7.4.4 Generation of Models and Code for Specific Platforms

In order to transform PIMs into PSMs, additional information about the platform is required. It can be provided as an additional model or it can be implicitly contained in the transformations. For mappings from UWE design models (PIMs) to PSMs for Web applications, we tested different model transformation languages. The query-view-transformation languages we use are ATL (Jouault and Kurtev, 2005), QVT-P (QVT-Partners, 2003), and QVT (QVT-Merge Group, 2004). For example, the following QVT-P transformation tackles the generation of J2EE elements from Java server pages of the integration model:

```
relation ServerPage2J2EE {
    domain { (IM.IntegrationModel)
            [(ServerPage)
                [name = nc,
                    services = { (WebService) [name = on,
                                                type = ot] },
                    views = { (View) [name = vn] }]] }
    domain { (JM.J2EEModel)
            [(JavaServerPage)
                [name = nc,
                    forms = { (Form) [name = on,
                                       type = ot] },
                    beans = { (JavaClass) [name = vn] }]] }
    when { services->forAll(s |
                WebService2Form(s, F1set.toChoice()))
            views->forAll(v |
            View2Bean(v, J1set.toChoice())) }
}
```

The ATL code below exemplifies a transformation rule that maps the element Anchor of the UWE presentation model to a JSP element. Note that the transformation rule also involves elements of the navigation model (NavigationLink).

```
rule Anchor2JSP {
  from
    uie : UWE!Anchor
          (not uie.presentationClass.oclIsUndefined() and
           not uie.navigationLink.oclIsUndefined())
  to
    jsp : JSP!Element
          (name <- 'a',
           children <- Sequence { hrefAttribute,
                                  contentNode }),
    hrefAttribute : JSP!Attribute
      (name <- 'href',
       value <- thisModule.createJSTLURLExpr
         (uie.navigationLink.target.name,'objID')),
    contentNode : JSP!TextNode
                (value <- uie.name)
}
```

7.5 CASE TOOL ARGOUWE

We have extended the CASE tool ArgoUML into a tool for UWE-based Web application development, called ArgoUWE (Knapp et al., 2003; www.pst.ifi.lmu.de/projekte/argouwe). We decided to extend ArgoUML as it is a feature-rich, open source tool and offers a plug-in architecture. The drawback of this decision is that the UWE meta-model cannot be used directly since ArgoUML is based on UML 1.3/4. However, a UML 1.x-compatible profile can easily be derived from the UWE meta-model along the same lines as sketched in Section 7.3.

ArgoUML provides support for designing Web applications in the phases of requirements elicitation and content, navigation, business process, as well as presentation modeling. It provides not only tailored editors for UWE diagrams, but also semiautomatic model transformations defined in the UWE development process. As these model transformations are based on the UWE meta-model, the tool ensures both consistency between the different models and integrity of the overall Web application model with respect to UWE's OCL constraints. ArgoUWE fully integrates the UWE meta-model (Koch and Kraus, 2003), provides XMI export, and thus facilitates data transfer with other UML-compliant tools. Design deficiencies, such as violations of the OCL constraints, are reported by an extension of the cognitive design critiques of ArgoUML and can also be checked upon request (see Section 7.5.2).

Working with ArgoUWE is intuitive for ArgoUML users, as ArgoUWE makes use of ArgoUML's graphical interface. In particular, the UML model

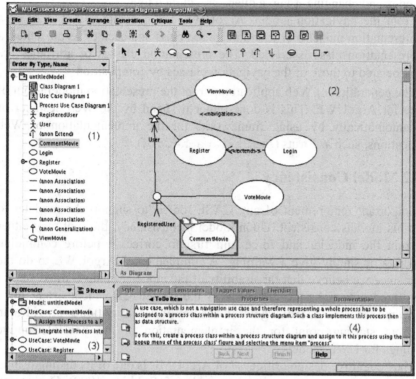

Figure 7.22. MUC case study: ArgoUWE screenshot of a fragment of the use case model.

elements and diagrams are structured in a tree view in the *explorer* [(1) in Figure 7.22]; the diagrams are edited in the *editor pane* (2); to-do items of the designer are listed in the *to-do pane* (3); tagged values, constraints, and documentation of the currently selected model as well as automatically generated code skeletons are shown in the *details pane* (4).

7.5.1 Model Transformations

ArgoUWE implements some of the aforementioned model transformations as semiautomatic procedures.

- In the content model, the designer may mark classes as navigation-relevant. ArgoUWE can then generate an initial navigation model by creating for each navigation-relevant class a navigation class and for each association between navigation-relevant classes a link between the corresponding navigation classes.

- In the navigation model, ArgoUWE can add indexes and menus automatically. The designer may add queries and guided tours between navigation nodes manually or, alternatively, by selecting a generated index and changing it into a query or a guided tour.
- From the navigation model, ArgoUWE can generate a first draft of a presentation model. For each navigation class and each of its attributes, a presentation class is created. The presentation classes of attributes are associated to those of the navigation classes by composition.

The generation of Web applications from the presentation model is out of scope for ArgoUWE. This is done either by hand by the Web designer or semiautomatically by using frameworks for the implementation of Web applications, such as Struts (struts.apache.org).

7.5.2 Model Consistency

An important requirement of any CASE tool is to support the modeler to keep his models consistent. Upon model inconsistency, the tool may either interrupt the modeler and force him first to correct it before continuing modeling or simply give a warning. We implemented ArgoUWE to do the latter since we believe that the usability of the modeler being warned yet not interrupted outweighs the drawback of the model being inconsistent for a short time. Moreover, the ArgoUML feature of design critiques provides an excellent starting point for the implementation of the non-interruptive warnings for UWE models.

The "cognitive design critiques" of ArgoUML is one of its distinguishing features compared to other modeling tools (cf. Robbins, 1999). During run time, a thread running in the background keeps checking if the current model shows deficiencies. For each deficiency found, a design critique item is created and added to the to-do pane. Design critiques not only warn the user that her design may be improved but can also, by means of a wizard, lead to a better design. The design critique items range from incompleteness, such as unnamed model elements, to inconsistency, such as name collisions of different attributes or operations in a class. Furthermore, design critiques also suggest the use of certain design patterns (Gamma et al., 1995). The issues of design critiques can be sorted by several criteria like priority or the model element causing the design critique. Design critiques are only warnings and do not interrupt the designer.

ArgoUWE inherits the feature of design critiques from ArgoUML. In fact, all well-formedness constraints of UWE have been fully integrated and are continuously checked by ArgoUWE in the background at run time. In Figure 7.22 the highlighted design critique indicates that the use case CommentMovie does not show a corresponding process class yet; this critique corresponds to the meta-model constraints shown in Section 7.3.

7.6 OUTLOOK

The UML-based Web Engineering (UWE) approach is continuously evolving. Evolution is due to improvement of existing features, such as personalization of Web systems; adaptation to new technologies, e.g. asynchronous client-server communication; and introduction of new software engineering techniques, like aspect orientation and model-driven principles. The challenge in all these cases is to provide a more intuitive and useful tool for the methodological development of Web systems, to increase Web systems quality, and to reduce development time.

The evolution we can currently observe is driven by a set of improvements that are being addressed and a set of extensions we are planning for UWE. The most important are

- specification of the transformations (at the meta-model level) of (nonfunctional) requirements to architecture models
- implementation of the "weaving" process for the integration of the aspect-oriented features in UWE models
- engineering of Rich Internet Applications (RIAs), e.g., Web applications based on asynchronous communication such as using AJAX (Garrett, 2005)
- tool support for transformations from CIM models to PIM models and for the UML 2.0 features in UWE
- integration of a QVT engine (when available) in the tool environment
- extension of UWE with test models

Our higher-level goal is the convergence of Web design/development methods. It is the only way to obtain a powerful domain-specific modeling and a development language that benefits from the advantages of the different methods. Obviously, there is a trend toward using UML as the common notation language. Some methods are moving from their proprietary notation to a UML-compliant one and introduce a UML profile; others define an MOF-based meta-model. It is currently hard to predict how far this converging trend will go and whether it will eventually lead to a "Unified Web Modeling Language."

ACKNOWLEDGEMENTS

Thanks go to Andreas Kraus for providing the ATL transformation rule and fruitful discussions. This work has been partially supported by the MAEWA project, "Model Driven Development of Web Applications" (WI841/7-1) of the Deutsche Forschungsgemeinschaft (DFG), Germany, and the EC 6th Framework SENSORIA project, "Software Engineering for Service-Oriented Overlay Computers" (FET-IST 016004).

REFERENCES

Baresi, L., Garzotto, F., Mainetti, L., and Paolini, P., 2002, Meta-modeling techniques meet Web application design tools. In R.-D. Kutsche and H. Weber, eds., *Proceedings Fifth International Conference on Fundamental Approaches to Software Engineering* (FASE'02), pp. 294–307.

Baumeister, H., Knapp, A., Koch, N., and Zhang, G., 2005, Modelling adaptivity with aspects. In D. Lowe and M Gaedke, eds., *Proceedings Fifth International Conference on Web Engineering* (ICWE'05), pp. 406–416.

Baumeister, H., Koch, N., and Mandel, L., 1999, Towards a UML extension for hypermedia design. In R. France and B. Rumpe, eds., *Proceedings Second International Conference on Unified Modeling Language* (UML'99), pp. 614–629. .

de Troyer, O., and Leune, C.J., 1998, WSDM: A user centered design method for Web sites. *Computer Networks*, **30**(1–7): 85–94.

Escalona, M.J., and Koch, N., 2006, Metamodeling the requirements of Web systems. *Proceedings Second International Conference on Web Information Systems and Technologies* (WebIST'06), Setubal, Portugal.

Filman, R.E., Elrad, T., Clarke, S., and Aksit, M., eds., 2004, *Aspect-Oriented Software Development*, Addison-Wesley, Reading, MA.

Gamma, E., Helm, R., Johnson, R., and Vlissides, J., 1995, *Design Patterns*, Addison-Wesley, Reading, MA.

Garrett, J.J., 2005, Ajax: A New Approach to Web Applications. http://www.adaptivepath.com/publications/essays/archives/000385.php.

Gómez, J., Cachero, C., and Pastor, O., 2001, Conceptual modeling of device-independent Web applications. *IEEE Multimedia*, **8**(2): 26–39.

Hennicker, R., and Koch, N., 2001, Systematic design of Web applications with UML. In K. Siau and T.A. Halpin, eds., *Unified Modeling Language: Systems Analysis, Design and Development Issues*, Idea Group, Hershey, PA, pp. 1–20.

Isakowitz, T., Stohr, E.A., and Balasubramanian, P., 1995, RMM: A methodology for structuring hypermedia design. *Communications of the ACM*, **38**(8): 34–44.

Jouault, F., and Kurtev, I., 2005, Transforming models with ATL. In J.-M. Bruel, ed., *Revised Selection of Papers on Satellite Events at the MoDELS 2005 Conference*, pp. 128–138.

Knapp, A., Koch, N., Moser, F., and Zhang, G., 2003, ArgoUWE: A CASE tool for Web applications. *Proceedings First International Workshop on Engineering Methods to Support Information Systems Evolution* (EMSISE'03), Geneva.

Knapp, A., Merz, S., and Rauh, C., 2002, Model checking timed UML state machines and collaborations. In W. Damm Werner and E.R. Olderog, eds., *Proceedings Seventh International Symposium on Formal Techniques in Real-Time and Fault Tolerant Systems*, pp. 395–416.

Knapp, A., and Zhang, G., 2006, Model transformations for integrating and validating Web application models. In H.C. Mayr and R. Breu, eds., *Proceedings Modellierung 2006* (MOD'06), pp. 115–128.

Koch, N., 2001, Software engineering for adaptive hypermedia systems: Reference model, modeling techniques and development process. PhD thesis, Ludwig-Maximilians-Universität, München.

Koch, N., and Kraus, A., 2002, The expressive power of UML-based Web engineering. In D. Schwabe, O. Pastor, G. Rossi, and L. Olsina, eds., *Proceedings Second Internatioanl Workshop on Web-Oriented Software Technology* (IWWOST'02), pp. 105–119.

Koch, N., and Kraus, A., 2003, Towards a common metamodel for the development of Web applications. In J.M.C. Lovelle, B.M.G. Rodríguez, L.J. Aguilar, J.E.L. Gayo, and M. del

Puerto Paule Ruiz, eds., *Proceedings Third International Conference on Web Engineering* (ICWE'03), pp. 495–506.

Koch, N., Kraus, A., and Hennicker, R., 2001, The authoring process of the UML-based Web engineering approach. In D. Schwabe, ed., *Proceedings First International Workshop on Web-Oriented Software Technology* (IWWOST'01). http://www.dsic.upv.es/~west2001/iwwost01/.

Koch, N., Zhang, G., and Escalona, M.J., 2006, Model transformations from requirements to Web system design. In D. Wolber, N. Calder, C. Brooks, and A. Ginige, eds., *Proceedings Sixth International Conference on Web Engineering* (ICWE'06), pp. 281–288.

Lowe, D., and Gaedke, M., eds., 2005, *Proceedings Fifth International Conference on Web Engineering* (ICWE'05).

Meliá, S., Kraus, A., and Koch, N., 2005, MDA transformations applied to Web application development. In D. Lowe and M. Gaedke, eds., *Proceedings Fifth International Conference on Web Engineering* (ICWE'05), pp. 465–471.

Object Management Group (2005). Unified Modeling Language. www.uml.org.

Object Management Group (2005). Unified Modeling Language: Superstructure, version 2.0. Specification, OMG. http://www.omg.org/cgi-bin/doc?formal/05-07-04.

Pressman, R., 2005, *Software Engineering—A Practitioner's Approach,* 6th edition, McGraw-Hill, Boston.

QVT-Merge Group (2004). Revised Submission for MOF 2.0 Query/Views/Transformations RFP (ad/2002-04-10). Submission, OMG. http://www.omg.org/cgi-bin/doc?ad/04-04-01.pdf.

QVT-Partners (2003). Revised Submission for MOF 2.0 Query/Views/Transformations RFP, version 1.1. http://qvtp.org/downloads/1.1/qvtpartners1.1.pdf.

Robbins, J.E., 1999, Cognitive support features for software development tools. PhD thesis, University of California, Irvine.

Schwabe, D., and Rossi, G., 1995, The object-oriented hypermedia design model. *Communications of the ACM,* **38**(8): 45–46.

Schwinger, W., and Koch, N., 2006, Modeling Web applications. In G. Kappel, B. Pröll, S. Reich, and W. Retschitzegger, eds., *Web Engineering: Systematic Development of Web Applications,* John Wiley, Hoboken, NJ, pp. 39–64.

Vilain, P., Schwabe, D., and de Souza, C.S., 2000, A diagrammatic tool for representing user interaction in UML. In A. Evans, S. Kent, and B. Selic, eds., *Proceedings Third International Conference on Unified Modeling Language* (UML'00), pp. 133–147.

Wirsing, M., Koch, N., Rossi, G., Garrido, A., Mandel, L., Helmerich, A., and Olsina, L., 1999, Hyper-UML: Specification and modeling of multimedia and hypermedia applications in distributed systems. In *Proceedings Second Workshop on German-Argentinian Bilateral Programme for Scientific and Technological Cooperation,* Königswinter, Germany.

Zhang, G., 2005, Towards aspect-oriented class diagrams. In *Proceedings 12th Asia Pacific Software Engineering Conference* (APSEC'05), pp. 763–768.

Chapter 8

DESIGNING MULTICHANNEL WEB APPLICATIONS AS "DIALOGUE SYSTEMS": THE IDM MODEL

Davide Bolchini[1] and Franca Garzotto[2]

[1]TEC-Lab, Faculty of Communication Sciences, University of Lugano, Via G. Buffi, 13 6900 Lugano, Switzerland
[2]HOC (Hypermedia Open Centre), Department of Information and Electronics, Politecnico di Milano, Milan, Italy

8.1 BACKGROUND

IDM, the design method discussed in this chapter, is the distillation of a long experience of building, using, and teaching models for hypermedia design. At the beginning of the 1990s, we started with HDM (Hypertext Design Model), (Garzotto el al., 1991; Garzotto and Paolini, 1993) which was the first model for the conceptual design of this class of applications that appeared in the literature. HDM was relatively simple and, in some respects, naïve. Still, it proposed some core concepts that inspired many subsequent models for (Web-based) hypermedia that we and other researchers proposed: the distinction among different conceptual design "dimensions" (content, navigation/interaction, presentation) and the proposal, for complex applications, of a "schema-based" design process, as opposed to "design-by-page" (or "design-by-instance"), which was the common practice at the time.

HDM progressively evolved into models (named HDM+, HDM2, and W2000) (Garzotto et al., 1994, 1995, 1999; Baresi et al., 2001a) that, to address the increasing complexity of hypermedia applications, were significantly richer and more sophisticated than their ancestor. These models provided a rich set of primitives that enabled designers to specify a wide spectrum of design solutions, at both a general level and a very detailed level. Unfortunately, the increase in expressive power had some drawbacks. In many graduate courses in different faculties (computer engineering, industrial design, and communication sciences), the difficulty of learning the theory and practice of our models did not completely pay off in terms of the increased design quality delivered by students' designs. Building design documentation in industrial projects became more and more time-consuming (since design specifications were more and more detailed), while its power as a communication medium among project stakeholders dramatically decreased (especially among persons who had no formal training in modeling). An empirical survey we carried on in the industrial arena confirmed that usability in general, and learnability and effectiveness in particular, are crucial factors for the acceptability and adoption of the design models and methods in the real world (Garzotto and Perrone, 2003).

Thus, after moving from simplicity (HDM) to complexity (W2000), we progressively moved back to simplicity, as oftentimes occurs in scientific research (in art, too). IDM (Bolchini and Paolini, 2006) is the "end" of this "parabola." It focuses on design concepts that are truly fundamental for making a design process cost-effective. It makes the "deep" meaning of design concepts more intuitive. It does not simply offer a specification tool for designers to render their creative design solutions: It helps them to create abstract, minimal, but expressive representations and, above all, to understand how they may think when they do design.

We like to quote the following sentence, attributed to Albert Einstein: "... A complex 'phenomenon' ... cannot be modeled as simple, but we (scientists) should try at least to give it a representation that is as simple as possible." Designing a complex hypermedia application is not simple. Our hope is that IDM makes it as simple as possible.

8.2 THE DIALOGICAL APPROACH OF IDM

"Design" (from the Latin *designare* = to mark out) is the process of developing plans or schemes; more particularly, a design may be a developed plan or scheme, ..., set forth as a drawing or model. ... A design is ordinarily conceived with a number of limiting factors in mind: the capacities of the material employed; ....; the effect of the end result on those who may see it, use it, or become involved in it.

The above quotation, from the *Encyclopaedia Britannica*, captures some essential aspects of the concept of "design"(which different authors defined in so many different ways) and provides us with a reference definition to better explain IDM.

Next, we should define the scope for design in the specific domain of hypermedia. Unfortunately, also in this restricted domain, the definition of the design scope is not obvious, being strongly related to the profile of who is making a design, to the goal of a design artifact, and to its users.

For a graphic designer, the scope of hypermedia design is the appearance of "pages." The goal of a design artifact is to convey a brand and identity "image," for discussing it with the customer: "Design" means defining (a schema for) the visual, directly perceivable properties of a hypermedia interface. For an interaction designer, the design scope is the definition of the interaction modalities available to the user to interact with the "pages" (e.g., form filling, menu selection, icons and direct manipulation capability, etc.); the goals of a design artifact are to render the tangible experience of the user with the application and to provide both the interaction requirements for the implementers and a preliminary "prototype" to be evaluated by usability experts. For an information architect, the scope is the organizational structures for the content delivered by the application; the goal is to provide both the content requirements for authors and the data requirements for implementors. For a computer engineer, the design scope is the definition of both the data structures for the contents and the functions provided by the systems. And so on.

For IDM, the "designer" is anyone who is translating the problem space represented by users' and stakeholders' requirements into a solution space represented by a design artifact. The goals of design are to reify requirements in terms of general properties of the application, to support early brainstorming among the different profiles of designers listed above (who must later add details to the design specs), as well as to discuss general solutions among them and among other stakeholders (customers and users).

To achieve these goals, we use a dialogue metaphor: We conceive user interactions with a hypermedia as a sort of dialogue, namely, as a sequence of question-answering "acts": The selection of a link is the operational counterpart to a question that the user "asks" herself and turns to "the system" (e.g., "who is the director of this movie?"). The effect of link selection, i.e., the display of the link destination page, is the answer is the system materially offers, according to the designers, on how to respond to the user's question. The scope of hypermedia design is therefore to shape the possible dialogues between the users and the system, and the design is the process concerning the construction of a dialogue plan. The different design activities are progressive steps in forming this plan, from a more general level of abstraction, to a more concrete level where the various limiting (or contextual) factors for the execution of the plan are progressively taken into account (including, among others, the characteristics of the delivery device, the actual context of use, the specific user's characteristics).

In general, we can say that a dialogue-based design offers a number of advantages:

- It is conceptually simple even for people who are not used to design (e.g., content experts and newcomer designers). We have experienced (as we will discuss in the conclusions) that a dialogue-metaphor is far more intuitive and natural (especially for the above profiles) than an information-navigation metaphor.
- It is very close to the way requirements are specified and therefore allows for better traceability, i.e., keeping track of how the different requirements were taken into account during the definition of the various design solutions.
- It captures the "essence" of the dialogues that the user can establish, easily avoiding all the details connected to technology and implementation.
- As a special case of the last point, it is suitable for paving the ground for specific versions of the dialogue aiming at users with special needs (e.g., aural interaction for visually impaired users).

8.3 IDM ACTIVITIES

The design process envisioned by IDM comprises three main activities: conceptual design, logical design, and page design. Each addresses different aspects of the application under design, at different levels of abstractions. For each activity, IDM provides a set of concepts and notations, as discussed and exemplified in the rest of this section.

8.3.1 Conceptual IDM (or C-IDM)

Assuming a dialogue-oriented perspective, the first set of issues that the designer should try to address can be summarized by the following questions:

1. What are the *dialogue subjects*, i.e., what can (should) the application say to the user?
2. What are the relevant *shifts of subjects* to be supported during the user/application dialogue?
3. What are the possible different ways to organize the dialogue, i.e., to group the different subjects through which the user may start the actual flow of conversation?

Precise and detailed answers to the above questions can be provided only when a specific channel of delivery has been chosen (determining factors like screen size, pointing mechanisms, available media, performances, etc.). Still, important decisions can be made in advance, in what we call "conceptual design."

In this initial phase, a *conceptual schema* of the interactive application must be defined to convey all the necessary "dialogue strategies," without (and before) digging into details that may depend on technical issues of the actual delivery device (and should be addressed in the following design activities).

At this stage, a conceptual schema has multiple uses:

1. to support brainstorming among designers
2. to allow traceability and comparison with requirements (e.g., needs and goals of the stakeholders) and therefore to support discussion with stakeholders (are we making the most appropriate design decisions?)
3. to provide a firm suggestion to the technical designers, who must add details to it

C-IDM (*Conceptual IDM*) is a model for the definition of conceptual schemas. It is simple to grasp and effective in representing the most relevant features of the application in terms of content of the dialogue and dialogue moves. Indeed, three basic design elements characterize C-IDM: "topic," "relationship," and "group of topics."

An interactive application may "talk about" a "topic" (e.g., a "movie" or an "actor"), or it may allow the user to switch the dialogue focus to a "related topic" (e.g., switching from the "actor" to the "movies" in which he starred), or it may allow the user to start from a "group of topics" (e.g., "the top at the box office movies" or "movies of 2006") and then lead the dialogue among the different topics within the group.

The "informative" quality of the dialogue comes from the choice of the topics and the "objective ways" of relating and grouping topics; the "argumentative" quality of the dialogues is based upon the choice of the specific content associated to each topic, upon the "subjective ways" of relating topics and grouping them.

More precisely, the above simple ideas have been translated into the following C-IDM design primitives:

- **Topic:** something that can be the subject of conversation between the user and the interactive application. "Mission: Impossible III," "Tom Cruise," and "Paramount Pictures" are examples of topics, i.e., possible subjects of a dialogue between the user and the application.

- **Kind of topic:** the category of possible subjects of conversation. "Movie," "Actor," and "Company" are kinds of topics. "Tom Cruise" is an example of "Actor."
- **Change of subject (or relevant relation):** it determines how the dialogue can switch from one kind of topic to another one. "Produced by" is a possible change of subject relating any Movie to one Company.
- **Group of topics:** it determines a specific group of topics, possible subjects of conversation. Announced Movies is a specific group of Movies, while All 2006 movies is another, larger, group.
- **Multiple group of topic:** it determines a family of group of topics. It could be nice, for example, to group the Movies according to genres. All the movies of the same genre are a group of topics; "Movies by Genre," overall, is a family of groups of topics (as many as there are Genres). Each multiple group of topics has a corresponding "higher-level" group of topics (e.g., "all genres"), which allows one to select the specific group of topics of interest (e.g., "Movies of the genre Comedy").

The above list of terms and concepts has a number of advantages over most of the current design models and methods:

1. The number of concepts is short and therefore easy to teach (and to learn).
2. Despite their limited number, the concepts are expressive enough for describing the content of most (information-intensive) applications.
3. The concepts (and terms) relate to the "human" dialogue experience, rather than to informatics; therefore, they can be more effectively conveyed to people without a computer science or engineering background.

The concepts are of the proper "level" to allow an in-depth comparison between requirements and design decisions (if requirements have been explicitly stated, of course).

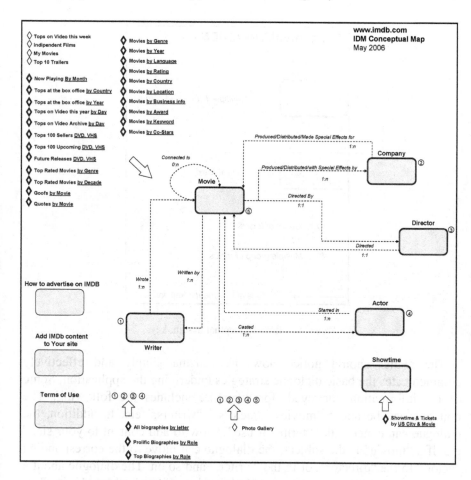

Figure 8.1. Conceptual IDM modeling of www.imdb.com.

Figure 8.1 describes a potential conceptual design for the IMDB (Internet Movie Database) Web site (www.imdb.com), presenting it as a possible modeling result through C-IDM. The graphical primitives of C-IDM are illustrated in Figure 8.2.

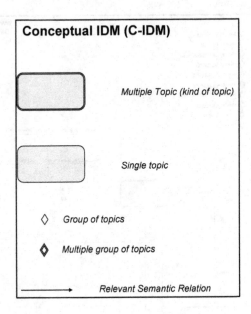

Conceptual IDM (C-IDM)

Multiple Topic (kind of topic)

Single topic

◊ Group of topics

◆ Multiple group of topics

——————▶   Relevant Semantic Relation

Figure 8.2. IDM conceptual design: key.

The reader should notice how the schema simply and effectively communicates the basic dialogue strategies underlying the application. Some of the information conveyed, for example, includes the following: The dialogue can be about "movies," "actors," "writers," etc. In addition, the dialogue can concern the "terms of use," "how to add content to your site," etc. If a "movie" is the subject, the dialogue can move to the corresponding "actor," to the "director," or to the "writer," and so on. The dialogue about a movie can start in various ways: "Independent Films," "My Movies," or selecting movies by rating, by country, by genre, the "now playing" movie, and so on. Guessing the rest is left to the reader as a simple exercise.

This schema, however, is not fully sufficient: Additional information needs to be provided for a fully satisfactory design document. Here is an outline of suggested additional information:

- *Topic*: description of the motivations (i.e., why has it been considered?; what's its purpose?); description of the content (i.e., what can be said when the topic is "selected" as subject of the dialogue?)
- *Kind of topic*: description of the motivations (see above); description of the content (see above); cardinality (i.e., an indication of the expected number of topics instances or exemplars: e.g., how many movies do we expect to have?)
- *Change of subject (relevant relation)*: description of the semantics (i.e., what is the actual meaning of the relations?) and motivations (i.e., why is

it considered important?); cardinality (i.e., an indication of the expected numbers; e.g., changing subject from a writer to the movie, how many movies should we expect to have—on average—for a given writer?)

- *Group of topics*: description of the motivations (i.e., why is this group of topics useful or interesting and to whom?); cardinality (i.e., expected number of topics to be part of the group)

Design documents do not always need to be complete. Designers often want to negotiate strategic decisions with stakeholders and to document those decisions, without being forced to commit on premature details early in the development. Nor do all the different choices need an adequate explanation: They may be obvious in a given context. In many situations design documents can be left "unfinished," still fulfilling their role of conveying most of the "crucial" ideas about the application. Even with the above enrichments indicated, a conceptual design document can be kept very simple, easy to write, and effective for the reader.

In synthesis, the main advantages of the dialogue map shown in Figure 8.1 may be summarized as follows:

1. The schema is quite simple, and it does not take too much time to write it down (any common editor tool may fit).
2. The schema expresses all the most relevant aspects of a "real-life" interactive application.
3. The schema conveys the basic interaction ideas, without commitment to a specific "channel" of delivery (whether it is the Web technology, a PDA, a Car Navigator System).
4. The schema can be used to brainstorm, debate alternatives, and discuss preliminary decisions.

As we will see in the next section, the conceptual schema can be translated into one or more logical schemas, according to the choices made for a specific channel of communication.

8.3.2 L-IDM Logical Design

Unlike conceptual design, logical design starts by making decisions that are typically dependent on a specific fruition channel through which the application may be conveyed (be it the traditional Web, an oral channel, an interactive TV, or a mobile channel).

Whereas a C-IDM conceptual design schema defines the overall interaction strategy to be supported during the dialogue of the application with the user, designers can develop one or more "logical" designs, one for each specific channel they want to design the application for. IDM "logical" design can be seen as a detailed version of the conceptual design, where details are decided on the basis of a variety of channel-dependent factors, such as the constraints imposed by the type of device available on a given channel (e.g., screen size), the pointing devices (e.g., keyboard, smart pen, mouse, scroller, audio input, touch pointers, eye-tracking pointers), the media that can be used (e.g., audio, visual text, images, graphics, or video), the expected performance, and—of utmost importance—the typical scenarios of use (e.g., home or office desktop use, walking or standing contexts, mobile use on car, etc.).

All these "technicalities" may influence key decisions for the user experience, which concern at the logical level the ways detailed pieces of content are split and structured and how and when navigation possibilities are made available and may be traversed.

Starting from C-IDM, logical design (called L-IDM) for a specific channel may be defined by answering two basic questions: What are the units of dialogue? How can units of dialogue be combined in a user experience? A unit of dialogue is an atomic object, in the sense that it will be delivered to the user in its totality.

These two basic questions, in order to be addressed, need a number of technical steps:

1. Organize each (kind of) topic into dialogue units, and organize the possible dialogue flows across them.
2. Organize the needed dialogue units that allow the shift of subjects.
3. Organize the dialogue units that allow the exploration of a group of topics

In order to provide all the answers, we have developed the design primitives of L-IDM, explained below.

- **Dialogue act:** a unit of the dialogue within a topic. The content of a topic is represented by either a single dialogue act or several of them. Decisions are based both on technical considerations (the relevant features of the channel) and on user profiles and/or needs.
- **Structural strategy:** the possible development of a dialogue for exploring a topic with more than one dialogue act. What must be specified are the initial dialogue act and the possibilities for changing the dialogue from one act to another one.
- **Transition act:** when changing the subject from a (kind of) topic (e.g., "movie") to another (kind of) topic (e.g., "director"), no additional dialogue is need, since the dialogue can immediately switch, upon request. When the new subject is multiple (e.g., switching from "movie" to its "actors"), an additional part of dialogue is needed, which we call

the *transition act*. A transition act is, in essence, a list of possible new topics (e.g., a list of actors who starred in that movie).

- **Transition strategy:** the existence of the transition act, as explained above, does not entirely solve all the problems. A dialogue substrategy must be developed to explain the way a user can explore all the new topics (all the "actors" starring in the movie, in the example).
- **Introductory act:** a piece of dialogue that allows the application (and the user) to consider the group of topics as a whole. It consists, in general, of an introduction followed by a list of the topics belonging to the group. Introductory acts are the unique *starting points* for the dialogue, in the sense that any dialogue starts with an introductory act. For example, the list of "Top of the Box Office Movies" may be introduced by some engaging text and a representative picture.
- **Subject strategy:** as was the case for transitions, creating introductory acts does not solve the problem of "engaging a conversation" about the group of topics. There must be a dialogue strategy coordinating how the conversation can involve the introductory act and support the exploration of all the topics belonging to the group.
- **Multiple introductory acts:** an introductory act corresponding to a "Multiple Group of Topics." It is a strange technicality, not difficult to explain: If there is a group of "movies" for each "genre," we need an introductory act for each genre (listing all the movies belonging to that genre), but we also need another introductory act listing all the genres (to let the user choose one genre), possibly with an introduction and/or an explanation accompanying that list. In other words, for a multiple group of topics we need a family of introductory acts (one for each theme, in the example) and a further introductory act (the list of genres in the example), holding the family together.

On the basis of the same C-IDM schema, Figure 8.3 provides the L-IDM graphical primitives, while Figure 8.4 illustrates L-IDM design for the IMDB Web site.

Whereas the C-IDM conceptual schema represents the utmost degree of interactivity potential (resembling the richest channel of the ones available, such as the Web, for example), the L-IDM design defines a subset of interactions that are sound and suitable for the channel at issue.

On the basis of our project experience, the common activities that can be undertaken to specialize the conceptual schema into a "channel-dependent" version are the following:

- Dialogue acts or entire topics may be removed.
- Relevant relations may be removed.
- Groups of topics may be removed or simplified.
- … Other adaptations are possible.

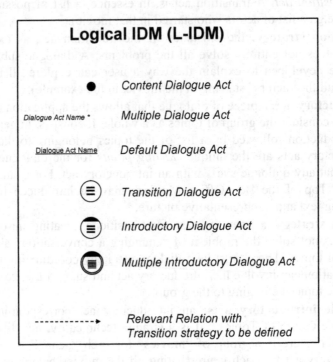

Figure 8.3. IDM logical design: key.

Based on the results of these decisions, the design should be refined without totally changing the overall dialogue pattern. In fact, the user should perceive that she is dealing with the same application across different channels. Design decisions made at this stage should cope with the trade-off between a unifying user experience and the constraints imposed by each specific channel.

As a demonstrative example, let us now assume to design a palm-held version of IMDB to support the following scenarios:

- A person waiting for the movie to start (outside the theater or not yet in the projection room) wants detailed information, anticipation, and trivia about the movie he is going to watch.
- A person wants to go to the movies tonight. She does not know yet which movie to watch. She would like to get an idea about the latest releases, browse the movies, and then see the showtimes in her town.
- A person has decided which movie to watch and wants to know the showtimes in his town.

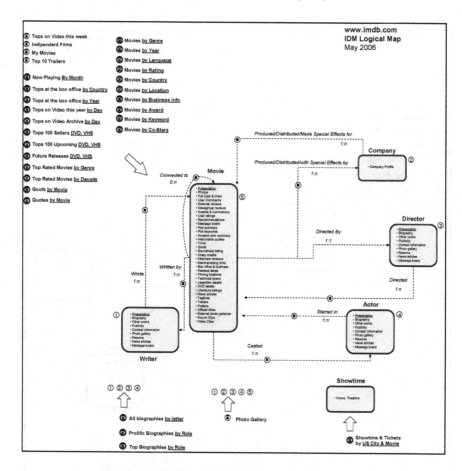

Figure 8.4. IDM logical modeling of www.imdb.com.

Figure 8.5 shows the IDM logical schema for a PDA-version IMDB application that we have designed to support the scenarios described above.

With respect to the conceptual design, the logical schema for the PDA shows that there have been changes "in-the-large" concerning the simplification of the content and the navigation possibilities, with the aim of supporting the above-described scenarios and focusing on those that are potentially the most "appealing" and useful for the situations of use envisioned. In particular, two multiple topics have been removed (company and writer) along with the attached relevant relations. The set of groups of topics has been dramatically reduced, decreasing from more than 20 to 5, thus offering few relevant options to browse the movies.

In comparison with the logical design for the Web, the logical schema for the PDA have been simplified in the perspective of offering a more usable, straightforward access to content and fewer but more relevant details about a movie and the correlated topics. Namely, the many dialogue acts for the

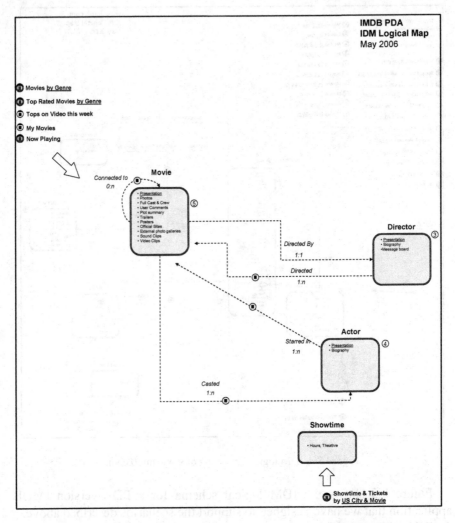

Figure 8.5. IDM logical schema for the PDA version of the IMDB application.

multiple topic "Movie" have been left out (e.g., soundtrack listing, crazy credits, alternate versions, etc.) with the aim of offering the user a selection of suggested content to browse. This design choice has also taken into account the fact that managing a huge set of dialogue acts (more than 25 in the Web version) would have made navigation within the topic very cumbersome in the PDA version, thus negatively affecting the usability of the application. Similarly, the decision to reduce the number of introductory acts for the PDA will have a positive effect on the page's design, which will have to provide access to fewer options.

8.3.3 P-IDM: From Logical Design to Pages

IDM page design (P-IDM) means defining the elements to be communicated to the user in a single dialogue act. With respect to previous decisions (see the L-IDM schema), designers now have to craft the actual pages containing the necessary elements to sustain the dialogue.

Note that page design should not yet go into wireframe design (defining the visual page grid) or into layout design (how elements are physically arranged in the grid) or into graphic design (actual rendering of the visual elements in the page). Whereas all these aspects contribute to define the visual communication strategy of the application, page design should provide the proper input to these activities just by specifying the important elements to be presented in the page.

In this view, there are simple guidelines for transitioning from L-IDM (channel design) to P-IDM (page design):

- Each dialogue act becomes a page type.
- Each introductory act becomes a page type.
- Each transition act becomes a page type.
- Relevant topics become landmarks [i.e., links present in (almost) any page]. Landmarks are usually either single topics or important groups of topics that are always accessible.
- Relevant groups of topics become landmarks.

Different page types can be easily derived from dialogue acts, introductory acts, and transition acts. We have a set of specific guidelines for page derivation. Let us consider the following excerpt of the guidelines, namely those specific for the page design of the dialogue acts. A page for a dialogue act (e.g., Presentation) for a kind of topic (e.g., Movie) should basically contain the elements listed in Table 8.1.

Table 8.1 Page Elements for a Dialogue Act

Page Element	Description
Content	The actual content of the dialogue act (e.g., text, graphics, voice, video, audio, or any combination of these)
Structural links (if any)	To pages of the other dialogue acts of the same topic
Transition links (if any)	To pages of related topic (1:1) or to pages of transition acts (1:n)
Group of topic links	Next-previous (in case of guided tour) or to pages of introductory acts/introductory act I came from
Orientation info (if any)	Messages communication "where I am"
Landmarks	To relevant sections of the site (pages of single topics) or a group of topics

These hints serve as a reminder for the designer about the elements to consider when building a page. Visual communication designers can then make layout and graphic decisions on the basis of this input to create mockup prototypes or the final rendered page.

Figures 8.6 and 8.7 describe two Web pages of the IMDB Web site, displaying, respectively, a Dialogue Act ("Presentation," of the multiple topic Movie) and an Introductory Act. Figure 8.8 shows the same dialogue act as it is rendered in the PDA version of the application.

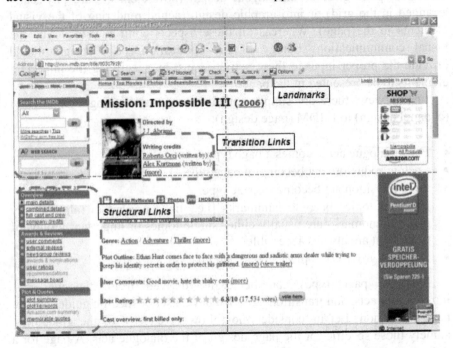

Figure 8.6. IDM page design elements on an instance of the multiple topic "Movie"—Dialogue Act "Presentation" (www.imdb.com—accessed June 2006).

Figure 8.7. IDM page design elements for the Introductory Act "Movies Now Playing" (www.imdb.com—accessed June 2006).

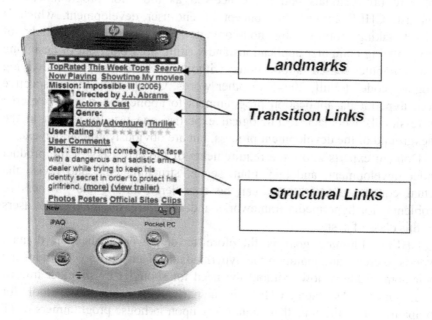

Figure 8.8. IDM page design elements on an instance of the multiple topic "Movie"—Dialogue Act "Presentation"—PDA version.

8.4 IDM IMPLEMENTATION TOOLS

By their very nature, IDM design specifications are "abstract" and semiformal: The main purpose of IDM is to act as a communication and brainstorming tool among the project stakeholders involved in the design process, and a number of details, especially those related to layout, are omitted. Therefore, generating running applications from IDM specifications cannot be performed in a totally automatic way. Still, we have built a number of tools that support the development of IDM applications and exploit some key concepts of the model. The last version of these tools is called CHEF, which stands for Cultural Heritage Enterprise Framework since it was originally built for a specific class of applications, in the cultural heritage domain, as described in Garzotto and Megale, 2006.

CHEF can be regarded as an IDM application framework. It provides a reusable implementation architecture for content-intensive multichannel hypermedia that are designed using IDM, and it supports an IDM-based design and development process. CHEF can be regarded as an application "skeleton" that can be customized to produce a specific application.

The main originality of CHEF stems from its "philosophy," which makes it rather different from most of the existing hypermedia application frameworks and development tools. The latter are traditionally designed by software professionals and are conceived as tools for programmers. In contrast, CHEF applies the concept of end-user development, which is "about taking control" by non-computer professionals, "not only of personalizing computer applications and writing programs, but of designing new computer based applications without ever seeing the underlying program code" (Wulf, 2004). In other words, CHEF shifts the perspective from hypermedia application programmers to application domain experts: professionals who lack technological expertise and usually remain in the background of the development process, but are obviously crucial players.

Domain experts know the requirements of the end users of the product under development, and they plan, select, structure, edit, and revise the actual contents. Indeed, they can be considered among the "owners of problems" for hypermedia frameworks and, therefore, the main target users for this class of systems.

CHEF's ultimate goal is therefore to empower application domain experts to create and maintain the hypermedia artifacts built to communicate their domain know-how, without the need for shoulder-by-shoulder trained programmers. As such, CHEF is a particularly appropriate tool for companies or institutions that cannot rely upon in-house programmers or IT departments; it helps them to avoid expensive outsourcing aid so that they can focus their financial resources on design and on high-quality content, rather than on code production.

CHEF has been conceived for and with domain specialists in different knowledge-intensive fields (e.g., cultural heritage, tourism, e-learning, e-commerce), during a requirements elicitation process that has tried to understand the (domain-independent) aspects of their process of information production, communication, and management. CHEF provides a user-friendly, easy-to-use, visual environment where domain experts can design "by reuse" their applications, instantiate the resulting design schemas with the proper multimedia contents (built using conventional multimedia authoring tools), and generate high-quality multidevice hypermedia applications without learning any specific implementation technology.

A simple interface guides the design process, which is carried on through the customization of a general design space. The systematic instantiation of the customized design is performed by a data entry interface that is automatically customized to become consistent with the actual schemas, without any implementation effort by the framework users. The paradigms of learning-by-examples and immediate visual feedback are supported by CHEF to facilitate the creation of a shared understanding within the development team of what is achievable and of the effects of the different design choices, leading to new insights, new ideas, and new artifacts.

More precisely, CHEF provides the following set of tools.

8.4.1 Customization Design Tool

This allows the domain expert to define IDM information, navigation, or presentation schemas. This work can be regarded as a *customization process* and comprises various activities.

During the definition of the information and navigation schemas, the designer can specialize a set of general design data structures, which are defined in the CHEF *meta-model*. This meta-model captures the general IDM abstractions needed to specify the actual information and navigation properties of the application under development. Information and navigation design involves various tasks:

- the definition of (kinds of) topics by selecting, in the corresponding meta-structure, the proper combination of attributes and cardinalities for the (kind of) topics under definition; definition of relevant associations, by specifying the association name and the kind of topics involved in the relationship.
- the definition of (multiple) groups of topics, by selecting the kinds of topic involved in each group under definition.

- the definition of the various categories of acts (Dialogue, Introductory, and Transition Acts), by mapping the attributes of the different kinds of topics (Topics) into the different acts.
- the definition of the various strategies, by mapping each (kind of) topic, (multiple) group, and relevant association to the proper *navigation pattern* (Garzotto et al., 1999). For this task, CHEF provides a *pattern library* that includes the most popular navigation design patterns (*Index, GuidedTour, Index+GuidedTour, All-to-all*), i.e., generic topologies that are acknowledged as successful solutions to allow users to navigate across groups of hypermedia "objects."

For page design, CHEF provides a library of *Presentation Meta Templates*—basically abstract layout "grids" such as the ones adopted by graphic designers during the very early stage of design. CHEF users can map acts and patterns to the different Meta Template components, also specifying landmarks elements and orientation information. The "concrete" layout can be defined by *decorating* the so-instantiated meta-template with specific visual or typographical properties (color, shape, size, etc.) and application-specific elements (e.g., logos) to meet the "corporate image" requirements of the application under development.

8.4.2 Instantiation Tool

This is a *schema-driven data entry tool* that supports the instantiation of the various types of information and navigation structures defined as conceptual and logical design in the different delivery devices.

For each instantiation task, the tools provide the editorial author with the proper data entry "form" that is *consistent* with the current C-IDM and L-IDM schemas of the application under development (and the proper delivery channel). These forms are automatically generated by CHEF according to the current design specifications (i.e., the parameters provided by the customization tool).

8.4.3 Feedback Tools

Two original tools are offered in CHEF to meet the need for continuous feedback during the design and instantiation activities process: the Mockupper and the Previewer.

The *Mockupper* is used at design time. It exploits a *fictitious* set of multimedia contents and links (prestored in CHEF) to *automatically instantiate* the schemas of the current design and, by means of the generation tool (discussed below), produces a fictitious application after a design schema has been defined. The result can be regarded as a running demo that allows the designer to experiment with the user interaction that results from his design choices, helping him to decide how to adjust or improve them.

The *Previewer* is used during the instantiation activity. When a new instance is created or updated, the Previewer allows developers to inspect the effects of their work. The developer can see and navigate across the pages for the instances created or updated *with the same layout and navigation capability that appears in the end-user application*.

8.4.4 Generation Tool

CHEF supports both the dynamic generation of the online application pages and the "batch" generation of "static" pages, which can be exploited for offline use of the application, e.g., when the application is delivered on CD-ROM or, more generally, when it cannot rely upon a client-server Web architecture.

Dynamic generation is triggered by HTTP requests when a page is needed during Web-based use of the application. In contrast, the generation tool creates a static version of the entire application, by repeatedly simulating a link activation and the corresponding page requests, invoking the dynamic generation capability of the framework, and storing all pages of the applications as they are generated.

The software architecture that implements CHEF tools is sketched in Figure 8.9. In this figure we highlight different user profiles for the CHEF framework:

- the *editorial designer*, i.e., the domain expert who shapes the general properties of the application and takes the main design choices (for the different channels)
- the *editorial author*, i.e., the domain expert who is responsible for identifying the proper "cultural objects" of the domain and for instantiating the design with the proper multimedia contents; the *end users* of the final application, who may use it on different technological contexts—Web-enabled or offline stationary workstation, and online or offline PDA

Indeed, the CHEF software environment is the same for all these profiles, since it serves both the execution of the customization and instantiation operations and the dynamic generation of the final application on the different technological contexts.

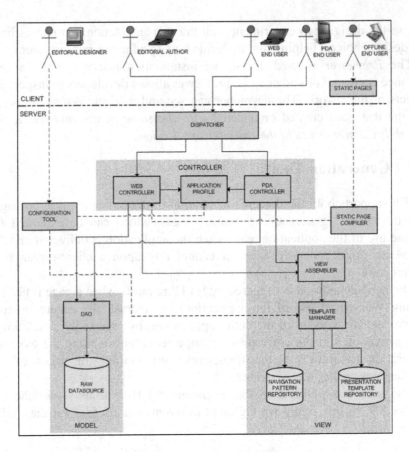

Figure 8.9. The architecture of CHEF—an IDM application framework.

As highlighted in Figure 8.9, the framework architecture is modeled according to the Model-View-Controller (MVC) design pattern. The MVC pattern divides an application into three logical categories of objects: model, view, and controller.

Model objects (collectively referred to as "Model") represent application domain data and the business rules that govern access and updates to this data. *View* objects are responsible for rendering the contents of the Model and forwarding user commands to the Controller.

Controller objects (collectively referred to as Controller) are responsible *for mapping user requests to operations* on the Model, for executing them, for building the proper View, and for returning them to the client. In Web applications, user "commands" appear as HTTP page requests.

View objects typically correspond to HTML pages. Based on the page request, the results of the operations on the Model, and the state of, the Model, the Controller generates the next HTML page.

The main logical components of CHEF comprise

- a module for the *configuration tool*. This component creates the configuration parameters for the customized design schemas and data entry forms (stored in the Application Profile component) and selects the proper navigation and presentation templates that will be used by the customized instantiation tools and by the final application.
- a *static compiler* that implements the functionalities of the static pages generation tool.
- a set of components for the *dynamic generation* of the pages requested by the editorial manager, during the instantiation activities, and by the end users of the final application. The dynamic generation approach exploits a well-known approach in Web Engineering, separating the application business logic from its presentation and control logic. The presentation logic, delegated to the client side, manages user interaction and data (dis)play. The control logic, delegated to the server side, interprets the requests from the presentation level, manages the functionality defined by the business logic (e.g., data retrieval or update, composition of the required HTML page), and returns an HTML page to the presentation level via the network infrastructure using the HTTP protocol.

So far, CHEF has been successfully implemented in three large projects, where, in most cases, the framework users had limited or no programming know-how:

- the EC project *MEDINA* #314 (MEDiterranean by INternet Access), which is developing the "Portal on Mediterranean Cultural Heritage" for Web-based stationary PCs (www.medinataproject.net) and PDAs, with the contribution of Ministries of Tourism and Culture, Cultural Tourism Associations, National Tourism Agencies, Museums and Cultural Institutions, of 9 countries in the Mediterranean basin (Morocco, Tunisia, Algeria, Cyprus, Malta, Lebanon, Palestinian Authority, Syria, Jordan)
- the *Bramantino* project, which produced hypermedia about the current exhibition on Bramantino's Adorations held in December 2005 at the Biblioteca Ambrosiana Museum in Milan, available on the Web (www.bramantino.it) and on CD-ROM for exhibition visitors
- *SYRIA DGAM*, which is developing the new Web site for the General Directorate of Syrian Antiquities and Musuem, sponsored by the Syrian Ministry of Tourism and the Syrian Ministry of Cultural Heritage, with the partial contribution of the European Union.

8.5 DISCUSSION AND CONCLUSIONS

Lightweight design processes and usability are being recognized, more and more, as relevant for all the design methodologies, and for the design of interactive applications in particular. Different factors are being implied here:

- It should be easy to teach the design methodology (and the design model) to anyone (from students to practitioners). Professionals, especially, do not have the time and resources to invest in learning new methodologies; one of the success factors of the "entity relationship" (probably the most successful design model, ever) stems from the fact that it was very easy to transmit its basic concepts, both in academia and in a professional environment.
- It must be possible to use the design model for brainstorming, i.e., for generating and discussing ideas among developers, with stakeholders, and with potential users. It is of little use to have a design model capable of representing only fully developed solutions.
- It must take little time to write down design ideas: Developers do not like to spend too many resources on preliminary activities.
- It must be possible to move, smoothly, from a general design to a more detailed design, without the need for excessive reworking and for completeness; in other words, even an incomplete design document must be useful and understandable.

IDM may appear to be an oversimplified model, with respect to other models discussed in this book. Still, its simplicity has been gained not at the expense of expressiveness, but at the expense of "technical details."

IDM is mainly intended as a model for *brainstorming design*, where people with different backgrounds (content experts, communication experts, computer scientists, graphic designers, marketing people, etc.) throw in ideas, which they then evaluate and discuss. A number of experiences (both in academia and in industry environments) have proved that IDM, by eliminating technical details and encouraging the expression of more semantic features, works beautifully for this purpose: It can be used from the very early stage of design (when decisions are still in the clouds) down to the moment when details start to surface.

Other, more technical models (e.g., W2000 and WEBML, for example) do not allow semantic annotation, but rather require the expression of a number of details that cannot be known at the brainstorming phase: They can be used to record decisions already made, rather than helping to make decisions.

A second point is that the *simplicity* and the dialogue-oriented terminology of IDM do not intimidate anyone and allow everybody around the table to discuss design issues. A more tech-oriented model, in the best case, may be used to "communicate" a design to nontechnical people, but nontechnical people cannot use it to freely discuss ideas.

A third, crucial, point is about the *usability* of a design model, which entails at least two key performance indicators: the amount of time required for teaching the model and the amount of time necessary to sketch the design of an application. The reduction in the time spent teaching the model has been astonishing: In an engineering environment the time has been cut down to 25% (moving from either W2000 or WEBML), with no loss at all in understanding the issues. The reduction of time required to sketch the design of an application (by several groups of students) can be estimated at approximately 50% (with a similar reduction in the amount of paper documentation being produced). Also, a few experiments in the "transfer" to industry have shown that a half-day is enough to convey effectively all important ideas in details, compared with the 1.5 or 2 days usually required for training on our previous models.

The fourth, and perhaps most important, issue of all is about the *quality of design*. We have verified something that was initially only a hypothesis: Simplifying the technique and encouraging brainstorming (besides being less "expensive" in terms of time) generally produce better design, in the sense of requirements and goals satisfaction. Designers can focus on and discuss the possible choices and their trade-offs, which leads to better solutions.

Currently, IDM is being used in seven different courses at Politecnico di Milano (three undergraduate and four graduate ones) and five different courses at the University of Lugano (two undergraduate and three graduate ones): It has shown to be tremendously effective, significantly reducing the teaching-learning effort and dramatically improving the quality of design.

We will discuss one example, to give an idea of what happened. TEC-CH (Technology-Enhanced Communication for Cultural Heritage) is an international master's program (in English) awarded by the University of Lugano (first edition: October 2004). We have enrolled 11 students (from Switzerland, Italy, Romania, Sri Lanka, Ghana, Nigeria, and the United States), 8 of whom have never designed an interactive application and only 1 of whom has experience in computer programming. An 8-hour lecture on IDM was sufficient to convey the technique; in a 3-week-long intensive class, these students were able to produce 3 complete projects (for real-life problems) that were technically correct and, above all, superb in terms of design solutions.

As far as non-academic environments are concerned, we had a number of episodes of transferring the methodology to industries (in the area of Milan, Rome, and Southern Italy): In all situations IDM was highly appreciated for its simplicity, expressiveness, and "efficiency." In these contexts we also used IDM for "reverse engineering," i.e., conceptualizing what existing applications do. Industry people were pleased by the possibility of easily visualizing a complex application and, through the IDM notation, discussing how their applications worked. As far as we know, those companies have plans for extensive internal use of IDM, outside the groups that initially cooperated with us.

APPENDIX: ONLINE APPLICATIONS DESIGNED USING IDM

IDM has been validated in both the academic and industry environments, in the design of a large number of content-intensive Web applications. The most recent and relevant are listed below:

- MEDINA: a multichannel transnational portal for cultural tourism in the Mediterranean, connecting the national Web sites for cultural tourisms of nine Mediterranean countries; see an example at http://www. medinaproject.net/tunisia/pages/
- MUNCH: a multichannel Web application for the Munch's Prints exhibition (State Museums of Berlin, April 2003); Web version: http://www.munchundberlin.org; PDA version: http://munchpda.sytes. net/simulatore.html (user id: 1)
- TEC-Lab: the Web site of the Technology-Enhanced Communication Laboratory at the University of Lugano (Faculty of Communication Sciences); http://www.tec-lab.ch
- SeRiAC: Web site for promoting accessibility research results and initiatives for the Public Administration in Italy; http://www.seriac.net
- BRAMANTINO: a multichannel Web application for the exhibition on Bramantino's Adorations (Museo Ambrosiano di Milano, Dec. 2005–Feb. 2006); http://hoc.elet.polimi.it/bramantino
- SYRIA TOURISM: official Web site of the Syrian Ministry of Tourism (under redesign); http://www.syriatourism.org
- UNIVERSITY OF LUGANO: Web site for the Faculty of Communication Sciences at the University of Lugano; http://www.com. unisi.ch

REFERENCES

Baresi, L., Garzotto, F., and Paolini, P. 2001a, Extending UML for modeling Web applications. In *Proceedings IEEE 34th International Conference on System Sciences*, Maui, January.

Baresi, L., Garzotto, F., and Paolini, P., 2001b, Supporting reusable Web design with HDM-Edit. In *Proceedings IEEE 34th International Conference on System Sciences*, Maui, January.

Bolchini, D., and Paolini, P., 2006, Interactive dialogue model: A design technique for multi-channel applications. *IEEE Transactions on Multimedia*, **8**(3).

Garzotto, F., Mainetti, L., and Paolini, P., 1994, HDM2: Extending the E-R approach to hypermedia application design. In *Proceedings ER'04—International Conference on the Entity Relationship Approach*, R.A.-E. Vram Kouramajian and B. Thalheim, eds.

Garzotto, F., Mainetti, L., and Paolini, P., 1995, Hypermedia design, analysis, and evaluation issues. *Communications of the ACM*, **38**(8).

Garzotto, F., and Megale, L., 2006, CHEF: A user-centered perspective for cultural heritage enterprise frameworks. In *Proceedings ACM AVI'06*, Venice, Italy, May.

Garzotto, F., and Paolini, P., 1993, A model-based approach to hypertext application design. *ACM Transactions on Information Systems*, **11**(1): 1–26.

Garzotto, F., Paolini, P., Bolchini, D., and Valenti S., 1999, "Modeling-by-patterns" of Web applications. In *Proceedings WWWCM'99—World-Wide Web and Conceptual Modeling*, ER'99 Workshop, Paris.

Garzotto, F., Paolini, P., and Schwabe, D., 1991, HDM—A model for the design of hypertext applications. In *Proceedings ACM Hypertext '91*, San Antonio, TX.

Garzotto, F., and Perrone, V., 2003, On the acceptability of conceptual design models for Web applications. In *Conceptual Modeling for Novel Application Domains—ER'03 Workshops Proceedings*, M. A. Jeusfeld and Ö. Pastor, eds., Chicago, October.

Wulf, V., Jarke, M., 2004, The Economics of End-User Development, *Communication of the ACM*, 47(49): P.31

Chapter 9

DESIGNING WEB APPLICATIONS WITH WEBML AND WEBRATIO

Marco Brambilla, Sara Comai, Piero Fraternali, Maristella Matera
Dipartimento di Elettronica e Informazione, Politecnico di Milano, Pizza L. da Vinci 32, 20133, Milan, Italy

9.1 INTRODUCTION

The Web Modeling Language (WebML) is a third-generation Web design methodology, conceived in 1998 in the wake of the early hypermedia models and the pioneering works on hypermedia and Web design, like HDM (Garzotto et al., 1993) and RMM (Isakowitz et al., 1995). The original goal of WebML was to support the design and implementation of so-called data-intensive Web applications (Ceri et al., 2002), defined as Web sites for accessing and maintaining large amounts of structured data, typically stored as records in a database management system, like online trading and e-commerce applications, institutional Web sites of private and public organizations, digital libraries, corporate portals, and community sites.

To achieve this goal, WebML reused existing conceptual data models and proposed an original notation for expressing the navigation and composition features of hypertext interfaces. WebML's hypertext model took an approach quite different from previous proposals: Instead of offering a high number of primitives for representing all the possible ways to organize a hypertext interface that may occur in data-intensive Web applications, the focus was on inventing a minimal number of concepts, which could be composed in well-defined ways to obtain an arbitrary number of application configurations.

This initial design choice deeply influenced the definition of the language and its evolution toward more complex classes of applications. Four major versions of WebML characterize the progression of the language:

- **WebML 1**: The original version comprised only a fixed set of primitives for representing read-only data-intensive Web sites; the focus was on the modular organization of the interface, navigation definition, and content extraction and publication in the interface.
- **WebML 2**: It added support for representing business actions (called operations) triggered by the navigation of the user; in this way, the expressive power was extended to support features like content management, authentication, and authorization.
- **WebML 3**: The introduction of the concept of model plug-ins transformed WebML into an open language, extensible by designers with their own conceptual-level primitives, as to widen the expressive power to cover the requirements of new application domains. This transition emphasized the role of component-based modeling and was the base of all subsequent extensions.
- **WebML 4**: The notion of a model plug-in was exploited to add orthogonal extensions to the core of WebML, covering sectors and applications not previously associated with model-driven development. For example, Web service interaction and workflow modeling primitives were added as plug-in components, to enable the modeling and implementation of distributed applications for multi-actor workflow enactment (Manolescu et al., 2005; Brambilla et al., 2006); other extensions pointed in the direction of multichannel and context-aware Web applications (Ceri et al., 2007).

A distinctive trait of the WebML experience is the presence of an industrial line of development running in parallel to the academic research. One of the original design principles of WebML was implementability, with the ultimate goal of bringing model-driven development (MDD) to the community of "real" developers. To achieve this objective, Politecnico di Milano spun off a company (called Web Models) in 2001, with the mission of implementing and commercializing methods and tools for model-driven development of Web applications, based on WebML. Even before then, WebML had been used for modeling and automatically implementing an industrial project, the Acer-Euro system (http://www. acer-euro.com), comprising the multilingual B2B and B2E content publishing and management applications of Acer, the number 4 PC vendor in the world.

The major result of the industrial R&D is WebRatio (WebModels, 2006), an integrated development environment supporting the modeling of applications with WebML and their implementation with model-driven code generators. Today WebRatio is a consolidated industrial reality: More than 100 applications have been developed by WebModels' customers, over 4,000 trial copies are downloaded per year, and many universities and institutions worldwide use the tool in their Web Engineering courses. In retrospect, the most fruitful and challenging aspect of the interplay of academic and industrial activity has been the continuous relationship between researchers and "real–world," "traditional" developers, which produced essential feedback on the definition of a truly usable and effective model-driven development methodology, which is (hopefully) reflected in the current status of WebML and its accompanying tools.

In this chapter we will overview the core features of WebML and some of its extensions and briefly comment on the usage experience. The chapter is organized as follows: Section 9.2 presents an overview of the WebML methodology and, in particular, introduces the WebML notations for the definition of conceptual schemas. Section 9.3 describes the implementation of the methodology and the architecture of the development tool supporting it. Section 9.4 presents extensions of WebML for supporting Web service composition and publication, workflow-driven Web applications, and context-aware Web applications. Section 9.5 shortly summarizes some of the lessons learned in the application of model-driven development with WebML in industrial projects. Finally, Section 9.6 presents the ongoing and future work and draws the conclusions.

9.2 THE WEBML METHODOLOGY

WebML is a visual language for specifying the content structure of a Web application and the organization and presentation of such content in a hypertext (Ceri et al., 2000, 2002).

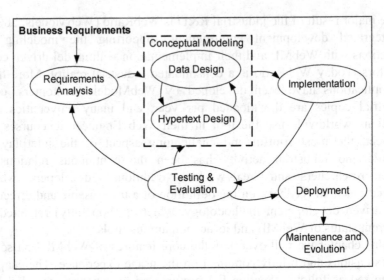

Figure 9.1. Phases in the WebML development process.

As reported in Figure 9.1, the WebML approach to the development of Web applications consists of different phases. Inspired by Boehm's spiral model (Boehm, 1988) and in line with modern methods for Web and software applications development (Beck, 1999; Booch et al., 1999; Conallen, 2000), the WebML process is applied in an iterative and incremental manner in which the various phases are repeated and refined until results meet the application requirements. The product life cycle therefore undergoes several cycles, each producing a prototype or a partial version of the application. At each iteration, the current version of the application is tested and evaluated and then extended or modified to cope with the previously collected requirements as well as the newly emerged requirements. Such an iterative and incremental life cycle appears particularly appropriate for the Web context, where applications must be deployed quickly (in "Internet time") and requirements are likely to change during development.

Out of the entire process illustrated in Figure 9.1, the "upper" phases of analysis and conceptual modeling are those most influenced by the adoption of a conceptual model. The rest of this section will introduce the WebML notations for the definition of conceptual schemas. It will then illustrate the different activities in the WebML development process, with special emphasis on conceptual modeling activities. Some issues about implementation through automatic code generation will be discussed in Section 9.3, by showing how conceptual schemas defined during the design phases can be translated into a running application using WebRatio.

9.2.1 Requirements Analysis

Requirements analysis focuses on collecting information about the application domain and the expected functions and on specifying them through easy-to-understand descriptions. The input to this activity is the set of business requirements that motivate the application development. The main results of this phase are

- the identification of the **groups of users** addressed by the application. Each group represents users having the same characteristics or playing the same role within a business process, i.e., performing the same activities with the same access rights over the same objects. The same individual user may play different roles, thus belonging to different groups.
- the specification of **functional requirements** that address the functions to be provided to users. For each group of users, the relevant activities to be performed are identified and specified.
- the identification of **core information objects**, i.e., the main information assets to be accessed, exchanged, and/or manipulated by users.
- the decomposition of the Web application into **site views**, i.e., different hypertexts designed to meet a well-defined set of functional and user requirements. Each user group will be provided with at least one site view supporting the functions identified for the group.

Analysts are expected to use their favorite format for requirements specification; for instance, tabular formats can be used for capturing the informal requirements such as group or site view descriptions; UML use case diagrams and activity diagrams can also be used as standard representations of usage scenarios and activity synchronization. In particular, functional requirements might be captured by activity flow, showing sequence, and parallelism and synchronization among the activities to be performed by different user groups.

9.2.2 Conceptual Modeling

Conceptual modeling consists of defining conceptual schemas, which express the organization of the application at a high level of abstraction, independently from implementation details. According to the WebML approach, conceptual modeling consists of data design and hypertext design.

Data design corresponds to organizing core information objects previously identified during requirements analysis into a comprehensive and coherent data schema, possibly enriched through derived objects.

Hypertext design then produces site view schemas on top of the data schema previously defined. Site views express the composition of the content and services within hypertext pages, as well as the navigation and the interconnection of components. For applications where different user groups perform multiple activities, or for multichannel applications, in which users can adopt different access devices, hypertext design requires the definition of multiple site views, addressing the user groups involved and their access requirements.

The models provided by the WebML language for data and hypertext design are briefly described in the following. A broader illustration of the language and its formal definition can be found in Ceri et al. (2000, 2002) and at http://www.webml.org.

9.2.2.1 WebML Data Model

Data design is one of the most traditional and consolidated disciplines of information technology, for which well-established modeling languages and guidelines exist. For this reason, WebML does not propose yet another data modeling language; rather, it exploits the entity-relationship data model, or the equivalent subset of UML class diagram primitives. The fundamental elements of the WebML data model are therefore entities, defined as containers of data elements, and relationships, defined as semantic connections between entities. Entities have named properties, called *attributes*, with an associated type. Entities can be organized in generalization hierarchies and relationships can be restricted by means of cardinality constraints.

In the design of Web applications it is often required to calculate the value of some attributes or relationships of an entity from the value of some other elements of the schema. Attributes and relationships so obtained are called *derived*. Derived attributes and relationships can be denoted by adding a slash character (/) in front of their name, and their computation rule can be specified as a logical expression added to the declaration of the attribute or relationship, as is customary in UML class diagrams (Booch et al., 1999). Derivation expressions can be written using declarative languages like OQL or OCL.

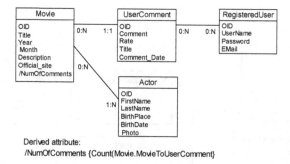

Figure 9.2. A fragment of data schema of the Movie database Web application.

Figure 9.2 shows a small fragment of the data schema of the Movie database example, containing the entities **Movie**, **UserComment**, **RegisteredUser**, **Actor**, and their relationships. The entity **Movie** contains one derived attribute **/NumOfComments**, which is computed as the value of the expression **Count(Movie.MovieToUserComment)**. This expression counts the number of comments associated with a movie according to the **MovieToUserComment** relationship role between the entities **Movie** and **UserComment**.

9.2.2.2 WebML Hypertext Model

The hypertext model enables the definition of the front-end interface, which is shown to a user in the browser. It enables the definition of pages and their internal organization in terms of components (called *content units*) for displaying content. It also supports the definition of links between pages and content units that support information location and browsing. Components can also specify operations, such as content management or user's login/logout procedures. These are called *operation units*.

The modular structure of an application front end is defined in terms of site views, areas, pages, and content units. A *site view* is a particular hypertext, designed to address a specific set of requirements. It consists of *areas*, which are the main sections of the hypertext, and comprises recursively other subareas or pages. *Pages* are the actual containers of information delivered to the user.

Several site views can be defined on top of the same data schema, for serving the needs of different user communities or for arranging content as requested by different access devices like PDAs, smart phones, and similar appliances.

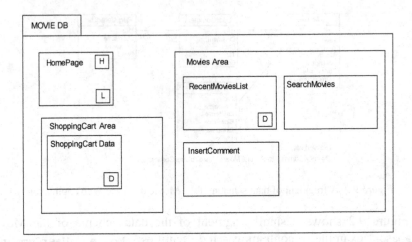

Figure 9.3. Example of site view modularization based on areas and pages.

Figure 9.3 gives an example of the organization of pages and areas in a site view, considering a fragment of the Movie database Web application. The site view is composed of a *home page*, which is the first page accessed when the user enters the application. The site view also comprises two areas: the shopping Cart area, including only one page through which the user manages his current shopping cart; and the Movies area, including three pages that show the list of recent movies, support the search of movies, and allow the user to enter comments.

Pages and areas are characterized by some relevance properties, which highlight their "importance" in the Web site. In particular, pages inside an area or site view can be of three types:

- The **home page** (denoted with a small "h" inside the page icon) is the page at the default address of the site view, or the one presented after the user logs into the application; it must be unique.
- The **default page** (denoted with a small "d" inside the page icon) is the one presented by default when its enclosing area is accessed; it must be unique within an area. In the example in Figure 9.3, the shopping Cart Data page and the Recent Movies List page are default pages for their enclosing areas. This implies that the two pages are entry points for the two areas.
- A **landmark page** (denoted with a small "l" inside the page icon) is reachable from all the other pages or areas within its enclosing module. For example, in Figure 9.3 the home page is also a landmark page, meaning that a link to it will be available from any other page of the site view.

Table 9.1. The Five Predefined Content Units in WebML

Data Unit	Multidata Unit	Index Unit	Scroller Unit	Entry Unit

Page composition. Pages are made of *content units*, which are the elementary pieces of information, possibly extracted from data sources, published within pages. Table 9.1 reports the five WebML predefined content units, representing the elementary information elements that may appear in the hypertext pages.

Units represent one or more instances of entities of the structural schema, typically selected by means of queries over the entity attributes or over relationships. In particular, *data units* represent some of the attributes of a given entity instance; *multidata units* represent some of the attributes of a set of entity instances; *index units* present a list of descriptive keys of a set of entity instances and enable the selection of one of them; *scroller units* enable the browsing of an ordered set of objects. Finally, *entry units* do not draw content from the elements of the data schema, but publish a form for collecting input values from the user.

Data, multidata, index, and scroller units include a *source* and a *selector*. The source is the name of the entity from which the unit's content is retrieved. The selector is a predicate, used for determining the actual objects of the source entity that contribute to the unit's content. The previous collection of units is sufficient to logically represent arbitrary content on a Web interface (Ceri et al., 2002). However, some extensions are also available, for example, the *multichoice* and the *hierarchical* indexes reported in Table 9.2. These are two variants of the index unit that allow one to choose multiple objects and organize a list of index entries defined over multiple entities hierarchically.

Link definition. Units and pages are interconnected by links, thus forming a hypertext. Links between units are called *contextual*, because they carry some information from the *source unit* to the *destination unit*. In contrast, links between pages are called *noncontextual*.

Table 9.2. Two Index Unit Variants

Multichoice Unit	Hierarchical Unit

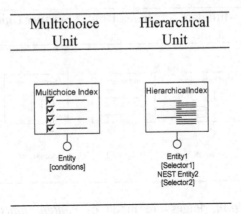

In contextual links, the binding between the source unit and the destination unit of the link is formally represented by link parameters, associated with the link, and by parametric selectors, defined in the destination unit. A *link parameter* is a value associated with a link between units, which is transported as an effect of the link navigation, from the source unit to the destination unit. A *parametric selector* is, instead, a unit selector whose condition contains one or more parameters.

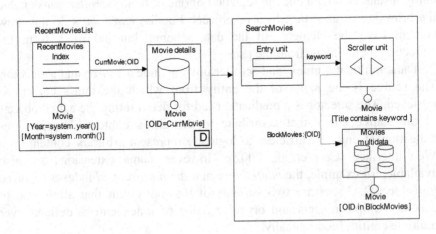

Figure 9.4. Example of contextual and noncontextual navigation.

As an example of page composition and unit linking, Figure 9.4 reports a simple hypertext, containing two pages of the **Movies** Area. The page **Recent Movies List** contains an index unit defined over the **Movie** entity, which shows the list of movies shown in the last month, and a data unit also defined over the Movie entity, which displays the details of the movie selected from the index. Two selectors ([Year=system.year()], [Month=system.month()]) are defined to restrict the selection only to the movies of the current month and year. The arrow between the two units is a contextual link, carrying the parameter CurrMovie, containing the object identifier (OID) of the selected item. The data unit includes a parametric selector ([OID=CurrMovie]), which uses the input OID parameter to retrieve the data of the specific movie.

OIDs of the objects displayed or chosen from the source unit are considered the default context associated with the link. Therefore, OID parameters over links and parametric selectors testing for OID values can be omitted and simply inferred from the diagram.

An example of a noncontextual link is shown from the Recent Movies List page to the Search Movies page: This link does not carry any parameter, because the content of the destination page does not depend on the content of the source page.

The page Search Movies shows an interesting hypertext pattern; it contains three units: an entry unit denoting a form for inserting the keyword of the title to be searched, a scroller unit defined over the Movie entity and having a selector for retrieving only the movies containing that keyword in their titles ([Title contains keyword]), and a multidata unit displaying a scrollable block of search results. Through the scroller unit it is possible to move to the first, previous, next, and last blocks of results.

Automatic and transport links. In some applications, it may be necessary to differentiate a specific link behavior, whereby the content of some units is displayed as soon as the page is accessed, even if the user has not navigated its incoming link. This effect can be achieved by using automatic links. An *automatic link,* graphically represented by putting a label "A" over the link, is "navigated" in the absence of a user's interaction when the page that contains the source unit of the link is accessed.

Also, there are cases in which a link is used only for passing contextual information from one unit to another and thus is not rendered as an anchor. This type of link is called a *transport link,* to highlight that the link enables only parameter passing and not interaction. Transport links are graphically represented as dashed arrows.

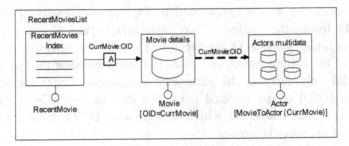

Figure 9.5. Example of automatic and transport links.

Consider the example in Figure 9.5, extending the content of the page `Recent Movies List` shown in Figure 9.4. The link between the index and the data unit has been defined as *automatic*: When the page is accessed, the details of the first movie appearing in the index will be shown to the user, without the need for her interaction. A multidata unit has been added to show the names of the actors playing in the selected movie. A *transport* link is used to pass the OID of the current movie to the multidata unit. This OID is used by the multidata unit in a parametric selector associated with the `MovieToActor` relationship defined between the entities `Movie` and `Actor` to retrieve only the actors associated with the current movie. Note that the automatic link admits the user's interaction for selecting a different movie and is thus rendered as an anchor; conversely, the output link of the data unit does not enable any selection and thus is defined as transport and is not rendered as an anchor.

Global parameters. In some cases, contextual information is not transferred point to point during navigation but can be set as globally available to all the pages of the site view. This is possible through *global parameters*, which abstract the implementation-level notion of session-persistent data.

Parameters can be set through the *Set unit* and consumed within a page through a *Get unit*. The visual representation of such two units is reported in Table 9.3. An example of use of the get unit will be shown in the next subsection.

Operations. In addition to the specification of read-only Web sites, where user interaction is limited to information browsing, WebML also supports the specification of services and content management operations requiring write access over the information hosted in a site (e.g., the filling of a shopping trolley or an update of the users' personal information). WebML offers additional primitives for expressing built-in update operations, such as creating, deleting, or modifying an instance of an entity (represented through the *create, delete,* and *modify* units, respectively) or adding or dropping a relationship between two instances (represented through the *connect* and *disconnect* unit, respectively). The visual representation of such units is reported in Table 9.4.

Table 9.3. The WebML Global Parameter Units

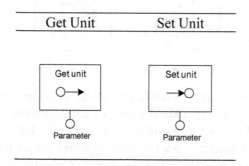

Table 9.4. The WebML Operation Units

Create Unit	Modify Unit	Delete Unit	Connect Unit	Disconnect Unit
Create	Modify	Delete	Connect	Disconnect
Entity <param := value>	Entity [Conditions] <param := value>	Entity [conditions]	Relationship	Relationship

Other utility operations extend the previous set. For example, *login* and *logout* units (see Table 9.5) are respectively used (1) for managing access control and verifying the identity of a user accessing the application site views and (2) for closing the session of a logged user.

Operation units do not publish the content to be displayed to the user but execute some processing as a side effect of the navigation of a link. Like content units, operations may have a source object (either an entity or a relationship) and selectors, may receive parameters from their input links, and may provide values to be used as parameters of their output links. The result of executing an operation can be displayed in a page by using an appropriate content unit, for example, a data or multidata unit, defined over the objects updated by the operation.

Table 9.5. Login and Logout Operations, Supporting Site View Access Control

Login Unit	Logout Unit

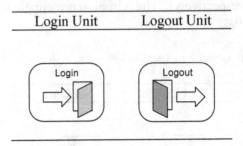

Regardless of their type, WebML operations may have multiple incoming contextual links, which provide the parameters necessary for executing the operation. One of the incoming links is the activating link (the one followed by the user for triggering the operation), while the others just transport contextual information and parameters, for example, the identifiers of some objects involved in the operation.

Two or more operations can be linked to form a chain, which is activated by firing the first operation. Each operation can have two types of output links: one *OK link* and one *KO link*. The former is followed when the operation succeeds; the latter when the operation fails. The selection of the link to follow (OK or KO) is based on the outcome of the operation execution and is under the responsibility of the operation implementation.

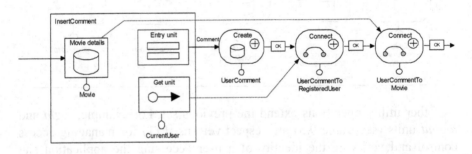

Figure 9.6. Example of content management.

The example in Figure 9.6 shows the content of the **Insert Comment** page in the **Movies** area. Through the entry unit the user can insert a comment for the movie currently displayed by the **Movie details** data unit. A get unit is defined to retrieve the data of the currently logged user, which have been stored in a global parameter after the login. When the user submits a comment, a chain of operations is triggered and executed: First, a new comment instance is created in the **UserComment** entity, containing the text inserted by the user; then, the new comment is associated to the current user (by creating a new instance of the relationship `UserCommentToRegisteredUser`) and to the current movie (relationship `UserCommentToMovie`). In the example, KO links are not explicitly drawn: By default, they lead the user to the page from which the operation chain has been triggered.

9.2.3 Other Development Phases

The phases following conceptual modeling consist of implementing the application, testing and evaluating it in order to improve its internal and external quality, deploying it on top of a selected architecture, and maintaining and possibly evolving the application once it has been deployed.

As described in more details in Section 9.3, the WebRatio development environment (WebModels, 2006) largely assists the implementation phase. First of all, it offers a visual environment for drawing the data and hypertext conceptual schemas. Such visual specifications are then stored as XML documents, which are the inputs for the WebML code generator, which then produces the data and hypertext implementation.

For space reasons, the remaining phases of the application life cycle are only hinted at in this chapter, but they are nonetheless well supported by WebML and WebRatio. In particular:

- The model-driven approach benefits the systematic testing of applications, thanks to the availability of the conceptual model and the model transformation approach to code generation (Baresi et al., 2005). With respect to the traditional testing of applications, the focus shifts from verifying individual Web applications to assessing the correctness of the code generator. The intuition is that if one could ensure that the code generator produces a correct implementation for all legal and meaningful conceptual schemas (i.e., combinations of modeling constructs), then testing Web applications would reduce to the more treatable problem of validating the conceptual schema. The research work conducted in this area has shown that it is possible to quantitatively evaluate the confidence in the correctness of a model-driven code generator, by formally measuring the coverage of a given test set (that is, of a set of sample conceptual schemas) with respect to the entire universe of syntactically admissible schemas. Different notions of coverage have been proposed, and heuristic rules have been derived for minimizing the number of test cases necessary to reach the desired coverage level of the testing process.
- Model-driven development also fosters innovative techniques for quality assessment. The research in this area has led to a framework for the model-driven and automatic evaluation of Web application quality (Fraternali et al., 2004; Lanzi et al., 2004; Meo and Matera, 2006). The

framework supports the *static* (i.e., compile-time) analysis of conceptual schemas and the *dynamic* (i.e., run-time) collection of Web usage data to be automatically analyzed and compared with the navigation dictated by the conceptual schema. The static analysis is based on the discovery in the conceptual schema of design patterns and on their automatic evaluation against quality attributes encoded as rules. Conversely, usage analysis consists of the automatic examination and mining of enriched Web logs, called *conceptual logs* (Fraternali et al., 2003), which correlate common HTTP logs with additional data about (1) the units and link paths accessed by the users, and (2) the database objects published within the viewed pages.

- In a model-driven process, maintenance and evolution also benefit from the existence of a conceptual model of the application. Requests for changes can in fact be turned into changes at the conceptual level, either to the data model or to the hypertext model. Then, changes at the conceptual level are propagated to the implementation. This approach smoothly incorporates change management into the mainstream production life cycle and greatly reduces the risk of breaking the software engineering process due to the application of changes solely at the implementation level.

9.3 IMPLEMENTATION

Application development with WebML is assisted by WebRatio (WebModels, 2006), a commercial tool for designing and implementing Web applications. The architecture of WebRatio (shown in Figure 9.7) consists of two layers: a *design layer*, providing functions for the visual editing of specifications, and a *run-time layer*, implementing the basic services for executing WebML units on top of a standard Web application framework.

The design layer includes a graphical user interface (shown in Figure 9.8) for data and hypertext design, which produces an internal representation in XML of the WebML models. A data mapping module, called Database Synchronizer, maps the entities and relationships of the conceptual data schema to one or more physical data sources, which can be either created by the tool or pre-existing. The Database Synchronizer can forward- and reverse-engineer the logical schema of an existing data source, propagate the changes from the conceptual data model to the physical data sources, and vice versa.

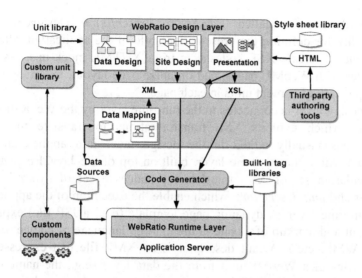

Figure 9.7. The WebRatio architecture.

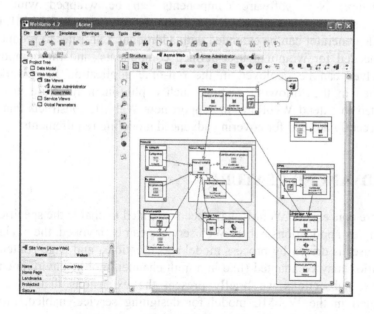

Figure 9.8. WebRatio's graphical user interface.

A third module (called *EasyStyler Presentation Designer*) offers functionality for defining the presentation style of the application, allowing the designer to create XSL stylesheets from XHTML mock-ups, associate XSL styles with WebML pages, and organize page layout, by arranging the relative position of content units in each page.

The design layer is connected to the run-time layer by the WebRatio code generator, which exploits XSL transformations to translate the XML specifications visually edited in the design layer into application code executable within the run-time layer, built on top of the Java2EE platform. In particular, a set of XSL translators produces a set of *dynamic page templates* and *unit descriptors*, which enable the execution of the application in the run-time layer. A dynamic page template (e.g., a JSP file) expresses the content and markup of a page in the markup language of choice (e.g., in HTML, WML, etc.). A unit descriptor is an XML file that expresses the dependencies of a WebML unit from the data layer (e.g., the name of the database and the code of the SQL query computing the population of an index unit).

The design layer, code generator, and run-time layer have a plug-in architecture: New software components can be wrapped with XML descriptors and made available to the design layer as custom WebML units, the code generator can be extended with additional XSL rules to produce the code needed for wrapping user-defined components, and the components themselves can be deployed in the run-time application framework. As described in the following section, such a plug-in architecture has been exploited to extend WebRatio to support new WebML constructs that have been recently defined for covering advanced modeling requirements.

9.4 ADVANCED FEATURES

The core concepts of WebML have been extended to enable the specification of complex applications, where Web services can be invoked, the navigation of the user is driven by process model specifications, and page content and navigation may be adapted (like in a multichannel, mobile environment). In the next subsections we briefly present the extensions that have been integrated in the WebML model for designing service-enabled, process-enabled, and context-aware Web applications.

9.4.1 Service-Enabled Web Applications

Web services have emerged as essential ingredients of modern Web applications: They are used in a variety of contexts, including Web portals for collecting information from geographically distributed providers or B2B applications for the integration of enterprise business processes.

To describe Web services interactions, WebML has been extended with Web service units (Manolescu et al., 2005), implementing the WSDL (W3C, 2002) classes of Web service operations.

We start by recalling some basic aspects of WSDL, providing the foundation of the proposed WebML extensions. A *WSDL operation* is the basic unit of interaction with a service and is performed by exchanging messages.

Two categories of operations are initiated by the client:

- *One-way* operations consist of a message sent by the client to the service.
- *Request-response* operations consist of one request message sent by the client and one response message built by the service and sent back to the client.

Two other operation categories are initiated by the service:

- *Notification operations* consist of messages sent to the service.
- *Solicit* and *response* operations are devised for receiving request messages sent to the service and providing messages as responses to the client.

WebML supports all four categories of operations. In particular, we interpret the operations initiated by the service as a means for *Web services publishing*. Therefore, we assume that these operations will not be used within the traditional hypertext schemas representing the Web site, but within appropriate *Service views*, which contain the definition of published services. The operations initiated by the client are instead integrated within the specification of the Web application. In the following subsections we will see how they can be specified in WebML and present some examples applied to the Movie database running case.

9.4.1.1 Modeling Web Applications Integrated with Web Services

The specification of Web service invocation from within a Web application exploits the request-response and one-way operations. Here we show an example of a request-response operation. Suppose we want to extend the Movie database Web application with the possibility of retrieving books related to a particular movie from a remote Web service (e.g., the Amazon

Web service). Assume that the request-response operation `SearchBooks` allows one to obtain a list of books meeting search criteria provided as input to the service (e.g., keywords contained in the title). The remote Web service responds with the list of books meeting the given search criteria.

The WSDL request-response operation is modeled through the request-response unit, whose graphical notation is shown in Figure 9.9. This operation involves two messages: the message sent to the service and the message received from the service. The corresponding unit is labeled with the Web service operation name and includes two arrows that represent the two messages. This operation is triggered when the user navigates one of its input links; from the parameters transferred by these links, a message is composed and then sent to a remote service as a request. The user waits until the arrival of the response message from the invoked service; then she can resume navigation from the page reached by the output link of the Web service operation unit.

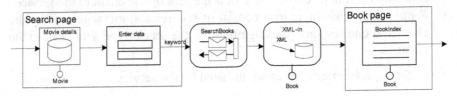

Figure 9.9. Example of usage of the request-response operation.

In the example in Figure 9.9, the user can browse to the `Search page`, where an entry unit permits the input of search criteria, preloaded from the currently selected movie. From this information, a request message is composed and sent to the `SearchBooks` operation of the Web service exposed by the service provider. The user then waits for the response message, containing a list of books satisfying the search criteria. From these options, a set of instances of the `Book` entity is created through the XML-in operation unit (which receives as input XML data and transforms them into relational data) and displayed to the user by means of the `Book Index` unit; the user may continue browsing, e.g., by choosing one of the displayed books. Further details about data transformations and about the storage of data retrieved from Web services can be found in recent publications (Manolescu et al., 2005).

One-way operations are modeled in a similar way: The main difference is that the service will not provide any response. Therefore, once the message is sent to the service, the user continues navigation without waiting for the response.

9.4.1.2 Modeling Web Services Publishing

WebML also supports the publication of Web services that can be invoked by third-party applications. From the application point of view, no user interaction is required in a published Web service. The actions to be performed when the notification or the solicit-response operations are triggered are not specified through pages, but as a chain of operations (e.g., for storing or retrieving data, or for executing generic operations such as sending emails). Therefore, the publishing of Web services can be specified separately from the site view of a Web application. We introduce the following concepts:

- *Service view*: a collection of ports that expose the functionality of a Web service through WSDL operations
- *Port*: the individual service, composed by a set of WSDL operations; each individual WSDL operation is modeled through a chain of WebML operations starting with a solicit-response and/or notification operation

Therefore, the business logic of a WSDL operation is described by a chain of WebML operations, specifying the actions to be performed as a consequence of the invocation of the service, and possibly building the response message to be sent back to the invoker. Each WSDL operation starts with a *solicit unit*, which triggers the service, and possibly ends with the *response unit*, which provides a message back to the service. Here we show an example of a solicit-response operation.

Suppose we want to extend the Movie database application with the publication of a service providing the list of movies satisfying search criteria. The WSDL operation is modeled through a chain of WebML operations starting with the solicit unit (**SearchSolicit**), shown in Figure 9.10. The solicit unit receives the SOAP message from the requester and decodes the search keywords, passing them as parameters to the next WebML operation in the sequence. This is a so-called XML-out (Manolescu et al., 2005) operation unit, which extracts from the database the list of movies that correspond to the specified conditions and formats it as an XML document. After the XML-out operation, the composition of the response message is performed through the *response unit* (**SearchResponse**).

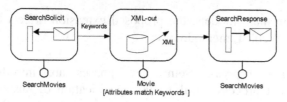

Figure 9.10. Example of usage of the solicit-response operation.

Notice that the schema of Figure 9.10 can be seen as the dual specification of the *SearchBooks* service invocation pattern, represented in Figure 9.9.

In addition to the above-mentioned examples, WebML also supports the exchange of asynchronous messages (Brambilla et al., 2004) and complex Web service conversations (Manolescu et al., 2005).

From the implementation standpoint, the deployment and publishing of Web services required the extension of the run-time WebRatio with a SOAP listener able to accept SOAP requests.

9.4.2 Process-Enabled Web Applications

Today the mission of Web applications is evolving from the support of online content browsing to the management of full-fledged collaborative workflow-based applications, spanning multiple individuals and organizations. WebML has been extended for supporting lightweight Web-enabled workflows (Brambilla, 2003; Brambilla et al., 2003, 2007), thus transferring the benefits of high-level conceptual modeling and automatic code generation also to this class of Web applications.

Integrating hypertexts with workflows means delivering Web interfaces that permit the execution of business activities and embodying constraints that drive the navigation of users. The required extensions to the WebML language are the following:

- *Business process model:* A new design dimension is introduced in the methodology. It consists of a workflow diagram representing the business process to be executed, in terms of its activities, the precedence constraints, and the actors/roles in charge of executing each activity.
- *Data model:* The data model representing the domain information is extended with a set of objects (namely, entities and relationships) describing the meta-data necessary for tracking the execution of the business process, both for logging and for constraints evaluation purposes.
- *Hypertext model:* The hypertext model is extended by specifying the business activity boundaries and the workflow-dependent navigation links.

Besides the main models, the proposed extension affects the following aspects of the WebML methodology:

- *Development process:* Some new phases are introduced in the development process, to allow the specification of business processes and their integration in the conceptual models (see Figure 9.11).

- *Design tools:* A new view shall be introduced for supporting the design of the workflow models within the WebML methodology.
- *Automatic generation tools:* A new transformer is needed for translating workflow diagrams into draft WebML specifications of the Web applications implementing the process specification.

Figure 9.11. Steps of the proposed methodology: Square boxes represent the design steps and the involved tools; bubbles represent the expected results of each step.

The following sections present the details of the process-related extensions, by referring to a specific aspect of the Internet movie database case study, namely the subscription process. Details will be provided about the new features of the development process, the business process modeling, and the data and hypertext modeling.

9.4.2.1 Extensions to the Development Process

The development process is enriched by a set of new design tasks and automatic transformations that addresses the workflow aspects of the application. Figure 9.11 shows the expected steps of the development, the results of each steps, and the involved tools: Through a visual workflow editor, the analyst specifies the business process model to be implemented; the designed workflow model can be processed by an automatic transformation that generates a set of hypertext skeletons implementing the specified behavior; the produced skeletons can be modified by designers by means of CASE tools for conceptual Web application modeling; the resulting models can be processed by automatic code generators that produce the running Web application.

9.4.2.2 Workflow Model and Design Tool

Many standard notations have been proposed to express the structure of business processes. For our purposes, we adopt the Business Process Management Notation (BPMN), which covers the basic concepts required by WfMC (Workflow Management Coalition) and is compatible with Web service choreography languages (e.g., BPEL4WS) and standard business process specification languages (e.g., XPDL). A visual design tool for business processes has been implemented for covering this design phase. The tool is an Eclipse plug-in and allows one to specify BPMN diagrams.

Figure 9.12 shows a subscription process that could apply to the Movie database scenario (the case study has been extended to avoid a simplistic example): The user specifies whether he is a private customer or a company, then he alternatively submits the company or his own personal information, and finally a user manager accepts the subscription.

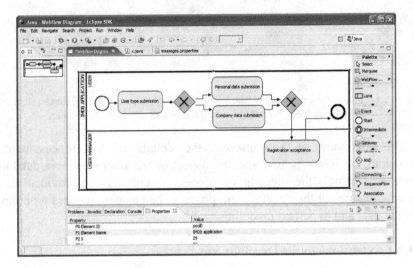

Figure 9.12. Subscription process represented in BPMN in the BP design tool.

9.4.2.3 Data Model Extensions: Workflow Meta-Data

The extensions to the data model include some standard entities for recording activities instances and process cases, thus allowing one to store the state of the business process execution and enacting it accordingly. The adopted meta-model is very simple (see Figure 9.13): The `Case` entity stores the information about each instantiation of the process, while the `Activity` entity stores the status of each activity instance executed in the system. Each activity belongs to a single case. Connections to user and application data can be added, for the purpose of associating domain information to the process execution. Typical requirements are the assignment of application objects to activity instances and the tracking of the relation between an activity and its executor (a user).

Notice that the proposed meta-model is just a guideline. The designer can adopt more sophisticated meta-data schemas or even integrate with underlying workflow engines through appropriate APIs (e.g., Web services) for tracking and advancing the process instance.

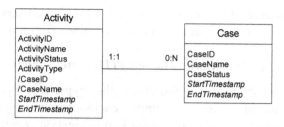

Derived attributes:
/CaseID {Self.Activity2Case.CaseID}
/CaseName {Self.Activity2Case.CaseName}

Figure 9.13. Workflow meta-data added to the data model.

9.4.2.4 Hypertext Model Extensions: Activities and Workflow Links

The hypertext model is extended with two new primitives:

- *Activity:* An activity is represented by an area tagged with a marker "A." The whole hypertext contained in the area is the implementation of the activity.
- *Workflow link:* Workflow links are links that traverse the boundary of any activity area. They are used for hypertext navigation, but their behavior includes workflow logic, which is not explicitly visible in the hypertext. Every link entering an activity represents the start of the execution of the activity; every outgoing link represents the end of the activity. The actual behavior of the workflow links is specified by a category associated with the link.

Incoming links can be classified as *Start link,* allowing an existing activity to start from scratch; *Start case link,* allowing one to create a new case and a new activity and to start them; *Create link,* allowing one to create a new activity and start it; *Resume link,* allowing one to resume the execution of an activity once it has been suspended.

Outgoing links can be classified as *Complete link,* which closes the activity and sets its status to completed; *Complete case link,* which closes the activity and the whole case, setting their status to completed; *Suspend link,* which suspends the execution of an activity (that can be resumed later through a resume link); *Terminate link,* which closes the activity and sets its status to terminated (e.g., for exception management).

Notice that *if* and *switch* units can be used to express navigation conditions. Moreover, a specific approach has been studied for managing exceptions within workflow-based Web applications (Brambilla et al., 2005; Brambilla and Tziviskou, 2005), but it is not discussed here for the sake of brevity. Moreover, by combining workflows and Web services extensions, the design of distributed processes can be obtained (Brambilla et al., 2006).

9.4.2.5 Mapping Workflow Schemas to Hypertext Models

Workflow activities are realized in the hypertext model by suitable configurations of pages and units, enclosed within an activity area. Workflow constraints must be turned into navigation constraints among the pages of the activities and into data queries on the workflow meta-data for checking the status of the process, thus ensuring that the data shown by the application and user navigation respect the constraints described by the process specification. The description of how the precedence and synchronization constraints between the activities can be expressed in the hypertext model is specified in Brambilla et al. (2003), which describes the mapping between each workflow pattern and the corresponding hypertext.

A flexible transformation, depending on several tuning and style parameters, has been included in the methodology for transforming workflow models into skeletons of WebML hypertext diagrams.

The produced WebML model consists of an application data model, workflow meta-data, and hypertext diagrams. The transformation supports all the main WfMC precedence constraints, which include sequences of activities, AND-, OR-, XOR- splits and joins, and basic loops.

Since no semantics is implied by the activity descriptions, the generated skeleton can only implement the empty structure of each activity and the hypertext and data queries that are needed for enforcing the workflow constraints. The designer remains in charge of implementing the interface and business logic of each activity. Additionally, it is possible to annotate the activities with a set of predefined labels (e.g., create, update, delete, browse), thus allowing the transformer tool to map the activity to a coarse hypertext that implements the specified behavior.

Once the transformation has been accomplished, the result can be edited with WebRatio (WebModels, 2006), thus allowing the designer to refine the generated hypertext and to implement the internal behaviour of each activity.

9.4.2.6 Workflow-Based Hypertext Example

Figure 9.14 shows the hypertext diagram for the Personal Data Submission activity, which is part of the example process depicted in Figure 9.12. Notice that the shown implementation is the final result of the two steps of automatic hypertext skeleton generation and of hypertext refinement by the designer. The link marked with the "..." label may come from any hypertext fragment in the site view.

Before starting the activity, a condition is checked for verifying that the `Company data submission activity` is not started yet, since it is defined as mutually exclusive with respect to the `Personal Data Submission` activity (a corresponding XOR-split decision gateway is shown in Figure 9.14). Hence, the condition to be checked before starting `Personal Data Submission` is that the instance of `Company data submission` activity within the current case has a status not yet *Active*. Notice that we assume an ordered set of possible values for the status (*Created* < *Inactive* < *Active* < *Suspended* < *Resumed* < *Completed*), and at most one instance of the activity `Company data submission` exists within a case, because of the construction rules of the instances of the workflow. Therefore, the condition extracts the activity of type `Company data submission` not yet started. If this instance exists, the *Start* link is followed and the `Personal Data Submission` activity is started (i.e., its status in the database is set to *Active*). The user submits his own information and the Modify unit updates the database, then the *Complete* link closes the activity and redirects the user to the home page.

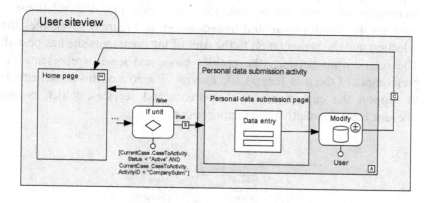

Figure 9.14. Example of hypertext representing the Personal data submission activity.

9.4.3 Context-Aware Web Applications

WebML has also been applied to the design of adaptive, context-aware Web applications (Ceri et al., 2003, 2006, 2007). The overall design process for context-aware applications follows the activity flow typically used for conventional Web applications. However, some new issues must be considered for modeling and exploiting the context at the data level and for modeling adaptive behaviors in the hypertext interface.

9.4.3.1 Modeling User and Context Data

During data design, the user and context requirements can be translated into three different subschemas complementing the application data (see Figure 9.15):

- The *User subschema*, which clusters data about users and their access rights to application data. In particular, the entity User provides a basic profile of the application's users, the entity Group allows access rights for a group of users to be managed, and the entity SiteView allows users (and user groups) to be associated with specific hypertexts. In the case of adaptive context-aware applications, users may require different interaction and navigation structures, according to the varying properties of the context.
- The *Personalization subschema*, which consists of entities from the application data associated with the User entity by means of relationships expressing user preferences for some entity instances, or the user's ownership of some entity instances. For example, the relationship between the entities User and UserComment in Figure 9.15 enables the selection and the presentation to the user of the comments she has posted. The relationship between the entities User and Movie represents the preferences of the user for specific movies. The role of this subschema is to support the customization of contents and services, which is one relevant facet of adaptive Web applications.

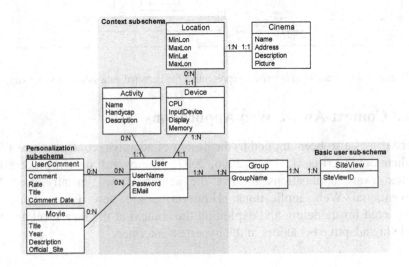

Figure 9.15. Three subschemas representing context data.

- The *Context subschema*, including entities such as `Device`, `Location`, and `Activity`, which describe context properties relevant for providing adaptivity. Context entities are connected to the entity `User` to associate each user with his (personal) context.

9.4.3.2 Identifying Context-Aware Pages

During hypertext design, adaptive requirements are considered to augment the application's front end with reactive capabilities. As illustrated in Figure 9.16, context-awareness in WebML can be associated with selected pages, and not necessarily with the whole application. Location-aware applications, for example, adapt "core" contents to the position of a user, but typical "access pages" (including links to the main application areas) might not be affected by the context of use.

We therefore tag adaptive pages with a *C* label (standing for "Context-aware") to distinguish them from conventional pages. This label indicates that some adaptivity actions must be associated with the page. During application execution, such actions must be evaluated prior to the computation of the page, since they can serve to customize the page content or to modify the navigation flow defined in the model.

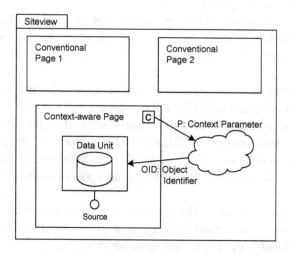

Figure 9.16. Hypertext schema highlighting context-aware pages. Context-aware pages are labeled with a "C" and are associated with a context cloud.

As shown in Figure 9.16, adaptivity actions are clustered within a *context cloud*. The cloud is external to the page, and the adaptivity actions that it clusters are kept separate from the page specification. Such a notation highlights the different roles played by pages and context clouds: The former act as providers of content and services, the latter act as modifiers of such content and services.

In order to monitor the state of the context and execute adaptivity actions, C-pages must be provided with autonomous intervention capabilities. The standard HTTP protocol underlying most of today's Web applications implements a strict pull paradigm. In the absence of a proper push mechanism, reactive capabilities can therefore be achieved by periodically refreshing the viewed page and by triggering the execution of adaptivity actions before the computation of the page content. This polling mechanism "simulates" the active behavior necessary for making pages sensitive to the context changes.

9.4.3.3 Specifying Adaptivity Actions in Context Clouds

Context clouds contain adaptivity actions expressed as sequences of WebML operations and are associated with a page by means of a directed arrow, i.e., a link, exiting the C label. This link ensures communication between the page logic and the cloud logic, since it can transport parameters derived from the content of the page, useful for computing the actions specified within the cloud. Vice versa, a link from the cloud to the page can transport parameters computed by the adaptivity actions, which might affect the page contents with respect to a new context.

The specification of adaptivity actions relies both on the use of the standard WebML primitives and on a few novel constructs, related to the acquisition and use of context data:

1. *Acquisition and management of context data.* This may consist of the retrieval of context data from the context model stored within the data source, or of the acquisition of fresh context data provided by device- or client-side-generated URL parameters, which are then stored in the application data source. These are the first actions executed every time a C-page is accessed, for gathering an updated picture of the current context.
2. *Condition evaluation.* The execution of some adaptivity actions may depend on some conditions, e.g., evaluating whether the context has changed and hence triggering some adaptivity actions.
3. *Page content adaptivity.* Parameters produced by context data acquisition actions and by condition evaluation can be used for page computation. They are sent back to the page by means of a link exiting the context cloud and going to the page. The result is the display of a page where the content is adapted to the current context.
4. *Navigation adaptivity.* The effect of executing the adaptivity actions within the context cloud can be the redirection to a different page. The

specification of context-triggered navigation just requires a link exiting the context cloud to be connected to pages other than the cloud's source page.

5. *Adaptivity of the hypertext structure.* To deal with coarse-grained adaptivity requirements, e.g., the change of device, role, or activity, the adaptivity actions may lead to the redirection toward a completely different site view.

6. *Adaptivity of presentation properties.* To support finer-grained adjustments of the interface, the adaptivity actions may induce the run-time modification of the presentation properties (look and feel, content position and visibility, and so on).

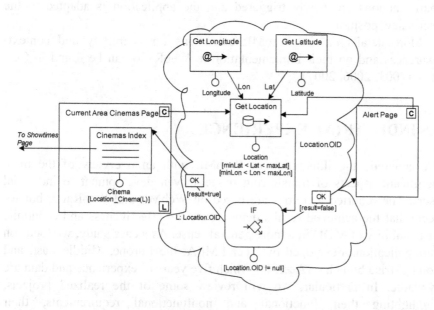

Figure 9.17. The WebML specification of adaptivity actions providing users with context-aware information about cinemas.

Figure 9.17 illustrates an example of adaptivity actions, applied to the **Current Area Cinemas** page. Upon page access, some adaptivity actions in the cloud are executed, which may change the content of the page based on the geographical position of the user. Specifically, the user's **Latitude** and **Longitude** are retrieved by the **Get Longitude** and **Get Latitude** units, which are examples of the *GetClientParameter* operation unit, introduced in WebML to access context data sensed at the client side. In the example, the two parameters **Longitude** and **Latitude** represent the position coordinates sensed through a user's device equipped with a GPS module. The retrieved position values are used by the **Get Location** unit to identify a (possible) location stored in the database for the current user's position. Get Location is a *Get Data* unit, a content unit for retrieving values (both scalars and sets) from an entity of the data model without displaying them on a page. The location OID is evaluated through an *If* unit: If it is not null (i.e., the sensed coordinates fall into a location stored in the application data source), the list of cinemas in that location is visualized in the Current Area Cinemas page; otherwise, the user is automatically redirected to the Alert page, where a message notifies of the absence of information about cinemas in the current area.

Figure 9.17 also models the Alert page as context-aware; in particular, this page shares its adaptivity actions with the Current Area Cinemas page. Therefore, as soon as an automatic refresh of the Alert page occurs, the shared actions are newly triggered and the application is adapted to the user's new position.

More details on the WebML extensions for adaptivity and context-awareness and on their implementation in WebRatio can be found in Ceri et al. (2003, 2006, 2007).

9.5 INDUSTRIAL EXPERIENCE

We conclude the illustration of WebML with an overview of the most significant aspects of transferring model-driven development to industrial users. The reported activities are based on WebML and WebRatio, but we deem that the achieved results demonstrate the effectiveness and economic sustainability of MDD in a more general sense. As a case study, we focus on the applications developed by Acer EMEA, the Europe, Middle East, and South Africa branch of Acer, for which five years of experience and data are available. In particular, we will review some of the realized projects, highlighting their functional and nonfunctional requirements, their dimensional parameters, and the key aspects of their development, deployment, evolution, and economic evaluation. The experience started with the first version of the Acer-Euro application (http://www.acer-euro.com), which aimed at establishing a software infrastructure for managing and Web-deploying the marketing and communication content of an initial group of 14 countries out of the 31 European Acer national subsidiaries. The content of Acer-Euro 1.0 included the following main areas: *About Acer, Products, News, Service & Support, Partner Area*, and *Where to buy*.

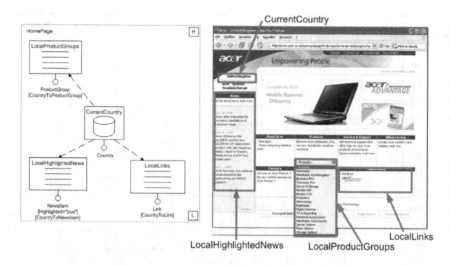

Figure 9.18. The WebML specification of the home page of a national site of Acer-Euro (left) and its rendition in HTML (right).

Figure 9.18 shows the home page of a national site of Acer-Euro (left) and its rendition in HTML generated by WebRatio. The Acer-Euro 1.0 system supported two main functions:

1. *Content publishing:* comprising the architecture, tools, and processes to make content about the Acer European Web sites available on the Web to the users of the target countries.
2. *Content management:* comprising the architecture, tools, and processes needed to gather, store, update, and distribute to the destination countries the content related to the Acer European Web sites.

Figure 9.19 shows the schedule and milestones of the Acer-Euro 1.0 project. Only 7 weeks elapsed from the approval of the new site map and visual identity to the publishing of the 14 national Web sites and to the delivery of the CMS to Acer employees. In this period, two distinct prototypes were formally approved by the management: Prototype 1, with 50% of functionality, was delivered at the end of week 2; prototype 2, with 90% of functionality, at week 5. Overall, nine prototypes were constructed in six weeks: two formal, seven for internal assessment.

The development team consisted of four persons: one business expert and one junior developer from Acer, and one analyst and one Java developer from Politecnico di Milano.

	Week 1	Week 2	Week 3	Week 4	Week 5	Week 6	Week 7
M0							
M1		◆PR1					
M2			◆PR2				
M3							
M4							
M5							
M6							
M7							
M8							
M9							
M10							
M11							
M12							
M13							

M0: agreement of site map and Visual Identity

M1: prototype 1.0 (50% of features) + initial CMS

M2: approval of prototype V.1 + change list

M3: prototype 2.0 (90% of feature) + revised CMS

M4: approval of prototype 2.0

M5: localized static texts and images

M6: localized dynamic database content

M7: information on data and traffic of countries

M8: initial stress test and tuning

M9: definition of application clustering policies

M10: network configuration and country clustering

M11: database and template installation

M12: content upload

M13: publishing of the 14 sites + CMS

Figure 9.19. The schedule and milestones of the Acer-Euro 1.0 project.

Figure 9.19 shows the most relevant figures of the project: only six weeks of development plus one week of testing were sufficient for analyzing, designing, implementing, verifying, documenting, and deploying a set of midsized, functionally complex, multilingual Web applications. As illustrated by the dimensional and economic parameters reported in Table 9.6, such result has to be ascribed to

1. The high degree of automation brought to the process by the use of the model-driven approach: More than 90% of the application and database code were synthesized automatically by the WebRatio development environment from the WebML models of the applications, without the need to manually intervene on the produced code.

2. The overall productivity of the development process: The productivity value is obtained by counting the number of function points (FPs) of the project and dividing this value by the number of staff-months

employed in the development. The result is an average productivity rate of 131.5 FP/staff month, which is 30% greater than the maximum value expected for traditional programming languages in the Software Productivity Research Tables (SPR, 2006). This latter result is a consequence of the former: High automation implies a substantial reduction of the manually written repetitive code and a high reuse of design patterns.

Table 9.6 Main Dimensional and Economic Parameters of the Acer-Euro Project

Class	Dimension	Value
Time & effort	Number of elapsed workdays	49
	Number of development staff-months (analysts and developers)	6 staff-months (6 weeks × 4 persons)
	Total number of prototypes	9
	Average elapsed man days between consecutive prototypes	5,4
	Average number of development man days per prototype	15,5
Size	Number of localized B2C Web sites	14
	Number of localized CMS applications	4 (Admin, News, Product, Other)
	Number of supported languages	12 for B2C Web sites, 5 for CMS
	Number of data entry masks	39
	Number of automatically generated database tables	46
	Number of automatically generated database views	82
	Number of automatically generated database queries	279 for extraction, 89 for update
	Number of automatically generated JSP page templates	48
	Number of automatically generated or reused Java classes	250
	Number of automatically generated Java lines of code	12,500 Noncommented lines of code
Degree of automation	Number of manually written SQL statements	17 (SQL constraints)
	Percentage of automatically generated SQL code	96%
	Number of manually written/adapted Java classes /JSP templates	10% JSP templates manually adapted
	Percentage of automatically generated Java and JSP code	90% JSP templates, 100% Java classes
Productivity	Number of function points	177 (B2C web site) + 612 (CMS) = 789
	Average number of FP delivered per staff-month	131.5

Another critical success factor has been the velocity in focusing the requirements, thanks to the rapid production of realistic prototypes. At the end of week 2, the top management could already evaluate an advanced prototype, which incorporated 50% of the requested functionality, and this initial round of requirement validation proved essential to the delivery of a compliant solution in such a limited time. With respect to traditional prototyping, which exploits a simplified architecture, WebRatio generates code directly for the actual delivery platform; in this way, stress test and architecture tuning could already start at week 1 on the very first prototype, greatly improving the parallelism of work and further reducing time to market.

The benefits of MDD were manifested not only in the development of the first version, but were even more sensible in the maintenance and evolution phase. Figure 9.20 shows the timeline of the additional releases and spin-off projects of Acer-Euro. Four major releases of Acer-Euro were delivered between 2001 and 2006, and the number of applications grew from the initial 5 to 13 intranet and Internet applications, serving more corporate roles and supporting more sophisticated workflow rules.

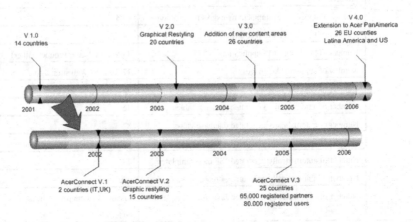

Figure 9.20. The evolution of the Acer-Euro project in five years.

At the end of 2005, Acer-Euro was rolled out in 26 European countries and extended also to the Acer Pan-American subsidiaries, including Latin America and the United States. As early as June 2001, an extension of the Acer-Euro platform was scheduled, to address the delivery and management of content for the channel operators (Acer partners). This spin-off project, called Acer Connect, is a multi-actor extranet application targeted to Acer partners, characterized by the following features:

1. the segmentation of the users accessing the site into a hierarchy of groups corresponding to both Acer's and partners' business functions
2. the definition of different access privileges and information visibility levels to groups

3. the provision of an Acer European administration role, able to dynamically perform via the Web all administrative and monitoring tasks
4. the provision of an arbitrary number of nation-based and partner-based administration roles, with responsibility for local content creation and publishing, and local user administration
5. a number of group-tailored Web applications (e.g., sales, marketing) targeting content to corporate-specific or partner-specific user communities
6. the management of administrative and business functions in multiple languages flexibly set by administrators and users
7. a security model storing group and individual access rights into a centrally managed database, to enforce global control over a largely distributed application
8. content personalization based on group-specific or user-specific characteristics, for ensuring one-to-one relationships with partners
9. advanced communication and monitoring functions for the effective tracking of partners' activity and of Acer's quality of services

The first version of Acer Connect was deployed in Italy and the UK in December 2001, after only seven months of development and with an effort of 24 staff-months. Today, Acer Connect is rolled out in 25 countries and hosts 65,000 registered partners, delivering content and services to a community of over 80,000 users. Acer Connect and Acer-Euro share part of the marketing and communication content, and therefore the former project was realized as an evolution of the latter; starting from the data model of Acer-Euro, the specific functions of Acer Connect were added, and new applications were modeled and automatically generated. The model-driven approach greatly reduced the complexity of integration, because the high-level models of the two systems were an effective tool for reasoning about the functionality to reuse and develop.

Besides Acer Connect, several other projects were spun off, to exploit the customer and partner communities gathered around these two portals. Figure 9.21 overviews the delivered B2C projects, which collectively total over 10,800,000 visits per month.

As a remark on the long-term sustainability of MDD, we note that, despite their complexity and multinational reach, both Acer-Euro and Acer Connect are maintained and evolved by one junior developer each, working on the project at part time. In total, only 5 junior developers, allocated to the projects at part time, maintain the 56 mission-critical Web applications implemented by Acer with WebML.

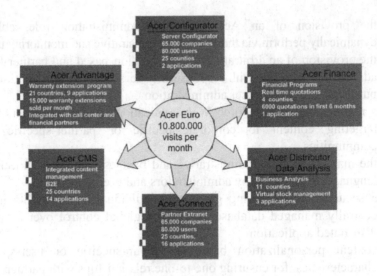

Figure 9.21. The main applications developed in Acer with WebML.

On the negative side of MDD, the initial training and switching costs have been reported as the most relevant barrier. MDD requires nontechnical knowledge on the modeling of software solutions, which must be acquired with a mix of conventional and on-the-job training. Furthermore, developers have their own previous consolidated skills and professional history, and switching to a completely new development paradigm is felt to be a potential risk. Acer estimates that it takes developers from 4 to 6 months to become fully acquainted and productive with MDD, WebML, and WebRatio. However, Acer's figures demonstrate that the initial investment in human capital required by MDD pays off in the mid-term. The number of applications developed and maintained per unit of development personnel increases with the developers' expertise and exceeds 10 fully operational, complex, and distributed Web applications per developer.

9.6 CONCLUDING REMARKS

In this chapter we have described the Web Modeling Language, a conceptual notation for specifying the design of complex, distributed, multi-actor, and adaptive applications deployed on the Web and on service-oriented architectures using Web services. WebML was born in academia but soon spun off to the industrial battlefield, where it faced the development of complex systems with requirements often exceeding the expressive power of the language. This fruitful interplay of academic design and industrial experience made the language evolve from a closed notation for data-centric

Web applications to an open and extensible framework for generalized component-based development. The core capability of WebML is expressing application interfaces as a network of collaborating components, which sit on top of the core business objects. WebML incorporates a number of built-in, off-the-shelf components for data-centric, process-centric, and Web service-centric applications and lets developers define their own components, by wrapping existing software artifacts and reverse-engineering them. In other words, the essence of WebML boils down to a standard way of describing components, their interconnection and passage of parameters, their exposition in a user interface, and the rules for generating code from their platform-independent model.

This flexibility allowed several extensions of the language, in the direction of covering both new application requirements and deployment architectures. The ongoing work is pursuing a number of complementary objectives:

1. Extending the model-driven approach to all the phases of the application life cycle: WebML is being used as a vehicle to investigate the impact of MDD on development activities like business requirement elicitation and reengineering, cost and effort estimation, testing, quality evaluation, and maintenance.
2. Extending the capability of the user interface beyond classical hypertexts: The expressive power of WebML is presently inadequate to express Rich Internet Applications and classical client-server applications; research is ongoing to identify the minimal set of concepts needed to capture the Web interfaces of the future.
3. Broadening the range of deployment platforms: WebML and WebRatio are being extended to target code generation for nonconventional infrastructures. A version of WebRatio for digital television has been already built, and experimentation is ongoing for deploying applications on top of embedded systems and mobile appliances for the DVB-H standard.

REFERENCES

Baresi, L., Fraternali, P., Tisi, M., and Morasca, S., 2005, Towards model-driven testing of a Web application generator. *Proceedings 5th International Conference on Web Engineering* (ICWE'05), Sydney, Australia, pp. 75–86.

Beck, K., 1999, Embracing change with extreme programming. *IEEE Computer*, **32**(10): 70–77.

Boehm, B., 1988, A spiral model of software development and enhancement. *IEEE Computer*, **21**(5): 61–72.

Booch, G., Rumbaugh, J., and Jacobson, I., 1999, *The Unified Modeling Language User Guide (Object Technology Series)*, Addison-Wesley, Reading, MA.

Brambilla, M., 2003, Extending hypertext conceptual models with process-oriented primitives. *Proceedings Conceptual Modeling* (ER 2003), Chicago, IL, pp. 246–262.

Brambilla, M., Ceri, S., Comai, S., Fraternali, P., and Manolescu, I., 2003, Specification and design of workflow-driven hypertexts. *Journal of Web Engineering*, **1**(2): 163–182.

Brambilla, M., Ceri, S., Comai, S., and Tziviskou, C., 2005, Exception handling in workflow-driven Web applications. *Proceedings World Wide Web International Conference* (WWW'05), Chiba, Japan, May 10–13, pp. 170–179.

Brambilla, M., Ceri, S., Fraternali, P., and Manolescu, I., 2007, Process modeling in Web applications. *ACM Transactions on Software Engineering and Methodology*. In print.

Brambilla, M., Ceri, S., Passamani, M., and Riccio, A., 2004, Managing asynchronous Web services interactions. *Proceedings ICWS 2004*, pp. 80–87.

Brambilla, M., and Tziviskou, C., 2005, Fundamentals of exception handling within workflow-based Web applications. *Journal of Web Engineering*, **4**(1): 38–56.

Ceri, S., Daniel, F., Facca, F., Matera, M., and the MAIS Consortium, 2006, Front-end methods and tools for the development of adaptive applications. In *Mobile Information Systems. Infrastructure and Design for Flexibility and Adaptivity*, B. Pernici, ed., Springer-Verlag, pp. 209–246.

Ceri, S., Daniel, F., and Matera, M., 2003, Extending WebML for modelling multi-channel context-aware Web applications. *Proceedings WISE '03 Workshops*, IEEE Press, pp. 225–233.

Ceri, S., Daniel, F., Matera, M., and Facca, F., 2007, Model-driven development of context-aware Web applications. *ACM Transactions on Internet Technology*, **7**(1), Article No. 2.

Ceri, S., Fraternali, P., and Bongio, A., 2000, Web Modeling Language (WebML): A modeling language for designing Web sites. *Computer Networks*, **3**(1–6): 137–157.

Ceri, S., Fraternali, P., Bongio, A., Brambilla, M., Comai, S., and Matera, M., 2002, *Designing Data-Intensive Web Applications*, Morgan Kaufmann, San Francisco.

Conallen, J., 2000, *Building Web Applications with UML (Object Technology Series)*, Addison-Wesley, Reading, MA.

Fraternali, P., Lanzi, P.L., Matera, M., and Maurino, A., 2004, Model-driven Web usage analysis for the evaluation of Web application quality. *Journal of Web Engineering*, **3**(2): 124–152.

Fraternali, P., Matera, M., and Maurino, A., 2003, Conceptual-level log analysis for the evaluation of Web application quality. *Proceedings LA-WEB 2003*, IEEE Press, pp. 46–57.

Garzotto, F., Paolini, P., and Schwabe, D., 1993, HDM—A model-based approach to hypertext application design. *ACM Transactions on Information Systems*, **11**(1): 1–26.

Kruchten, P., 1999, *The Rational Unified Process: An Introduction*, Addison-Wesley, Reading, MA.

Isakowitz, T., Sthor, E.A., and Balasubranian, P., 1995, RMM: A methodology for structured hypermedia design. *Communications of the ACM*, **38**(8): 34–44.

Lanzi, P.L., Matera, M., and Maurino, A., 2004, A framework for exploiting conceptual modeling in the evaluation of Web application quality. *Proceedings ICWE 2004*, Springer-Verlag, pp. 50–54.

Manolescu, I., Brambilla, M., Ceri, S., Comai, S., and Fraternali, P., 2005, Model-driven design and deployment of service-enabled Web applications. *ACM Transactions on Internet Technology*, **5**(3): 439–479.

Meo, R., and Matera, M., 2006, Designing and mining Web applications: A conceptual modeling approach. In *Web Data Management Practices: Emerging Techniques and Technologies*, A. Vakali and G. Pallis, eds., Idea Group Publishing, Hershey, PA.

SPR (Software Productivity Research), 2006, SPR Programming Language Table—Version PLT2005a. Retrieved February 2006 from http://www.spr.com.

WebModels, 2006. WebRatio Tool Suite. Retrieved October 2006 from http://www.webratio.com.

W3C, 2006, WSDL Web Service Description Language. Retrieved October 2006 from https://www.w3.org/2002/ws/desc.

Chapter 10

HERA

Geert-Jan Houben,[1,2] Kees van der Sluijs,[1] Peter Barna,[1] Jeen Broekstra,[1,3] Sven Casteleyn,[2] Zoltán Fiala,[4] Flavius Frasincar[5]

[1]*Technische Universiteit Eindhoven, PO Box 513, 5600 MB Eindhoven, The Netherlands, {g.j.houben, k.a.m.sluijs, p.barna, j.broekstra}@tue.nl*
[2]*Vrije Universiteit Brussel, Pleinlaan 2, 1050 Brussels, Belgium, {Geert-Jan.Houben, Sven.Casteleyn}@vub.ac.be*
[3]*Aduna, Prinses Julianaplein 14b, 3817 CS Amersfoort, The Netherlands, jeen@aduna.biz*
[4]*Technische Universität Dresden, Mommsenstr. 13, D-01062, Dresden, Germany, zoltan.fiala@inf.tu-dresden.de*
[5]*Erasmus Universiteit Rotterdam, PO Box 1738, 3000 DR Rotterdam, The Netherlands, frasincar@few.eur.nl*

10.1 INTRODUCTION

This chapter illustrates a method for Web information systems (WIS) design that found its origins in an approach for hypermedia presentation generation. It was also this focus on hypermedia presentation generation that gave the first engine complying with this method its name, HPG (Frasincar, 2005). The method distinguishes three main models that specify the generation of hypermedia presentations over available content data. With a model for the content, a model for the hypermedia navigation construction, and a model for the presentation construction, the method enables the creation of a hypermedia-based view over the content. Originally, in the first generation of the method and its toolset, the models specified a transformation from the content to the presentation. The engine that was compliant with this definition was based on XSLT and is therefore known as HPG-XSLT.

One of the characteristic aspects that HPG-XSLT supported was adaptation. As an illustrative example, we show in Figure 10.1 how the engine could produce different presentations from a single design in which the "translation" to formats such as HTML, SMIL, and WML was dealt with generically.

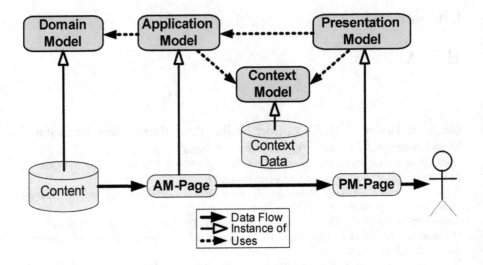

Figure 10.1. Hera models.

Characteristic for the Hera models was not only their focus on user- and context-adaptation support, but also the choice to base the models on the resource description framework (RDF) (Klyne and Carrol, 2004) and RDF schema (RDFS) (Brickley and Guha, 2004). The use of Web standards such as RDF and RDFS as a modeling paradigm facilitates easy deployment on very heterogeneous data sources: The only assumption made is that a semistructured description (in RDF) of the domain is available for processing. Not only is such a representation less costly to develop than any alternative, but it also enables the reuse of existing knowledge and flexible integration of several separate data sources into a single hypermedia presentation.

During further research into the development of the method, support was extended for more advanced dynamics. Whereas the first XSLT-based approach primarily transformed the original content data into a hypermedia document, with which the user could interact by following links with a Web browser, the subsequent engine version allowed the inclusion of form processing, which led to the support of other kinds of user interaction while retaining the hypermedia-based nature. Out of this effort, a Java-based version of the engine became available that used RDF queries to specify the data involved in the forms.

The experience from these HPG-based versions and the aim for further exploitation of the RDF-based nature of the models have led to a further refinement of the approach in what is now termed Hera-S. The Hera-S-compliant models do combine the original hypermedia-based spirit of the Hera models with more extensive use of RDF querying and storage. Realizing this, RDF data processing using the Sesame framework (Broekstra et al., 2002) and its query language SeRQL (Broekstra, 2005) caters for extra flexibility and interoperability.

In the current version of the Hera method that we present in this chapter, we aim to exemplify the characteristic elements included in the method. As we mentioned before, there is the RDF-based nature of the models. There is certainly also the focus on the support for adaptation in the different model elements. Adapting the data processing to the individual user and the context that the user is in (in terms of application, device, etc.) is a fundamental element in WIS design and one that deserves the right attention: Managing the different design aspects and thus controlling the complexity of the application design is crucial for an effective design and implementation.

In this chapter we first address the main characteristics of the method and then we explain the models, i.e., the main design artifacts, for the book's running example. We present the implementation of the hypermedia presentation generation process induced by the models. We also consider some extensions to the basic approach that can help the design process in certain scenarios.

10.2 METHOD

We discuss the Hera approach and illustrate it by means of examples from the Hera models for the running example (in this case we use Hera-S-compliant versions of those models). In this section we will capture the main elements of the key models used in the example before we go into details in the next section.

The purpose of Hera is to support the design of applications that provide navigation-based Web structures (hypermedia presentations) over semantically structured data in a personalized and adaptive way. The design approach centers on *models* that represent the core aspects of the application design. Figure 10.2 gives an overview of these models. With the aid of a tool for executing those models (e.g., HPG-XSLT or Hera-S), we can also generate the application, as depicted in this figure. Thus, the appropriate pipeline of models captures the entire application design, leaving room for the designer to change or extend the implementation where desired. In this section we give a short overview over the different models and associated modeling steps, while each of them is presented in more detail in subsequent sections.

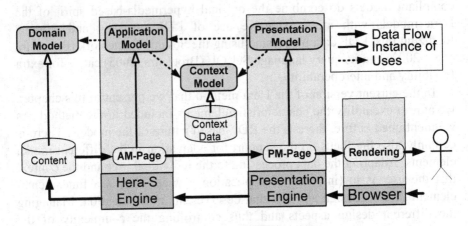

Figure 10.2. Hera-S models and tool pipeline.

Before we can create a model to specify the core design of the application, we need as a starting point in Hera a *domain model* (DM) that describes the structure of the content data. The sole purpose of the DM is to define how the designer perceives the semantical structure of the content data: It tells us what we need to know about the content over which we want the application to work. Based on this DM, the designer creates an *application model* (AM) that describes a hypermedia-based navigation structure over the content. This navigation structure is devised for the sake of delivering and presenting the content to the user in a way that allows for (semantically) effective access to the content.

In turn, this effective access can imply the personalization or adaptation that is deemed relevant. Hera allows dynamic personalization and adaptation of the content. For this purpose, context data are maintained (under control of the application) in a so-called context model (CM). These context data are typically updated based on the (inter)actions of the user as well as on external information.

Thus, on the basis of DM and CM, the AM serves as a recipe that prescribes how the content is transformed into a navigational structure. To be more precise, instantiating the AM with concrete content results in AM (instance) *pages* (AMP). These AMPs can be thought of as pages that contain content to be displayed and navigation primitives (based on underlying semantic relations from the DM) that the user can use to navigate to other AMPs and thus to semantically "move" to a different part of the content. An AMP itself is not yet directly suitable for a browser, but can be transformed into a suitable presentation by a presentation generator, i.e., an engine that executes a specification, for example, a presentation model (PM) of the concrete presentation design in terms of layout and other (browser-specific) presentation details. In Section 10.7 we demonstrate that both proprietary and external engines can be used for this task. For the Hera method, this presentation-generation phase itself is not specific and may be done in whatever way is preferred. So, the AM specifies the (more conceptual or semantical) construction of the navigational structure over the content, while the subsequent presentation phase, possibly specified by a PM, is responsible for the transformation of this structure into elements that fit the concrete browsing situation.

AMP creation is conceptually *pull-based*, meaning that a new AMP is constructed in the Hera pipeline only upon request (in contrast to constructing the whole instantiation of the AM at once, which was done, for example, in the implementation by the HPG-XSLT engine). Through navigation (link-following) and forms submission, the user triggers the feedback mechanism, which results in internally adapting (updating) the Web site navigation or context data and the creation of a new AMP.

As indicated in the introduction, Hera models use RDF(S) to represent the relevant data structures. In the next sections we will see this for the specification of the data in DM, CM, and AM. In the engines these RDF(S) descriptions are used to retrieve the appropriate content and generate the appropriate navigation structures over that content. In HPG-XSLT the actual retrieval was directly done by the engine itself, whereas in HPG-Java this was done with the aid of expressions that are based on SeRQL (Broekstra, 2005) queries. In Hera-S the actual implementation exploits the fact that we have chosen to use RDF(S) to represent the model data and allows us to use native *RDF querying* to access data, for example, the content (DM) and context (CM) data. For this Hera-S allows the application (AM) to connect to the content and context data through the Sesame RDF framework. This solution, combining Hera's navigation design and Sesame's data processing by associating SeRQL queries to all navigation elements, allows us to effectively apply existing Semantic Web technology and a range of its solutions that is becoming available. We can thus include background knowledge (e.g., ontologies, external data sources), and we can connect to third-party software (e.g., for business logic) and to services through the RDF-based specifications. We can also use the facilities in Sesame for specific adaptation to the data processing and to provide more extensive interaction processing (e.g., client-side, scripting). The dynamics and flexibility required in modern Web information systems can thus be met by accommodating the requirements that evolve from an increasing demand for personalization, feedback, and interaction mechanisms. We point out that

Hera-S models in principle are query- and repository-independent. We only require a certain type of functionality; if a repository fulfills these requirements, it can be used for implementation of Hera-S models.

10.3 DATA MODELING

Before the application design can consider the personalized navigation over the domain content, the relevant data need to be specified. As a necessary first step in the approach, the *data modeling* step leads to the construction of the data models for the domain content and the context of the user.

The modeling of the domain content uses RDF(S) and is primarily targeted toward capturing the semantical structure of the domain content. With the Hera-S engine we even allow the model to be an OWL (Dean and Schreiber, 2004) ontology (without restrictions). If we look at the UML representation for the IMDb example that is used throughout the book, this can be easily modeled as an RDFS or OWL definition. In this case this could be done by using a UML-to-OWL conversion process (several papers have been written on the relations between UML and OWL) (Hart et al., 2004). We could, however, also create this model ourselves, e.g., by using an ontology editor like Protégé.[1] Figure 10.3 contains a screenshot of the UML model translated into an RDFS hierarchy together with its properties and OWL restrictions in Protégé. We divided the UML model into four parts. One part, with the prefix imdb, contains the "core" of the movie domain, describing the movies and the persons involved with those movies. Another part, with the prefix cin, models the cinemas that show the movies that are modeled in the imdb part.

In this figure we also see prefixes starting with cm. They relate to the *context* modeling. The CM is modeled and implemented in a similar way as the DM. The main difference between the two is that the content data are meant to be presented to the user, while the context data are meant to support the context-dependent adaptation of the application. So, the content data typically contain the information that in the end is to be shown to the user, while the context data typically contain information used (internally) for personalization and adaptation of content delivery. This distinction might not always be strict, but as it is only a conceptual distinction in Hera-S, the designer may separate content and context in whatever way he desires. As a consequence, we assume that context data are under direct control of the engine, while the content often is not. In the IMDb example, the context model is modeled in the same way as the domain. We first maintain a model,

---

[1] http://protege.stanford.edu.

with the prefix cm1, that contains users and their comments on movies in the imdb part. The second part, with the prefix cm2, contains a description of tickets bought by the user for a particular movie showing in a particular cinema.

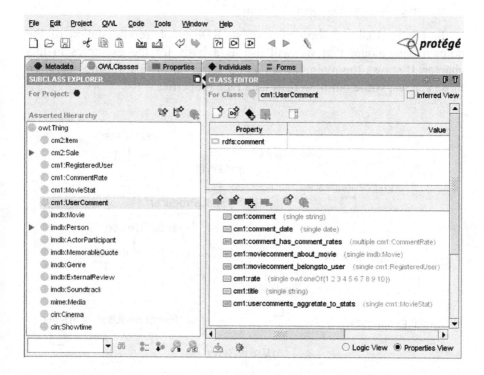

Figure 10.3. Protégé screenshot for the IMDb data modeling.

Considering the role and function of the context data, we can identify different aspects of context. We will come back to context data later when we discuss adaptation in the AM, but we now address the context data modeling. Even though the designer is free to choose any kind of context data, we discern three types in general: session data, user data, and global data.

- *Session data* are relevant to a certain session of a certain user. An example of such data is the current browsing context, such as the device that is used to access the Web application or the units browsed in the current session.
- *User data* are relevant to a certain user over multiple sessions (from initial user data to data collected over more than one session). User (profile) data can be used for personalization (even at the beginning of a

new session). Note that for maintaining these user data over time, the application needs some authentication mechanism.

- *Global data* are usage data relevant to all users over all sessions. Global data typically consist of aggregated information that gives information about groups of people. Examples include "most visited unit" or "people that liked item x, also browsed item y."

In Figure 10.4 we show part of an RDF-graph representation of the domain data model that we will use as a basis for the examples in this chapter. It shows the main classes and a selection of relationships between those classes, while omitting their data type properties.

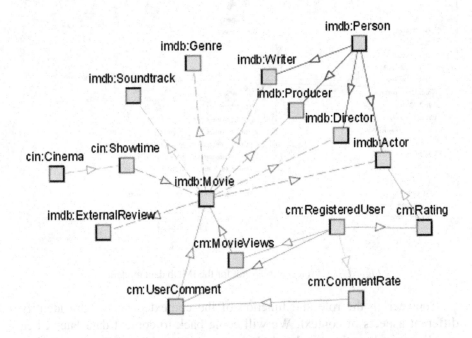

Figure 10.4. RDF-graph representation of IMDb domain and context data.

Both the DM and CM data are implemented in Hera-S using a Sesame repository. For the CM, which is under direct control of the application, this allows the application to manage and update the context as it perceives this context. Next to this, it also provides the means for other processes to use and update (parts of) this information. The context data could, for instance, be manipulated by business logic software for the sake of adaptation, or by external user-profiling software.

Another great advantage of using Sesame is the possibility to combine several data sources (both content and context data) at the same time. In this way, designers can couple additional data sources to the already existing ones and can thus easily extend the domain content. This also offers possibilities to exploit additional knowledge when performing a search. Currently, we are involved in the exploitation of the WordNet ontology[2] (Miller, 1995), time ontologies (Hobbs and Pan, 2004), and geographic ontologies[3] (Chipman et al., 2005). In this way, a keyword search can be extended with synonyms extracted from the WordNet ontology, or a search for a city can be extended with surrounding cities from a geographic ontology. By supporting unrestricted RDFS or OWL DMs, Hera-S is particularly suited to (re-)use existing domain ontologies. Moreover, many existing data sources that are not yet available in RDFS or OWL format can be used via Semantic Web wrapping techniques[4] (Thiran et al., 2005). In the latter case Sesame can be used as a mediator between such a data source and Hera-S.

As we will see in detail in the next section, the access to the data from the DM or CM is part of the application definition. It means that the access to the RDF data is part of the model. In principle, we assume that the concepts from the DM and CM are associated with concrete data elements in the data storage structure. As we use the Sesame RDF framework as our back-end repository, these data can be exploited and reasoned upon. Accessing the content data in Hera-S will be done via explicit SeRQL queries; by making them explicit in the models, we support customizable access via customizable SeRQL queries. Thus, the full potential of the SeRQL query language can later be used in the AMP creation. For the purpose of defining the content and context, we can abstract from the SeRQL queries, but for the support of different types of adaptation, we benefit from making this SeRQL access explicit.

10.4 APPLICATION MODELING

Based on the domain definition, application modeling results in the application model (AM) that specifies the navigational behavior of the Web application. The AM enables designers to specify how the (navigational) access to the data (dynamically retrieved from the domain) is structured by describing which data are shown to the user and what Web pages the user can navigate to. At the same time, the AM allows this specification to be dynamic, such that the navigational access to the data can be personalized to a user and adapted for a specified context.

---

[2] http://www.semanticweb.org/library/.
[3] http://reliant.teknowledge.com/DAML/Geography.owl.
[4] http://simile.mit.edu/RDFizers/.

Since in the AM we use Turtle and SeRQL syntax, we first highlight in Section 10.4.1 the most relevant elements from those languages. In Section 10.4.2 we present the basic AM constructs and exemplify them based on the IMDb example as discussed in the previous section. In Section 10.4.3 we give examples of adaptation expressed in the AM. Section 10.4.4 contains a number of more advanced modeling primitives. In Section 10.4.10 we illustrate a model builder that offers designers a visual tool to help create the domain models and the AM and produce the correct RDF serialization for those graphical representations.

10.4.1 Queries and Syntax

10.4.1.1 Turtle

Turtle (Terse RDF Triple Language) (Beckett, 2004) is an RDF syntax format designed to be compact, easy to use, and easy to understand by humans. Although not an official standard, it is widely accepted and implemented in RDF toolkits.

In Turtle, each part of the triple is written down as a full URL or as a qualified name (using namespace prefixes). In our examples, we will mostly use the latter form, for brevity. For example,

> my:car rdf:type cars:Volvo

denotes the RDF statement "my car is of type Volvo." "my:" and "cars:" in this example are namespace prefixes that denote the vocabulary/ontology from which the term originates. Turtle also introduces the predicate "a" as a shortcut for the "rdf:type" relation.

> my:car a cars:Volvo

denotes the same RDF statement as the first example.

In order to list several properties of one particular subject, we can use the semicolon to denote branching:

> my:car a cars:Volvo ;
>   my:color "Red"

denotes two statements about the car: that it is of type "Volvo" and that its color is red (denoted by a string literal value in this example).

When the value of a property is itself an object with several properties, we can denote this by using square brackets ([and]). In RDF terms, such brackets denote a blank node (which can be thought of as an existential qualifier). For example:

```
my:car a cars:Volvo ;
    my:hasSeat [
                              a my:ComfortableSeat ;
             my:material "Leather"
    ]
```

denotes that the car has a seat that is "something" (a blank node) that has as its type "my:ComfortableSeat" and that has leather as the material.

In the next sections, we will regularly use Turtle syntax forms in various examples.

10.4.1.2 SeRQL

SeRQL (Broekstra et al., 2002; Broekstra, 2005) (Sesame RDF Query Language) is an RDF query and transformation language that uses graph templates (in the form of path expressions) to bind variables to values occurring in the queried RDF graph. It is an expressive language with many features and useful constructs.

An SeRQL query consists of a set of clauses (SELECT, FROM, and WHERE). As in SQL, the SELECT clause describes the projection, i.e., the ordered set of bound values that is to be returned as a query result. The FROM clause describes a graph template that is to be matched against the target graph, and the WHERE clause specifies additional Boolean constraints on matching values. A simple example query that selects all instances of the class "Volvo" is

```
SELECT aCar
FROM {aCar} rdf:type {cars:Volvo}
```

As one can see, the path expression syntax bears a strong resemblance to Turtle syntax, except that in SeRQL, each node in the graph is surrounded by braces ({ and }). In the above query, "aCar" is a variable that is to be matched in the target graph against all statements that conform to the pattern, i.e., those that have "rdf:type" as their predicate and "cars:Volvo" as their object.

As in Turtle, SeRQL paths can be branched (using a semicolon) as well as chained. For example, in the following query we use both chaining and branching to select a car, its color, its owner, and the address of that owner:

```
SELECT aCar, color, owner, address
FROM {aCar} rdf:type {cars:Volvo} ;
            my:color {color} ;
            my:owner {owner} my:address {address}
```

Additionally, we can use the WHERE clause to specify additional constraints on the results. To adapt the above query to return results only for those cars whose color is red, we could add a WHERE clause:

```
WHERE color = "Red"
```

10.4.2 Units, Attributes, and Relationships

Now we will discuss the constructs that we provide in our AM. We will start in this section with the basic constructs that are sufficient to build basic Web applications and then move on to more complex constructs for realizing richer behavior.

The AM is specified by means of *navigational units* (shorthand: units) and *relationships* between those units. The instantiation of units and relationships is defined by (query) expressions that refer to the (content and context) data, as explained in Section 10.3.

The unit can be used to represent a "page." It is a primitive that (hierarchically) groups elements that will be shown to the user together. Those elements shown to the user are called "attributes," and so units build hierarchical structures of attributes.

An attribute is a single piece of information that is shown to the user. This information may be constant (i.e., predefined and not changing), but usually it is based on information inside the domain data. If we have a unit for a concept c, then typically an attribute contained in this unit is based on a literal value that is directly associated with c (for example, as a data type property). Note that literals may denote not only a string type, but also other media by referring to a URL. Furthermore, we offer a built-in media class (denoted as hera:Mime) that can be used to specify an URL and the MIME type of the object that can be found at the URL. This can be used if the media type is important during later processing.

Below we give an example of the definition of a simple unit, called "MovieUnit," to display information about a movie. We mention two elements in this definition:

- From the second until the seventh line, we define which data instantiate this unit. These data are available as input (am:hasInput) from the environment of this unit, e.g., passed on as a link parameter or available as a global value. In this case we have one variable, "M": The fourth line specifies the (literal) name of the variable, while the fifth line indicates the type of the variable. In this case, a value from the imdb:Movie class concept from the domain will instantiate this unit.

- In the 8th until the 14th line, starting with am:hasAttribute, we decide to display an attribute of this movie, namely a title. We label this attribute "Title" (so that later we can refer to it), and we indicate (with "am:hasQuery") how to get its value from the data model. This query uses the imdb:movieTitle (datatype) property applied to the value of M. Note that in the query "$M" indicates that M is a Hera variable, i.e., outside the scope of the SeRQL query itself. The output of the SeRQL query result is bound to the Hera variable T (implicitly derived from the SELECT list).

In our RDF/Turtle syntax the definition looks like the following:

```
:MovieUnit a am:NavigationUnit ;
  am:hasInput [
    am:variable [
      am:varName "M" ;
      am:varType imdb:Movie
    ]
  ] ;
  am:hasAttribute [



    rdfs:label "Title" ;
    am:hasQuery
      "SELECT T
      FROM {$M} rdf:type {imdb:Movie};
              imdb:movieTitle {T}"
  ]
```

For the attribute value instead of the simple expression (for which we can even introduce a shorthand abbreviation), we can use a more complicated query expression, as long as the query provided in "am:hasQuery" returns a data type property value.

Relationships can be used to link units to each other. We can use relationships to contain units within a unit, thus hierarchically building up the "page" (we call these *aggregation relationships*), but we can also exploit these relationships for navigation to other units (we call these *navigation relationships*).

As a basic example, we include in the unit for the movie not only its title but also a (sub)unit with the name and photo of the lead actor and a navigational relationship that allows us to navigate from the lead-actor information to the full bio-page (unit) for that actor. Note that from now on we omit namespaces in our text when they appear to be obvious.

- We have separated here the definitions of "MovieUnit" and "ActorUnit" (which allows later reuse of the ActorUnit), but we can also define subunits inside the unit that contains them.
- In the definition of the MovieUnit, one can notice, compared to the previous example, that we have an additional subunit with its label LeadActor, with its type ActorUnit, and with the query that gives the value with which we can instantiate the subunit.
- In the definition of the ActorUnit. one can notice its input variable, two attributes, and a navigation relationship. This navigation relationship has a label "Actor-Bio," targets a "BioUnit," and, with the query based on the "imdb:actorBio" property, determines to which concrete BioUnit this ActorUnit offers a navigation relationship. Note that in this case the variable $B is passed on with the navigational relationship (it is also possible to specify additional output variables that are passed on with the relationship).

```
:MovieUnit a am:NavigationUnit ;
  am:hasInput [ am:variable [ am:varName "M";
                                      am:varType imdb:Movie]] ;
  am:hasAttribute [ rdfs:label "Title" ; ... ] ;
  am:hasUnit [
    rdfs:label "LeadActor" ;
    am:refersTo :ActorUnit ;
    am:hasQuery
      "SELECT L
      FROM {$M} rdf:type {imdb:Movie};
                  imdb:movieLeadActor {L} rdf:type {imdb:Actor}"
]

:ActorUnit a am:NavigationUnit ;
  am:hasInput [ am:variable [ am:varName "A" ;
                                      am:varType imdb:Actor]] ;
  am:hasAttribute [
    rdfs:label "Name";
    am:hasQuery
      "SELECT N
      FROM {$A} rdf:type {imdb:Actor};
                  imdb:actor_name {N}" ] ;
```

```
       am:hasAttribute [
          rdfs:label "Photo" ;
          am:hasQuery
          "SELECT P
          FROM {$A} rdf:type {imdb:Actor};
                        imdb:actorPhoto {P}" ] ;
       am:hasNavigationRelationship [
          rdfs:label "Actor-Bio" ;
          am:refersTo :BioUnit ;
          am:hasQuery
          "SELECT B
          FROM {$A} rdf:type {imdb:Actor};
                        imdb:actorBio {B}"
       ]
```

Thus, in these examples we see that each element contained in a unit, whether it is an attribute, a subunit, or a navigational relationship, has a query expression (hasQuery) that determines the value used for retrieving (instantiating) the element.

Sometimes we know that in a unit we want to contain subunits for each of the elements of a set. For example, in the MovieUnit we might want to provide information for all actors from the movie (and not just the lead actor). Below we show a different definition for MovieUnit that includes a *set*-valued subunit element (am:hasSetUnit). In its definition, one can notice

- the label "Cast" for the set unit
- the indication that the elements of the set unit are each an "ActorUnit"
- the query that determines the set of concrete actors for this movie to instantiate this set unit, using the imdb:movie_actor object property

```
       :MovieUnit a am:NavigationUnit ;
          am:hasInput [am:variable [am:varName "M" ;
                                    am:varitype imdb:Movie]] ;
          am:hasAttribute [rdfs:label "Title" ; ... ] ;
          am:hasSetUnit [
             rdfs:label "Cast" ;
             am:refersTo ActorUnit ;
             am:hasQuery
             "SELECT A
             FROM {$M} rdf:type {imdb:Movie} ;
                           imdb:movieActor {A}"
          ]
```

So, we see that a set unit is just like a regular unit, except that its query expression will produce a set of results, which will cause the application to arrange for displaying a set of (in this example) ActorUnits.

Likewise, we can have set-valued query expressions in navigational relationships, and with am:tour and am:index we can construct guided tours and indexes, respectively. With these the order of the query determines the order in the set, and with the index an additional query is used to obtain anchors for the index list.

10.4.3 Adaptation Examples

Adaptation and personalization are important aspects within the Hera methodology. For this purpose, the query expressions can be used to include conditions that provide control over the instantiation of the unit. Typically, these conditions use data from the context model (CM) and thus depend on the current user situation. For example, we can use U as a (global) variable that denotes the current (active) user for this browsing session (typically, this gets instantiated at the start of the session). Let us assume that in the CM for each Actor there is a cm:actorRating property that denotes U's rating of the actor (from 1 to 5 stars) and that the user has indicated to be interested only in actors with more than 3 stars. We could then use this rating in adapting the Cast definition in the last example:

```
am:hasSetUnit [
  rdfs:label "Cast";
  am:refersTo ActorUnit ;
  am:hasQuery
    "SELECT A
     FROM {$U} cm:actorRating {} cm:stars {V} ;
                cm:ratingOnActor {A} imdb:playsIn {$M}
     WHERE V > 3"
]
```

Here we see how we can influence (personalize) the input to an element (in this case a set) by considering the user context in the query that determines with which values the element is constructed. To be precise, in this example we state inside the movie unit what actors of the cast this user will be provided with, i.e., which values we "pass on."

Another user adaptation example would be that the user has indicated not to be interested in photos from actors. We could then change the query for the photo attribute accordingly:

```
:ActorUnit a am:NavigationUnit ;
  am:hasInput [ am:variable [ am:varName "A" ;
                              am:varType imdb:Actor]] ;
  ...
  am:hasAttribute [
    rdfs:label "Photo" ;
    am:hasConditionalQuery [
      am:if "SELECT *
             FROM {$U} cm:showElement {}
                         cm:showAbout {imdb:actorPhoto}"

      am:then "SELECT P
               FROM {$A} imdb:actorPhoto {P}"
    ]
  ] ;
  ... .
```

Here we see that with "am:hasConditionalQuery" the attribute becomes "conditional," i.e., the photo attribute is only shown when the condition (am:if) query produces a non-empty result. We can also add an "am:else" part here and display, for example, the string "no photo displayed." We point out that this query can be written in one single (nested) SeRQL query, but for the clarity of adaptation specification we use this syntax sugaring.

Finally, we present a more complex example of adaptation. Consider again the ActorUnit from the previous section, which showed an actor's name, his picture, and a link to his bio. Now imagine we would like to add the list of movies in which the actor played. However, because some movies are age-restricted, we would like to restrict this list so that adult-rated movies are only shown to registered users that are 18 or older. As in the previous adaptation examples, this adaptation can be achieved by tweaking the SeRQL query that computes the list of movies:

```
:ActorUnit a am:NavigationUnit ;
  am:hasInput [ am:variable [ am:varName "A" ;
                  am:varType imdb:Actor]] ;
  ...
  am:hasSetUnit [
  rdfs:label "Movies Played In";
  am:refersTo MovieUnit ;
  am:hasConditionalQuery [
  am:if "SELECT *
    FROM      {$U} cm:age {G}
    WHERE G > 17"
```

```
      am:then "SELECT M
             FROM {$A} imdb:actorMovie {M},
                    {M} rdf:type {imdb:Movie}"
      am:else "SELECT M
          FROM {$A} imdb:actorMovie {M},
                    {M} rdf:type {imdb:Movie}; imdb:mpaaRating {R}
                    WHERE R != "NC-17""
   ]]
```

First, notice in the code excerpt the am:hasSetUnit, which represents the list of movies for the active actor (A). This list is defined by a conditional query, in which it is verified whether the active user (U) is registered and whether his age is over 17 (am-if). If this condition holds (am:then), all movies of the particular actor are computed. If the condition does not hold (am:else), the computed movie list is restricted to movies that are not MPAA (Motion Picture Association of America)-rated as "NC-17" (No Children Under 17 Admitted).

10.4.4 Other Constructs

Earlier we explained the basic constructs. In this section we will look at some additional features of Hera-S that also allow designers to use some more advanced primitives in order to construct richer applications.

10.4.5 Update Queries

For the sake of adaptation, we need to maintain an up-to-date context model. In order to do so, we need to perform updates to this data. For this, we have the functionality to specify an am:onLoad update query and an am:onExit update query within every unit; these are executed on loading (navigating to) and exiting (navigating from) the unit. Furthermore, we allow an update query to be attached to a navigation relationship so that the update query is executed when a link is followed. In all cases, the designer may also specify more than one update query.

In our example we could, for instance, maintain the number of page views (visits) of a certain movieUnit and update this information if the movieUnit is loaded using the "onLoad" query:

```
   :MovieUnit a am:NavigationUnit ;
      ...
   am:onLoad [
      am:updateQuery
```

```
    "UPDATE {V} cm:amount {views+1}
      FROM {$U} rdf:type {cm:RegisteredUser};
               cm:userMovieViews {V} cm:amount {views};
               cm:viewsOfMovie {$M}"
];
.... .
```

10.4.6 Frame-Based Navigation

We explained earlier that units can contain other units. The root of such an aggregation hierarchy is called a *top-level unit*. The default semantics of a navigational relationship (that is defined somewhere inside the hierarchy of a top-level unit) is that the user navigates from the top-level unit to the top-level unit that is the target of the relationship. In practice, this often means that in the browser the top-level unit is replaced by the target unit. However, we also allow specify that the navigation should only consider the (lower-level) unit in which the relationship is explicitly specified, so that only that unit is replaced while the rest of the top-level unit remains unchanged.

This behavior is similar to the frame construct from HTML. We specify this behavior by explicitly indicating the source unit for the relationship. Inspired by the HTML frame construct, we allow the special source indications "_self" (the unit that contains the relation), "_parent" (the unit that contains the unit with the relation), and "_top" (the top-level unit—the default behavior). Alternatively, relations may also indicate another containing unit by referring to the label of the contained unit. An example of a navigational relationship with a source indication looks like

```
am:hasNavigationRelationship [
   ...
   am:source am:_self ;
   ... ]
```

10.4.7 Forms

Besides using relationships (links) for navigation, we also support applications that let the user provide more specific feedback and interact. For this we provide the form unit. A form unit extends a normal unit with a collection of input elements (that allow the user to input data into the form) and an action that is executed when the form is submitted. In a form a navigational relationship typically has a button that activates the submission.

Below we give an example of a form that displays the text "Search Movie:" (line 3) with one text input field (lines 5 to 11) to let the user enter the movie she wants to browse to. If the user enters a value in this field, it is bound to the variable movieName (line 9). After submitting the form via a button with the text "Go" (lines 14 and 15), the user navigates to the MovieUnit (line 14) that will display the movie for which the name was entered in the input field, which is specified in the query (starting in line 20) using the variable movieName.

```
:MovieSearchForm a am:FormUnit ;
  am:hasAttribute [


    am:hasValue "Search Movie: "
];
  am:formElement [
    rdfs:label "Search Input";
    am:formType am:textInput;
    am:binding[
        am:variable [am:varName "movieName" ;
                     am:varType xsd:String ]]
];
  am:formElement [
    rdfs:label "Submit Button";
    am:formType am:button;
    am:buttonText "Go";
    am:hasNavigationRelationship [
      rdfs:label "Search Form-Movie" ;
      am:refersTo :MovieUnit ;
      am:hasQuery
        "SELECT M
         FROM {M} rdf:type {imdb:Movie};
                      imdb:movieTitle {X}
         WHERE X = $movieName"
    ]
  ]
]
```

10.4.8 Scripting Objects

Current Web applications offer users a wider range of client-side functionality by different kinds of scripting objects, like Javascript and VBscript, stylesheets, HTML+TIME timing objects, etc. Even though WIS methods like Hera concentrate more on the creation of a platform-independent hypermedia presentation than a data domain, and these scripts are often (but not always) browser-/platform-specific, we still provide the designer a hook to insert these kinds of scripting objects.

The designer can specify within a scripting object whatever code she wants, as this will be left untouched in generating the AMPs out of the AM. Furthermore, the designer can add an am:hasTargetFormat property to specify one or more target formats for format-specific code, e.g., HTML or SMIL. This allows us later in the process to filter out certain format-specific elements if these are not wanted for the current presentation. The scripting objects can use the variables that are defined within the scope of the units. Scripting objects can be defined as an element within any other element (i.e., units and attributes). Furthermore, it can be specified whether or not the script should be an attribute of its superelement (e.g., similar to elements in HTML that have attributes and a body). The need to place some specific script on some specific place is, of course, decided by the designer.

10.4.9 Service Objects

An application designer might want to use additional functionality that cannot be realized by a client-side object but that involves the invocation of external server-side functionality. Therefore, we provide so-called service objects (am:serviceObject) to support Web services in the AM. The use of a service object and the reason to provide support for it are similar to that of scripting objects. The designer is responsible for correctness and usefulness of the service object.

Think of utilizing a Web service from an online store selling DVDs in order to be able to show on a movie page an advertisement for buying the movie's DVD. A service object needs three pieces of information:

- a URL of the Web service one wants to use
- a SOAP message that contains the request to the Web service
- a definition of the result elements

A service object declaration can be embedded as a part of every other element. If a unit is navigated to ("created"), first the service objects will be executed. The results of the service object either will be directly integrated into the AM and treated as such, or the result can be bound to variables. Service objects can use unit variables in their calls.

10.4.10 Model Builders

In most RDF serializations it can become difficult to see which structures
belong together and what the general structure of the document is, especially
as the documents get larger. This also applies to the Hera models and has the
consequence that manually creating them can become error-prone. It is
therefore beneficial to offer the designer tool support for creating those
models graphically. Based on a given HPG version, Hera Studio (Figure
10.5) contains a domain, context, and application model editor in which the
designer can specify the models in a graphical way. All these models can
subsequently be exported to an RDF serialization that can be used by Hera.

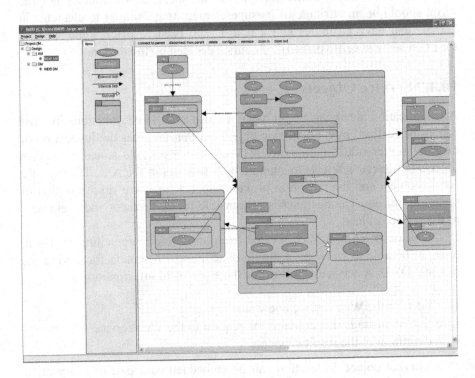

Figure 10.5. Hera Studio.

Note that Hera Studio is not a general-purpose OWL or RDF(S) editor
such as Protégé, for instance; rather, it is a custom-made version specialized
for Web applications designed through Hera models.

In the DM editor (Figure 10.6), designers can define classes and object
properties between those classes. For every class, a number of data type
properties can be given that have a specified media type (e.g., String, Image,
etc.). Furthermore, inheritance relations for classes and properties can be

denoted. In addition, instances of the classes and properties can be specified. Note that if more complex constructs are needed, the designer could also use a general-purpose OWL/RDF editor like Protégé.

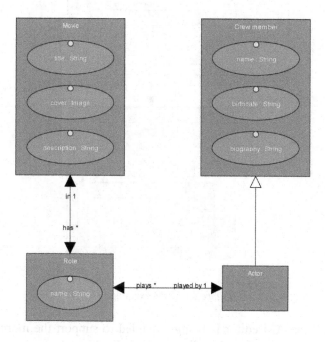

Figure 10.6. DM example.

The AM editor provides a graphical way for specifying an AM (Figure 10.7 gives an example). It specifically allows organizing the units and the relationships between them. Per unit, elements can be defined and displayed. Detailed information like queries is hidden in the graphical view and can be configured by double-clicking the elements. For the simpler constructs, the editor provides direct help: For example, when defining a data type property, the editor gives the designer a straightforward selection choice from the (inherited) data type properties of the underlying context and domain models. However, for the more complex constructs, the designer has the freedom to express his own queries and element properties. In addition, the designer can control the model's level of detail to get a better overview of the complete model.

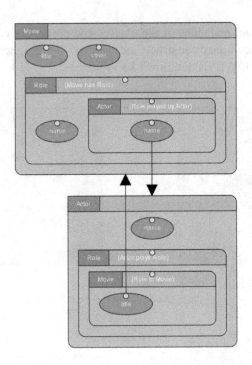

Figure 10.7. AM example.

Currently, the AM editor is being extended to support the more specific Hera-S constructs mentioned in this section. In this process, we will also extend the model-checking functionality that allows the designer to check if the Web application fulfills certain requirements. Furthermore, we plan to extend the builders with an optional lightweight presentation component.

10.5 ASPECT ORIENTATION IN MODEL DESIGN

Before we continue with presentation design and implementation, we make a side step and turn to an element of design support that we are currently working on and that uses principles from aspect orientation.

As described in the previous sections, Hera-S provides conceptual WIS design support on the basis of data contained in an RDF repository like Sesame and that are accessed and manipulated through an RDF query language like SeRQL. In this setting, adaptation is specified by SeRQL queries that, based on (DM and) CM data, conditionally instantiate navigational units in the AM. Examples of such an adaptation can be found in Section 10.4.3. In most cases, the desired adaptation is expressed by expressions that are embedded in the SeRQL query and that have the explicit purpose of restricting the set of instances; we can call these expressions *adaptation conditions*. We observe that often these adaptation conditions can conceptually be detached from the rest of the SeRQL queries and explicitly specified at (AM) model level. In this way, with each AM modeling element (i.e., units, relationships) we can nicely associate its adaptation conditions that explicitly denote the restriction of this element according to the user model's attributes/values.

Typically, in a Web application several adaptation issues need to be taken into account in parallel (e.g., age-group restriction, accessibility, device dependence). Adaptation engineering thus constitutes a significant effort in specifying the application's functionality. Moreover, although the adaptation conditions for an adaptation issue can occur at one specific place in the design (e.g., to restrict adult-rated material on a certain page), it is (more) often the case that they cannot be pinpointed to one particular element (e.g., when one does not want anything on the site to show adult-rated material to minors) and need to be applied at different places in the design (models). Concretely, consider the last example from Section 10.4.3, which restricts the list of movies starring a particular actor. Obviously, the designer may be required to specify other lists of movies (e.g., in the am:CinemaUnit, to denote the movies played in a particular cinema) also at other places in the design. To enforce the age-group restriction policy throughout the application or Web site, the designer thus needs to incorporate the necessary conditions in all SeRQL queries involving the selection of movies (or any other content that may be age-restricted, e.g., adult actors).

A similar observation was made in (regular) software development, when considering different design concerns of an application: Some concerns cannot be localized to a particular class or module; instead they are inherently distributed over the whole application. Such a concern is called a *cross-cutting* concern. To cleanly separate the programming code addressing this concern from the regular application code, aspect-oriented programming (Kiczales et al., 1997) was introduced. Inspired by the principles of aspect orientation, Hera-S provides (adaptation) design support to specify, in an aspect-oriented way, the different cross-cutting adaptation concerns by means of an aspect-oriented adaptation specification.

Applying aspect orientation to extend an AM with different additional adaptation concerns is thus done by modeling each concern as an *aspect*. Each aspect is composed of a number of advice-pointcut pairs. In this setting, the notions of advice and pointcut are as follows:

- *Advice*: Advice specifies a particular transformation in terms of modifications to the different (navigational) elements of the AM. In most cases, a single modification will add a single adaptation condition to certain navigational units or relationships in the form of an SeRQL query.

- *Pointcut*: A pointcut defines a query on the set of navigational units and relationships of an application model, which specifies exactly the elements to which certain advice should be applied.

These advice-pointcut pairs can thus be used to inject adaptation conditions to (certain elements of) the AM. It is a current research topic to investigate the limitations of this process of transforming these adaptation conditions in the corresponding SeRQL queries, a restricted form of what is called *weaving* in aspect terminology.

To exemplify this approach, we illustrate how two additional adaptation concerns, age-group (restriction) and device dependence, can be specified in an aspect-oriented way over an (existing, in this case non-adaptive) AM. For the first adaptation aspect, namely age-group (restriction), let us express the motivating example mentioned earlier in this section: Restrict visibility of all adult-rated, i.e., NC-17-rated, content throughout the application, and only show it when the user's age has been confirmed to be above 17. In an aspect-oriented way, this adaptation strategy is specified as follows:

```
POINTCUT SET WITH PARENT cm:movie
ADVICE
  SELECT M
  FROM {M} am:MPAA-rating {R}; rdf:type {imdb:Movie}
  WHERE R != 'NC-17'
  OR EXISTS
    (SELECT * FROM  {$U} cm:age {G}
    WHERE G > 17)
```

This pointcut-advice pair specifies first the pointcut: wherever in the AM a navigational unit is used that represents a set of movie elements (i.e., the pointcut part). In all these places (in the advice) a condition is added in the form of an SeRQL expression, which denotes that the age (an attribute from the CM) should be over 17 to view NC-17-rated material. Similar pointcut-advice pairs can be specified to restrict visibility of items with other MPAA ratings. Note that any movie set, wherever it appears in the AM, is restricted: The adaptation is not localized to one particular navigational unit and is thus truly cross-cutting.

The semantics of this condition addition is that this query expression is performed after the one that was defined originally for this element. Concretely, interpretation and execution of the above aspect result in modification of the SeRQL queries instantiating (a set of) movies. Note that the last example of Section 10.4.3 is one particular occurrence of such a set of movies, for which the adaptation was manually specified by the designated SeRQL query. However, to achieve automatic *weaving* of aspects, a more generic *pipeline approach* is best suited. In this approach, the original (non-adaptive) query expression Q producing the set of instances (i.e., movies in this case) is taken as a starting point. Subsequently, each adaptation condition C_i specified for this set gives rise to an SeRQL query Q_i that takes as input the result of the previous query $Q_{(i-1)}$ and filters from this result the element according to the adaptation condition C_i. For adaptation conditions C_1 ... C_n specified for a set, and possibly originating from different adaptation issues, the resulting query will thus be of the form $Q_n \circ Q_{(n-1)} \circ ... \circ Q_1 \circ Q$. Evidently, other approaches, such as query rewriting or query merging, are possible.

A second example concerns device dependence: In order not to overload small-screen users (e.g., PDA users), we decided not to show pictures. Therefore, we can specify the following pointcut-advice pair:

```
POINTCUT ATTRIBUTE
ADVICE
  SELECT P
  FROM {P} hera:Mime {} hera:mimeType {T}
  WHERE T != 'image\*'
  OR EXISTS
    (SELECT * FROM {$U} cm:device {D}
                WHERE D != 'pda')
```

In the pointcut, all attributes from the AM are selected. For these attributes, in the advice part, the picture attributes (denoted by the mime-type specification as mentioned in Section 10.4.2) are filtered out for PDA users, restricting their visibility for these PDA users. Note that, once again, our example addresses a truly cross-cutting concern: Anywhere in the AM where a picture attribute is used, it will be filtered out for PDA users.

To conclude this section on aspect-oriented adaptation support, we would like to point out that the primary way of defining adaptation, namely to manually specify it in the AM by means of SeRQL queries, as was illustrated in Section 10.4, is still available to the designer. The aspect-oriented support presented here merely offers the designer an additional and alternative means of specifying, in a straightforward and distributed way, the adaptation conditions for (sets of) AM elements.

10.6 IMPLEMENTATION

After illustrating the AM design, we now turn to the engine implementing the model, i.e., generating the hypermedia views over the content according to what is specified in the AM. As explained in Section 10.1, we distinguish three implementations for the Hera models. The Hera-S implementation is based on our previous experiences with the Hera Presentation Generator (HPG) (Frasincar, 2005), an environment that supports the construction of WIS using the Hera methodology. Considering the technologies used to implement Hera's data transformations, we distinguish two variants of the HPG: HPG-XSLT, which implements the data transformations using XSLT stylesheets, and HPG-Java, which implements the data transformations using Java. In HPG-XSLT we employed as an XSLT processor Saxon, one of the most up-to-date XSLT processors implementing XSLT 2.0. In HPG-Java we used two Java libraries, the Sesame library for querying the Hera models and the Jena library for building the new models. Hera-S resembles in many ways HPG-Java, but it is based on the revision of the Hera models presented in this paper.

10.6.1 HPG-XSLT and HPG-Java

First we take a look at the tools for HPG-XSLT and HPG-Java that build the foundation for Hera-S. HPG-XSLT has an intuitive designer's interface, visualizing the Hera pipeline for the development of a Web application (see Figure 10.8). The user is guided in a sequence of steps to create the complete Web application, which, generated with XSLT stylesheets, results in a concrete, but static, Web site for a given platform. In the interface we see that each step in this advanced HPG view is associated with a rectangle labeled with the step's name (e.g., Conceptual Model, Unfolding AM, Application Adaptation, etc.). In each step a number of buttons are connected with within-step arrows and between-step arrows that express the data flow. Such a button represents a transformation or input/output data depending on the associated label (e.g., Unfold AM is a transformation, Unfolding sheet AM is an input, and Unfolded AM is an output). The arrows that enter into a transformation (left, right, or top) represent the input, and the ones that exit from a transformation (bottom) represent the output. The last step is the generation of the presentation in the end format (e.g., HTML).

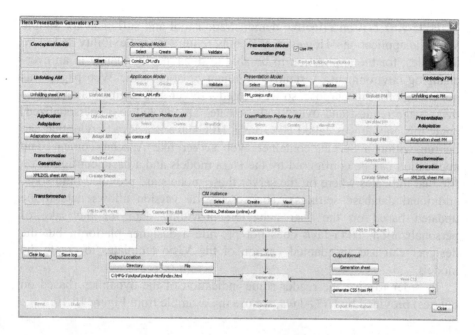

Figure 10.8. Screenshot from HPG-XSLT.

The models for HPG-XSLT can be created by hand but also with the help of Microsoft Visio templates, which provide a graphical environment to aid the correct construction of the different models (see Figure 10.9 for an example of the corresponding AM builder).

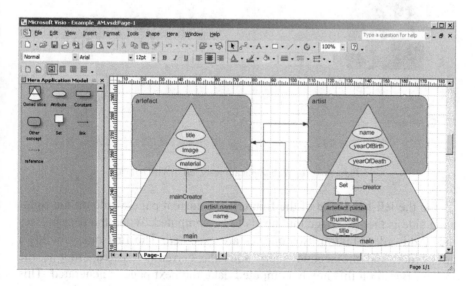

Figure 10.9. Visio templates HPG-XSLT.

HPG-XSLT is an effective demonstration tool and sufficient for simple Web site applications. However, WIS may require more flexibility and more dynamics, for the application to be able to dynamically change in an ever-changing environment. A standalone client creating static Web pages was not enough for this purpose, so we created a server-side engine that evaluates every page request and dynamically creates an adapted (e.g., personalized) page; this engine was called HPG-Java. HPG-Java is a Java Servlet that can be run within a Servlet container Web server like Apache Tomcat. The application can be configured by the Hera models and a basic configuration file that indicates where on the server these models are provided (and some additional database settings). The server-side version allows data to be updated based on the user behavior, providing data for the sake of personalization. HPG-Java does not provide a designer platform, but the designer can use an adapted version of the Visio templates to create the models.

In order to give the reader some indication of the dynamics (based on queries) provided by HPG-Java, we use the example from Figure 10.10.

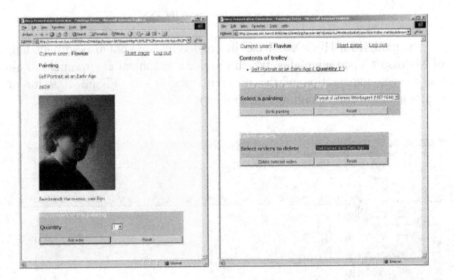

Figure 10.10. Web application served by HPG-Java.

On the left-hand side of the figure is the current page, while on the right-hand side is the next page that needs to be computed. When the user presses the "Add order" button, two queries are executed. The first query builds a new order, and the second query adds the currently created order to the trolley. Based on this newly computed data, the next page is generated. This new page displays the list of ordered paintings (based on the orders in the trolley) and also provides two forms. The first form allows the user to select the next painting, and the second form enables the user to delete an order previously added to the trolley.

10.6.2 Hera-S

As we have explained earlier, the architecture of the Hera-S version is similar to that from the earlier HPG-Java version, but obviously it accommodates the newer Hera-S AMs with their SeRQL queries. A major difference is that the AM is less tightly coupled to the domain, in the sense that the designer has more freedom to select elements and concepts in the domain by the use of the SeRQL queries. Furthermore, we allow the domain to be any repository of RDF data (i.e., no proprietary data model). Note that this does not only apply to the domain, but also to the context. The implementation is again a Java servlet; however, storage and manipulation of all the meta-models are now handled by different Sesame repositories.

Furthermore, the Hera-S implementation concentrates on the application-model level only. Several presentation modules exist (Section 10.7 will go into more details) that can configure the presentation of AM data, each with outstanding features that might be more appropiate in different situations. Having separate implementations allows a presentation module to be plugged into the pipeline that fits the situation, thus also making Hera-S more platform-independent.

In Figure 10.11 we see the main components that make up the Hera-S implementation architecture. The domain model (DM), application model (AM), and all context data are realized as Sesame repositories, exploiting Sesame's capability that enables storage, reasoning, and querying of RDF and OWL data.

The content is interfaced to the rest of the system through the DM repository. A major advantage of this approach is that integrated querying of both schema and instance data becomes possible. To enable this, the content has to be represented as RDF statements. For non-RDF content repositories, this can be achieved in various ways. The simplest and most straightforward case is an offline translation of the data to RDF and simply storing that RDF in a Sesame repository. However, this approach has a drawback for certain cases by duplicating data, which means that updates to the data need to happen in two places. An alternative way of realizing the link between DM and data is by creating a wrapper component around the actual data source that does online back-and-forth translation. The Sesame architecture caters for this scenario by having a storage abstraction layer called the SAIL API (Broekstra et al., 2002). A simple wrapper component around virtually any data source

can be realized as a SAIL implementation and then be integrated effortlessly
into the rest of the Sesame framework and thus into our Hera-S environment.

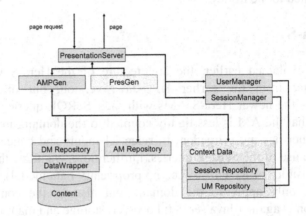

Figure 10.11. Hera-S architecture.

The entire system has an event-driven architecture. When a request for a
certain page comes in at the PresentationServer component, the request is
translated to a request for an AMP. At the same time, the UserManager and
SessionManager components are informed of the request. These two
manager components can then take appropriate actions in updating the
context data repositories [specifically, the UM (user model) Repository, and
the Session Repository].

Independently from this, the so-called AMPGen component retrieves the
requested part of the AM that contains the conceptual specification that is
the basis for the next AMP. It then starts the AMP creation process by
following that specification.

The actual AMP is internally implemented as a volatile (in-memory)
Sesame repository, which means that all transformation operations on it can
simply be carried out as RDF queries and graph manipulations using the
SeRQL query language. When the AMP has been fully constructed, it is sent
back to the presentation-generation component. This presentation-generation
component can then transform the AMP into an actual page (in terms that a
thin client such as a Web browser can understand, e.g., XHTML). The result
is then finally sent back to the client (as the response).

In the Hera-S system, SeRQL query expressions are extensively used to
define mappings and filters between the different data sources and the
eventual AMP. Since all these data are expressed as RDF graphs, an RDF
query/transformation language is a natural choice as a mapping tool.

In Section 10.7 we will describe a presentation-generation process that uses the AMP as input to generate a presentation for different user platforms. It will also show a screenshot from an application that can be generated with the Hera-S engine in combination with that presentation-generation solution. Via the feedback mechanism, built-in as parameters in the links, user actions will trigger subsequent actions in the Hera-S engine (i.e., presentation generation typically does not interfere with this process).

10.7 PRESENTATION DESIGN

In this section we address one particular approach to presentation design. The presentation design step of Hera bridges the gap between the logical level from the AM and the actual implementation. If needed, the presentation model (PM) can specify the details of this transformation. Complementary to the AM, where the designer is concerned with the structure of the information and functionality as it needs to be presented to the user (by identifying navigational units and relationships), the PM specifies how the content of those navigation units is displayed. According to these specifications, AMPs can be transformed to a corresponding Web presentation in a given output format, e.g., XHTML, cHTML, WML, etc. We do stress that we foresee multiple alternative ways to render AMPs in specific output formats, and the designer is free to choose a way to configure this transformation of AMPs into output. In this section we illustrate one particular way, which uses a PM to detail the presentation design and which is implemented using a particular document format for adaptive Web presentations.

10.7.1 Presentation Model Specification

The PM is defined by means of so-called regions and relationships between regions. Regions are abstractions for rectangular parts of the user display and thus satisfy browsing platform constraints. They group navigational units from the AM; like navigation units, regions can be defined recursively. They are further specified by a layout manager, a style, and references to the navigational units that they aggregate. We note that the usage of layout managers was inspired by the AMACONT project's component-based document format (Fiala et al., 2003), adopting its abstract layout manager concept in the Hera PM. As will be explained in Section 10.7.2, this enables us to use AMACONT's flexible presentation capabilities for the generation of a Web presentation.

Figure 10.12 shows an excerpt of the PM for the running example, i.e., the regions associated to the MovieUnit navigational unit and its subregions.

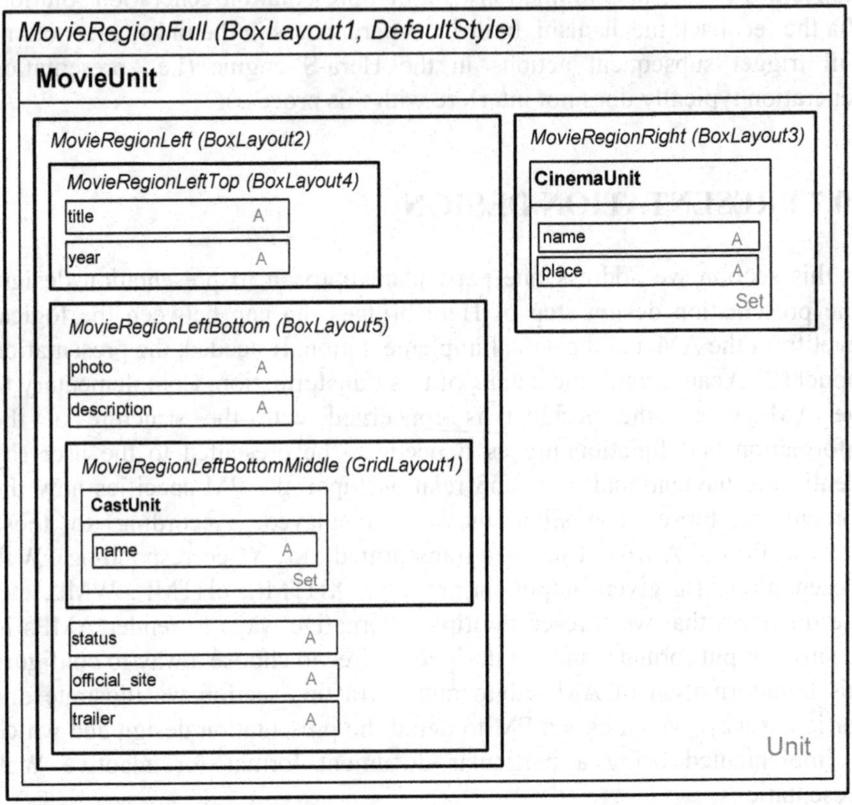

Figure 10.12. Presentation model for the MovieUnit navigational unit.

The MovieUnit navigational unit is associated with the region called MovieRegionFull. It uses the layout manager BoxLayout1 for the arrangements of its subregions (MovieRegionLeft and MovieRegionRight) and the style given by DefaultStyle. BoxLayout1 is an instance of the layout manager class BoxLayout that allows us to lay out the subregions of a region either vertically or (as in this case) horizontally. The style describes the font characteristics (size, color), background (color), hyperlink colors, etc. to be used in a region. The definition of styles was inspired by Cascading Style Sheets (CSS) (Bos et al., 2005). We chose to abstract the CSS formatting attributes because (1) not every browser supports CSS at the current moment and (2) we would like to have a representation of the style that can be customized based on user preferences.

Both MovieRegionLeft and MovieRegionRight use BoxLayout's with a vertical organization of their inner regions. For the title and year attributes, BoxLayout4 is used, which specifies a horizontal arrangement. For photo, description (the region containing the names in the cast), status, official_site, and trailer, BoxLayout5 is used, which indicates a vertical arrangement. The names in the cast are organized using GridLayout1 (an instance of the layout manager class GridLayout), a grid with four columns and an unspecified number of rows. The number of rows was purposely left unspecified, as one does not know a priori (i.e., before the presentation is instantiated and generated) how many names the cast of a movie will have. The regions that do not have a particular style associated with them inherit the style of their container region. Note that in Figure 10.12 we have omitted constant units [e.g., (,), Cast, etc.] in order to simplify the explanation.

Besides the layout manager classes exemplified in Figure 10.12, the definition of PM supports additional ones. BorderLayout arranges subregions to fit in five directions: north, south, east, west, and center. OverlayLayout allows us to present regions on top of each other. FlowLayout places the inner regions in the same way as words are placed on a page: The first line is filled from left to right, and the same is done for the second line, etc. TimeLayout presents the contained regions as a slide show and can be used only on browsers that support time sequences of items, e.g., HTML+TIME (Schmitz et al., 1998) or SMIL (Bulterman et al., 2005). Due to the flexibility of the approach, this list can be extended with other layout managers that future applications might need.

The specification of regions allows us to define the application's presentation in an implementation-independent way. However, to cope with users' different layout preferences and client devices, Hera-S also supports different kinds of adaptation in presentation design. As an example, based on the capabilities of the user's client device (screen size, supported document formats, etc.), the spatial arrangement of regions can be adapted. Another adaptation target is the corporate design (the "look-and-feel") of the resulting Web pages. According to the preferences and/or visual impairments of users, style elements like background colors, fonts (size, color, type), or buttons can be varied. For a thorough elaboration of presentation-layer adaptation, the reader is referred to Fiala et al. (2004).

Turning back to our running example, we now consider how to adapt the PM for the MovieUnit navigational unit to the typical small display size and horizontal resolution of a handheld device. In this respect, we aim at replacing the layout managers BoxLayout1 and GridLayout1 with BoxLayout's specifying vertical arrangements for their containment elements. Note that the PM facilitates specifying such adaptations by the assignment of multiple layout or style alternatives (variants) as simple conditions attached to "region-layout manager assignments," in correspondence with the adaptation conditions of the AMACONT document format. These conditions are simple Boolean expressions consisting of constants, arithmetic and logical operators, as well as references to context model parameters.

10.7.2 Presentation Generation Implementation

After the specification of the PM, we now turn to its implementation. As mentioned above, we illustrate it by using the AMACONT project's component-based document model, which is perfectly suited for this task as this PM was based on AMACONT presentation principles in the first place. This approach aims at implementing personalized ubiquitous Web applications by aggregating and linking configurable document components. These are instances of an XML grammar representing adaptable content on different abstraction levels. Media components encapsulate concrete media assets (text, structured text, images, videos, HTML fragments, CSS) by describing them with technical meta-data. Content units group media components by declaring their layout in a device-independent way. Document components define a hierarchy from content units to fulfill a semantic role. Finally, the hyperlink view defines links that are spanned over components. For more details on the AMACONT document model, the reader is referred to Fiala et al. (2003).

Whereas the AMACONT document model provides different adaptation mechanisms, in this chapter we focus on its presentation support. For this purpose it allows us to attach XML-based abstract layout descriptions (layout managers) to components. Document components with such abstract layout descriptions can be automatically transformed to a Web presentation in a given Web output format. As mentioned above, the PM was specified by adopting AMACONT's layout manager concept to the model level. This enables the automatic translation of AMPs to a component-based Web presentation based on a PM specification. The corresponding presentation generation pipeline is illustrated in Figure 10.13.

In a first transformation step (AMP to component) the AMPs are translated to hierarchical AMACONT document component structures. In doing so, both the aggregation hierarchy and the layout attributes of the created AMACONT components are configured according to the PM configuration. Beginning at top-level document components and visiting their subcomponents recursively, the appropriate AMACONT layout descriptors (with adaptation variants) are added to each document component. This transformation can be performed in a straightforward way and was already described in detail by Fiala et al. (2004). The automatically created AMACONT documents are then processed by AMACONT's document generation pipeline. In a first step, all adaptation variants are resolved according to the current state of the context model. Second, a Web presentation in a given Web output format (e.g., XHTML, XHTML Basic, cHTML, or WML) is created and delivered to the client.

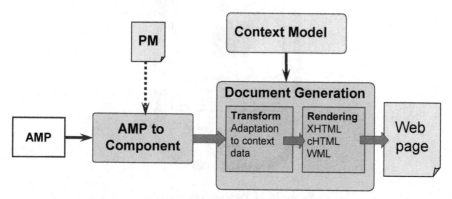

Figure 10.13. Presentation generation with AMACONT.

Figure 10.14 illustrates the XHTML page generated for the PC version of our running example. It represents an instantiation of the Movie navigational unit with data used for "The Matrix" movie. It also shows the cinemas that are currently playing this movie.

Note that the presentation of content elements corresponds to the PM specification that was illustrated in Figure 10.12.

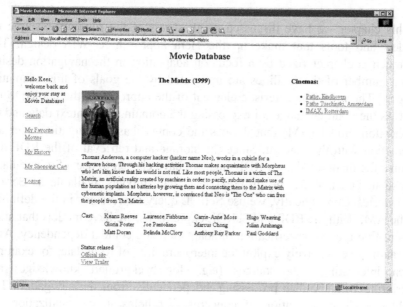

Figure 10.14. Presentation on a PC.

Figure 10.15. Presentation on a PDA.

As an alternative, Figure 10.15 shows the same page as presented on a PDA, exemplifying the layout adaptation. As can be seen, the resulting presentation is in correspondence with the PM adaptation specified above, i.e., all content elements are displayed below each other.

10.8 SUMMARY

In this chapter we have discussed on the basis of the running example the models and tools that make up the Hera approach to WIS design. This approach is characterized by a focus on adaptation in the navigation design, and a number of the facilities are motivated by the goals of this adaptation support. The most characteristic element of the approach is the choice to use RDF as the main language for expressing the domain and context data and the application model (AM) that defines the context-based navigation over and interaction with the content. Since the storage and retrieval of the RDF data involve the manipulation of RDF data, we have chosen to use a Sesame-based approach, i.e., making the different RDF data models available as Sesame repositories. Consequently, we use SeRQL query expressions in the definition of the AM. With the RDF and SeRQL expressions, we have models that allow a more fine-grained specification of adaptation and context dependency. Also, we can more extensively exploit the interoperability of RDF data, for example, when integrating data sources (e.g., for background knowledge) and interfering with the data processing independently from the navigation. This enables a clean separation of concerns that helps in personalization and adaptation and in the inclusion of external data sources.

REFERENCES

Beckett, D., 2004, *Turtle: Terse RDF Triple Language.* Technical report. http://www.dajobe.org/2004/01/turtle/.

Bos, B., Çelik, T., Hickson, I., and Lie, H.W., 2005, *Cascading Style Sheets, level 2 revision 1*, CSS 2.1 specification, W3C Working Draft, June 13.

Brickley, D., and Guha, R.V., 2004, *RDF Vocabulary Description Language 1.0: RDF Schema.* W3C Recommendation, Feb. 10. http://www.w3.org/TR/rdf-schema/.

Broekstra, J., Kampman, A.. and van Harmelen, F., 2002, Sesame: An architecture for storing and querying RDF and RDF schema. *Proceedings First International Semantic Web Conference, ISWC2002*, Sardinia, Italy, June 9-12, Springer-Verlag Lecture Notes in Computer Science (LNCS) no. 2342, pp. 54–68. http://www.openrdf.org/.

Broekstra, J., 2005, SeRQL: A second-generation RDF query language. Chapter 4 in Storage, Querying and Inferencing for Semantic Web Languages, PhD thesis, Vrije Universiteit Amsterdam, ISBN 90-9019-236-0. http://www.openrdf.org/doc/SeRQLmanual.html.

Bulterman, D., Grassel, G., Jansen, J., Koivisto, A., Layaïda, N., Michel, T., Mullender, S., and Zucker, D., 2005, *Synchronized Multimedia Integration Language (SMIL 2.1)*, W3C Recommendation Dec. 13.

Chipman, A., Goodell, J., Harpring, P., Beecroft, A., Johnson, R., and Ward, J., 2005, *Getty Thesaurus of Geographic Names: Editorial Guidelines.* Available at http://www.getty.edu/research/conducting_research/vocabularies/guidelines/tgn_1_contents_intro.pdf.

Dean, M., and Schreiber, G., 2004, *The OWL Web Ontology Language Reference.* W3C Recommendation, Feb. 10. http://www.w3.org/TR/owl-ref/.

Fiala, Z., Frasincar, F., Hinz, M., Houben, G.J., Barna, P., and Meissner, K., 2004, Engineering the presentation layer of adaptable Web information systems. *International Conference on Web Engineering, ICWE 2004*, July 28-30, Munich, Germany, Springer-Verlag Berlin Heidelberg, LNCS 3140, pp. 459–472.

Fiala, Z., Hinz, M., Meißner, K.. and Wehner, F., 2003, A component-based approach for adaptive, dynamic Web documents. *Journal of Web Engineering,* **2**(1&2): 58–73.

Frasincar, F., 2005, Hypermedia Presentation Generation for Semantic Web Information Systems, PhD thesis, Chapter 4 (Hera Presentation Generator), Eindhoven University of Technology Press Facilities, ISBN 90-386-0594-3, pp. 67–87.

Hart, L., Emery, P., Colomb, B., Raymond, K., Taraporewalla, S., Chang, D., Ye, Y., Kendall, E., and Dutra, M., 2004, OWL full and UML 2.0 compared. http://www.itee.uq.edu.au/~colomb/Papers/UML-OWLont04.03.01.pdf.

Hobbs, J.R., and Pan, F., 2004, An ontology of time for the Semantic Web. *ACM Transactions on Asian Language Information Processing, TALIP,* 3(1): 66–85.

Kiczales, G., Lamping, J., Mendhekar, A., Maeda, C., Lopes, C., Loingtier, J.M., and Irwin, J., 1997, Aspect-oriented programming. *Proceedings 11th European Conference on Object-Oriented Programming, ECOOP'97*, Jyväskylä, Finland, pp. 220–242.

Klyne, G.. and Carrol, J., 2004, *Resource Description Framework (RDF): Concepts and Abstract Syntax.* W3C Recommendation, Feb. 10. http://www.w3.org/TR/rdf-concepts/.

Miller, G.A., 1995, Wordnet: A lexical database for English. *Communications of the ACM,* **38**(11): 39–41.

Schmitz, P., Yu, J., and Santangeli, P., 1998, *Timed Interactive Multimedia Extensions for HTML (HTML+TIME)*, W3C Note Sept. 18.

Thiran, P., Hainaut, J.L., and Houben, G.J., 2005, Database wrappers development: Towards automatic generation. *Ninth European Conference on Software Maintenance and Reengineering, CSMR'05*, Manchester, UK, IEEE CS Press, pp. 207–216.

Chapter 11

WSDM: WEB SEMANTICS DESIGN METHOD

Olga De Troyer, Sven Casteleyn, Peter Plessers
Research Group WISE, Department of Computer Science, Vrije Universiteit Brussel, Pleinlaan 2, 1050 Brussels, Belgium

11.1 WSDM OVERVIEW

WSDM was introduced by De Troyer and Leune in 1998 (De Troyer and Leune, 1998). At that time the acronym stood for **Web Site Design Method** and only targeted information-providing Web sites. In the meantime, the method has evolved a great deal and now also allows traditional Web applications as well as Semantic Web applications to be designed, hence the renaming of the method into **Web Semantics Design Method**.

More than other Web design methods, WSDM is a methodology, i.e., it not only provides modeling primitives that allow a Web developer to construct models that describe the Web site/application from different perspectives and at different levels of abstraction, but it also provides a systematic way to develop the Web application. Developing a Web site/application with WSDM starts with the formulation of the so-called mission statement and follows a well-defined design philosophy that offers the designer the necessarily support to structure the Web site. The method consists of a sequence of phases. Each phase has a well-defined output. For each phase, a (sub)method describing how to derive the output from its input is provided. The output of one phase is the input of a following phase. As already indicated, currently the method allows the development of Web sites as well as Web applications. For the sake of simplicity, we will use the term "Web systems" to indicate both Web sites and Web applications. It is also important to notice that WSDM allows us to develop Web systems that are semantically annotated, in this way effectively enabling the Semantic Web. Content-related (semantic) annotations as well as structural annotations can be generated. Content-related annotations make the semantics of the content explicit. Structural annotations are annotations that explicitly describe the semantics of the different structural elements of the Web systems. Structural annotations can be exploited by third parties to transcode the Web system to a different format, for example to formats appropriate for a screen reader, or they can be exploited by search engines for their page segmentation [see, e.g., Deng et al. (2004) for an overview of page segmentation by search engines].

WSDM follows an *audience-driven* design approach. An audience-driven design philosophy means that the different target audiences (visitors) and their requirements are taken as starting point for the design and that the main structure of the Web site is derived from this. Concretely, this results in different navigation paths (called audience tracks) offered from the home page, one for each different kind of visitor.

Figure 11.1 shows an overview of the different phases of WSDM. The different phases are shown sequentially. However, in practice, the design process is rather iterative. In this section a brief description of the different phases is given. In the following sections the different phases are explained into more detail and illustrated with examples from this book's common example, the Internet Movies Database Web site,[1] or IMDb for short. Note that it is not realistic and also not the purpose to redesign the entire system here. Simplifications made were necessarily to reduce the size of the drawings and the examples.

In the first phase of the method, the mission statement specification, the mission statement for the Web system is formulated. The goal of this phase is to identify the purpose of the Web system, as well as the subject and the target users. Without giving due consideration to the purpose, there is no proper basis for making design decisions or for evaluating the effectiveness of the Web system. The target users are the users whom we want to address or who will be interested in the Web system. The subject of the Web system is, of course, related to the purpose and the target users of the Web system. The subject must allow fulfilling the purpose of the Web system, and it must be adapted for the target users. The output of this phase is the *mission statement*. It is formulated in natural language and must describe the purpose, subject, and target users of the Web systems. In fact, the mission statement establishes the borders of the design process. It allows (in the following phases) deciding which information or functionality to include or exclude, how to structure it, and how to present it.

---

[1] http://www.imdb.com.

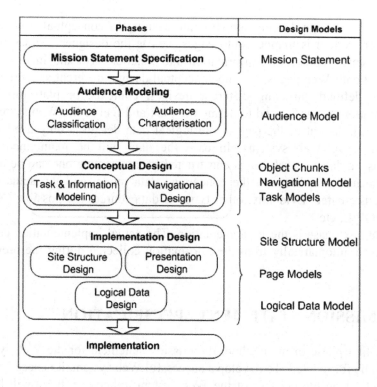

Figure 11.1. WSDM overview.

The next phase is the audience modeling phase. The target users identified in the mission statement are refined into *audience classes*. This means that the different types of users are further identified and classified into audience classes. The classification is based on the requirements of the different users. Users with the same information and functional requirements become members of the same audience class. Users with additional requirements form audience subclasses. In this way a hierarchy of audience classes is constructed. For each audience class, relevant characteristics (e.g., age, experience level) are given.

The next phase, the conceptual design, is used to specify the information, functionality, and structure of the Web system at a conceptual level. A conceptual design makes an abstraction from any implementation technology or target platform. The information and functionality are specified during the task & information modeling subphase. The overall conceptual structure including the navigational possibilities for each audience class is specified during the navigational design subphase.

During the implementation design phase, the conceptual design models are complemented with information required for an actual implementation. It consists of three subphases: site structure design, presentation design, and logical data design. During site structure design, the conceptual structure of the Web system is mapped onto pages, i.e., is the designer decides which components (representing information and functionality) and links will be grouped onto Web pages. For the conceptual design, different site structures can be defined, targeting different devices, contexts, or platforms. The presentation design is used to define the look and feel of the Web system as well as the layout of the pages. The logical data design is only needed for data-intensive Web systems. In case the data will be maintained in a database, a database schema is constructed (or an existing one can be used), and the mapping between the conceptual data model and the actual data source is created. Evidently, other types of data sources are possible (XML, RDF, OWL, etc.).

The last phase is the implementation. The actual implementation can be generated automatically from the information collected during the previous phases.

11.2 MISSION STATEMENT SPECIFICATION

In the first phase of the method, the mission statement for the Web system should be formulated. To develop a successful Web system, it is necessary to first reflect on the purpose of the Web system; otherwise, there will be no proper basis for making design decisions or for evaluating the effectiveness of the Web system. For example, for a company, the purpose may range from simply "having an identity on the Web," to "advertising some of its products," to "provide a full-fledged e-shop"; for public and local authorities, it may range from providing general information to a full-fledged e-government system that allows users to arrange official matters (e.g., apply for official documents) using the Web. The purpose should be established in consultation with the different stakeholders.

The different stakeholders should also agree on the topics that should be covered by the Web system. Even if the purpose is clear, it may be necessary to explicitly name the topics the system will deal with. For example, a company may decide to offer online information about products but only for their products in a higher price range. Another example is a high school that decides only to offer information about its educational system and courses, but not about its research activities.

Furthermore, the target users should also be identified. In principle, everybody can visit a public Web site, including people for whom the Web site is not relevant. However, it is impossible to satisfy the expectations of each possible visitor. It is better to focus on the users needed to make the Web system successful, called the *target users*. For example, consider a company that only sells very specialized technical items. In this case, the

Web site should focus on the people who need these products. These people are likely not the general public but instead probably very technical and specialized people. When building a Web system for a university, an important group of users you probably want to address are potential students.

It is clear that the purpose, subject (topics), and the target users are highly related. The subject and the target users of the Web system must allow the purpose to be fulfilled, and the subject must be suitable for the target users. So, one may argue that if the purpose is stated, the topics and target users are implicitly stated as well. However, to avoid misunderstandings, it is better to explicitly identify all three aspects of the mission statement. The mission statement is formulated in natural language.

Later on, in the following phases, the mission statement serves as the basis to decide what information or functionality to include (or not), how to structure it, and how to present it. Information or functionality that is not needed for the purpose or is not covered by the subject should not be considered. How to present and structure information and functionality is highly dependent on the target users, e.g., information should be presented and organized differently to professionals than to a common public. In addition, the mission statement can be used during validation to check if the Web system has indeed achieved the formulated purpose.

To illustrate this phase, we have formulated a mission statement for the example Web system. Currently, imdb.com mainly focuses on movies, but there is also a part about games. Therefore, the mission statement is formulated as follows:

> To be the biggest and best movie and game site on earth. For movies, this will be achieved by providing as much information as possible on movies, including their actors, directors, and producers, as well as to provide news, allow exploring show times, buy tickets in selected cinemas, and to share personal opinions about movies. For games, information about games is offered as well as news, and game lovers should be able to exchange information.

This mission statement defines the purpose, subject, and target users as follows:

- **Purpose**: to be the biggest and best movie and game site by (1) providing information and news on movies and games, (2) allowing users to explore show times of movies and to buy tickets, and (3) allowing movie lovers and game lovers to share personal opinions and exchange information.
- **Subject**: movies and related information such as actors, directors, and producers; selected cinemas; games.
- **Target users**: movie lovers and game lovers.

As you may have noticed, the purpose may involve multiple goals. Here, the stakeholders want to realize their long-term purpose (to be the biggest and best movie and game site) by means of three (related) goals. The subject may also deal with different topics. Here, movies as well as cinemas and games are considered. Also, the target users may be composed of different groups. Here, two different groups of users are involved: movie lovers and game lovers.

11.3 AUDIENCE MODELING

The mission statement formulated in the first phase is only a first and very incomplete description of the system that should be developed. Because WSDM is an audience-driven design method, the first concern that is elaborated is the set of target users. The target users identified in the mission statement are refined into *audience classes*. This is done by means of two subphases: the audience classification and the audience characterization. During audience classification, the different types of users are identified in more detail and classified into so-called audience classes. During audience characterization, relevant characteristics are specified for each audience class. We describe each subphase in more detail in the following subsection, but first we discuss why it is important to distinguish between different types of users.

In general, a Web system has different types of visitors who may have different needs. Consider as an example a university's Web site. Typical users of such a Web site are potential students, enrolled students, and researchers. Potential students are looking for general information about the university and the content of the different programs of study. The enrolled students need detailed information about the different courses, timetables, and contact information of the lecturers (telephone extension, room number, and contact hours). Researchers look for information on research projects and publications and general information on the researchers (full address, research interests, and research activities). This illustrates that different types of users (WSDM uses the term *audience class*) may have different information and/or functional requirements. To ensure good usability, this should be reflected in the Web system. For example, a student should be able to follow a navigation path that leads him to the information he is interested in without having to travel through pages of other (for him) nonrelevant information. If this is not the case and all information is provided to all users, a user has to scan the page(s) in order to find the links, the pages, and the pieces of information or functionality that are relevant for him. Providing too much nonrelevant information enhances the lost-in-hyperspace syndrome.

Next to the fact that different types of users may have different informational and functional requirements, it may be necessary to represent the (same) information or functionality in different ways to different kinds of users. This depends on the characteristics of the users. As an example, we again consider the university example. Potential students, especially secondary school students, are not familiar with the university jargon and should be addressed in a young and dynamic way. Also, by preference, the information should be offered in the native language. The enrolled students are familiar with the university jargon. They also prefer to have the information in the native language; however, for foreign students (e.g., who follow exchange programs) English should be used as the communication language. For researchers, it may be sufficient to use English. When the information and functionality are grouped based on the requirements of the different types of users, it is also possible to adapt the presentation to the characteristics of the different type of users without the need to rely on adaptive Web systems or personalization (Brusilovsky, 1996). Although for some situations, personalization may be undoubtedly the best solution, in other situations it may be less appropriate.

11.3.1 Audience Classification

The target users informally identified in the mission statement are the input for the audience classification. These target users are refined and classified into audience classes based on differences in their informational and functional requirements. All members of an audience class must have the same set of informational and functional requirements.

Sometimes, the set of informational and functional requirements of one audience class is a subset of the set of requirements of another audience class. To accommodate such situations, the concept of *audience subclass* is used. Figure 11.2 gives the graphical representation of an audience class and an audience subclass. Audience class B is an audience subclass of audience class A, which means that audience class B has all the same informational and functional requirements as audience class A but also some extra requirements. In other words, the set of requirements of audience class A is a subset of the set of requirement of audience (sub)class B. From the point of view of their populations, the population of the audience subclass is a subset of the population of the audience superclass. Indeed, the members of the audience subclass have more requirements than the members of the audience superclass, so these can only be fewer people.

Figure 11.2. Graphical representation of audience class and subclass.

WSDM prescribes two alternative methods for discovering the audience classes. The first method uses the activities of the organization for which the Web system needs to be developed and the role people play in these activities. Only activities that are related to the subject of the Web system are considered. Each activity involves people, who may be potential users for the Web system. These people should be identified. If they belong to the target users of the Web system, their requirements (informational as well as functional, usability, and navigational requirements) are formulated (in an informal way and at a high level). Users with the same informational and functional requirements become members of the same audience class. Whenever the informational and functional requirements of a set of users differ, a new audience class is defined or, if possible, an audience subclass is introduced. If possible, the activities are decomposed in order to refine the audience classes. This may introduce audience subclasses. The decomposition stops if no new subclasses emerge or if decomposition is not possible anymore. In summary, the method is as follows:

Step 1: Consider the activities of the organization related to the purpose of the Web system.
Step 2: For each activity,

1. Identify the people involved.
2. Restrict them to the target users.
3. Identify their requirements.
4. Divide them into audience classes based on different informational or functional requirements.
5. Decompose the activity if possible, and repeat Step 2.

In this way a hierarchy of audience classes is constructed. At the top of this *audience class hierarchy* we always place the audience class *Visitor*. The Visitor audience class represents all target users. The requirements associated with the Visitor class are the requirements that are common to all users.

The second method starts with identifying all possible informational and functional requirements of the target users, without wondering how to classify them into audience classes. The different audience classes and the subclass relations between them are derived from a matrix that is constructed using the different requirements as dimensions of the matrix. The cells in the matrix answer the question, "Does every user who has the requirement of this row also (always) have the requirement of this column?" Informally, every row i of such a matrix characterizes the users having the requirement associated with this row in terms of the other requirements they have. From this requirements matrix, the audience class hierarchy can be (automatically) derived as follows.

If two or more rows are exactly the same, this means that the users represented by these rows are the same in terms of possible requirements, and thus the users having these requirements should belong to the same audience class. If the set of "Y" entries of a row k is a subset of the "Y" entries of another row l, this means that the users represented by row l have the same requirements as the users represented by row k and some extra requirements. So, the audience class represented by row l is an audience subclass of the audience class represented by the row k.

This algorithm is formally specified in Casteleyn and De Troyer (2001). In summary, it looks as follows:

Step 1. Construct the audience class matrix based on all the requirements formulated for the Web system to be built.

Step 2. Determine the equivalence rows. Each set of equivalence row represents an audience class. The user requirements for this audience class are the requirements associated with the rows. Meaningful names should be given to the audience classes.

Step 3. Identify subset relations between the rows of the different equivalence classes. These subset relations result in audience subclass relations.

Step 4. Construct the integrated audience class hierarchy (using the audience classes and the audience subclass relations).

We now illustrate the audience classification phase for the IMDb example. We first illustrate the activity-based method and then the method based on the requirements matrix.

We suppose that IMDb is run by a separate organization. In this case, the activities of this organization could be

- Provide information about movies and games.
- Sell cinema tickets.
- Maintain information about movies and games.

The people (and other organizations) involved in these activities are movie lovers, game lovers, cinemas, and the organization's database administrators. Figure 11.3 illustrates this.

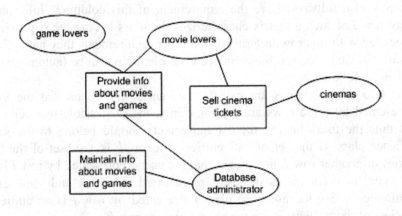

Figure 11.3. Activity diagram for the IMDb example.

The organization's database administrators are not part of the target users, and maintaining the information about movies and games is also not part of the purpose of the Web system. Therefore, the database administrators are not considered in the audience classification. The cinemas are involved in the activity "Sell cinema tickets" because the information about the movies, show times, and available seats must be synchronized with the ticket information of the cinemas. However, we suppose that this synchronization is done by means of interactions with the cinemas' information systems, for which no manual intervention is needed. Therefore, cinemas can also be discarded. This leaves us with the movie lovers and the game lovers. The requirements for these users can be specified as follows:

Movie lovers
1. To get an overview of the movies currently playing
2. To get an overview of the movies coming soon
3. To find a movie by means of a search function
4. To browse the movie database
5. To get an overview of new DVDs
6. To get an overview of DVDs coming soon
7. To obtain information about a movie
8. To obtain information about a person involved in a movie
9. To read news about movies
10. To have links to other interesting sites in relation to movies

11. To explore show times at different cinemas of movies currently playing
12. To buy tickets for a show time in a selected cinema
13. To manage a personal movie list
14. To post messages on the movie message boards
15. To enter a comment about a movie

Game lovers
1. To get an overview of games
2. To get information about a game
3. To read news about games
4. To have links to other interesting sites in relation to games
5. To post messages on the game message boards

The requirements for these two groups are sufficiently different to put them in separate audience classes. This results in two different audience classes: Movie Lover and Game Lover. Note that these classes don't need to be disjoint: A person may be a movie lover as well as a game lover. However, such a person will in general not want to look for movie information and game information at the same time. Also, in general, a movie lover is not necessarily a game lover, and vice versa.

There is no useful further decomposition for these activities. The resulting audience class hierarchy is shown in Figure 11.4. Note that Visitor is the top of the hierarchy.

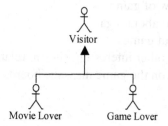

Figure 11.4. Audience class hierarchy for the IMDb example.

Some parts in the IMDb system require authorization to access and are protected by a login. Therefore, additional (authorization) requirements are needed. A user must be able to register; once he is registered, he is able to log in. Also logout must be possible. These are requirements common to the movie lovers and the game lovers and are therefore assigned to the Visitor class.

Visitor
1. To register
2. To log in
3. To log out

To use the matrix method to derive the (final) audience class hierarchy, we first have to list all informational and functional requirements of the target users, here being movie lovers and game lovers. These are defined as follows:

1. To get an overview of the movies currently playing
2. To get an overview of the movies coming soon
3. To find a movie by means of a search function
4. To browse the movie database
5. To get an overview of new DVDs
6. To get an overview of DVDs coming soon
7. To obtain information about a movie
8. To obtain information about an actor
9. To obtain information about a director
10. To read news about movies
11. To obtain links to other interesting sites in relation to movies
12. To explore show times at different cinemas of movies currently playing
13. To buy tickets for a show time in a selected cinema
14. To manage a personal movie list
15. To post messages on the movie message boards
16. To enter a comment about a film
17. To get an overview of games
18. To get information about a game
19. To read news about games
20. To obtain links to other interesting sites in relation to games
21. To post messages on the game message boards
22. To register
23. To log in
24. To log out

Then the requirements matrix is constructed. For each requirement, a row and a column are created. Then the cells are filled by answering the question, "Does every user who has the requirement of this row also (always) have the requirement of this column?" For example, for row 1 (requirement 1), we obtain the following answers:

- For columns 1 to 16: "Y"
- For columns 17 to 21: "N"
- For columns 22 to 24: "Y"

The other cells are filled in a similar way. Table 11.1 shows a reduced version of the matrix where equal rows and columns are displayed as a single row or column.

Table 11.1. Reduced Requirements Matrix

	1–16	17–21	22–24
1–16	Y	N	Y
17–21	N	Y	Y
22–24	N	N	Y

The following audience classes can be derived from this matrix (equal rows):

- Rows 1 to 16: Movie Lover
- Rows 17 to 21: Game Lover
- Rows 22 to 24: Visitor (this audience class only has the requirements that are common to all users)

The following subclass relations can be derived (subset between rows):

- Movie Lover (rows 1–16) is an audience subclass of Visitor (rows 22–24).
- Game Lover (rows 17–21) is an audience subclass of Visitor (rows 22–24).

This result is the same audience hierarchy as the one given in Figure 11.4.

Once the audience classes are identified, it should be investigated if the members of those audience classes have special usability or navigational requirements. Different examples of navigational requirements can be found in the IMDb example. For example, for the Movie Lover audience class, we can formulate the following navigational requirements:

- The user should be able to navigate directly from the information of a movie to the show times and the ordering of tickets when the movie is currently played.
- If more information about some item shown is available, then the user should always be able to directly navigate to this information; e.g., from the movie information to the information about its directors, its actors, its genre, etc.

11.3.2 Audience Characterization

In the second subphase of the audience modeling, the audience characterization, relevant characteristics should be specified for each audience class. Examples of characteristics are level of experience with Web sites in general, frequency of use, language issues, education/intellectual abilities, age, income, lifestyle, etc. Some of the characteristics may be translated into usability requirements, while others may be used later on in the implementation design phase to guide the design of the "look and feel" of the navigation tracks of the different audience classes, e.g., choice of colors, fonts, graphics, etc.

The target users of the IMDb example are a very broad audience; they don't have very specific characteristics. There are also no differences worth mentioning between the characteristics of the audience class Game Lover and the audience class Movie Lover. Therefore, the characteristics for all audience classes are specified as follows:

Characteristics for all audience classes in the IMDb example :
• Able to communicate in English
• Have reasonable experience with the Web
• Are young people or adults

11.4 CONCEPTUAL DESIGN

So far in the method, the informational, functional, usability, and navigational requirements as well as the characteristics of the potential visitors have been identified and different audience classes have been defined. The goal of the conceptual design is to turn these informal requirements into high-level, formal descriptions that can be used later on to generate (automatically or semiautomatically) the Web system.

During conceptual design, we concentrate on the **conceptual** "what and how" rather than on the visual "what and how." The conceptual "what" is covered by the task & information modeling subphase and deals with the modeling of the content and functionality of the Web system; the conceptual "how" is covered by the navigational design subphase and specifies the conceptual structure of the Web system and the navigation. We describe these two subphases in more detail in the next subsections.

11.4.1 Task and Information Modeling

Instead of starting with an overall conceptual data model, like most Web design methods do, WSDM starts by analyzing the requirements of the different audience classes. This will result in a number of tiny conceptual descriptions, called *object chunks*, which model the information and functionality needed to satisfy these requirements. These conceptual descriptions are integrated into an overall conceptual model. This approach is used because WSDM follows the audience-driven design philosophy. It has the following advantages:

- The developer is forced to concentrate on the actual needs of the users rather than on the information (and functionality) already available in the organization. In this way, the chance that information is missing in the actual system will be less than in a data-driven approach where the available data are taken as the starting point. In addition, the information and functionality already available in the organization are not necessarily what the users need. Also, the way the information is organized and structured in the organization is not necessarily the way external users need it.
- It gives consideration to the fact that different types of users may have different requirements and that it may be necessary to use different structures or terminology for different types of users. By modeling the requirements for each audience class separately, we can give due consideration to this.

The output of the task & information modeling subphase is a collection of *task models* and associated *object chunks*. We first explain the task modeling and afterwards the information modeling.

11.4.1.1 Task Modeling

The purpose of task modeling is to model in detail the different tasks the members of each audience class need to be able to perform and to formally describe the data and functionality that are needed for those tasks. The tasks that a member of an audience class needs to be able to perform are based on the requirements formulated for the audience class during audience classification, i.e., for each informational and functional requirement formulated for an audience class, a task is defined that should allow one to satisfy this requirement. Each task is modeled into more details using an adapted version of the task-modeling technique CTT (Paterno et al., 1997; Paterno, 2000). Essentially, in CTT, tasks are decomposed into subtasks until elementary tasks are obtained. In addition, temporal relationships between subtasks are specified to indicate the order in which the subtasks need to be performed. The result is a *task model*.

CTT was developed in the context of human–computer interaction to describe user activities. CTT looks like hierarchical task decomposition, but it distinguishes four different categories of tasks (user tasks, application tasks, interaction tasks, and abstract tasks). CTT also has an easy-to-grasp graphical notation. However, we do not completely follow the original specifications of CTT, but have adopted them slightly to better satisfy the particularities of the Web and Web design:

1. WSDM does not consider user tasks. User tasks are tasks performed by the user without using the application (such as thinking on or deciding

about a strategy). They are not useful to consider at this stage of the design. This means that we only use the following categories of tasks (see Figure 11.5 for the graphical notation):

- *Application tasks*: tasks executed by the application. Application tasks can supply information to the user or perform some calculations or updates, e.g., checking username and password is typically an application task.
- *Interaction tasks*: tasks performed by the user by interaction with the system, e.g., entering information using a form.
- *Abstract tasks*: tasks that consist of complex activities and thus require decomposition into subtasks, e.g., ordering tickets for a movie.

2. A (complex) task is decomposed into (sub)tasks. The same task can be used in different subtrees. Tasks are identified by means of their name. CTT prescribes that if the children of a task are of different categories, then the parent task must be an abstract task. WSDM does not follow this rule. We use the category of the task to explicitly indicate who will be in charge of performing the task. For an interaction task, the user will be in charge; for an application task, the application will be in charge. In this way, we can indicate at a conceptual level who will initiate a subtask, or who will make a choice between possible subtasks.

3. CTT has a number of operators to express temporal relations among tasks. For some of the operations, we have changed the meaning slightly and an extra operator for transactions has been added:

- *Order-independent* (T1 |=| T2): The tasks can be performed in any order.
- *Choice* (T1 [] T2): One of the tasks can be chosen and only the chosen task can be performed.
- *Concurrent* (T1 ||| T2): The tasks can be executed concurrently.
- *Concurrent with information exchange* (T1 |[]| T2): The tasks can be executed concurrently, but they have to synchronize in order to exchange information.
- *Deactivation* (T1 [> T2): The first task is deactivated once the second task is started.
- *Enabling* (T1 >> T2): The second task is enabled when the first one terminates.
- *Enabling with information exchange* (T1 []>> T2): The second task is enabled when the first one terminates, but, in addition, some information is provided by the first task to the second task.
- *Suspend-resume* (T1 |> T2): This indicates that T1 can be interrupted to perform T2; when T2 is terminated, T1 can be reactivated from the state reached before the interruption.

- *Iteration* (T*): The task can be performed repetitively. In CTT the meaning is that the action is performed repetitively: When the action terminates, it is restarted automatically until the task is deactivated by another task. The interpretation in WSDM is that the task can be repeated several times and ends when the one in charge decides not to repeat the task (e.g., the user who decides not to redo the task but to continue with the next task).
- *Finite iteration* (T(n)): indicates if the task has to be repeated a fixed number of times (number known in advance).
- *Optional* ([T]): indicates that the performance of the task is optional.
- *Recursion*: occurs when the subtree that models a task contains the task itself. This means that performing the task can be a recursive activity.
- *Transaction* (-> T <-): The task must be executed as a transaction. This means that if the task, or in case of a complex task one of the tasks in the task's subtree, is not completed successfully, the whole task will not be successful and all activities should be rolled back (i.e., "all or nothing").

4. In WSDM, the level of detail provided in the task model is less than in the original CTT method. The reason for this is the use of the object chunks. As we will explain, with each elementary task, an object chunk can be associated that further describes the task in terms of informational and functional needs.

Interaction Task   Application Task   Abstraction Task

Figure 11.5. Graphical notation for the different types of tasks.

We illustrate the task modeling for some of the requirements formulated for the IMDb example. Figure 11.6 shows the task model for the tasks defined for the requirement "To find a movie by means of a search function" of the audience class Movie Lover. For this requirement, the task "Search IMDB" is defined. This abstract task is decomposed into three sequential tasks: "Specify Query," "View Results," and "Show Movie." The task "Show Movie" is optional and is further decomposed into "Show Movie Info" (to show information like title, director, etc.) and "Provide Extras." This task allows the user to choose among "Show Photos" (to display photos of the movie), "Add to My List" (to add the movie to the user's personal movie list), and "Post Message" (to post messages on the message boards associated with the movie). The task "Add to My List" is composed of an application task "Update My List" that will add the movie to the user's personal movie list and to the task "Manage My List." In order not to overload the figure, the abstract tasks "Manage My List" and "Post Message" are not further elaborated in this CTT.

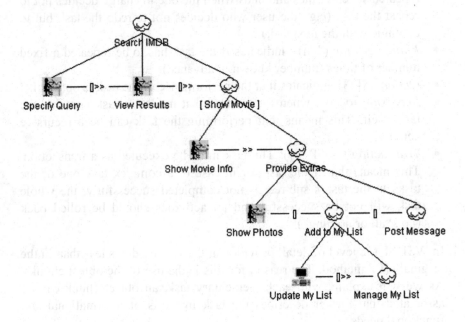

Figure 11.6. Task model for the task "Search IMDB."

Figure 11.7 shows the task model for the task defined for the requirements "To obtain show times of movies currently playing" and "To buy tickets for a show time in a selected cinema" of the audience class Movie Lover. We decided to support both requirements by a single task, as buying tickets requires knowing the show time, and offering the possibility to buy tickets while exploring show times may stimulate the sale of tickets. The task "Showtimes & Buy Tickets" is decomposed into two sequential tasks. First, the location must be specified using the "Specify Location" task. This is done by means of an interaction task to enter the location and the movie(s) (task "Enter Location Movie"), optionally followed by an interaction task to choose the location if more than one location exists for the information entered (task "Choose Location"). Next, the user can explore the show times and optionally buy tickets by means of the task "Select Showtime & Buy Tickets." This task is decomposed into the task "Explore Show Times," which can be repeated, followed by the optional task "Buy Tickets." For the task "Explore Show Times," first the show times associated with the requested location, movie(s), and date are showed ("View

Showtimes"), and then the user may change these parameters ("Change Parameters") and obtain the show times again.

The task models created in this way allow a first-level description of the functionality to be provided by the Web system (i.e., they describe a kind of workflow). More details are given by means of the object chunks. The object chunks are described in the next section.

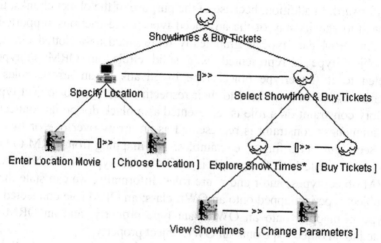

Figure 11.7. Task model for the task "Show Times & Buy Tickets."

11.4.1.2 Information Modeling

When a task model is completed, an object chunk is created for each elementary task in this model. The main purpose of an object chunk is to formally describe the information and functionality needed by the user when he has to perform the associated task. If the requirement associated with the task is a pure informational requirement (i.e., the user is only looking for information; she doesn't need to perform actions), then the object chunk can be considered as the conceptual description of the information that will be displayed on (a part of) the screen. For this purpose, a standard conceptual modeling language is sufficient. However, to be able to deal with functionality (e.g., filling in a form and processing it), a data manipulation language is also needed. We first discuss the modeling of informational requirements and then discuss what is needed to allow modeling functionality.

WSDM uses OWL[2] to model the information needs. OWL is becoming the standard for the Semantic Web. Its use as a specification language for the object chunks allows an easy integration with and use of existing domain ontologies and allows making the object chunks available as local application

---

[2] www.w3.org/TR/owl-features.

ontology in case no relevant domain ontology already exists. It also provides the basis for the generation of semantic annotations (see Section 11.6). Note that, as there isn't yet a generally used and compact graphical notation for OWL, we use the ORM graphical notation (Halpin, 2001) to give a graphical representation of OWL. We have opted for the ORM notation because ORM is very close to OWL, and therefore the mapping from ORM to OWL is straightforward. In addition, because of the purpose of the object chunks, there is no need to specify any of the advanced types of restrictions supported by OWL. An ORM data type is graphically represented as a dotted circle, an ORM object type is represented as a solid circle, an ORM subtype is connected to its supertype object type by means of an arrow, roles are represented as boxes connected to their respective data type or object type, a mandatory constraint on a role is represented as a black dot on its connection, and a uniqueness constraint is represented as an arrow over one or two role boxes. See Figure 11.8 for some examples. The mapping from ORM to OWL is sketched in Table 11.2. Suppose L is an ORM data type; N, N', N1, and N2 are ORM object types; and r and r' are roles. Informally, we can state that an ORM object type is mapped onto an OWL class; an ORM role connected to a data type is mapped onto an OWL data type property; and an ORM role connected to an object type onto an OWL object property.

As already indicated, the use of OWL allows an easy way of coupling the concepts used in the object chunks to concepts in existing (external) ontologies. This coupling is later on (in the implementation phase—see Section 11.6) used to generate semantic annotations. The namespace mechanism of OWL is used to refer in an object chunk to concepts defined in ontologies. To refer to a concept in an ontology, the identifying prefix of the ontology is used to qualify the names of the concept. For example, "FOAF:Person" refers to the class Person defined in the ontology identified by the prefix FOAF.

Figure 11.8 shows an example object chunk "ShowMovie." This object chunk is associated with the elementary task "Show Movie Info" of the task model "Search IMDB" given in Figure 11.6. In this object chunk the use of two external ontologies is illustrated: a basic IMDB ontology[3] (prefixed with "IMDB") and the well-known FOAF ontology[4] (prefixed with "FOAF" and used to describe persons). For example, the classes "IMDB:Movie," "FOAF:Image," "IMDB:Genre," and "FOAF:Person" refer to classes from these ontologies. Also, properties can refer to properties defined in ontologies; e.g., "IMDB:genres" refers to such a property.

---

[3] http://www.csd.abdn.ac.uk/~ggrimnes/dev/imdb/IMDB.rdfs.
[4] http://www.foaf-project.org/.

Table 11.2. Mapping Between ORM and OWL

ORM	OWL
N	<Class rdf:ID="N"/>
N' subtype of N	<Class rdf:ID="N'">
	<subClassOf rdf:resource="#N"/>
	</Class>
(N1, r, L)	<DatatypeProperty rdf:ID="r"/>
	<Class rdf:about="#N1">
	<subClassOf>
	<Restriction>
	<onProperty rdf:resource="#r"/>
	<allValuesFrom rdf:resource="L"/>
	</Restriction>
	</subClassOf>
	</Class>
(N1, r', N2)	<ObjectProperty rdf:ID="r"/>
	<Class rdf:about="#N1">
	<subClassOf>
	<Restriction>
	<onProperty rdf:resource="#r'"/>
	<allValuesFrom rdf:resource="N2"/>
	</Restriction>
	</subClassOf>
	</Class>
(r,r')	<Property rdf:about="#r">
	<inverseOf rdf:resource="#r'"/>
	</Property>
	(for object properties only)
Mandatory role r	...
	<Restriction>
	<onProperty rdf:resource="#r"/>
	<someValuesFrom
	rdf:resource="..."/>
	</Restriction>
	...
Uniqueness constraint of role r	...
	<Restriction>
	<onProperty rdf:resource="#r"/>
	<maxCardinality> 1
	</maxCardinality>
	</Restriction>
	...

To allow communication between tasks, parameters (input as well as output parameters) can be specified for object chunks. For example, the object chunk "ShowMovie" (Figure 11.8) has an instance of type "IMDB:Movie" as input parameter (represented by *m). Input parameters are used in general to restrict the information that should be presented to the user. For instance, the input parameter *m of type IMDB:Movie is used to express that only the information related to this particular movie should be shown. This is graphically represented by putting this parameter in the corresponding class. In fact, placing the parameter *m in the class "IMDB:Movie" restricts the complete schema to a view.

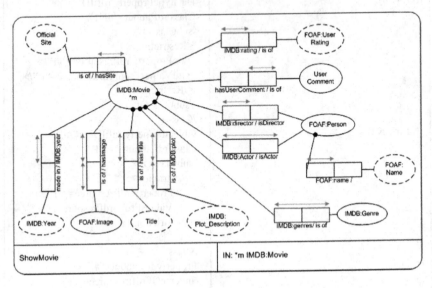

Figure 11.8. Object chunk "ShowMovie."

To be able to deal with functionality (e.g., fill in a form or update, add, or delete information), a (conceptual) data manipulation language is needed. WSDM provides a graphical conceptual data manipulation language. However, notice that this language has limited expressive power and does not intend to allow complex functionality to be specified. We don't believe that a graphical language is appropriate for this. However, using the primitives provided by the language, most commonly used functionalities for Web systems, such as adding, deleting, and changing information, can be specified. For more complex functionality, WSDM supports the use of (external) Web services. More in particular, the conceptual data manipulation language of WSDM provides support for

- specifying that the user can select one or several instances from a class or a property (e.g., to allow the user to select an actor from the list of available actors in the IMDb example). For this, the symbols "!" (single selection) and "!!" (multiple selection) are used.
- expressing interactive input (e.g., needed to fill in a form). The symbol "?" is used for the input of a single value, while "??" is used for

expressing interactive input of more than one value. Note that these symbols can only be applied to value types (data type properties). Class instances cannot be entered directly. They should be created using the "NEW" operator (see next bullet).

- To manipulate the data itself, a number of primitive operators are available. "NEW" indicates the creation of a new class instance; "REMOVE" is used to indicate the removal of one or more class instances; the symbol "+" above a relation indicates the addition of a property (and its inverse), and the symbol "-" indicates the removal of properties.
- Furthermore, an assignment operator ("=") is available to assign values to variables (also called *referents*), as well as several built-in functions and default referents. For example, *USER is available to refer to the current user of a session.

A more detailed description of this graphical language can be found in De Troyer and Casteleyn (2001) and De Troyer et al. (2005).

Figure 11.9 shows an object chunk involving functionality: adding a movie to the personal movie list of the user. This object chunk is created for the elementary (application) task "Update My List" in the task model "Search IMDB" given in Figure 11.6. The movie instance that needs to be added to the personal list is given by means of the input parameter *m (and passed to this task after the user has opted for the task "Add to My List" in the task "Show Movie" where the user was viewing a certain movie). The list to which the movie needs to be added is denoted by the referent *l and refers to the "My List" instance that "belongs to" the "User" instance *USER (which is the predefined referent used to refer to the current user). The "+" below the object properties "is in" and "has" specified the addition of the relationship (i.e., instantiation of both object properties for *l and *m). Note that *l is returned as output parameter because in the task "Add to My List" this information need to be passed to the task "Manage My List."

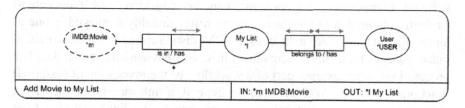

Figure 11.9. Object chunk "Add Movie to My List."

11.4.2 Navigational Design

The goals of the navigational design are to define the conceptual structure of the Web system and to model how the members of the different audience classes can navigate through the Web system and perform their tasks. Because of the audience-driven approach of WSDM, a *navigation track* is created for each audience class. Such an audience track can be considered as a subsystem containing all and only the information and functionality needed by the members of the associated audience class. The internal structure of an audience track is derived from the task models made for this audience class. In addition, navigational requirements formulated during audience modeling are also taken into account. In the next subsection we explain in detail how a navigational track is created. Next, all audience tracks are combined into a basic conceptual navigation structure by means of *structural links* (see Section 11.4.2.2). In WSDM, the structure defined between the audience tracks corresponds to the hierarchical structure defined between the audience classes in the audience class hierarchy.

Once the main conceptual navigation structure has been derived, *semantic* and *navigational aid links* are added (see also Section 11.4.2.2). Semantic links are navigational links based on semantic relationships that exist between objects in the domain and that are modeled in the object chunks by means of object properties. Semantic links express task-independent navigation (which may have been expressed in the form of navigational requirements during audience modeling). Navigational aid links are links that enhance navigation, such as home links, landmarks, quick links, etc. In contrast to structural links and semantic links, navigational aid links are strictly speaking not necessary but are added to enhance the usability of the Web system. A more detailed discussion on the different types of links used in WSDM can be found in De Troyer and Casteleyn (2003a, 2003b).

The output of the navigational design phase is the *navigational model*. The navigational model is expressed in term of *components* and *links* between components. Components can be considered as (conceptual) navigation units that group the information/functionality conveyed in one or more object chunks. As indicated, WSDM distinguishes between structural links, process logic links, semantic links, and navigational aid links. The process logic links express part of a workflow or the invocation of (external) functionality (e.g., a Web service). In general, a link may be defined from one component to one (other) component (one-to-one link), but also from one component to a set of components (one-to-many link), or from a set of components to one single component (many-to-one link), or from a set of components to a set of components (many-to-many link). As typical implementation formats, such as HTML, do not support one-to-many, many-to-one, or many-to-many links, these kinds of links need to be implemented as a collection of one-to-one hyperlinks when generating (HTML) output. However, these kinds of links are useful to consider during conceptual design because they allow abstracting from the current implementation limitations and provide more semantics. For example, in the presentation design (see Section 11.5.2) a one-to-many link can be represented as a single menu, and structural annotations can be generated to indicate the semantics of the links (see Section 11.6).

Note that the links specified in the navigational model are actually link types. That means that even a one-to-one link may result in different hyperlinks in the actual Web system. For example, if we specify in the navigational model that the user can navigate from a "Movie" component to an "Actor" component, this is modeled by means of a one-to-one link between these two components. However, a movie may involve several actors; therefore, for each individual movie, the one-to-one link may give rise to several hyperlinks, one to each of its actors.

Links can have parameters to indicate that relevant information should be passed from the source component to the target component when a user follows the link. A parameter is usually an output parameter from an object chunk connected to the source component.

Next to parameters, conditions can also be specified for links. A condition allows restricting the availability of the link to different users, devices, or timeframes. For example, a link may become unavailable after a certain date, or only users who are logged in are presented certain links. To some extent, conditional links allow for adaptation of the Web system.

The graphical representation of components and the different kinds of links are given in Figure 11.10. An external component refers to an external system or a Web service.

Note that the navigational model only provides the *conceptual* structure (including navigation) of the Web system. The mapping of this conceptual structure onto (Web) pages and hyperlinks is specified during site structure design, which is part of the implementation design phase (see Section 11.5.1).

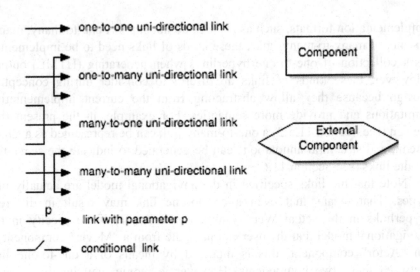

Figure 11.10. Graphical representation of components and links.

11.4.2.1 Creating the Navigational Tracks

To create a navigational track for an audience class, for each task a *task navigational model* is created. A task navigational model is the translation of the task model (represented by means of a CTT) into a navigational structure.

A task navigational model is created by defining a component for each elementary interaction task defined in the hierarchical decomposition of the task. The object chunk that was created for the elementary task is connected to this component. See Figure 11.11 for the graphical representation. Also, object chunks created for application tasks can be attached to components. In fact, components are a kind of placeholder for the object chunks (which represents the actual information and/or functionality). By linking components instead of object chunks, it is possible to use the same object chunk in different task navigational models and even in different navigational tracks without losing the modeling context of the different links.

Next, process logic links between components are used to express the workflow or process logic, which is expressed in the task model by means of the temporal CTT relations. In fact, the temporal CTT relations are translated into links (one-to-one, one-to-many, many-to-one, or many-to-many links; conditional or nonconditional links). Components and process logic links can be grouped into a *transaction* to indicate that they constitute a conceptual unit (for which the all-or-nothing property holds). To avoid complex diagrams, complex subtasks may be modeled separately, in *subtask navigational models*.

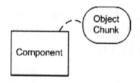

Figure 11.11. An object chunk connected to a component.

Until now, we permitted the designer to neglect the fact that not all information and functionality should be freely available. In many Web systems, parts of the information and functionality need to be protected in some way. This can be modeled during the navigational design by means of a *protection area*. Graphically, this is represented by including the component(s) (together with their associated object chunks) that need to be protected into a named box labeled with a key symbol (an example can be found in Figure 11.12). In a similar way, it is possible to indicate that some information transfer needs to be secure. This protection area concept for expressing security and validation allows abstracting (in the different navigational models) from how to achieve the validation or security. If relevant, how this must be achieved can be specified by means of a separated navigational model. An example is given in Figure 11.14 and is explained later on.

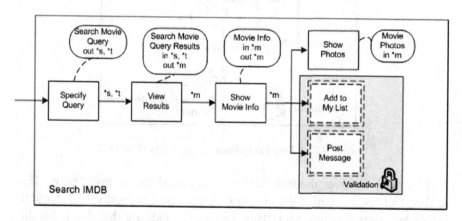

Figure 11.12. Task navigational model for the task "Search IMDB."

We illustrate the task navigational models by means of some examples. Figure 11.12 shows the task navigational model for the task "Search IMDB." Its task model was given in Figure 11.6. The navigational subtask models "Add to My List" and "Post Message" are protected by the "Validation" protection area. These parts of the Web system can only be accessed after the user has been authorized. How this must be done is specified in the task navigation model given in Figure 11.14, which has been derived from the task model given in Figure 11.13.

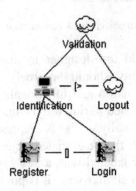

Figure 11.13. Task model "Validation."

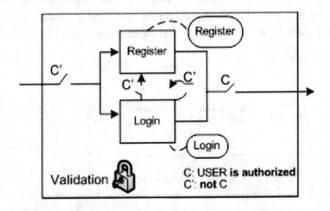

Figure 11.14. Task navigational model for "Validation."

Figure 11.15 gives the task navigational model for the task "Show Time & Buy Tickets" for which the task model was given in Figure 11.7. Note the use of an external component "Buy Tickets" to indicate that this is handled by an external service. Link parameters as well as input and output parameters are omitted in this diagram.

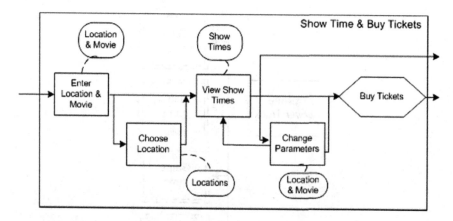

Figure 11.15. Task navigational model for the task "Show Time & Buy Tickets."

Once the task navigational models are constructed for the different tasks of an audience class, they should be composed into a navigational track using structural links. This can be done by first making a task model of how the members of the audience class are allowed to select the different tasks and then translating this task into a task navigational model. In the simple case that, at any moment in time, a member of the audience class can freely select between the different tasks, this modeling process can be reduced to the introduction of a new component that is linked to the different task navigational models by means of a one-to-many link. This principle is illustrated in Figure 11.16, which shows the navigational track for the Game Lover audience class of the IMDb example. For the sake of simplicity, the navigational models are represented by means of their shorthand notation (dotted double-lined rectangles). The newly introduced component is not connected to an object chunk, because it does not provide any information or functionality itself. Instead, its sole role is to allow navigation to the different tasks. In the actual Web system, this may result in a menu that provides links to the different tasks. However, if there are a lot of tasks for an audience track, it may be better (from a usability point of view) to structure the tasks in some way and to provide groups of tasks (which may result in groups of menus).

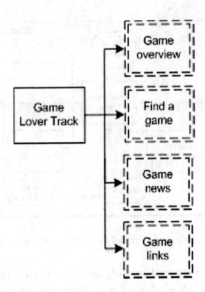

Figure 11.16. Navigational track for the Game Lover audience class.

11.4.2.2 Creating the Navigational Model

Once the navigational tracks for the different audience classes are constructed, they need to be composed into a single structure. This will be the main conceptual structure of the Web system. Because WSDM is audience-driven, the structure between the audience tracks must correspond to the hierarchical structure defined between the audience classes in the audience class hierarchy. We illustrate this with the IMDb example. The navigational model for the IMDb example is given in Figure 11.17. Note that for space limitations the different task navigational models are given by means of their shorthand notation and that the navigational track for the Movie Lover is also given by means of its shorthand notation (a double-lined rectangle). Note the correspondence with the audience class hierarchy given in Figure 11.4.

During navigational design, we also define semantic links that will enhance the navigation. Semantic links are based on semantic relationships that exist between objects in the application domain and that are modeled in the object chunks by means of object properties. For example, in the IMDb example, there are semantic relationships between movie and actor, between movie and director, and between movie and cinema. Also, in the navigational requirements for the Movie Lover audience class, it was stated

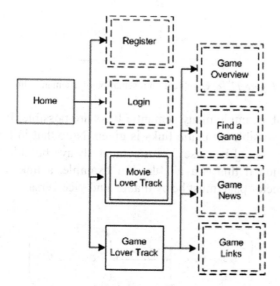

Figure 11.17. Main conceptual navigation structure for the IMDb example.

that the user should be able to navigate directly from the movie to the information of each of these related items. This facility can be modeled by means of semantic links. A semantic link is a link between two object chunks and must be based on the existence of a semantic relationship between two classes (e.g., movie having director). The source object chunk should contain the object property that expresses this semantic relationship between the two classes (movie having director). The target object chunk should provide the request information (information about director). We illustrate this with an example. Consider the object chunk "ShowMovie" as shown in Figure 11.8. For a movie we decided to provide the name of the director (modeled in "ShowMovie"). Suppose that the object chunk "Director Info" models the information provided for a director. Then, based on the object property "IMDB:director," we can define a semantic link from the object chunk "ShowMovie" to the object chunk "Director Info." See Figure 11.18 for a graphical representation. If needed, the link can be labeled with the name of the property used. Semantic links are independent of a particular task. This means that in each task where the chunk "ShowMovie" is used, the link will be available. Therefore, they don't need to be represented in the different task navigation models, and they will not overload these diagrams.

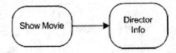

Figure 11.18. Graphical representation of a semantic link.

In the IMDb example many semantic links are possible. In Figure 11.19, a selection of possible semantic links is given. Note that in this example all links are bidirectional because the user must always be able to navigate to more information if this is available. For example, a link from the movie page to the director page must be available, and vice versa.

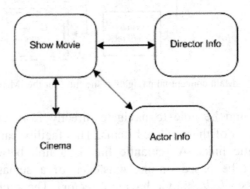

Figure 11.19. Some example semantic links for the IMDb example.

On top of the conceptual structure defined by means of the structural links, and the navigation possibilities defined by the process logic links and the semantic links, navigational aid links can be added to ease the navigation even more and to enhance the usability. From the viewpoint of being able to reach information and functionality, they are strictly speaking not needed; all information and functionality should also be reachable by means of the navigational tracks. Navigational aid links can be compared to adding an index and post-it pointers to chapters in a book: The information in and the structure of the book stay the same, but the user is provided with shortcuts to access the information more easily. A typical example of a navigational aid link is the home link, which can often be found on each page of a Web site. Also, landmarks are examples of navigational aid links. Not to overload the diagrams, the home component and the landmark components are represented by means of a symbol. Later on, during the implementation phase, home links and landmark links can be generated. In Figure 11.20 the conceptual structure of the IMDb example is enhanced with navigational aid links (home and landmarks and a link from the "Login" navigational task model to the "Register" navigational task model).

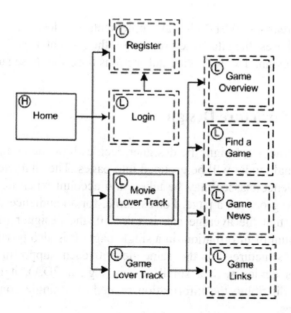

Figure 11.20. Navigational aid links.

11.5 IMPLEMENTATION DESIGN

The goal of the implementation design is to complement the conceptual design with the necessary details for the implementation. In principle, it would be possible to generate an implementation from the conceptual design, but this is not realistic for several reasons. First, the Web is very visually oriented, and the standards for presentation have become very high in recent years. Professional Web systems need to have a professional look and feel, and graphical designers are usually involved to achieve this. If the Web system is generated directly from the conceptual design, only standard and rather simplistic presentations can be obtained. Therefore, a presentation design is needed. Second, the information provided on the Web system may already be available from some data source (e.g., a relational database). In this case, no new data source needs to be created, but a mapping should be defined from the conceptual description of the information (the object chunks) to the actual data source. Third, Web users don't like to make unnecessary clicks (clicks that don't lead to new information), but, on the other hand, too much information on a single page will overload the page and also decrease the usability. Therefore, information and functionality should be grouped onto pages in such a way that a good balance is reached between the amount of information on a page and the number of clicks needed to reach information.

For these reasons, WSDM has an implementation design phase consisting of three subphases: the site structure design, the presentation design, and the logical data design. The following subsections describe these subphases into more detail.

11.5.1 Site Structure Design

During site structure design, the designer decides how the components from the navigational model will be grouped into pages. The characteristics of the different audience classes may be taken into account when deciding which information to group on a page. For example, for an audience class with the characteristic that the average age is over 50, the designer might want to limit the amount of information on a single page. It is also possible to define different site structures for the same design, each supporting a different device. For a device with a small screen (e.g., a PDA), it may even be necessary to distribute the information related to a single component onto different pages.

By default, each component (with its associated object chunks and links) is placed on a single page. However, the designer can decide to group different components on a single page or to use different pages for a single component. When components are grouped on a page, the designer should respect the conceptual structure expressed by means of the different links; e.g., if a component cannot be reached by a link from another component, these two components cannot be placed on the same page.

The output of this phase is the *site structure model*. The site structure is graphically presented by drawing pages over the components that should be grouped. Figure 11.21 illustrates a part of the site structure design for the IMDb example. The Home component and the links from this component are placed on a single page; Register and Login are each on a different page; and the components "Find a Game" and "Game Links" and all links coming from the "Game Lover Track" component are also put together on a single page. The rest has been left unspecified in this figure.

Note that the pages defined during the site structure design are abstract pages. Each abstract page will give rise to one or a set of concrete pages when the actual implementation is generated. For example, the page containing the "ShowMovie" object chunk will result (in the case of a static Web site) in many different concrete pages, one for each movie.

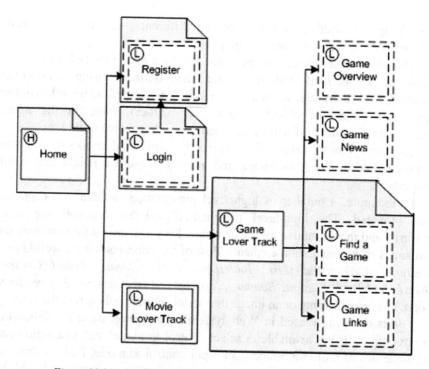

Figure 11.21. Part of the site structure design for the IMDb example.

11.5.2 Presentation Design

During presentation design, the look and feel of the Web system, as well as the layout of the pages (i.e., positioning of page elements), is defined. To enhance a consistent look and feel, templates are used. Therefore, page templates are defined. Typically, a Web system may require different kinds of pages, e.g., a home page, a title page, leaf page. For each of these page types, a template can be created. These templates are subsequently used in the page design, where the layout is defined for each of the pages defined in the site structure model. The layout describes how the information and functionality (modeled by means of the object chunks) and assigned to a page (by means of the components) should be laid out on the page.

For both the template and page design, a number of presentation-modeling concepts are available. To position information, the concept of a *grid* is used. A grid contains *rows* with *cells*. A cell contains a *multimedia value*, another grid (nesting of grids), or a *referent* from an object chunk assigned to the page [remember that a referent refers to an instance/value (or a set of instances/values) from a class or a property]. Absolute and relative height and width can be specified for grids, rows, and cells. By nesting grids, specifying the width and height of the different grids, rows, and cells, information can be positioned on the page.

The value of a cell can be associated with a *hyperlink* (which must be based on a link contained in the page and defined during navigational modeling). Furthermore, when a grid or cell is associated with a referent that represents a set (of object instances or values), then, in the actual implementation, the grid will be repeated for each instance of this set.

To display multimedia values correctly, additional properties may be required. For instance, an image and a video require a height and width property.

Furthermore, a number of high-level presentation-modeling concepts are also provided. The high-level presentation-modeling concepts are more powerful and more intuitive for the designer. They also are useful to capture the semantics of a presentation element. Most of the concepts have a well-known meaning: *OrderedBulletList, BulletList, Table, Menu, TableOfContent, BreadcrumbTrail, Section, Banner, Copyright, Advertisement, Figure, Icon, Logo, Marquee* (a string or an image that scrolls horizontally across the screen).

Forms are widely used in Web systems. To support them the following control concepts are available: a select control to model that a selection can be made out of multiple options, an input control to model that a value can be entered, and an action control to specify that an action should be performed. These controls can be associated with a presentation concept. Types of select controls are a *RadioButton*, a *CheckBox*, a *ListBox*, and a *DropDown* box. An input control is either a *TextBox* or a *SecretTextBox* (typically used for entering passwords). A typical action control is a *PushButton*. The behavior associated with an action control is defined by associating an event and an action to the control. It expresses the fact that when the specified event occurs for the associated presentation concept, the specified action will be performed. Possible events are *OnClick, OnLoad*, and *onHoover*; possible actions are *PopUp, Show, Scroll, Reset, Submit*, and *Cancel*. A popup menu, for instance, can be defined using the Menu presentation concept with associated *OnClick* event and associated *PopUp* action; an expandable menu can be defined using the Menu presentation concept, where the elements of the menu are associated with the event *OnClick* and the action *Show*.

Templates are specified using the presentation-modeling concepts mentioned. A template can also be composed out of a *Header, Footer, SideBar*, and/or *ContentPane*. Each template furthermore contains at least one *editable region*. An editable region denotes an area that one needs to specify further when the template is used for a page design. An editable region can be placed anywhere in a grid.

To specify style, WSDM currently relies on Cascading Style Sheets (CSS).[5] This allows style specification for any particular element and has enough expressive power to describe most styles commonly found in Web systems.

For each page, the designer chooses a template and then specifies how the links and the information (specified by means of the object chunks) will be positioned in the editable regions of the template. This is done using the presentation-modeling concepts mentioned. For each object chunk connected to a component included in the page, a grid is constructed. Each data type property of an object chunk is placed in a cell of the grid. For functionality, control concepts are used. If needed, multimedia values can be added to enhance the presentation (e.g., titles, labels, graphics, etc.).

For each link contained in the page, the designer needs to specify the anchor. This is done by adding the link to the relevant cell of the grid. Note how this linking mechanism does not differentiate between the type of anchors (e.g., a text element, an image, a table): A link is uniformly specified on a cell of a grid, no matter what its content is.

The characteristics and usability requirements of the audience classes should be taken into account when designing the different templates and pages.

The output of this phase is the *presentation model* consisting of a set of *templates*, a set of *styles,* and, for each page defined in the site structure model, a *page model.*

Figure 11.22 shows a simple example template and Figure 11.23 a simple example page model.

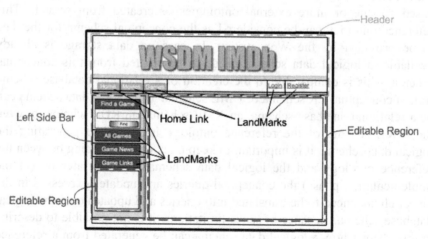

Figure 11.22. Example template for the IMDb example.

---

[5] www.w3.org/Style/CSS/.

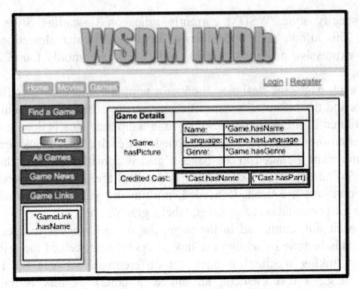

Figure 11.23. Template page model for the IMDb example.

11.5.3 Logical Data Design

The information provided by the Web system is described by means of the different object chunks made during task & information modeling. The different object chunks are related by means of the *reference ontology* that contains the different concepts used in the different object chunks. The object chunks are views on the reference ontology that is incrementally constructed during information modeling. The reference ontology may be based on one or more external ontologies or created from scratch. This reference ontology can be considered as the conceptual schema for the data to be provided by the Web system. In case no data storage is already available, a logical data schema needs to be created from this conceptual schema. This is comparable to the creation of a relational database schema from a conceptual ER schema or UML schema. The logical data schema can be a relational database schema, an XML schema, an RDF schema, or even the OWL schema of the reference ontology itself. While generating the logical data schema, it is important to keep track of the mapping between the reference ontology and the logical data schema, because later on (in the implementation phase) the conceptual queries and updates expressed in the object chunks need to be translated into queries and updates onto the logical database schema. Because of space limitations, it is not possible to describe in this chapter how a logical data schema can be generated from a reference ontology and how the mappings can be expressed. Normally, this process should be supported by a CASE tool, in which case the designer is not burdened with the creation of the logical data schema and the mappings.

In a second scenario, an existing data store is available. In this case it is only needed to define the mapping between the reference ontology and this data store.

The output of this phase is a *logical data schema* and a *data source mapping*.

11.6 IMPLEMENTATION

The actual implementation can be generated automatically from the information collected during the different design phases by means of the different design models. As proof-of-concept, a transformation pipeline (using XSLT) has been defined, which takes as input the object chunks (with corresponding data source mapping), navigational, site structure, style & template, and page models and outputs the actual implementation for the chosen platform and implementation language. This transformation is performed fully automatically. A description of this transformation pipeline is out of the scope of this chapter. An overview can be found in Plessers et al. (2005b). An example of a page (showing game details) is given in Figure 11.24.

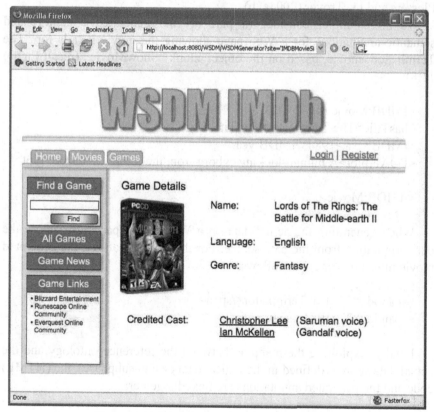

Figure 11.24. Example page from the IMDb example.

Important to notice is that, based on the design information collected, semantic annotations can be generated. More in particular, the use of one or more external ontologies during the conceptual design allows expressing explicitly the semantics of the presented data by means of content-related semantic annotations using these ontologies. However, it is also possible to annotate the Web system such that the semantics of its structure are also made explicit. Dedicated ontologies [e.g., the WAfA ontology (Yesilada et al., 2004) developed in the context of accessibility for visually impaired user] can be used to make the semantics of the different structural elements (e.g., a navigation menu, a logo, an advertising banner) explicit. These so-called structural annotations can be exploited by third parties that require specific knowledge about the Web system's structure: page transcoders to transcode a Web page in, for example, a format more appropriate for screen readers or search engine indexers. Structural annotations can be generated without any additional effort from the designer by exploiting the design information captured by means of the design models. How the content-related and structural annotations are generated is outside the context of this chapter. A description of this can be found in Plessers et al. (2005a, b) and Plessers and De Troyer (2004a, b).

As an example, consider (a part of) the generated content-related semantic annotations for a Web page showing the movie details for "The Terminator" movie, based on the object chunk "ShowMovie" (recall Figure 11.8):

```
<IMDB:Movie rdf:ID="23">
<hasTitle>The Terminator</hasTitle>
<IMDB:year>1984</IMDB:year>
<FOAF:plot>A human-looking cyborg from the future ...<FOAF:plot>
...
</IMDB:Movie>
```

When generating the actual data on a Web page, span tags enclose the data originating from the data source. For the example above, the generated movie title and year are as follows:

```
<span id="1">The Terminator</span>
<span id="2">1984</span>
```

Finally, exploiting the mapping between the reference ontology and the actual data source (defined in the logical data design subphase), the (HTML) code and the generated annotations are linked together:

page.html#xpointer(id("1"))<=>page.owl#xpointer(id("23")/hasTitle)
page.html#xpointer(id("2"))<=>page.owl#xpointer(id("23")/IMDB:year)

11.7 FURTHER ISSUES

WSDM has been extended in different directions. The most important ones are the extensions to support localization (De Troyer and Casteleyn, 2004) and the extensions for adaptation (Casteleyn, 2005). We will briefly describe the principles used for these extensions.

11.7.1 Localization of Web Systems

Public Web systems are accessible from all over the world. This offers opportunities for companies and organizations to attract visitors from across international borders and to do business with them. Two different approaches are possible to address this issue: Develop one single Web system to serve everyone, or develop "localized" Web systems for particular localities. The "one-size-fits-all" approach may be appropriate for particular communities (e.g., researchers), but in general it will be less successful. In general, it is recommended to localize a global Web system, i.e., to create different versions and adapt those versions to the local communities they target. Members of a community share not only a common language, but also common cultural conventions. Since measurement units, keyboard configurations, default paper sizes, character sets, and notational standards for writing time, dates, addresses, numbers, currency, etc. differ from one culture to another, it is self-evident that local Web systems should address these issues. Some jokes, symbols, icons, graphics, or even colors may be completely acceptable in one country but trigger negative reactions in another country. Sometimes even the style or tone of the site's text might be considered offensive by a particular cultural entity, resulting in the text's needing to be rewritten rather than merely translated. Next to cultural differences, it may also be necessary to adapt the content to regional differences, such as differences in the services and products offered, differences in price, and differences in regulations.

As for classical software, Web system localization is often done once the Web system is completely developed and available for a particular community. We believe that the globalization process[6] could benefit from

---

[6] According to LISA (Localization Industry Standards Association; http://www.lisa.org), localization of a thing is adapting it to the needs of a given locality. Globalization is about spreading a thing to several different countries, and making it applicable and usable in those countries.

taking localization requirements into consideration while designing the Web system. Then it may be easier to actually realize globalization because the internationalization activities[7] may already be considered and prepared for during the design process. For this reason, WSDM was extended to support Web localization. We shortly explain how the different (sub)phases have been adapted.

11.7.1.1 The Mission Statement Specification

To be able to take localization into account during the design process, the mission statement should also mention the different localities for which the Web system needs to be developed. A locality describes a particular place, situation, or location. Localities are identified by means of a name and a label. Examples of localities are the Unied States, Japan, and the Flemish community in Belgium.

As an example, suppose that next to the English version (which is targeted to Americans), we also want localized versions of the IMDb Web system for France and Germany. Then, the mission statement can be reformulated as follows:

> To be the biggest and best movie and game site on earth. For movies, this will be achieved by providing as much information as possible on movies including their actors, directors, and producers, as well as to provide news, allow exploring show times, buy tickets in selected cinemas in the United States, and to share personal opinions about movies. For games, information about games is offered as well as news, and game lovers should be able to exchange information. Next to the U.S. version, localized versions for France and Germany should be offered; information dependent on the country, such as the movies currently playing, should be adapted for each version. Exploring show times and buying tickets are only available for the United States.

Here, the localities that are targeted are the United States, France, and Germany.

11.7.1.2 Audience Modeling

To support localization, a distinction is made between requirements and characteristics typical for an audience class and those typical for a locality.

The requirements and characteristics that are typical for a locality are related to the language, culture, habits, or regulations of the locality. Some examples of locality requirements are that an address should always include the state; for each price it should be indicated if tax is included and, if not,

---

[7] Internationalization consists of all preparatory tasks that will facilitate subsequent localization.

the percentage of tax that needs to be added should be mentioned. Locality characteristics will typically deal with issues such as language use, reading order, use of color, and use of symbols.

Then the localities are linked to the different audience classes. An audience class may span different localities. For example, in the IMDb example all classes identified so far are applicable for all localities, but in fact only people within the United States should be able to explore show times and buy tickets. Therefore, we can refine the audience class hierarchy and introduce a new subclass for the people who can explore show times and buy tickets. Then this class only needs to be supported in the U.S. locality.

11.7.1.3 Conceptual Modeling

During task modeling, a task model is defined for each requirement. Now, we also have requirements formulated for the different localities. These requirements also need to be considered during task modeling. When constructing the task models, we need to inspect the locality requirements to check if additional or different steps are needed when decomposing a task. If a task must be completely different for a specific locality (which is rarely the case), a different CTT must be created and labeled with this locality. If only some additional steps are needed, then these steps are labeled with the localities for which they are needed.

Also, when constructing the object chunks, we need to inspect the locality requirements to check if additional information is needed. If this is the case, this information is added to the object chunk and labeled with the locality for which it is needed. In the object chunks, we should also indicate which information is dependent on the locality. For example, in the IMDb example, the description of a movie needs to be given in the language of the locality, and the movies currently played and the movies coming soon will be different for each locality. Labeling the classes and properties that are locality-dependent indicates this. In the navigational design, the audience tracks are labeled with all the localities for which they are applicable.

11.7.1.4 Implementation Design

Usually, the site structure design will be independent of the locality, i.e., for each locality the site structure will be the same. However, if some task models are very different for different localities, a different site structure may be needed.

During the presentation design, the localization characteristics formulated during audience modeling need to be taken into consideration. Different templates should be created for different localities if this is needed (e.g., different colors, different labels).

When creating a logical data schema, we need to take into account that the information may be different for different localities, as indicated by the labeling of and within the object chunks. Depending on the situation, different data sources for each locality may be needed or only different fields for some properties. Many different solutions are possible; we will not go into details here. More information can be found in De Troyer and Casteleyn (2004).

11.7.2 Adaptation

WSDM provides flexible design support for the specification of (automatic) reorganization of structure and content of the Web system (at run time), based on the way users access and use the Web system. Note that this type of adaptation, also called *optimization* (Perkowitz and Etzioni, 1997), differs from personalization (which is what is usually intended when the term "adaptation" is used): Optimization improves the Web system as a whole (for all users), whereas personalization adapts the Web system for a single user (i.e., the current user). The possibility to take into account and anticipate during design the actual use of the Web system at run time offers the following advantages:

1. **Anticipate and react on run-time browsing behavior**: For example, make popular pages more directly available (add navigational aids links).
2. **Evaluate and use design alternatives automatically**: For example, merge audience tracks if their separation seems to be less useful.
3. **Detect and correct design flaws**: For example, detect and correct misplaced information.
4. **Better tailor the Web system to satisfy business goals:** For example, add or replace strategic business information in such a way that it appears on the most popular pages.

To specify this type of adaptive behavior, a dedicated language, called the Adaptation Specification Language (ASL), was introduced. ASL is a high-level, rule-based adaptation specification language that allows the designer to specify adaptation strategies (i.e., *which* adaptation needs to be done) and adaptation policies (i.e., *when* adaptation needs to be done). ASL is event-based: User-generated *events* (e.g., clicking a link, visiting a page, starting a session) will trigger the adaptation strategies. The strategies themselves are specified using *rules* (e.g., iterations, conditional execution of an action, predefined transformations on the relevant design models). By allowing the designer to specify which event(s) need(s) to be tracked, and when and how adaptation should be performed based upon these events, the designer has a powerful mechanism to specify how the organization and structure of the Web system should be improved (at run time) based on the actual use of the Web system. The remainder of this section explains an example of a useful adaptation strategy (and policy) and highlights some interesting features of ASL. For an in-depth discussion of ASL (including formal specification, example strategies, experimentation results), we refer to Casteleyn (2005).

Consider as an example adaptation strategy the *promotion* strategy, discussed in the context of WSDM in Casteleyn et al. (2003). Promotion of a component makes the component easier to find by moving it closer to the root (e.g., the home page) of the Web system. Here, the promotion is based on the popularity of the components: The most popular component(s) [the component(s) with the highest number of accesses] are promoted. ASL allows specifying for which components the number of accesses needs to be tracked and how this should be done (i.e., per session, per load, per click). For the IMDb example, a useful adaptation strategy might be to promote the movie and game visited most often (overall) during the past month. Therefore, the accesses to each individual movie and game need to be counted. A general script for counting the access to the elements of some set (of design elements) is used for this. This script can be used in different adaptation strategies:

```
script trackAmountOfAccesses(Set) :
    forEach element in Set
    begin
            addTrackingVariable element.amountOfAccesses ;
            monitor load on element do element.amountOfAccesses :=
                            element.amountOfAccesses + 1
    end
```

Intuitively, the for-each rule in this script states that a tracking variable *amountOfAccesses* is declared (i.e., addTrackingVariable) and attached to each element of the given set. Furthermore, load events on the elements (i.e., for all users and for all sessions) will give rise to the increment of the *amountOfAccesses* tracking variable of that particular element.

The actual promotion in this case consists of linking the most popular movie and game to the root of the Web system. First, a script implementing the general principle of promotion is given. Here, the original links to the promoted component are kept (so only a navigational aids link is added). Alternative promotion strategies can be defined. The promotion script is specified as follows in ASL (note that in ASL the shorter term "node" is used instead of "component"):

```
script promoteNode(Set, promoteTo) :
    begin
    let promoteNodeMaxAccesses be
    max(Set [MAP on element: element.amountOfAccesses]);
    forEach node in Set :
        if node.amountOfAccesses = promoteNodeMaxAccesses
        then addLink (navigationAid, promoteTo, node)
    end
```

Having defined the adaptation strategy, we are able to specify the adaptation policy, i.e., *when* the adaptation should be performed. In this example, we collect the accesses to movies/games for one month and perform a promotion once every month:

```
when initialization do
    begin
            call trackAmountOfAccesses(ALL MovieDetailNode);
            call trackAmountOfAccesses(ALL GameDetailNode)
    end

when 1 month from now do
    begin
            call promoteNode(ALL MovieDetailNode, root);
            call promoteNode(ALL GameDetailNode, root)
            reset(ALL MovieDetailNode
                [MAP on element: element.amountOfAccesses]);
            reset(ALL GameDetailNode
                [MAP on element: element.amountOfAccesses]);
    end
```

Note that the ALL keyword is used to obtain a set of all instances of a particular (conceptual) component. In this case, all concrete Movie and Game Detail nodes (i.e., each individual movie or game detail page) are the subjects of the adaptation strategy. The first part of the adaptation policy specifies that when the Web system is initialized, the number of accesses to Movie and Game Detail nodes is initialized. The second policy specifies that after one month (note that this will be repeated each month), the promotion strategy is applied, and the components containing the most popular movie and game are promoted to the root. Finally, all tracking variables are reset for the next month of tracking.

11.8 SUMMARY

WSDM is a Semantic Web design method based on an audience-driven design philosophy. This means that the requirements of the target audience, rather than the data available in the organization or its internal organization, are the starting point of the modeling process. The different audience classes and their different requirements are also reflected in the actual structure of the Web system. This approach is used to offer the designer a well-defined method to identify the information and functionality needed for a Web system and to structure it in an appropriate way. This must prevent the developers from only providing information that happened to be available and structuring it in a way that is obvious only for them. The method is based on the principle that a Web system should be designed for and adapted to its target audiences.

The method also makes a clear distinction between the conceptual design and the implementation design. Issues like grouping of information and functionality in pages and graphical presentation and layout are not considered to be conceptual issues but implementation design issues, because more than one grouping into pages or more than one presentation design is possible for the same conceptual design.

Last but not least, WSDM allows developing Web systems that are semantically annotated by means of one or more ontologies. Next to the regular content-related semantic annotations, structural annotations can also be generated. These are annotations that describe the semantics of the different structural elements of the Web system and can be exploited by other applications to transcode the Web system to formats more suitable for purposes other than human reading.

Furthermore, the clear separation of design concern by means of different design concepts and models as well as a clear separation between conceptual issues and implementation issues have shown to pay off: The modeling of a new design concern can easily been added. This has been demonstrated for adding localization and adaptation.

REFERENCES

Brusilovsky, P., 1996, Methods and techniques of adaptive hypermedia. *User Modeling and User-Adapted Interaction*, 6(2–3), Springer Science+Business Media B.V., New York, ISSN 0924-1868, pp. 87–129.

Casteleyn, S., 2005, Designer specified self re-organizing Web sites, PhD thesis, Vrije Universiteit, Brussels.

Casteleyn, S., and De Troyer, O., 2001, Structuring Web sites using audience class hierarchies. *Conceptual Modeling for New Information Systems Technologies, ER 2001*

Workshops, HUMACS, DASWIS, ECOMO, and DAMA, Lecture Notes in Computer Science, **2465**, Springer-Verlag, ISBN 3-540-44-122-0, pp. 198–211.

Casteleyn, S., De Troyer, O., and Brockmans, S., 2003, Design time support for adaptive behavior in Web sites. *Proceedings 18th ACM Symposium on Applied Computing,* ACM, ISBN 1-58113-624-2, pp. 1222–1228.

Deng, C., Yu, S., Wen, J.-R., and Ma, W.-Y., 2004, Block-based Web search. *SIGIR 2004: Proceedings 27th Annual International ACM SIGIR Conference on Research and Development in Information Retrieval,* Sheffield, UK, July 25-29, M. Sanderson, K. Järvelin, J. Allan, and P. Bruza, eds., ACM, ISBN 1-58113-881-4, pp. 456–463.

De Troyer, O., and Casteleyn, S., 2001, The conference review system with WSDM. *First International Workshop on Web-Oriented Software Technology, IWWOST'01* (also http://www.dsic.upv.es/~west2001/iwwost01/), O. Pastor, ed., Valencia University of Technology, Spain.

De Troyer, O., and Casteleyn, S., 2003a, Modeling complex processes for Web applications using WSDM. *Proceedings Third International Workshop on Web-Oriented Software Technologies (held in conjunction with ICWE2003), IWWOST2003* (also http://www.dsic.upv.es/~west/iwwost03/articles.htm), D. Schwabe, O. Pastor, G. Rossi, and L. Olsina, eds., Oviedo, Spain.

De Troyer, O., and Casteleyn, S., 2003b, Exploiting link types during the conceptual design of Web sites. *International Journal of Web Engineering Technology (IJWT),* **1**(1): 17–40.

De Troyer, O., and Casteleyn, S., 2004, Designing localized Web sites. *Proceedings 5th International Conference on Web Information Systems Engineering (WISE2004),* X. Zhou, S. Su, M.P. Papazoglou, M.E. Orlowska, and K.G. Jeffery, eds., Springer-Verlag, Brisbane, Australia, ISBN 3-540-23894-8, pp. 547–558.

De Troyer, O., Casteleyn, S., and Plessers, P., 2005, Using ORM to model Web systems. *On the Move to Meaningful Internet Systems 2005: OTM 2005 Workshops, International Workshop on Object-Role Modeling (ORM'05), Lecture Notes in Computer Science,* **3762**, Springer, ISBN 3-540-29739-1, pp. 700–709.

De Troyer, O., and Leune, C., 1998, WSDM: A user-centered design method for Web sites. *Computer Networks and ISDN Systems, Proceedings 7th International World Wide Web Conference,* Elsevier, Brisbane, Australia, pp. 85–94.

Halpin, T., 2001, *Conceptual Schema and Relational Database Design: From Conceptual Analysis to Logical Design,* Morgan Kaufmann, San Francisco.

Paterno F., 2000, *Model-Based Design and Evaluation of Interactive Applications,* Springer-Verlag, New York.

Paterno, F., Mancini, C., and Meniconi, S., 1997, ConcurTaskTrees: A diagrammatic notation for specifying task models. *Proceedings INTERACT 97,* Chapman & Hall, pp. 362–366.

Perkowitz, M., and Etzioni, O., 1997, Adaptive Web sites: An AI challenge. *Proceedings 15th International Joint Conference on Artificial Intelligence,* Morgan Kaufmann, pp. 16–23.

Plessers, P., Casteleyn, S., and De Troyer, O., 2005a, Semantic Web development with WSDM. *Proceedings 5th International Workshop on Knowledge Markup and Semantic Annotation (SemAnnot 2005),* Galway, Ireland.

Plessers, P., Casteleyn, S., Yesilada, Y., De Troyer, O., Stevens, R., Harper, S., and Goble, C., 2005b, Accessibility: A Web engineering approach. *Proceedings 14th International World Wide Web Conference (WWW2005),* A. Ellis and T. Hagino, eds., ACM, Chiba, Japan, ISBN 1-59593-046-9, pp. 353–362.

Plessers, P., and De Troyer, O., 2004a, Web design for the Semantic Web. *Proceedings WWW2004 Workshop on Application Design, Development and Implementation Issues in the Semantic Web, CEUR Workshop Proceedings, Vol. 105 Web, WWW2004 Workshop,* C. Bussler, S. Decker, D. Schwabe, and O. Pastor, eds., ISBN 1613-0073, New York.

Plessers, P., and De Troyer, O., 2004b, Annotation for the Semantic Web during Web site development. *Proceedings ICWE 2004 Conference, Lecture Notes in Computer Science,* **3140**, N. Koch, P. Fraternali, and M. Wirsing, eds., Springer, Munich, Germany, ISBN 3-540-22511-0, pp. 349–353.

Yesilada, Y., Harper, S., Goble, G., and Stevens, R., 2004, Screen readers cannot see (ontology-based semantic annotation for visually impaired Web travelers). *Web Engineering, 5th International Conference, ICWE 2005, Sydney, Australia, July 27-29, 2005, Proceedings, Lecture Notes in Computer Science,* **3579**, Springer, ISBN 3-540-27996-2, pp. 445–458.

Chapter 12

AN OVERVIEW OF MODEL-DRIVEN WEB ENGINEERING AND THE MDA

Nathalie Moreno,[1] José Raúl Romero,[2] Antonio Vallecillo[1]
[1]Dept. *Lenguajes y Ciencias de la Computación, University of Málaga, Spain*
[2]Dept. *Informática y Análisis Numérico, University of Córdoba, Spain*

12.1 INTRODUCTION

Model-Driven Software Development (MDSD) is becoming a widely accepted approach for developing complex distributed applications. MDSD advocates the use of models as the key artifacts in all phases of development, from system specification and analysis to design and implementation. Each model usually addresses one concern, independently from the rest of the issues involved in the construction of the system. Thus, the basic functionality of the system can be separated from its final implementation; the business logic can be separated from the underlying platform technology, etc. The transformations between models enable the automated implementation of a system from the different models defined for it.

Web Engineering is a specific domain in which MDSD can be successfully applied. Most of the technology is here to implement systems that exploit the Web paradigm, but the effective design of Web applications is still a concern: The complexity and requirements of Web applications are constantly growing, while the supporting technologies and platforms rapidly evolve.

Existing model-driven Web Engineering (MDWE) approaches already provide excellent methodologies and tools for the design and development of most kinds of Web applications. They address different concerns using separate models (navigation, presentation, data, etc.) and are supported by model compilers that produce most of the application's Web pages and logic based on the models. However, these proposals also present some limitations, especially when it comes to modeling further concerns, such as architectural styles or distribution. Furthermore, current Web systems need to interoperate with other external applications, something that requires their integration with third-party Web services, portals, and also with legacy systems. Finally, many of these Web Engineering proposals do not fully exploit all the potential benefits of MDSD, such as complete platform independence, model transformation and merging, or meta-modeling. Miller and Mukerji (2003) from the Object Management Group (OMG™) have introduced a new approach for organizing the design of an application into (yet another set of) separate models so that portability, interoperability, and reusability can be obtained through architectural separation of concerns. MDA covers a wide spectrum of topics and issues (MOF-based meta-models, UML profiles, model transformations, modeling languages and tools, etc.) and also promises the interoperability required between models and tools from separate vendors. On the other camp, Software Factories (Greenfield and Short, 2004) provide effective concepts and resources for the model-based design and development of complex applications, and it is our belief that they can be successfully used for Web Engineering, too.

In this chapter we will introduce the main concepts involved in MDWE and discuss its current strengths, weaknesses, and major challenges, especially in the context of the MDA initiative.

12.2 DOMAIN-SPECIFIC MODELING

Domain-specific modeling (DSM) is a way of designing and developing systems that involves the systematic use of domain-specific languages (DSLs) to represent the various facets of a system. Such languages tend to support higher-level abstractions than general-purpose modeling languages and are closer to the problem domain than to the implementation domain. Thus, a DSL follows the domain abstractions and semantics, allowing modelers to perceive themselves as working directly with domain concepts. Furthermore, the rules of the domain can be included in the language as constraints, thereby disallowing the specification of illegal or incorrect models.

DSLs play a cornerstone role in DSM. In general, defining a modeling language involves at least two aspects: the domain concepts and rules (abstract syntax), and the notation used to represent these concepts (concrete syntax—let it be textual or graphical). Each model is written in the language of its meta-model. Thus, a meta-model will describe the concepts of the language, the relationships between them, and the structuring rules that constrain the model elements and combinations in order to respect the domain rules. We normally say that a model conforms to its meta-model (Bézivin, 2005).

Meta-models are also models, and therefore they need to be written in another language, which is described by its meta-meta-model. This recursive definition normally ends at that level, since meta-meta-models conform to themselves.

A typical example of a meta-model-defined DSL is ATL (Jouault and Kurtev, 2006b), which is a transformation language. A large library of ATL transformations is available from the Eclipse meta-model open source library. The interested reader can consult the work by Bézivin (2005) for a more complete and detailed introduction to these topics.

DSM often also includes the idea of code generation: automating the creation of executable source code directly from the DSM models. Being free from the manual creation and maintenance of source code implies significant improvements in developer productivity, reduction of both defects and errors in programs, and a better resulting quality. Moreover, working with models of the problem domain instead of models of the code raises the level of abstraction, hiding unnecessary complexity and implementation-specific details, while putting the emphasis on already familiar terminology.

A DSM environment may be thought of as a meta-modeling tool, i.e., a modeling tool used to define a modeling tool or CASE tool. The domain expert only needs to specify the domain-specific constructs and rules, and the DSM environment provides a modeling tool tailored for the target domain. The resulting tool may either work within the DSM environment or, less commonly, may be produced as a separate standalone program. Using a DSM environment can significantly lower the cost of obtaining tool support for a DSM language, since a well-designed DSM environment will automate the creation of program parts that are costly to build from scratch, such as domain-specific editors, browsers, and components.

Examples of DSM environments include commercial ones such as MetaEdit+; open source environments, such as the Generic Eclipse Modeling System; or academic ones such as the Generic Modeling Environment (GME; http://www.isis.vanderbilt.edu/projects/gme/). The increasing popularity of DSM has led to DSM frameworks being added to existing integrated development environments, such as the Eclipse Modeling Project (EMP) and Microsoft's DSL Tools for Software Factories.

12.3 MDA

One of the best known MDSD initiatives is called Model-Driven Architecture (MDA®), which is an approach to software development produced and maintained by the OMG, a consortium that produces and maintains computer industry specifications for interoperable enterprise applications. MDA is a registered trademark of the OMG, together with its related acronym, model-driven development (MDD), another OMG trademark.

The goal of MDA is one that is often sought: to separate business and application logic from its underlying execution platform technology so that (1) changes in the underlying platform do not affect existing applications and (2) business logic can evolve independently from the underlying technology. A tool that implements the MDA concepts will allow developers to produce models of the application and business logic and also generate code for a target platform by means of transformations.

The major benefit of this approach is that it raises the level of abstraction in software development. Instead of writing platform-specific code in some high-level language, software developers focus on developing models that are specific to the application domain but independent of the platform. In a nutshell, MDA is a broad conceptual framework that describes an overall approach to software development.

MDA is not to be confused with MDSD. MDA is the OMG implementation of MDSD, using the set of tools and standards defined by OMG. These OMG standards include UML® (Unified Modeling Language), MOF (Meta-Object Facility), XMI (XML Metadata Interchange), and MOF/QVT (Query/View/Transformations), among others. All these standards can be obtained from the OMG Web site (www.omg.org).

12.3.1 The MDA Framework

The MDA framework is basically organized around the so-called platform-independent models (PIMs) and platform-specific models (PSMs) and on the model transformations between them. The PIM is a specification of a system in terms of domain concepts. These domain concepts exhibit a specified degree of independence of different platforms (e.g., CORBA, .NET, and J2EE). The system can then be compiled using any of those platforms as a target by transforming the PIM to a platform-specific model (PSM). Thus, the PSM specifies how the system uses a particular type of platform. Finally, the application's code is considered a form of PSM (at the lowest level).

In MDA, a platform is a set of subsystems and technologies that provides a set of functionality through interfaces and specified usage patterns, which any application supported by that platform can use without concern for the details of how the functionality provided by the platform is implemented (Miller and Mukerji, 2003). As in MDSD, each model in MDA conforms to a meta-model, which in MDA can be defined using MOF.

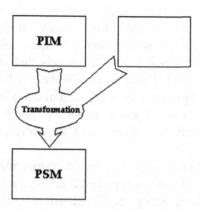

Figure 12.1. The MDA pattern.

In addition to models, transformations are also at the heart of MDA. Model transformation is the process of converting one model to another model of the same system (see Figure 12.1). Such transformations can be done following many ways: using types, marks, templates, etc. In MDA, software development becomes an iterative model transformation process: Each step transforms one PIM of the system at one level into one PSM at the next level, until a final system implementation is reached, with the particularity that each PSM of a transformation can become the PIM of the next transformation (within another level of abstraction). In this context, the implementation is just another model, which provides all the information necessary to construct the system and put it into operation.

12.3.2 OMG Approaches for Defining DSLs

Both PIMs and PSMs are models and are therefore defined using modeling languages. Although in theory MDA's models can be defined using any modeling language, OMG strongly suggests that models are specified using UML or any other MOF-compliant language (i.e., whose meta-meta-model is MOF). This interest for being MOF- and UML-compliant arises from the increasing need to be able to interoperate with other notations and tools, and to exchange data and models, thus facilitating and improving reuse.

OMG defines three main possible approaches for defining domain-specific languages. The first solution is to develop a meta-model that is able to represent the relevant domain concepts. This means creating a new domain language, an alternative to UML, using the MOF meta-modeling facilities provided by OMG for defining object-based visual languages (i.e., the same mechanisms that have been used for defining UML and its meta-model). In this way, the syntax and semantics of the elements of the new language are defined to faithfully match the domain's specific characteristics. The problem is that standard UML tools will not be able to deal with such a new language (to edit models that conform to the meta-model, compile them, etc.). This approach is the one followed by languages such as the CWM (Common Warehouse Metamodel) or the W2000 (Baresi et al., 2006b) notations, since the semantics of some of these languages' constructs do not match the semantics of the corresponding UML model elements.

The second and third solutions are based on extending UML. Extensions of the UML can be either heavyweight or lightweight. The difference between lightweight and heavyweight extensions comes from the way in which they extend the UML meta-model. Heavyweight extensions are based on a modified UML meta-model with the implication that the original semantics of modeling elements is changed, and therefore the extension might no longer be compatible with UML tools.

Lightweight extensions are called UML *profiles* and are based on the extension mechanisms provided by UML (OMG, 2005b; Fuentes and Vallecillo, 2004) (stereotypes, tag definitions, and constraints) for specializing its meta-classes, but without breaking their original semantics. UML profiles may impose new restrictions on the extended meta-classes, but they should respect the UML meta-model without modifying the original semantics of the UML elements (i.e., the basic features of UML classes, associations, properties, etc. will remain the same, only new constraints can be added to the original elements). Syntactic sugar can also be defined in a profile, in terms of icons and symbols for the newly defined elements. One of the major benefits of profiles is that they can be handled in a natural way by UML tools.

In UML profiles, stereotypes define particularizations of given UML elements, adding some semantics to them. For instance, we can define the stereotype <<persistent>> that extends UML classes to represent persistent elements in a particular domain. Tag definitions specify the possible attributes of stereotypes (e.g., the name of the table where the persistent element should be stored). Finally, constraints define the domain rules that the stereotyped UML elements should obey in order to make up correct models (e.g., suppose that we do not want abstract classes to be stereotyped as persistent). Figure 12.2 graphically shows the UML specification of this example stereotype.

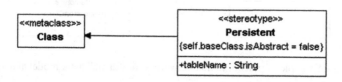

Figure 12.2. An example of a UML 2.0 stereotype specification.

Constraints on stereotypes are normally specified using OCL (Object Constraint Language) (OMG, 2006), whose current version (2.0) is fully aligned with UML. Constraints can be either directly attached to the modeling elements (as shown in the figure) or separately specified and then related to the element to which they apply by identifying their context:

context Persistent **inv:**
self.baseClass.isAbstract = false

Perhaps the best-known example of customizing UML for a specific domain is SysML, a DSL for systems engineering (www.sysml.org). In addition, there is a whole set of UML profiles that customize UML to deal with the specific concepts required in several relevant application domains (e.g., real-time, business process modeling, finance, etc.) or implementation technologies (such as .NET, J2EE, or CORBA).

The main advantage of UML profiles is probably not the extension of the UML meta-model (which is already too large and complex to be used in full) but that they allow "restricting" the set of UML elements that need to be used in a given domain, particularizing the semantics of those elements in order to capture the semantics and structuring rules of the domain-specific elements they represent. It is important to repeat that such a particularization can only be done by refinement, and without changing the original semantics of UML elements.

Finally, meta-transformations that transform back and forth from the profile definition to the meta-model definition can also be specified, as shown in Figure 12.3.

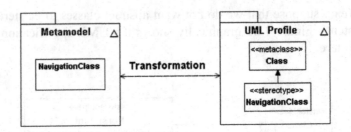

Figure 12.3. Example of transformation between a "profilable" meta-model and a profile.

12.3.3 Model Transformations

A model transformation can be viewed as a transformation between two models that describes how elements in the source model are converted into elements in the target model. This is done by relating the appropriate meta-model elements in the source and target meta-models and defining constraints and guards on such relations (e.g., the preconditions on the transformation to take place). It is important to notice that model transformations are also models, and therefore they conform to a meta-model that describes the language in which they are expressed.

MDA describes a wide variety of models and transformations between models. While there are many kinds of transformations, they can fit broadly into two main categories:

- Vertical mappings (or *refinements*), which relate system models at different levels of abstraction—such as PIM to PSM mappings, or reverse-engineering mappings. Until now, vertical transformations have in most cases been developed within modeling tools using Web tool-specific proprietary languages. For the same reason that domain know-how should not be tied to a particular platform, it is thus critical that model transformations are not dependent on a given CASE tool.
- Horizontal mappings, which relate or integrate models covering different aspects or domains within a system, but at the same level of abstraction. Horizontal mappings maintain the consistency between levels, guaranteeing that an entity needs to be consistent with what is said about the same entity in any other specification at the same level of abstraction. This includes the consistency of that entity's properties, structure, and behavior.

In MDA, OMG proposes MOF-QVT (Query/View/Transformation) (OMG, 2005a) as the standard language for specifying model transformations. Many other model transformation languages, like VIATRA by the University of Budapest, ATL by INRIA, RubyTL (Sánchez and García-Molina, 2006) by the University of Murcia, etc., are also available, with different levels of compliance to the QVT standard (Jouault and Kurtev, 2006a). The interested reader can visit the "Model Transformation" Web site (www.model-transformation.org) for a complete listing of model transformation languages and tools.

12.4 MODEL-DRIVEN WEB ENGINEERING PROPOSALS

As mentioned in the introduction, Web Engineering is a specific domain in which MDSD can be successfully applied, due to its particular characteristics: There is a precise set of concerns that need to be addressed (navigation, presentation, business processes, etc.); the basic kinds of Web applications is well known (Kappel et al., 2006) (document-centric, transactional, workflow-based, collaborative, etc.); and the set of architectural patterns and structural features used in Web systems is reduced and precisely defined. In fact, existing model-based Web Engineering approaches—most of which have been described in this book—already provide excellent methodologies and tools for the design and development of most kinds of Web applications.

These approaches come basically from two main areas. First, a few proposals are based on hypermedia design methods, introducing the required expressiveness and mechanisms to capture relevant Web-specific elements, such as navigation. Prominent examples of these initiatives are HDM (Garzotto et al., 1993), RMM (Frasincar, 2001), WebML (Ceri et al., 2002), W2000 (Baresi et al., 2006b), WSDM (De Troyer and Leune, 1998), Hera (Vdovjak et al., 2003), and Webile (Di Ruscio, 2004), the majority of which are based on the classic E/R model or on extensions of it. Another group of more recent approaches emerged as extensions of conventional object-oriented development techniques, adapting them to cope with the particular characteristics of Web systems. In this group we can find methods such as EORM (Lange, 1994), OOHDM (Schwabe et al., 1999), UWE (Koch, 2001), OOWS (Pastor et al., 2006), OO-Method (Pastor et al., 2001), OO-H (Gómez and Cachero, 2003), and MIDAS (De Castro et al., 2006).

These proposals are model-driven because they address the different concerns involved in the design and development of a Web application using separate models (such as content, navigation, and presentation) and then are supported by model compilers that produce most of the application's Web pages and logic from the original models. Furthermore, most of them count with development processes that support their notations and tools and have been successfully used in commercial environments for building many different kinds of Web systems. And although all methodologies adopt different notations and propose their own constructs, they all share a common ground of concepts—and thus they might be considered as somehow based on a common meta-model, as suggested by Koch and Kraus (2003).

However, as the complexity of Web applications grows (to be able to deliver, e.g., large e-commerce, e-learning, or e-government applications), and new requirements are imposed on Web systems, most of these proposals show some limitations:

- They are usually tied to particular architectural styles and technologies, i.e., they do not allow the parameterizable construction of Web applications using different platform technologies and architectural styles—they typically build client-server applications only, and based on very specific platform technologies (PHP, ASP, EJB, or JSP). The problem is that these architectural styles and target technologies are no longer relevant when, for example, mobility and nomadic features are required for some types of Web applications.
- Most of these proposals were originally conceived to deal with particular kinds of Web applications (such as Web information systems, hypermedia applications, or adaptive Web applications), so they deal with a fixed set of common concerns (navigation, presentation, etc.). Therefore, they are very good at modeling certain aspects, but very weak at modeling others. In addition, they are difficult to extend to model further aspects (such as internal processes, distribution, and some other extra-functional concerns) in a natural, modular, and independent way.

Finally, Web applications currently need to interoperate with other external systems. This requires their integration with third-party Web services, portals, and legacy systems—meaning, among other things, that their processes, choreography, and part of their business logic must be explicitly available for integration with these external systems (Moreno and Vallecillo, 2005a). Not all MDWE proposals address this issue at the model level; the integration is mostly achieved at the implementation level.

Solving all these limitations is not a trivial task. We are currently observing how some Web Engineering proposals are evolving to cope with some of these issues. For instance, some of them are developing extensions to address more and more aspects. Examples include UWE and OO-H, which have incorporated a process model into their original approaches (Koch et al., 2004) and are working to deal with the architectural style of the final application, too (Cáceres et al., 2006). WebML has also evolved to be able to deal with legacy systems and for context-awareness (Ceri et al.,

2007). The problem with these incremental extensions is that, unless their efforts to include new concerns are made in a very well-organized and interoperable manner, we may end up with proposals that have grown by adding too many new features in an unnatural and artificial way, and therefore may become too complex and brittle.

Another problem that some of these proposals are also facing is their use of proprietary notations and tools. This forces customers and developers to buy and use "yet-another" modeling tool (with the learning costs and efforts involved in the process) if they want to take advantage of them. Even worse, these proprietary tools do not interoperate with the rest of the tools being used by the customer, which forces him to work with a whole set of isolated development environments, each one different (and incompatible) from the rest—something that the customer is not going to tolerate.

Thus, we are witnessing how the Web Engineering community considers the use of standard UML notation, techniques, and supporting tools for modeling Web systems, including the adaptation of their own modeling languages, representation diagrams, and development processes to UML. There is a need to be able to be compatible and to interoperate with other notations and tools, and to seamlessly exchange data and models with them. This is the case for WebML, which is defining UML-based representations of its modeling language so that the WebML notation and its development process can be smoothly integrated into standard UML development environments (Moreno et al., 2006; Schauerhuber et al., 2006).

The advent of the model-driven architecture (MDA) initiative may also bring significant benefits here and may help to address most of the limitations cited above in a natural way. As mentioned in the preceding section, MDA provides an approach for organizing the design of an application into separate models so that portability, interoperability, and reusability can be achieved through architectural separation of concerns. In addition, the new modeling notation UML 2.0 incorporates a whole new set of diagrams and concepts that are more appropriate for modeling the specific structure and behavior of software systems, in particular of Web applications (e.g., the new structuring mechanisms, or the improved specification and semantics of state machines and activities).

Of course, the use of UML and MDA for model-driven Web Engineering is not free from problems. As any other initiative, it brings along both benefits and drawbacks and also has both supporters and detractors. The next two sections are dedicated to explaining these ideas in detail.

12.5 MDA-BASED WEB ENGINEERING

MDA provides several interesting opportunities to improve current Web Engineering approaches, helping them to overcome some of the limitations cited above.

12.5.1 Becoming UML- and MOF-Compliant

As previously mentioned, there is an increasing need to be able to interoperate and be compatible with other notations and tools, and to integrate with already existing modeling environments—in particular, with the UML tools that today are commonplace in many customer settings. Of course, other DSM environments are already being developed—some of them probably much better than those supporting the UML notation—but the problem is that they have not reached the level of acceptance and are not as widespread as UML modeling tools are today. And we are faced with the need to be able to offer a solution to our customers today.

In this sense, a very promising approach is the definition of UML profiles for representing proprietary Web Engineering modeling languages. This is the case with WebML, which has recently defined a meta-model and a UML profile (Moreno et al., 2006; Schauerhuber et al., 2006) for its notation. This allows the WebML language and its development process (supported by the WebRatio tool) to be smoothly integrated with standard UML development environments.

In addition, counting on a meta-model for WebML will allow its integration with other MDA tools as soon as they are available (editors, validators, metric evaluators, etc.) and also with other MDSD approaches and tools (using model transformations that allow the conversion of MOF-meta-models to other meta-modeling approaches, such as KM3 or Ecore).

12.5.2 Organizing Models According to the MDA Principles

We are also witnessing how other approaches that were originally UML-based are making use of the new MDA principles to reorganize their models in a modular manner, in such a way that each model focuses on one specific concern and then formulates its development processes in terms of model transformations and model merges.

Probably the most representative example is UWE, which has successfully restructured its original set of models (which represented the different concerns involved in the design and development of a Web application) in terms of meta-models, and the UWE development process in terms of transformations between them (Koch, 2006; Kraus, 2007). This has significantly enhanced the original proposal with better modularity, expressiveness, and reuse. Furthermore, the use of specification techniques for the transformations will allow UWE to redefine and improve many of the aspects of its development process, especially those that were originally hard-coded in the UWE supporting CASE tool, in order to benefit from model transformation rules defined at a higher abstraction level, e.g., using graph transformations or transformation languages.

Another interesting outcome of the work done by the UWE group when adopting the MDA principles into their proposal is the analysis of the models (and model transformations) that comprise the MDSD process for Web applications, focusing on the classification of the model transformations in terms of type, complexity, number of source models, involvement of marking models, implementation techniques, and execution type (Koch, 2006). This analysis could be very useful to other model-based Web Engineering methods if they decide to reformulate their proposals in terms of independent models and transformations between them. Other proposals, such as MIDAS, have also started to adopt such an approach by specifying the development process of Web information systems in terms of (meta)models and transformations between them (Cáceres et al., 2006).

12.5.3 Adding New Concerns

This reformulation of model-based Web Engineering proposals is also proving other benefits, such as the modular addition of further aspects into their designs. Most of these concerns were not contemplated originally, and integrating them was difficult because of the (usually ad hoc) internal structure of their supporting processes and tools.

One representative example is OO-H, whose authors realized that they had to be able to deliver Web applications with different software architectures and to different platforms, depending on the customers' specific requirements—in this case the customers were the ones demanding such features. The OO-H team managed to successfully reformulate part of their internal structure and methods, making the representation of the software architecture of the system a separate concern that could be captured as a separate model, and then merged (using QVT transformations) with the rest of the models of the system (such as navigation, presentation, etc.) (Meliá and Gómez, 2006).

UWE and OO-H have also investigated the explicit representation of the business processes of a Web application, as separate models (Koch et al., 2004). Their joint findings are very encouraging, because they managed to define a common way for modeling them for both proposals. This shows that reuse of meta-models across Web Engineering proposals is feasible.

Finally, UWE has also shown recently how other concerns, such as the user requirements (Koch et al., 2006), can be expressed as UML models and connected to the approach. This is one of the benefits they obtained once they fully reorganized their proposal as a set of separate models, related through model transformations (Kraus, 2007).

All these findings support the thesis that a common meta-model is possible for Web Engineering, as originally proposed by Koch and Kraus (2003). Furthermore, in the next section we will see how the existence of a common meta-model could allow the definition of a framework for building Web applications, which in the context of the MDA would also enable the exchange of models and tools between MDWE proposals.

12.6 WEI: A MODEL-BASED FRAMEWORK FOR BUILDING WEB APPLICATIONS

In this section we shall identify a general set of common concerns involved in the development of Web applications and present a model-driven Web architectural framework (WEI) for organizing and relating the different models that represent these concerns. Each WEI model focuses on one particular concern (navigation, presentation, architectural style, distribution) and at different levels of abstraction (platform-independent, platform-specific). The set of meta-models that define such models can be considered as a common meta-model for WEI.

MDWAF is also supported by a development methodology for building Web applications, which conforms to the MDA principles—in the sense that it is defined in terms of models and the relationships between them, so transformations can be easily formalized among the models until the final implementation is reached.

12.6.1 Identifying Reference Models for Web Applications

In general, the kinds of concerns involved in the development of a Web application will directly depend on the type of Web application being designed and also on the project requirements. Web applications have already been classified by complexity and development history (Kappel et al., 2006):

1. *Document-centric Web sites*, which are hierarchical collections of static HTML documents (basically, plain text and images) that offer read-only information based on a set of structured content, navigation patterns, and presentation characteristics designed and stored a priori.

The simplicity and stability of these systems limit the scope of Web modeling to three models: a **user interface structure** model that deals with the content of the information delivered to the client; a **navigation** model that points out the network of paths within the Web application; and a **presentation** model that refers to the visual elements that comprise the Web pages.

2. *Transactional Web applications*, which incorporate support for persistent data store, information location, concurrency control, failure, and configuration management. In addition to the navigation aspects of any hypermedia application, development of transactional Web applications implies the need for an effective **information structure** model, which is capable of capturing the processes of inserting, updating, and deleting data, and also a **distribution** model, which enables the establishment of alternatives for carrying out transactions. A clearer separation between data design, among behavioral aspects of the application, and from the user interface concerns is required.

3. *Interactive Web applications*, which are browser-based applications that allow dynamic content of Web pages, hence providing users with personalized information. This feature requires a **process** model that describes how business classes manage the information stored (i.e., the elements of the information structure model) and also requires that the navigation and presentation models are parameterizable to provide tailor-made information to individual users according to their preferences, goals, and knowledge. Furthermore, this type of application emphasizes modeling not only the information structure itself and its future consumers (i.e., the **users** model), but also the relationships or bridges between the information structure model, navigation model, and **business** model.

4. *Workflow-based Web applications*, which provide support for modeling structured business processes, activity flows, business rules, interactions among actors, roles, and a high-performance infrastructure for data storage (content management). Information is needed not only for the system actors but also for its processes. For this kind of Web applications, at a minimum the following models are required: a user interface structure model, a navigation model, a presentation model, an information structure model, a business model (i.e., the description of how functionality is encapsulated into business components and services), a process model (with a description of the behavior of the internal processes), and a **software architecture** model identifying the subsystems, components, and connectors (software and hardware) the application should have.

5. *Collaborative Web applications*, which are those executed by different groups of users that access Web resources to accomplish a specific task. They entail a modeling decomposition of the Web application

design into **views** or workspaces based on different **user roles**. For each group of users, the functional requirements, task, and activities to be performed must be specified. These issues involve **modularity** and **distribution** requirements on the process model. Finally, the information assets to be manipulated by views must also be modeled.

6. *Portal-oriented Web applications,* which integrate resources (data, applications, and services) from different sources in a single point. From an end-user perspective, a portal is a Web site with pages that are organized by some form of navigation. Pages can display either static HTML content or complex Web services. Personalization, behavior tracking of users, as well as message flows in Web service collaborations are extremely relevant in portal-oriented Web applications. Therefore, a **choreography** model needs to express the expected behavior of both the system processes and the **external services** in order to check their compatibility and interoperability to compose them to build the portal aggregated.

7. *Ubiquitous Web applications,* which need to be accessible at any time, from anywhere, and in any media, i.e., they must run on a variety of platforms, including mobile phones, personal digital assistants (PDAs), desktop computers, etc. This implies that their **presentation** and **navigational** models should be **adaptable** not only to different kinds of users, but also to different kinds of platforms and contexts. Consequently, this kind of application requires modeling the separation between **platform-independent** and **platform-specific** concerns.

Based on the set of concerns identified above, each one represented by one model, we have built an architectural framework for model-driven Web application development (WEI). Its basic structure is depicted in Figure 12.4. It is organized in three main layers (User Interface, Business Logic, and Data), each one corresponding to a viewpoint. In turn, each layer is composed of a set of models, which specify the entities relevant to each concern.

Far from being "yet another Web methodology," the aims of WEI can be summarized as follows:

1. to be able to represent, in terms of models and relationships between them, the concerns required for designing and developing Web applications—following an architectural separation of concerns as prescribed by MDA
2. to integrate and harmonize the models and practices proposed by existing approaches, addressing their concerns
3. to be extensible so that new concerns could be easily added

4. to provide as a common framework (and meta-model) in which current proposals could be integrated and formulated in terms of the MDA principles, hence allowing them to smoothly interoperate (by defining, e.g., interoperability bridges between compatible models coming from different proposals, whenever this is possible) and complement each other, share tools, etc.

At a high architectural design level, the whole WEI concept space is captured by 13 meta-models, organized in 3 main packages as shown in Figure 12.4. It is important to note that the models that comprise the framework have not been arbitrarily chosen but are based on the concerns covered by existing Web Engineering proposals (see also Table 12.1 later on) and our previous experience with the development of large distributed applications.

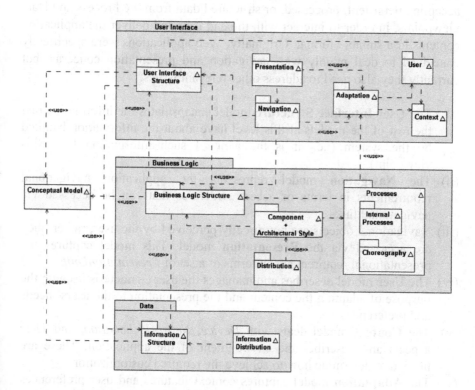

Figure 12.4. Models representing the concerns involved in the development of Web applications.

At the bottom level, the **Data Structure** package describes the organization of the information managed by the application (by means of, e.g., a database system) and provides a mechanism for storing it persistently. Information is depicted in terms of the data elements that constitute its information base and the semantic relationships between these elements. This level is organized in two models:

(i) The **Information Structure** model deals with the information that has to be made persistent, i.e., stored in a database.
(ii) The **Information Distribution** model describes the distribution and replication of the data being modeled, since information can be fragmented in *nodes* or replicated in different *locations*.

Then, the **User Interface** focuses on the facilities provided to the end user for accessing and navigating through the information managed by the application and describes how this information is presented depending on the context and the user profile. The User Interface level is responsible for accepting persistent, processed, or structured data from the Process and Data viewpoints, in order to interact with the end user and deliver the application contents in a suitable format. Originally, Web applications were specifically conceived to deal mainly with navigation and presentation concerns, but currently they also need to address other relevant issues:

(i)   The **User Interface Structure** model encapsulates the information that the rest of the models at this level have about the information handled by the system (i.e., it is the *view* of such information from this viewpoint).
(ii) The **Navigation** model represents the application navigational requirements in terms of access structures that can be accessed via navigational links.
(iii) Navigational objects are not directly perceived by the user; rather, they are accessed via the **Presentation** model. This model captures the presentational requirements in terms of a set of *PresentationUnits*.
(iv) The **User** model describes and manages the user characteristics with the purpose of adapting the content and the presentation to the users' needs and preferences.
(v)   The **Context** model deals with *Device, Network, Location,* and *Time* aspects and describes the environment of the application. These are needed to determine how to achieve the required customization.
(vi) The **Adaptation** model captures context features and user preferences to obtain the appropriate Web content characteristics (e.g., the number of embedded objects in a Web page, the dimension of the base-Web page without components, or the total dimension of the embedded components). Adaptation policies are usually specified in terms of ECA rules.

Finally, the **Business Logic** package encapsulates the business logic of the application, i.e., how the information is processed and how the application interacts with other computerized systems.

(i) The **Business Logic Structure** model describes the major classes or component types representing services in the system (*BusinessProcessInformation*), their attributes (*Attributes*), the signature of their operations (*Signature*), and the relationships between them (*Association*). The design of the Structure model is driven by the needs of the processes that implement the business logic of the system, taking into account the tasks that users can perform.

(ii) The **Internal Processes** model specifies the precise behavior of every *BusinessProcessInformation* or component as well as the set of activities that are executed in order to achieve a business objective. For a complete description of a business process, apart from the Structure model, we need information related to the *Activities* carried out by the *BusinessProcessInformation*, expressing their behavior and the *Flows* that pass around objects or data.

(iii) The **Choreography** model defines the valid sequences of messages and interactions that the different objects of the system may exchange. The choreography may be individually oriented, specifying the contract a component exhibits to other components (*PartialChoreography*), or it may be globally oriented, specifying the flow of messages within a global composition (*GlobalChoreography*).

(iv) The **Distribution** model describes how its basic entities, the *nodes*, are connected by means of point to point connections or *links*. While the Information Distribution model of the Data layer specifies the distribution of the data, this model describes the distribution of the processes that achieve the business logic of the system.

(v) The **Component+Architectural Style** model defines the fundamental organization of a system in terms of its components, their relationships, and the principles guiding its design and evolution, i.e., how functionality is encapsulated into business components and services.

The emphasis in each of these levels will depend on the kind of Web application being modeled (data-intensive, user interface-oriented, etc.).

A central model of the WEI framework is the **Conceptual Model**, which can be used for specifying the basic structure and contents on the Web application (so the rest of the "views" can relate to the elements of that model) and also for maintaining the consistency of the model specifications, establishing how the different viewpoints merge and complement each other.

Note that, in addition to the models, the framework predefines some dependencies between the models which determine those cases in which the definition of a model requires the previous specification of some other models. At a different level, the dependencies may also imply how the framework instantiation process should be carried out. Furthermore, these dependencies also specify correspondences between the elements from different models of the framework, especially when they may have been independently developed by different parties, or when they represent the system from different viewpoints, and therefore the same element is specified in different ways in different models (each one offering a partial view of the whole). In these cases, correspondences between model elements may also be subject to certain consistency rules, which check that the views do not impose contradictory requirements on the elements they share.

12.6.2 Modeling These Concerns

In order to formally define the framework, we have built an MOF meta-model for each model, which describes its entities and their relationships (http://www.lcc.uma.es/~nathalie/WEI/). MOF was selected as a meta-modeling language because of our interest in being MDA-compliant. Other alternatives were, of course, possible (using, e.g., KM3 or Ecore), but it was important for us to try to use OMG's notations and tools, to exercise the MDA approach. MagicDraw was selected as a modeling tool. The selection of a UML tool is really important, because they do not interoperate well, and therefore the tool you use may greatly condition your project.

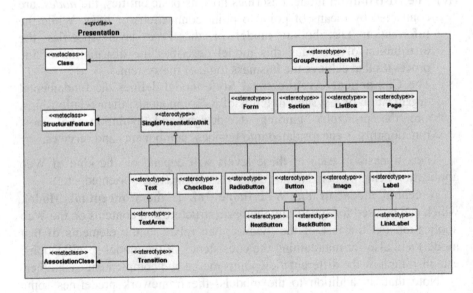

Figure 12.5. The WEI Presentation profile.

But the meta-models are just one part of the puzzle. Unlike other approaches, OMG does not provide a solution for directly building correct models from meta-models. Instead, you have to define your own DSL associated to these meta-models. In our case we defined lightweight extensions of UML, i.e., UML profiles, for representing these models (Moreno et al., 2005). As an example of it, Figure 12.5 shows the profile for the WEI presentation meta-model.

12.6.3 How the Framework is Used

WEI can be instantiated to build Web applications both from scratch and based on existing models (including those defined using other methodologies, e.g., UWE, WebML, or OO-H).

12.6.3.1 Building Applications from Scratch with WEI

The straightforward application of the framework in the context of MDA to develop a Web system from scratch has already been documented in detail (Moreno et al., 2005a, b; Moreno and Vallecillo, 2005c) and successfully applied to define and implement several kinds of Web applications such as the *Conference Review System* or the *Travel Agency Application*.

As a brief summary, the WEI methodology process involves the definition of at least three PIMs, each one corresponding to a viewpoint, as illustrated in Figure 12.6(b). Each PIM is composed of the set of models described in the previous section and is developed following the process depicted in Figure 12.6(a).

Once the three top-level PIMs have been appropriately defined, we need to mark them using the appropriate profile(s) for the target platform(s) and technologies. Once marked, we need to follow the MDA transformation process from PIMs to PSMs, applying a set of mapping rules (one for each mark and for each marked element). The result of the application of such mapping rules is a set of UML models of the application according to the target technologies (e.g., Java, JSP, Oracle, etc.). Finally, the PSMs are translated to code, applying a transformation process again.

It is important to note that *bridges* should be specified among the three PIMs and among their corresponding PSMs, and for which transformations are also required. Bridges are the key elements to maintain consistency between the different models at the same level of abstraction and to be able to provide links between them. A very interesting work by the group of Alfonso Pierantonio at the University of L'Aquila (Chicchetti et al., 2006) shows how model weaving can be effectively used to specify and implement such bridges, being able to connect the different artifacts and models produced during the development of Web applications—in particular, the models describing the data, navigation, and presentation aspects, whose connections are usually defined in an ad hoc manner, and their consistency manually maintained. Although their work is carried out using non-OMG notations and standards, it can be easily ported to the MDA context, using MOF meta-models and QVT transformations for establishing correspondences between elements from different views.

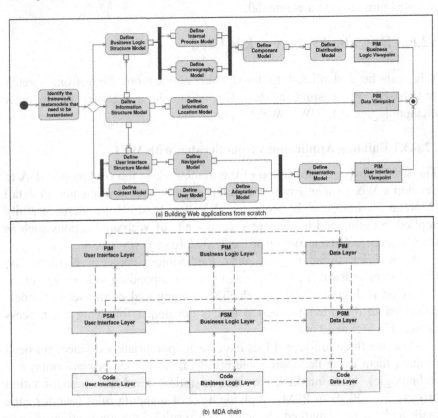

(a) Building Web applications from scratch

(b) MDA chain

Figure 12.6. The WEI process.

12.6.3.2 Designing Web Applications by Reusing Models from Other Methodologies

One of the major advantages of our proposal is its ability to design and implement applications reusing both models and tools (e.g., model compilers) defined by other Web methodologies. Thus, a Web application developer could use, for instance, UWE or OO-H for designing the models of the User Interface layer, and WebML for designing the Data layer, or vice versa. Furthermore, models could be already defined for other applications and reused here for building fast prototypes.

Reusing models conforming to other Web methodologies requires the definition of interoperability bridges between "compatible" models coming from different methodologies and the appropriate models of our framework. Usually, the source and target entities defined in different approaches do not differ much. In addition, neither the models nor the entities described in our framework were arbitrarily chosen: Instead, they try to generalize the entities and models defined by most Web Engineering proposals (see Table 12.1). Thus, the interoperability bridges between models from different proposals are a priori feasible and even quite straightforward using WEI as a reference framework.

Table 12.1 Concerns and Models Covered by Current Web Engineering Proposals

Layer	Model	OOHDM	W2000	UWE	WebML	WSDSM	OOWS	OOH
User Interface	Structure	√	~	√	~	~	√	√
	User	~		√	√	√	√	
	Context	~		√	√			
	Adaptation			√	√		√	
	Navigation	√	√	√	√	√	√	√
	Present.	√	√	√	√	√	√	√
Business Logic	Structure		~	~		√	√	~
	Processes		√	√			√	√
	Choreogr.						√	
	Architect.			√	√			√
	Distribution							
Data	Inf. Struct.	√	√	√	√	√		√
	Inf. Distrib.							

There are, however, some issues that need to be addressed, which are similar to the traditional problems that appear when integrating models that represent different views of the same system. First, we may find models using different names to refer to the same elements. Second, we may find that one model may assume the existence of other models that either provide some services (e.g., the precise behavior that needs to be executed when a navigation link is traversed) or represent external systems or legacy applications that our Web system should be able to work with (by, e.g., exchanging data or invoking services). Third, the majority of Web Engineering proposals apply (almost the same) separation of concerns, but the problem is that their levels of abstraction and granularity do not always coincide. Fourth, some of the models that we want to reuse may deal with more than one of our framework concerns. And finally, we may find some aspects and concerns that have not been modeled, because they are implicitly assumed in the proposals' models (the most typical example is behavior).

The way in which we address the first four issues is by specifying bridges (either correspondences or transformations) between the elements living in different models. Such bridges have been defined using QVT relations. The last issue, i.e., the lack of models for representing some concerns, needs to be addressed by the explicit specification of such elements, in order to supply the "missing" information. This case currently happens when models to be reused come from methodologies that do not have all their information explicitly modeled, but that is hardwired into their supporting CASE tools. Thus, the models to be reused assume some information and semantics that are not available if we try to use them in a different environment. This problem is alleviated by the explicit representation of all concerns in the WEI framework, because all the information has to be supplied there.

12.7 ISSUES AND CHALLENGES FOR MDWE AND MDA

So far we have discussed how MDA and its related concepts and mechanisms can help in the effective design and development of Web applications. This section describes the major challenges faced by the introduction of MDA in the Web Engineering domain.

12.7.1 Maturity of MDA Standards and Tools

One of the major problems that any person approaching MDA discovers is the lack of maturity of the current standards and tools. For example, some standards considered key to MDA are not currently supported by tools, and some others have not even been finalized. Probably the most representative example is QVT, for which there is not a complete implementation available as of today. This is really frustrating and needs to be urgently addressed in order to avoid the dissatisfaction it produces to potential users.

12.7.2 Lack of Interoperability Between UML Tools

Despite the interoperability goals of the OMG, current UML modeling tools cannot properly interoperate, and exchanging models and diagrams between them is almost impossible. XMI is supposed to provide the solution to this problem, but most UML tool vendors fail to generate fully XMI-compliant specifications of the models they produce. What we currently see is that most vendors add proprietary extensions to the XMI tags, which cannot be understood by other tools. This is another sign of the current immature status of the MDA initiative, which we expect can be resolved soon (otherwise the vendors may kill this opportunity with their incompatibilities).

12.7.3 Need to Improve the Support for DSLs

As mentioned above, UML profiles are a very interesting option to define DSLs, not only because they are relatively simple to define, but also because, once defined, they can be (in theory) used by any UML tool to produce models that conform to that profile.

The current situation is not so bright, however. Actually, most UML tools provide support for defining UML profiles (in terms of their corresponding stereotypes, tag definitions, and constraints) but fail to be able to guarantee the constraints on the models because they do not support OCL checks. Therefore, you can specify a UML profile that represents a given application domain (that is, a DSL for that domain), but then there is no way of checking that the models users produce respect the structuring rules of that DSL, i.e., users can easily create wrong models. It is similar to defining a language but without providing a compiler that could check the grammar of the programs produced.

Another improvement that is also required is a better support for relating MOF meta-models with profiles, i.e., to map the meta-model of a DSL to its corresponding profile, as suggested at the end of Section 12.3.2. This would allow meta-models to be imported from other sources as well as our being able to use standard UML tools to easily draw models that conform to them. There are some academic proposals in this respect (Abouzahra et al., 2005), although this kind of mechanism should be implemented in most UML tools as part of their profiling facilities.

12.7.4 The Complexity of UML

The size and technical complexity of UML have been held responsible for hampering its wide adoption in many industrial environments. UML is a general-purpose modeling language for software-intensive systems that is designed to support many kinds of applications. Consequently, in contrast to specific DSM languages, UML is used for a wide variety of purposes across a broad range of domains. Thus, it counts with many modeling elements and diagrams, and even provides support to cope with different semantic variants, through the *semantic variation points* defined for some of its elements. This mechanism increases the potential adoption of UML in many different kinds of environments, but at the high cost of increasing its complexity and introducing a lack of focus and precision ("maximizing reuse minimizes use"). This kind of mechanism also has a strong impact on the learning curve of UML, and on the efforts required by system modelers to master and effectively use the UML notation.

12.7.5 The Ways in Which Modelers Work

Many of today's modelers are still casual in their approach; MDSD (and in particular MDA) requires increased rigor to produce models that are amenable to automatic generation of code. This means that users need to be very precise when designing their models—which in MDA implies plenty of training in UML modeling.

Note that this issue and the previous one could be greatly alleviated by the use of UML profiles that restricted the set of UML elements that can be used to model a domain-specific application and only allowed users to draw correct models with regard to the DSL meta-model (i.e., the profile). This is why very compact, precise, and specific UML-based DSLs, with a reduced number of elements and strong structuring rules, are being perceived as a key factor to the success of MDSD (Bézivin et al., 2005). However, current UML tools do not provide complete support for UML profiles (including the validation of their OCL constraints) as mentioned above. In addition, the use that average modelers make of UML stereotypes and profiles is not always correct, especially because this extension mechanism is not as simple as it might seem at first sight. Different studies have tried to analyze the way in which stereotypes are currently used, and the most common mistakes made by modelers when defining and using them (Atkinson et al., 2003; Henderson-Sellers and González-Pérez, 2006).

Another tendency that we also perceive in normal modelers is the use of DSLs that support agile methodologies and rapid prototyping for designing and developing Web applications. For instance, the use of Ruby is gaining acceptance in many areas (Schwabe, 2006), and experience shows that the increase in development performance and reduction in costs might be worth its use, especially when combined with frameworks such as Rails (Thomas et al., 2006).

12.7.6 MDA is not Just About Modeling

It is unrealistic to expect 100% code generation for every computing problem, and no vendor today can realistically offer a complete MDA solution. Thus, if you expect too much of MDA, it will fail. What MDA offers is just a way of approaching the design and development of systems, using a set of standard notations and tools to achieve interoperability and reuse across vendors and platform independence. But to realize the full benefits of MDA, organizations should not just introduce some modeling practices in their development processes; they must support the full software lifecycle development process, from analysis and requirements management through design, development, implementation, deployment, and maintenance. Otherwise, the full advantages of MDA will be lost.

12.7.7 Modeling Further Concerns

Finally, and especially in the case of more data-intensive Web applications (usually called Web-based information systems), we see a trend toward the incorporation of emerging initiatives like the Semantic Web, with supporting technologies such as (Semantic) Web services, and (Semantic) Web rule languages, which aim at fostering application interoperability. Semantic Web languages [e.g., RDF(S) or OWL] facilitate the description of models for such domains. However, the integration of all these models with the rest of the model-based Web Engineering approaches is still unresolved. This is not only a problem for MDA, but for any MDSD approach.

Further concerns, such as user requirements, as well as the role that the computation-independent model (CIM) defined by MDA plays in MDWE, need to be investigated, too.

12.8 CONCLUSIONS

In this chapter we have presented an overview of the current state of model-driven software development, and of model-driven Web Engineering in particular, especially in the context of MDA. We have analyzed the key concepts and mechanisms that these approaches provide and how the development of Web systems can benefit from them. Apart from introducing the advantages and opportunities that MDA can bring to MDWE, we have also discussed the current problems and threats that MDA faces for its successful adoption in industrial settings. Addressing and resolving them properly is possibly the major challenge for MDA today.

In summary, we have seen that there is a real need to integrate with UML environments, which are the ones currently demanded in many customer settings, and that MDA can help reformulate and reorganize current Web Engineering proposals in terms of models and transformations between them. MDWE can significantly benefit from the facts that each model can address a concern, that these concerns can be explicitly represented, and that they can be specified in a platform-independent manner—hence achieving the modularity, portability, reusability, and interoperability required for any competitive Web Engineering proposal. MDWE solutions cannot survive isolated any longer; they need to interoperate among themselves and be integrated into the customers' development environments. And these are precisely the issues that MDA can help them address in a very successful way.

ACKNOWLEDGMENTS

We would like to acknowledge the work of many MDSD, MDA, and MDWE experts who have been involved in investigating and addressing the problems of model-Web Engineering. Although the views in this chapter are the authors' solely responsibility, they could not have been formulated without the many long and clarifying discussions with these experts. In particular, we would like to thank Nora Koch, Jaime Gómez, Vicente Pelechano, Piero Fraternali, Oscar Pastor, Daniel Schwabe, Gustavo Rossi, Geert-Jan Houben, Joaquin Miller, Jean Bézivin, Alfonso Pierantonio, Bryan Wood, and many others too numerous to be named here. We would also like to thank both the organizers and the participants of the past editions of the Model-Driven Web Engineering (MDWE) workshop at the last ICWE conferences, where some of the issues presented here were originally raised and discussed.

This work has been supported by Spanish Projects TIN2005-25886-E and TIN2005-09405-C02-01.

REFERENCES

Abouzahra, A., Bézivin, J., Del Fabro, M.D., and Jouault, F., 2005, A practical approach to bridging domain specific languages with UML profiles. *Proceedings Best Practices for Model Driven Software Development* (OOPSLA'05), San Diego, CA.

Atkinson, C., Kühne, T., and Henderson-Sellers, B., 2003, Systematic stereotype usage. *Software and Systems Modelling*, 2(3): 153–163.

Baresi, L., Colazzo, S., Mainetti, L., and Morasca, S., 2006a, Model-based Web application development. In *Web Engineering*, Springer, Heidelberg, pp. 303–334.

Baresi, L., Colazzo, S., Mainetti, L., and Morasca, S., 2006b, W2000: A modelling notation for complex Web applications. In *Web Engineering: Theory and Practice of Metrics and Measurement for Web Development*, Springer, New York, pp. 335–408.

Bézivin, J., Jouault, F., Rosenthal, P., and Valduriez, P., 2005, Modelling in the large and modelling in the small. *Proceedings European MDA Workshops: Foundations and Applications* (MDAFA 2003 and MDAFA 2004), Springer, LNCS 3599, pp. 33–46.

Bézivin, J., 2005, On the unification power of models. *Software and Systems Modelling* (SoSym), 4(2): 171–188.

Cáceres, P., De Castro, V., Vara, J.M., and Marcos, E., 2006, Model transformations for hypertext modelling on Web information systems. *Proceedings ACM/SAC 2006 Track on Model Transformations* (MT2006), Dijon, France, pp. 1256–1261.

Ceri, S., Fraternali, P., Bongio, A., Brambilla, M., Comai, S., and Matera, M., 2002, *Designing Data-Intensive Web Applications*, Morgan Kaufmann, San Francisco.

Ceri, S., Daniel, F., Matera, M., and Facca, F., 2007, Model-driven development of context-aware Web applications. *ACM Transactions on Internet Technology* (TOIT), 7(1).

Chicchetti, A., Di Ruscio, D., and Pierantonio, A., 2006, Weaving concerns in model-based development of data-intensive Web applications. *Proceedings ACM/SAC 2006 Track on Model Transformations* (MT2006), Dijon, France, pp. 1256–1261.

De Castro, V., Marcos, E., and López Sanz, M., 2006, A model-driven method for service composition modelling: A case study. *International Journal of Web Engineering and Technology*, **2**(4): 335–353.

De Troyer, O., and Leune, C.J., 1998, WSDM: A user centered design method for Web sites. *Proceedings 7th International Conference on World Wide Web*, Amsterdam, Elsevier Science Publishers B.V., pp. 85–94.

Di Ruscio, D., Muccini, H., and Pierantonio, A., 2004, A data modelling approach to Web application synthesis. *International Journal of Web Engineering and Technology*, **1**(3): 320–337.

Frasincar, F., Houben, G., and Vdovjak, R., 2001, An RMM-based methodology for hypermedia presentation design. *Proceedings 5th East European Conference on Advances in Databases and Information Systems* (ADBIS '01), London, Springer-Verlag, pp. 323–337.

Fuentes, L., and Vallecillo, A., 2004, An introduction to UML profiles. *UPGRADE, The European Journal for the Informatics Professional*, **5**(2): 5–13.

Garzotto, F., Paolini, P., and Schwabe, D., 1993, HDM—A model-based approach to hypertext application design. *ACM Transactions on Information Systems*, **11**(1): 1–26.

Gómez, J., and Cachero, C., 2003, *OO-H Method: Extending UML to Model Web Interfaces*, Idea Group Publishing, Hershey, PA, pp. 144–173.

Greenfield, J., and Short, K., 2004, *Software Factories: Assembling Applications with Patterns, Frameworks, Models & Tools*, Wiley, New York.

Henderson-Sellers, B., and González-Pérez, C., 2006, Uses and abuses of the stereotype mechanism in UML 1.x and 2.0. *Proceedings MODELS 2006*, Italy.

Jouault, F., and Kurtev, I., 2006a, On the architectural alignment of ATL and QVT. *Proceedings ACM Symposium on Applied Computing*, Dijon, France, ACM Press.

Jouault, F., and Kurtev, I., 2006b, Transforming models with ATL. *Proceedings Model Transformations in Practice Workshop at MoDELS 2005*, Montego Bay, Jamaica. Springer, LNCS 3844, pp. 128–138.

Kappel, G., Pröll, B., Reich, S., and Retschitzegger, W., 2006, *Web Engineering—The Discipline of Systematic Development of Web Applications*, Wiley, New York.

Koch, N., 2001, Software engineering for adaptive hypermedia systems: Reference model, modelling techniques and development process. *Softwaretechnik—Trends*, **21**(1).

Koch, N., and Kraus, A., 2003, Towards a common metamodel for the development of Web applications. *Proceedings 3rd International Conference on Web Engineering* (ICWE 2003). Springer, LNCS 2722, pp. 497–506.

Koch, N., Kraus, A., Cachero, C., and Meliá, S., 2004, Integration of business processes in Web applications models. *Journal of Web Engineering* (JWE), **3**(1): 22–49.

Koch, N., Zhang, G., and Escalona, M.J., 2006, Model transformations from requirements to Web system design. *Proceedings 6th International Conference on Web Engineering* (ICWE 2006), Palo Alto, CA, ACM Press, pp. 281–288.

Koch, N., 2006, Transformation techniques in the model-driven development process of UWE. *Proceedings 2nd Model-Driven Web Engineering Workshop* (MDWE 2006), Palo Alto, CA.

Kraus, A., 2007, Model-driven software engineering for Web applications, PhD Thesis. Institut für Informatik, Ludwig-Maximilians-Universität, Munich.

Lange, D.B., 1994, An object-oriented design method for hypermedia information systems. *Proceedings 27th Annual Hawaii International Conference on System Sciences* (HICSS-27), Maui, IEEE Computer Society, pp. 366–375.

Meliá, S., and Gómez, J., 2006, The WebSA approach: Applying model-driven engineering to Web applications. *Journal of Web Engineering* (JWE), **5**(2): 121–149.

Miller, J., and Mukerji, J., 2003, The MDA Guide. Draft v. 2.0, OMG doc. ab/2003-01-03.

Moreno, N., and Vallecillo, A., 2005a, A model-based approach for integrating third-party systems with Web applications. *Proceedings 5th International Conference on Web Engineering* (ICWE 2005), Springer, LNCS 3579, pp. 441–452.

Moreno, N., Romero, J.R., and Vallecillo, A., 2005b, Incorporating cooperative portlets in Web application development. *Proceedings 1st Model-Driven Web Engineering Workshop* (MDWE 2005), Sydney, Australia, pp. 70–79.

Moreno, N., and Vallecillo, A., 2005c, Modelling interactions between Web applications and third-party systems. *Proceedings IWWOST 2005,* Porto, Portugal, pp. 441–452.

Moreno, N., Fraternalli, P., and Vallecillo, A., 2006, A UML 2.0 profile for WebML modelling. *Proceedings 2nd Model-Driven Web Engineering Workshop* (MDWE 2006), Palo Alto, CA.

OMG, 2005a, MOF QVT Final Adopted Specification, OMG doc. ptc/05-11-01.

OMG, 2005b, UML 2.0 Superstructure Specification v. 2.0, OMG doc. formal/05-07-04.

OMG, 2006, OCL 2.0, OMG doc. ptc/06-05-01.

Pastor, O., Gómez, J., Insfran, E., and Pelechano, V., 2001, The OO-Method approach for information systems modelling: From object-oriented conceptual modelling to automated programming. *Information Systems,* **26**(7): 507–534.

Pastor, O., Fons, J., Abrahao, S., and Pelechado, V., 2006, Conceptual modelling of Web applications: The OOWS approach. In *Web Engineering,* E. Mendes and N. Mosley, eds., Springer, New York, pp. 277–302.

Sánchez, J., and García-Molina, J., 2006, A plugin-based language to experiment with model transformation. *Proceedings 9th International Conference MoDELS 2006,* Genova, Italy, Springer, LNCS 4199, pp. 336–350.

Schauerhuber, A., Wimmer, M., and Kapsammer, E., 2006, Bridging existing Web modelling languages to model-driven engineering: A metamodel for WebML. *Proceedings 2nd Model-Driven Web Engineering Workshop* (MDWE 2006), Palo Alto, CA.

Schwabe, D., 2006, Rapid prototyping of Web applications combining domain specific languages and model driven design. *Proceedings 6th International Conference on Web Engineering* (ICWE 2006), Palo Alto, CA, ACM Press.

Schwabe, D., Pontes, R.A., and Moura, I., 1999, OOHDMWeb: An environment for implementation of hypermedia applications in the WWW. *SigWEB Newsletter,* **8**(2).

Thomas, D., and Heinemeier, D., 2006, *Agile Web Development with Rails: A Pragmatic Guide,* 2nd ed., Pragmatic Bookshelf, Raleigh, NC.

Vdovjak, R., Frasincar, F., Houben, G., and Barna, P., 2003, Engineering Semantic Web information systems in Hera. *Journal of Web Engineering* (JWE), **2**(1–2): 3–26.

PART III

QUALITY EVALUATION AND EXPERIMENTAL WEB ENGINEERING

Chapter 13

HOW TO MEASURE AND EVALUATE WEB APPLICATIONS IN A CONSISTENT WAY

Luis Olsina, Fernanda Papa, Hernán Molina

GIDIS_Web, Engineering School, Universidad Nacional de La Pampa, Calle 9 y 110, (6360) General Pico, LP, Argentina, {olsinal,pmfer,hmolina}@ing.unlpam.edu.ar

13.1 INTRODUCTION

A recurrent challenge many software organizations face is to have a clear establishment of a measurement and evaluation of a conceptual framework useful for quality assurance processes and programs. While many useful approaches for and successful practical examples of software measurement programs exist, the inability to clearly and consistently specify measurement and evaluation concepts (i.e., the meta-data) could unfortunately hamper the progress of the software, and Web Engineering as a whole, and could hinder their widespread adoption.

Software and Web organizations introducing a measurement and evaluation program—maybe as part of a measurement and analyses process area and quality assurance strategy (CMMI, 2002)—need to establish a set of activities and procedures to specify, collect, store, and use trustworthy measurement and indicator data sets and meta-data. Moreover, to ensure, for analysis purposes, that measurement and indicator data sets are repeatable and comparable among different measurement and evaluation projects, appropriate meta-data of metrics and indicators should be adapted and recorded.

Therefore, in the present chapter we argue that at least three pillars are necessary to build, i.e., to design and to implement, a robust and sound measurement and evaluation program:

1. a process for measurement and evaluation, i.e., the main managerial and technical activities that might be planned and performed
2. a measurement and evaluation framework that must rely on a sound conceptual (ontological) base
3. specific model-based methods and techniques in order to carry out the specific project's activities

A measurement or evaluation process prescribes or informs a set of main phases, activities, and their input and output that might be considered. Usually, it says what to do but not how to do it; that is, it says nothing about the particular methods and tools in order to perform the specific activities' descriptions. Regarding measurement and evaluation processes for software, the *International Standard Organization* (ISO) published two standards: the ISO 15939 document issued in 2002 (ISO, 2002), which deals with the software measurement process, and the ISO 14598-5 issued in 1998 (ISO, 1998), which deals with the process for evaluators in its part 5. On the other hand, the CMMI (*Capability Maturity Model Integration*) initiative is also worthy of mention as another source of knowledge, in which specific support process areas such as measurement and analyses, decision analyses and resolution, among others, are specified. The primary aim of these documents was to reach a consensus about the issued models, processes, and practices. However, in Olsina and Martin (2004) we observe that very often a lack of consensus exists about the used terminology among the ISO standards.

Considering our second statement, we argue that in order to design and implement a robust measurement and evaluation program, a sound measurement and evaluation conceptual framework is necessary. Very often organizations start measurement programs from scratch more than once because they did not pay too much attention to the way metrics and indicators should be designed, recorded, and analyzed.

A well-established framework has to be built on a sound conceptual base, that is, on an ontological base. In fact, an ontology explicitly and formally specifies the main concepts, properties, relationships, and axioms for a given domain. In this direction, we have built an explicit specification of measurement and indicator meta-data, i.e., an ontology for this domain (Olsina and Martin, 2004). The sources of knowledge for this ontology stemmed from different software-related ISO standards (ISO, 1999, 2001, 2002) and recognized research articles and books (Briand et al., 2002; Kitchenham et al., 2001; Zuse, 1998), in addition to our own experience backed up by previous works on metrics and evaluation processes and methods (Olsina et al., 1999; Olsina and Rossi, 2002).

However, the metrics and indicators ontology itself is not sufficient to model a full-fledged measurement and evaluation framework but rather is the ground and rationale to building it. In Olsina et al. (2006b), the INCAMI framework (Olsina et al., 2005) is thoroughly analyzed in the light of its ontological roots. INCAMI is an organizational purpose-oriented measurement and evaluation framework that enables consistently saving not only meta-data of metrics and indicators but also values (data sets) for concrete real-world measurement and evaluation projects. It is made up of five main conceptual components, namely: the requirement, measurement, and evaluation of projects definition; the nonfunctional requirements definition and specification; the measurement design and execution; the evaluation design and execution; and the conclusion and recommendation components. We argue that this framework can be useful for different qualitative and quantitative evaluation methods and techniques with regard to the requirements, measurement, and evaluation concepts and definitions (Olsina et al., 2008).

On the other hand, the growing importance the Web currently plays in such diverse application domains as business, education, government, industry, and entertainment have heightened concerns about the quality and quality of delivered Web applications. It is necessary to have not only robust development methods to improve the building process (one of the main aims of this book) but also consistent ways to measure and evaluate intermediate and final products as well. In this sense measurement and evaluation methods and tools that are grounded on the quoted conceptual framework are the third pillar of our proposal.

There are different categories of methods (e.g., inspection, testing, inquiry, simulation, etc.) and specific types of evaluation methods and techniques such as the heuristic evaluation technique (Nielsen et al., 2001), the Web Quality Evaluation Method (WebQEM) (Olsina and Rossi, 2002) as a concept model-centered evaluation methodology for the inspection category, to name just a few. We argue that a method or technique is usually not enough to assess different information needs for diverse evaluation purposes. In other words, it is true that one size does not fit all needs and preferences, but an organization might at least adopt a method or technique in order to know the state of its quality and quality in use for understanding and improving purposes.

In order to illustrate the above three main points, this chapter is organized as follows. In Section 13.2 we present an abridged overview of the state-of-the-art of measurement and evaluation processes as well as a basic process that is akin to our framework. In Section 13.3 we analyze the main components of the INCAMI framework regarding the metrics and indicators ontological base; at the same time, as proof of these concepts, an external quality model to measure and evaluate the shopping cart component of a typical e-commerce site is employed. In Section 13.4, using the specific models, procedures, and processes, the WebQEM inspection methodology is illustrated with regard to the previous case study. Finally, additional discussions about the flexibility of the framework as well as concluding remarks are drawn in Section 13.5.

13.2 OVERVIEW OF MEASUREMENT AND EVALUATION PROCESSES

As previously mentioned, a measurement or evaluation process specifies a set of main phases, activities, their input and output, and sometimes control points that might be considered. Usually, a process says what to do but not how to do it.

For instance, the ISO 14598-5 standard prescribes an evaluation process to assess software quality which is a generic abstract process customizable for different evaluation needs; however, it does not prescribe or inform about specific evaluation methods and tools in order to perform the activities' descriptions.

On the other hand, it is important to remark that no unique ISO standard that integrates in one document the measurement and evaluation process as a whole exists. Instead, there are two separate standards: one for the evaluation process, issued in 1998 (ISO, 1998), and another for the measurement process, issued in 2002 (ISO, 2002). Regarding the former, in an introductory paragraph it says, "The primary purpose of software product evaluation is to provide quantitative results concerning software product quality that are comprehensible, acceptable to and can be dependable on by any interested party"; it continues, "This evaluation process is a generic abstract process that follows the model defined in ISO/IEC 9126."

In the ISO 14598-5 standard, the evaluation process comprises the five activities listed in Figure 13.1 (see ISO, 1998, for a detailed description):

1. *establishment of evaluation requirements*
2. *specification of the evaluation* based on the evaluation requirements and on the product provided by the requester
3. *design of the evaluation,* which produces an evaluation plan on the basis of the evaluation specification
4. *execution of the evaluation plan,* which consists of inspecting, modeling, measuring, and testing the products and/or its components according to the evaluation plan
5. *conclusion of the evaluation,* which consists of the delivery of the evaluation report

Figure 13.1. The main activities specified in the ISO 14598-5 evaluation process standard.

The ISO 15939 standard that deals with the measurement process says, "Software measurement is also a key discipline in evaluating the quality of software products and the capability of organizational software processes"; in addition,

Continual improvement requires change within the organization. Evaluation of change requires measurement. Measurement itself does not initiate change. Measurement should lead to action, and not be employed purely to accumulate data. Measurement should have a clearly defined purpose. . . , This standard defines the activities and tasks necessary to implement a software measurement process ... each activity is comprised of one or more tasks. This International Standard does not specify the details of how to perform the tasks included in the activities.

In this standard two activities (out of four) are considered to be the core measurement process, namely: *plan the measurement process*, and *perform the measurement process*. These two activities are comprised of the following tasks (see Figure 13.2 and also ISO, 2002, for a detailed description):

1. Plan the Measurement Process:
    1.1 Characterize organizational unit
    1.2 Identify information needs
    1.3 Select measures
    1.4 Define data collection, analysis, and reporting procedures
    1.5 Define criteria for evaluating the information products and the measurement process
    1.6 Review, approve, and provide resources for measurement tasks
    1.7 Acquire and deploy supporting technologies
2. Perform the Measurement Process:
    2.1 Integrate procedures
    2.2 Collect data
    2.3 Analyze data and develop information products
    2.4 Communicate results

Figure 13.2. The two core measurement processes specified in the ISO 15939 measurement process standard.

Lastly, the CMMI (CMMI, 2002) initiative[1] is also worthy of mention. This initiative specifies support process areas such as *measurement and analyses*, among others. It says, "The purpose of measurement and analysis is to develop and sustain a measurement capability that is used to support management information needs", Figure 13.3 shows the two specific goals

---

[1] There is a related ISO 15504 initiative named SPICE (*Software Process Improvement and Capability dEtermination*).

for this process area and its specific practices (which can be considered as activities or specific actions).

  1   Align Measurement and Analysis Activities
          1.1   Establish measurement objectives
          1.2   Specify measures
          1.3   Specify data collection and storage procedures
          1.4   Specify analysis procedures
  2   Provide Measurement Results
          2.1   Collect measurement data
          2.2   Analyze measurement data
          2.3   Store data and results
          2.4   Communicate results

Figure 13.3. The two specific goals and related practices for the CMMI Measurement and Analyses process area.

As the reader could observe in the previous figures, there is in principle no clear integrated proposal about measurement and evaluation activities even though both are closely intertwined, as we discuss in our framework later on. However, a common denominator between activities and tasks outlined in the previous figures can be observed. For instance, there are the definition and specification of requirements, e.g., activities 1 and 2 in Figure 13.1 deal with the establishment and specification of evaluation requirements; tasks 1.1 and 1.2 in Figure 13.2 are about measurement requirements, as is practice 1.1 in Figure 13.3. There are also design activities, i.e., defining, specifying, or ultimately planning activities; then, execution or implementation activities of the designed evaluation or measurement; and lastly, activities about the conclusion and communication of results.

On the other hand, we have been developing the WebQEM methodology since the late 1990s (Olsina et al., 1999; Olsina and Rossi, 2002). The underlying WebQEM process integrates activities for requirements, measurement, evaluation, and recommendations. Figure 13.5 shows the evaluation process, including the phases, main activities, input, and output. This model followed to some extent the ISO's process model for evaluators (ISO, 1998). The main activities are grouped into the following four major technical phases (see Figure 13.4):

  1. *Nonfunctional Requirements Definition and Specification*
  2. *Measurement and Elementary Evaluation* (both Design and Implementation stages)
  3. *Global Evaluation* (both Design and Implementation stages)
  4. *Conclusion and Recommendations*

Figure 13.4. The four phases underlying the WebQEM methodology and the INCAMI framework. Note that the specific activities are not listed in the figure.

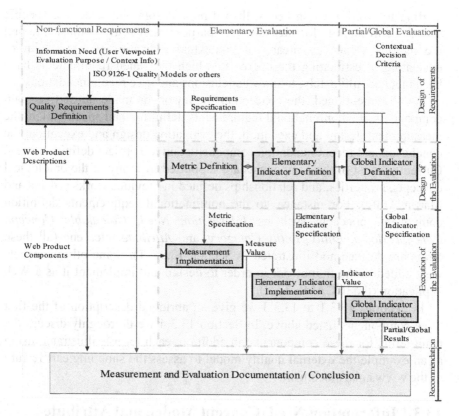

Figure 13.5. The basic measurement and evaluation process underlying the WebQEM methodology. The technical phases, main activities, and their input and output are represented (it might be assumed that some activities are iterative).

In the next section we thoroughly discuss the measurement and evaluation framework (the second pillar proposed in Section 13.1) in the light of its conceptual root and the above measurement and evaluation process. As an additional remark, in Olsina and Martin (2004) we observed that very often there is a lack of consensus about the used terminology among the quoted ISO standards, and some terms used mainly for the evaluation domain are missing.

13.3 FRAMEWORK FOR MEASURING AND EVALUATING NONFUNCTIONAL REQUIREMENTS

The proposed INCAMI (*Information Need, Concept model, Attribute, Metric,* and *Indicator*) framework (Molina et al., 2004; Olsina et al., 2005) is based upon the assumption that for an organization to measure and evaluate in a purpose-oriented way it must first specify nonfunctional requirements starting from information needs, then it must design and select the specific set of useful metrics for measurement purpose, and lastly it must interpret the metrics values by means of contextual indicators with the aim of evaluating or estimating the degree to which the stated requirements have been met and, ultimately, to draw conclusions and give recommendations.

As aforementioned, the conceptual framework is made up of five main components: the nonfunctional requirements definition and specification; the measurement design and execution; the evaluation design and execution; the conclusion and recommendation component; and the project definition itself. Currently, most of the components are supported by many of the ontological concepts, properties, and relationships defined in previous works (Olsina and Martin, 2004). For instance, to the nonfunctional requirements definition component, concepts such as *Information Need, Calculable Concept, Concept Model, Entity, Entity Category,* and *Attribute* intervene (all these terms are defined and illustrated in Section 13.3.4.1). Some other concepts were added to the framework in order to design and implement it as a Web application (the INCAMI_Tool).

In Sections 13.3.1 to 13.3.3 we give an abridged description of the first three components listed above. In Section 13.3.4 we thoroughly discuss the main terms for these components; in addition, each term is illustrated using as an example the external quality model to assess the shopping cart feature of the www.amazon.com site.

13.3.1 Information Need, Concept Model, and Attribute

First, for the nonfunctional requirements definition and specification component, the *Information Need* to a measurement and evaluation *Project* must be agreed upon. Information need is defined as the insight necessary to manage objectives, goals, risks, and problems. Usually, information needs come from two organizational project-level sources: goals that decision makers seek to achieve, or obstacles that hinder reaching the goals; e.g., obstacles involve basically risks and problems. The *InformationNeed* class (see Figure 13.6) has three properties: the *purpose*, the user *viewpoint*, and the *contextDescription*. (Note that from the process standpoint, outlined in the previous section, and particularly for the *Nonfunctional Requirements Definition and Specification* phase, we can represent an activity named *Identify Information Needs* and in turn tasks such as *Establish measurement/evaluation purpose*; *Establish the user viewpoint*; and *Specify the context of the measurement/evaluation.*)

Additionally, the *InformationNeed* class has two main relationships with the *CalculableConcept* and the *EntityCategory* classes, respectively. A calculable concept can be defined as an abstract relationship between attributes of entities' categories and information needs; in fact, internal quality, external quality, cost, etc. are instances of a calculable concept. In turn, a calculable concept can be represented by a *ConceptModel*; for example, ISO 9126-1 specifies quality models for the internal quality, external quality, and quality in use, respectively.

On the other hand, a common practice is to assess quality by means of the quantification of lower abstraction concepts such as *Attributes* of entities' categories. The attribute term can be defined in brief as a measurable property of an *EntityCategory* (e.g., categories of entities of interest to software and Web Engineering are resource, process, product, service, and project as a whole). An entity category may have many attributes, though only some of them may be useful just for a given measurement and evaluation project's information needs.

In summary, this component allows the definition and specification of nonfunctional requirements in a sound and well-established way. It has an underlying organizational strategy that is purpose-oriented by information needs and is concept model-centered and evaluator-driven by domain experts and users.

13.3.2 Metrics and Measurement

Regarding the measurement component, purposeful metrics should be selected in the process. In general, each attribute can be quantified by one or more metrics, but in practice just one metric should be selected for each attribute of the requirements tree, given a specific measurement project.

The *Metric* concept contains the definition of the selected *Measurement* or *Calculation Method* and the *Scale* (see Figure 13.8). For instance, the measurement method is defined as the particular logical sequence of operations and possible heuristics specified for allowing the realization of a metric description by a measurement; while the scale is defined as a set of values with defined properties. Thus, the metric m represents a mapping m: A->X, where A is an empirical attribute of an entity category (the empirical world), X is the variable to which categorical or numerical values can be assigned (the formal world), and the arrow denotes a mapping. In order to perform this mapping, a sound and precise measurement activity definition is needed by explicitly specifying the metric's method and scale. We can apply an *objective* or *subjective* measurement method for *Direct Metrics*; conversely, we can perform a calculation method for *Indirect Metrics*, that is, when a *Formula* intervenes.

Once the metric has been selected, we can perform (execute or implement) the measurement process, i.e., the activity that uses a metric definition in order to produce a measure's value (see Figure 13.5). The *Measurement* class allows the date/time stamp, the information of the owner in charge of the measurement activity, and the actual or estimated yielded value to be recorded.

However, since the value of a particular metric will not represent the elementary requirement's satisfaction level, we need to define a new mapping that will produce an elementary indicator value. One fact worthy of mention is that the selected metrics are useful for a measurement process as long as the selected indicators are useful for an evaluation process in order to interpret the stated information need.

13.3.3 Indicators and Evaluation

For the evaluation component, contextual indicators should be selected. Indicators are ultimately the foundation for the interpretation of information needs and decision making. There are two types of indicators: *elementary* and *global indicators* (see Figure 13.9).

In Olsina and Martin (2004) the indicator is described as "the defined calculation method and scale in addition to the model and decision criteria in order to provide an estimate or evaluation of a calculable concept with respect to defined information needs." In particular, we define an elementary indicator as one that does not depend upon other indicators to evaluate or estimate a concept at a lower level of abstraction (i.e., for associated attributes to a concept model). On the other hand, we define a partial or global indicator as one that is derived from other indicators to evaluate or estimate a concept at a higher level of abstraction (i.e., for subconcepts and concepts). Therefore, the elementary indicator represents a new mapping coming from the interpretation of the metric's measured value of an attribute (the formal world) into the new variable to which categorical or numerical values can be assigned (the new formal world). In order to perform this mapping, elementary and global model and decision criteria for a specific user information need should be designed.

Therefore, once we have selected a scoring model, the aggregation process follows the hierarchical structure defined in the concept model, from bottom to top. Applying a stepwise aggregation mechanism, we obtain a global schema; this model lets us compute partial and global indicators in the execution stage. The global indicator's value ultimately represents the global degree of satisfaction in meeting the stated requirements (information need) for a given purpose and user viewpoint.

13.3.4 Definition and Exemplification of the INCAMI Terms

In this section (from Sections 13.3.4.1 to 13.3.4.3) we define the main terms that intervene in the above INCAMI framework's components, i.e., the requirement, measurement, and evaluation components. Each one is modeled by a class diagram (Figures 13.6, 13.8, and 13.9), where many (but not all) terms in the diagrams come from the metrics and indicators ontology. Note that for space reasons, we do not define each class attribute and relationships among classes, as is done in Olsina and Martin (2004).

In addition, for illustration purposes, we use an external quality model with associated attributes specified to the shopping cart of Web sites. We have conducted a case study in order to assess the shopping cart feature of the www.amazon.com site (details of this study will be given in Section 13.4).

13.3.4.1 Requirements Definition and Specification Model

As shown in Figure 13.6, this model includes all the necessary concepts for the definition and specification of requirements for measurement and evaluation projects. Nonfunctional requirements are the starting point of the measurement and evaluation process, so that a *requirement project* should be defined.

Definition 13.1. *RequirementProject* is a project that allows us to specify nonfunctional requirements for measurement and evaluation activities.

In our example the project *name* is "ExternalQuality_Amazon_05"; the *description* is "requirements for evaluating the external quality for the shopping cart feature of the www.amazon.com site"; with a starting date "2005/12/19" and an ending date "2005/12/30" and in charge of "Fernanda Papa" with the "pmfer@ing.unlpam.edu.ar" *contact* email.

Next, the *information need* should be specified. For this study, a basic information need may be "understand the external quality of the shopping cart component of a typical e-store, for a general visitor viewpoint, in order to incorporate the best features in a new e-bookstore development project."

Definition 13.2. *InformationNeed* is the insight necessary to manage objectives, goals, risks, and problems.

In our example the *information need* is stated by the *purpose* (i.e., to understand), the *user viewpoint* (i.e., a general visitor), in a given *context* of use (e.g., bandwidth constraints, among other contextual descriptions). In addition, an *entity category*, which is the *object* under analysis, and the *calculable concept*, which is the *focus* of *the information need,* must be defined.

Definition 13.3. *Entity Category* is the object category that is to be characterized by measuring its attributes.

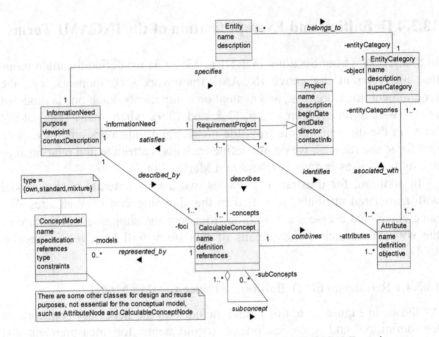

Figure 13.6. Key terms and relationships that intervene in the INCAMI requirements component for the definition and specification of nonfunctional requirements.

Definition 13.4. *Entity,* synonym Object, is a concrete object that belongs to an entity category.

Therefore, given the *entity category* (i.e., an e-commerce application, of which *superCategory* is a product), a concrete object *name* that belongs to this category is the "Amazon's shopping cart" Web component.

Definition 13.5. *CalculableConcept,* synonym Measurable Concept in ISO (2002), defines the abstract relationship between attributes of entity categories and information needs.

In the example the *calculable concept name* is "external quality" and its *definition* is "the extent to which a product satisfies stated and implied needs when used under specified conditions" (ISO, 1999). The external quality concept has *subconcepts* such as "usability", "functionality", "reliability", "efficiency", "portability", and "maintainability".

For instance, the "functionality" subconcept is defined in ISO (2001) as "the capability of the software product to provide functions which meet stated and implied needs when the software is used under specified conditions". In turn, the calculable concept (characteristic) "functionality" is split into five subconcepts (subcharacteristics): "suitability", "accuracy", "interoperability", "security", and "functionality compliance." Suitability is defined as "the capability of the software product to provide an appropriate set of functions for specified tasks and user objectives"; and accuracy as "the capability of the software product to provide the right or agreed results or effects with the needed degree of precision." See Figure 13.7, where these two subconcepts in the requirements tree are included as "Function Suitability" and "Function Accuracy", respectively (we used the name "function suitability" instead of "suitability" alone, in order to distinguish it from the name "information suitability", which is a subconcept of the Content characteristic).

On the other hand, the calculable concept can be *represented by* a *concept model*.

Definition 13.6. ConceptModel, synonym Factor or Feature Model, is the set of subconcepts and the relationships between them, which provide the basis for specifying the concept requirement and its further evaluation or estimation.

As mentioned earlier, INCAMI is a concept model-centered approach; the concept model *type* can be either a standard-based model or an organization own-defined model, or a mixture of both. The concept model used in the example is of the "mixture" *type* that is based mainly on the ISO external quality model (*reference* "(ISO, 1999)"), and the *specification* is shown in Figure 13.11 (note that the model also shows *attributes* combined to the *subconcepts*).

Definition 13.7. Attribute, synonym Property, Feature, is a measurable physical or abstract property of an entity category.

Note that the selected attributes are those properties relevant to the agreed-upon information need. The abridged representation in Figure 13.7 shows attribute *names* such as "Capability to delete items" (2.1.2) and "Precision to recalculate after deleting items" (2.2.2), among others.

2. Functionality
    2.1. Function Suitability
        2.1.1.   *Capability to add items from anywhere*
        2.1.2.   *Capability to delete items*
        2.1.3.   *Capability to modify an item quantity*
        2.1.4.   *Capability to show totals by performed changes*
        2.1.5.   *Capability to save items for later/move to cart*
    2.2. Function Accuracy
        2.2.1.   *Precision to recalculate after adding an item*
        2.2.2.   *Precision to recalculate after deleting items*
        2.2.3.   *Precision to recalculate after modifying an item quantity*

Figure 13.7. An excerpt (taken from Figure 13.11) of an instance of the external quality model with associated attributes specified for measurement and evaluation of the shopping cart component; for instance, the 2.1 and 2.2 codes represent specific calculable concepts and subconcepts; and the rest (in italic) are associated attributes to the above subconcepts. The model as a whole is depicted as a requirements tree.

For instance, the "Capability to delete items" attribute is defined (see the field *definition* in the Attribute class in Figure 13.6) as "the capability of the shopping cart to provide functions in order to delete appropriately items one by one or to the selected group at once."

The INCAMI_Tool, which is a prototype tool that supports this framework, currently implements concept models in the form of requirements trees. It also allows partially or totally previously edited requirements trees to be imported for a new project.

13.3.4.2 Measurement Design and Execution Model

The measurement model (see Figure 13.8) includes all the necessary concepts for the design and implementation of the measurement as a part of the *Measurement and Elementary Evaluation* phase shown in Figure 13.4. First, a *measurement project* should be defined.

Definition 13.8. *MeasurementProject* is a project that allows us, starting from a requirement project, to select the metrics and record the values in a measurement process.

Once the measurement project has been created, with similar information as that of a requirement project, the attributes in the requirements tree can be quantified by *direct* or *indirect metrics*.

Consider that for a specific measurement project just one metric should be selected for each attribute of the concept model. In the INCAMI_Tool, each metric is selected from a catalogue (Molina et al., 2004).

On the other hand, note that many measurement projects can rely on the same requirements, for instance, in a longitudinal analysis. In this case the starting and ending dates should change for each project.

Definition 13.9. *Metric*[2] is the defined measurement or calculation method and the measurement scale.

Definition 13.10. *DirectMetric*, synonym Single, Base Metric, is a metric of an attribute that does not depend on a metric of any other attribute.

---

[2] The "metric" term is used in ISO (1999, 2001) but not in ISO (2002). Furthermore, ISO (1999, 2001) uses the terms "direct measure" and "indirect measure" (instead of "direct" or "indirect metric"), while ISO (2002) uses "base measure" and "derived measure." In some cases we could state that they are synonymous terms, but in others such as "metric", which is defined in ISO (1999) as "the defined measurement method and the measurement scale", there is no term with exact matching meaning in ISO (2002). Furthermore, we argue that the measure term is not synonymous with the metric term. The measure term is defined in ISO (1999) (the meaning we adopted) as "the number or category assigned to an attribute of an entity by making a measurement" or in ISO (2002) as the "variable to which a value is assigned as the result of measurement" reflects the fact of the measure as the resulting value or output for the measurement activity (or process). Thus, we argue that the metric concept represents the specific and explicit definition of the measurement activity.

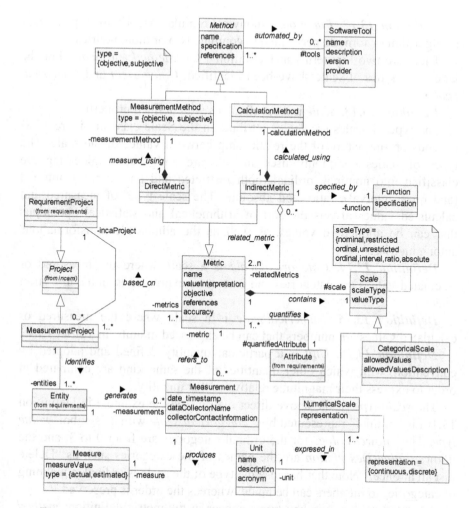

Figure 13.8. Key terms and relationships that intervene in the INCAMI measurement component for the definition of metric and measurement concepts.

For example, to the "Capability to delete items" attribute (coded 2.1.2 in Figure 13.7) we designed a direct metric named "Degree of the capability to delete items" that specifies four categories, namely:

0. Does not delete items at all
1. Delete just all at once
2. Delete one by one
3. Delete one by one or delete the selected group at once

Definition 13.11. *IndirectMetric,* synonym Hybrid, Derived Metric, is a metric of an attribute that is derived from the metrics of one or more other attributes.

Definition 13.12. *Function,* synonym Formula, Algorithm, Equation, is an algorithm or formula performed to combine two or more metrics.

There are two key terms in Definition 13.9: *Method* and *Scale.* For the latter, two types of scales have been identified: *Categorical* and *Numerical Scales:*

Definition 13.13. *Scale* is a set of values with defined properties.

The type of scales (*scaletype* attribute in the Scale class in Figure 13.8) depends on the nature of the relationship between values of the scale. The types of scales commonly used in software and Web Engineering are classified into nominal, ordinal (both restricted and unrestricted), interval (and quasi-interval), ratio, and absolute. The scale type[3] of measured and calculated values affects the sort of arithmetical and statistical operations that can be applied to values, as well as the admissible transformations among metrics.

Definition 13.14. *CategoricalScale* is a scale where the measured or calculated values are categories and cannot be expressed in units, in a strict sense.

Definition 13.15. *NumericalScale* is a scale where the measured or calculated values are numbers that can be expressed in units, in a strict sense.

Definition 13.16. *Unit* is a particular quantity defined and adopted by convention, with which other quantities of the same kind are compared in order to express their magnitude relative to that quantity.

The *scale type* of the above direct metric (see the example in Definition 13.10) is "ordinal" represented by a *categorical scale* with a "symbol" *value type.* The *allowedValues* for the ordinal categories are from 0 to 3, and the *allowedValuesDescription* are the names of the categories such as "Delete just all at once." Note that because the type of the scale is ordinal, a mapping of categories to numbers can be made, whereas the order is preserved.

As stated earlier, two key terms appear in the metric definition: *method* and *scale.* In the sequel, the method-related terms are defined.

Definition 13.17. *Method,* synonym Procedure, is a logical sequence of operations and possible heuristics, specified generically, for allowing the realization of an activity description.

Definition 13.18. *SoftwareTool,* synonym Software Instrument, is a tool that partially or totally automates a measurement or calculation method.

For example, the INCAMI_Tool, the current prototype tool that supports the WebQEM methodology, allows us to calculate indirect metrics (from direct metrics and parameters) in addition to calculating elementary and global indicators from elementary and global models. A previous tool for WebQEM was the WebQEM_Tool (Olsina et al., 2001). Different

---

[3] See a deeper discussion about type of scales in Chapter 14, Section 14.2.

commercial tools for data collection of direct metrics are widely well known and available for download.

Definition 13.19. *MeasurementMethod,* synonym Counting Rule, Protocol, is the particular logical sequence of operations and possible heuristics specified for allowing the realization of a metric description by a measurement.

To the exemplified direct metric (see the example in Definition 13.10), the counting rule was clearly specified as well as the measurement method *type*. The type of method can be either "subjective" i.e., where the quantification involves human judgment, or "objective" i.e., where the quantification is based on numerical rules. Generally, an objective measurement method type can be automated or semiautomated by a software tool. Nevertheless, for our example of a direct metric, even though the type is objective, no tool can automate the collection of data, and so a human must perform the task.

Definition 13.20. *CalculationMethod* is the particular logical sequences of operations specified for allowing the realization of a formula or indicator description by a calculation.

Definition 13.21. *Measurement* is an activity that uses a metric definition in order to produce a measure's value.

Definition 13.22. *Measure* is the number or category assigned to an attribute of an entity by making a measurement.

A *measurement* activity must be performed for each metric that intervenes in the project. It allows the *date/time stamp*, the *collector information* in charge of the measurement activity, and the *measure,* the "actual" or "estimated" value *type,* and the yielded *value* itself to be recorded.

Ultimately, for a specific measurement project, at least all the above concepts and definitions of the measurement model are necessary in order to specify, collect, store, and use trustworthy metrics' values and meta-data.

13.3.4.3 Evaluation Design and Execution Model

As introduced in Section 13.3.2, the value of a particular metric will not represent the elementary requirement's satisfaction level. Thus, we need to define a new mapping that will produce an elementary indicator value.

As aforementioned, the selected metrics are useful for designing and performing the measurement process as long as the selected indicators are useful for designing and executing the evaluation process for the stated information need, which is represented specifically in the concept model. The main concepts involved in the elementary and global evaluation are depicted in the model in Figure 13.9.

Definition 13.23. *EvaluationProject* is a project that allows us, starting from a measurement project and a concept model of a requirement project, to select the indicators and perform the calculations in an evaluation process.

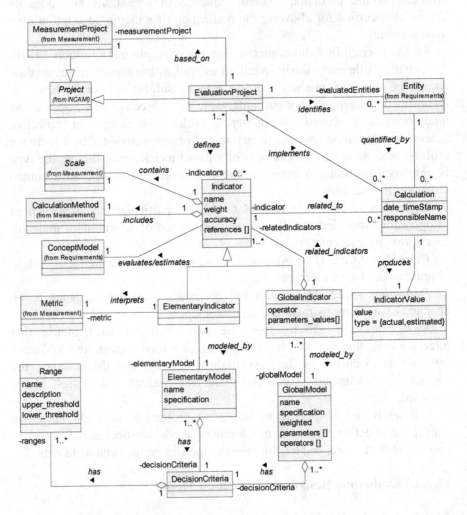

Figure 13.9. Key terms and relationships that intervene in the INCAMI.evaluation component for the definition of indicators and related concepts.

Once a measurement project has been created, one or more evaluation projects can in turn be created, relying on the recorded measurement values and meta-data, by adding related information with *indicators*.

Definition 13.24. *Indicator*, synonym Criterion, is the defined calculation method and scale in addition to the model and decision criteria in order to provide an estimate or evaluation of a calculable concept with respect to defined information needs.

Definition 13.25. *ElementaryIndicator,* synonym Elementary Preference, Elementary Criterion, is an indicator that does not depend upon other indicators to evaluate or estimate a calculable concept.

Therefore, an elementary indicator for each attribute of the concept model, i.e., for each leaf of the requirements tree, can be defined. For instance, to the 2.1.2 attribute of Figure 13.7, the *name* of the elementary indicator is "Performance Level of the Capability to Delete Items" (CDI_PL).

The elementary indicator interprets the metric's value of the attribute. To this end, an *elementary model* is needed.

Definition 13.26. *ElementaryModel,* synonym Elementary Criterion Function, is an algorithm or function with associated decision criteria that model an elementary indicator.

The *specification* of the elementary model can look like this: CDI_PL = (0.33 * CDI) * 100; where CDI is the direct metric for the *Capability to Delete Items* attribute (see Definition 13.10).

Note that, like a metric, an indicator has a *Scale* (see Definition 13.13). To the above example we considered a *numerical scale* where the *Unit* (see Definition 13.16) can be a normalized "percentage" scale. As mentioned, the elementary indicator interprets the metric's value of an attribute (an attribute as an elementary requirement). Then, the above elementary model interprets the percentage of the satisfied elementary requirement.

Definition 13.27. *DecisionCriteria,* synonym Acceptability Levels, are the thresholds, targets, or patterns used to determine the need for action or further investigation, or to describe the level of confidence in a given result.

Definition 13.28. *Range* is the threshold or limit values that determine the acceptability levels.

The decision criteria that a model of an indicator may have are the agreed-upon acceptability levels in given ranges of the scale; for instance, it is "unsatisfactory" if the *range* (regarding *lower_threshold* and *upper_threshold*) is "0 to 45", respectively; "marginal" if it is "greater than 45 and less or equal than 70"; otherwise, "satisfactory." A *description* or interpretation for "marginal" is that a score within this range indicates a need for improvement. An "unsatisfactory" rating means change actions must take high priority.

Definition 13.29. *GlobalIndicator,* synonym Global Preference, Global Criterion, is an indicator derived from other indicators to evaluate or estimate a calculable concept.

Definition 13.30. *GlobalModel,* synonym Aggregation Model, Scoring Model, or Function, is an algorithm or function with associated decision criteria that model a global indicator.

In order to enact the concept model (see Definition 13.6) for elementary, partial, and global indicators, an *aggregation model* and *decision criteria* must be selected. The quantitative aggregation and scoring models aim at making the evaluation process well structured, objective, and comprehensible to evaluators. For example, if our procedure is based on a "linear additive scoring model," the aggregation and computing of partial/global indicators (P/GI), considering relatives *weights* (*W*), is based on the following *specification*:

$$P/GI = (W_1\, EI_1 + W_2\, EI_2 + ... + W_m\, EI_m);\qquad\qquad (13.1)$$

such that if the elementary indicator (EI) is in the percentage scale and unit, the following holds:

$$0 \le EI_i \le 100;$$

and the sum of weights for an aggregation block must fulfill

$$(W_1 + W_2 + ... + W_m) = 1$$

if $W_i > 0$; for i = 1, . . ., *m*, where *m* is the number of subconcepts at the same level in the tree's aggregation block (see Figure 13.11).

The basic arithmetic aggregation *operator* for input in Eq. (13.1) is the plus (+) connector. Besides, this model lets us compute partial and global indicators in the execution stage. Other nonlinear aggregation models or functions can be used such as logic scoring of preference (Dujmovic, 1996), fuzzy model, and neural models, among others.

Definition 13.31. *Calculation,* synonym Computation, is an activity that uses an indicator definition in order to produce an indicator's value.

Definition 13.32. *Indicator Value,* synonym Preference Value, is the number or category assigned to a calculable concept by making a calculation.

As a final remark, for a specific evaluation project, all the above concepts and definitions of the evaluation model are necessary in order to specify, calculate, store, and use trustworthy indicator values and meta-data. When the execution of the measurement and evaluation activities for a given project has been performed, decision makers can analyze the results and draw conclusions and recommendations with regard to the established information need. Ultimately, we argue that this framework can be useful for different qualitative and quantitative evaluation methods and techniques with regard to the requirements, measurement, and evaluation concepts and definitions discussed previously.

13.4 ASSESSING WEB QUALITY USING WEBQEM: A CASE STUDY

In Section 13.1, we stated that in order to build a robust and clear measurement and evaluation program, at least three pillars are necessary, namely (1) a process for measurement and evaluation, which is outlined in Section 13.2, (2) a measurement and evaluation framework based on an ontological base, which is analyzed in Section 13.3, and (3) specific model-based methods and techniques in order to perform the specific program or project's activities, which are the aim of this section.

While a measurement or evaluation process specifies what to do (i.e., a clear specification of activities' descriptions, input and output, etc.), a method specifies how to do and perform such activities' descriptions relying on specific models and criteria.

As mentioned, there are different categories of methods (for example, categories for inspection, testing, inquiry, simulation, etc.) and specific types of evaluation methods and techniques such as the heuristic evaluation technique, analyses of log files, or concept model-centered evaluation methods, among many others.

In this section we present the Web Quality Evaluation Methodology (WebQEM) (Olsina and Rossi, 2002) as a model-centered evaluation methodology for the inspection category, that is, inspection of concepts, subconcepts, and attributes stemming from a quality or quality-in-use requirement model, among others. In addition, WebQEM relies on the metric and indicator concepts for measurement and evaluation in order to draw conclusions and give recommendations. We have been developing the WebQEM methodology since the late 1990s. It has been used to evaluate Web sites in several domains, as documented elsewhere (Olsina et al., 1999, 2000, 2006a), in addition to evaluating some industrial Web sites.

In order to illustrate WebQEM and its applicability, we conducted an e-business case study by evaluating the external quality of the shopping cart feature of the Amazon Web site, taking into account a general visitor standpoint. Note that users are redirected to the Amazon Web site (www.amazon.com) from the IMDb, the Internet Movie Database Web site (www.imdb.com), when trying to buy a DVD.

13.4.1 External Quality Requirements Specification

Many potential attributes, both general and domain-specific, can contribute to the Web's external quality. However, as mentioned earlier, evaluation must be organizational, purpose-oriented for an identified information need. Let us establish that the purpose in the present study is to understand the external quality of the shopping cart component of a typical e-store, for a general visitor viewpoint, in order to incorporate the best features in a new e-bookstore development project. For this aim, a successful international site such as Amazon was chosen. On the other hand, recall that the ISO 9126-1 standard models the software quality from three related approaches, which can be summarized as follows:

- *Internal quality*, which is specified by a quality model (ISO, 2001; prescribing a set of six characteristics and a set of subcharacteristics for each characteristic) and can be measured and evaluated by static attributes of documents such as specification of requirements, architecture, or design; pieces of source code, and so forth. In the early phases of a software or Web life cycle, we can evaluate and control the internal quality of these early products, but assuring internal quality is not usually sufficient to assure external quality.
- *External quality*, which is specified by a quality model (likewise as in the previous cited model) and can be measured and evaluated by dynamic properties of the running code in a computer system, i.e., when the module or full application is executed in a computer or network simulating the actual environment as closely as possible. In the late phases of a software life cycle (mainly in different kinds of testing, or even in the acceptance testing, or furthermore in the operational state of a software or Web application), we can measure, evaluate, and control the external quality of these late products, but assuring external quality is usually not sufficient to assure quality in use.
- *Quality in use*, which is specified by a quality model (ISO, 2001; prescribing a set of four characteristics) and can be measured and evaluated by the extent to which the software or Web application meets a specific user's needs in an actual, specific context of use.

A point worthy of mention is the important difference between measuring and evaluating external quality and quality in use; see Olsina et al. (2006a) for an in-depth discussion on Web quality and these ISO models. The former generally involves no real users but rather experts, as long as the latter always involves real end users. The advantage of using expert evaluation without extensive user involvement is minimizing costs and time, among other features. Deciding whether or not to involve end users should be carefully planned and justified. On the other hand, without the end user's participation, it is unthinkable to conduct a task testing in a real context of use for quality-in-use evaluation. Nielsen et al. (2001) indicate that it is common for three to five subjects in the testing process for a given audience to produce meaningful results that minimize costs; however, they recommend running as many small tests as possible.

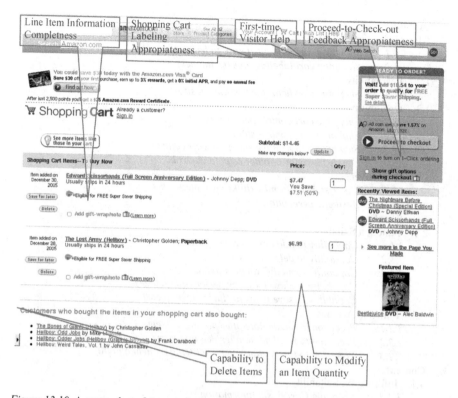

Figure 13.10. A screenshot of Amazon's shopping cart page with several attributes highlighted.

Considering the present study, Figure 13.10 shows a screenshot of Amazon's shopping cart page with several highlighted attributes, which intervene in the quality requirements tree of Figure 13.11.

To the external quality requirements definition, we considered 4 main characteristics: *Usability* (1), *Functionality* (2), *Content* (3), and *Reliability* (4), and 32 attributes related to them (see Figure 13.11). For instance, the Usability characteristic splits into subcharacteristics such as *Understandability* (1.1), *Learnability* (1.2), *Operability* (1.3), and *Attractiveness* (1.4).

Instead of previous quoted case studies, we now consider two separate characteristics: *Functionality* and *Content*. The *Functionality* characteristic splits into *Function Suitability* (2.1) and *Accuracy* (2.2), while the *Content* characteristic splits into *Information Suitability* (3.1) and *Content Accessibility* (3.2). As the reader can observe in Figure 13.11, we relate five measurable attributes to the *Function Suitability* subcharacteristic and three to *Function Accuracy*. In the latter subcharacteristic, we mainly consider precision attributes to recalculate values after making supported operations. On the other hand, in Olsina et al. (2006a) we also justified the inclusion of the *Content* characteristic for assessing the Web.

The following categories can help to evaluate information quality requirements of Web sites and applications (see also Lee et al., 2002):

1.   Usability
   1.1.   Understandability
      1.1.1.   Shopping cart icon/label ease to be recognized
      1.1.2.   Shopping cart labeling appropriateness
   1.2.   Learnability
      1.2.1.   Shopping cart help (for first-time visitor)
   1.3.   Operability
      1.3.1.   Shopping cart control permanence
      1.3.2.   Shopping cart control stability
      1.3.3.   Steady behavior of the shopping cart control
      1.3.4.   Steady behavior of other related controls
   1.4.   Attractiveness
      1.4.1.   Color style uniformity (links, text, etc.)
      1.4.2.   Aesthetic perception

2.   Functionality
   2.1.   Function Suitability
      2.1.1.   Capability to add items from anywhere
      2.1.2.   Capability to delete items
      2.1.3.   Capability to modify an item quantity
      2.1.4.   Capability to show totals by performed changes
      2.1.5.   Capability to save items for later/move to cart
   2.2.   Function Accuracy
      2.2.1.   Precision to recalculate after adding an item
      2.2.2.   Precision to recalculate after deleting items
      2.2.3.   Precision to recalculate after modifying an item quantity

3.   Content
   3.1.   Information Suitability
      3.1.1.   Shopping Cart Basic Information
         3.1.1.1.   Line item information completeness
         3.1.1.2.   Product description appropriateness
      3.1.2.   Shopping Cart Contextual Information
         3.1.2.1.   Purchase Policies Related Information
            3.1.2.1.1.   Shipping and handling costs information completeness
            3.1.2.1.2.   Applicable taxes information completeness
            3.1.2.1.3.   Return policy information completeness
         3.1.2.2.   Continue-buying feedback appropriateness
         3.1.2.3.   Proceed-to-check-out feedback appropriateness
   3.2.   Content Accessibility
      3.2.1.   Readability by Deactivating the Browser Image Feature
         3.2.1.1.   Image title availability
         3.2.1.2.   Image title readability
      3.2.2.   Support for text-only version

4.   Reliability
   4.1.   Nondeficiency (Maturity)
      4.1.1.   Link Errors or Drawbacks
         4.1.1.1.   Broken links
         4.1.1.2.   Invalid links
         4.1.1.3.   Reflective links
      4.1.2.   Miscellaneous Deficiencies
         4.1.2.1.   Deficiencies or unexpected results dependent on browsers
         4.1.2.2.   Deficiencies or unexpected results independent of browsers

Figure 13.11. Specifying the external quality requirements tree to the shopping cart component from a general visitor standpoint.

- *Information accuracy.* This subcharacteristic addresses the very intrinsic nature of the information's quality. It assumes that information has its own quality per se. Accuracy is the extent to which information is correct, unambiguous, authoritative (reputable), objective, and verifiable. If a Web site becomes famous for inaccurate information, the Web site will likely be perceived as having little added value and will result in reduced visits.

- *Information suitability.* This subcharacteristic addresses the contextual nature of the information quality. It emphasizes the importance of conveying the appropriate information for user-oriented goals and tasks. In other words, it highlights the quality requirement that contents must be considered within the context of use and the intended audience. Therefore, suitability is the extent to which information is appropriate (appropriate coverage for the target audience), complete (relevant amount), concise (shorter is better), and current (see the specified attributes in Figure 13.11).

- *Accessibility.* It emphasizes the importance of technical aspects of Web sites and applications in order to make Web contents more accessible for users with various disabilities (see the specified attributes in Figure 13.11).

- *Legal compliance.* The capability of the information product to adhere to standards, conventions, and legal norms related to contents and intellectual property rights.

The INCAMI_Tool records all the information for a measurement and evaluation project. Besides the data in the project itself, it also saves to the *InformationNeed* class (see Figure 13.6) the purpose, user viewpoint, and context description meta-data; for the *CalculabeConcept* and *Attribute* classes, it saves all the names and definitions, respectively.

The *ConceptModel* class permits us to instantiate a specific model, that is, the external quality model in our case, allowing evaluators to edit and relate specific concepts, subconcepts, and attributes (the whole instantiated model looks like that in Figure 13.11, and an INCAMI_Tool screenshot of it appears in Figure 13.12).

13.4.2 Designing and Executing the Measurement and Elementary Evaluation

As mentioned in Section 13.2, the evaluators should design, for each measurable attribute of the instantiated external quality model, the basis for the measurement and elementary evaluation process by defining each specific metric and elementary indicator for the information needed accordingly.

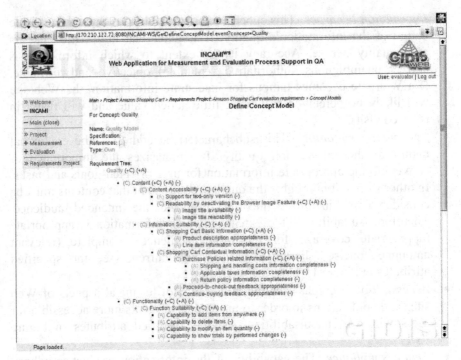

Define Concept Model

Figure 13.12. INCAMI_Tool screenshot to the instantiated concept model. Attributes are labeled with "A" on the left side of the tree; concepts and subconcepts with "C." In addition, "+C" and "+A" mean adding concepts or attributes, respectively, and "-" removing them.

In the design phase we record all the information for the selected metrics and elementary indicators regarding the conceptual schema of the *Metric* and *Elementary Indicator* classes shown in Figures 13.8 and 13.9, respectively. In addition, in Sections 13.4.2 and 13.4.3 the metric and indicator meta-data for the "Capability to delete items" attribute were illustrated. Finally, Figure 13.13 shows the name of the attributes and the name of each metric that quantifies them. Note that we can assign a metric for a given attribute by selecting it from the semantic catalogue (Molina et al., 2004); see the "Assign Metric" link in the figure.

Lastly, in the execution phase, we record for the *Measurement* and *Calculation* classes' instances the yielded final values for each metric and indicator. The data collection for the measurement activity was performed from December 19 to 30, 2005. From the metrics' values, the elementary indicators' values were calculated according to the respective elementary models.

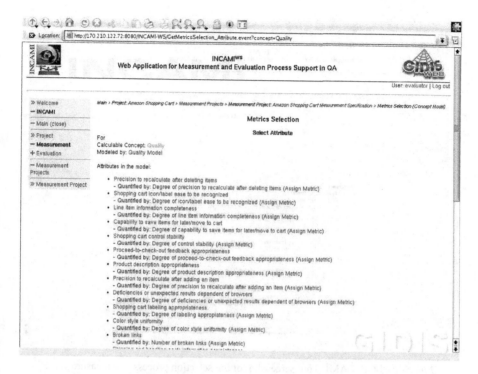

Figure 13.13. INCAMI_Tool screenshot of the metric selection process.

Figure 13.14 shows the selection process of a measurement value from a specific measurement project, which will be the input to the respective elementary indicator function in order to produce the indicator value (recall that for the same measurement project we can record measurement values at different times).

Once evaluators have designed and implemented the elementary evaluation, they should consider not only each attribute's relative importance but also whether the attribute (or subcharacteristic) is mandatory, alternative, or neutral. For this global evaluation task, we need a robust aggregation and scoring model, described next.

13.4.3 Designing and Executing the Partial/Global Evaluation

In the design of the global evaluation phase we select and apply an aggregation and scoring model (see *GlobalModel* class in Figure 13.9). Arithmetic or logic operators will then relate the hierarchically grouped attributes, subconcepts, and concepts accordingly.

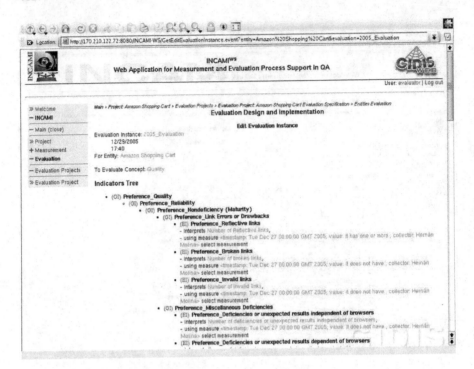

Figure 13.14. INCAMI_Tool screenshot of the selection process of a measure value for a given elementary indicator.

As mentioned earlier (see Definition 13.30), the INCAMI_Tool supports a linear additive or a nonlinear multicriteria scoring model (even other models can be used for designing the global evaluation such as fuzzy logic or neural networks not supported currently by the tool). We cannot use the additive scoring model to model input simultaneity (an *and* relationship among inputs) or replaceability (an *or* relationship), however, because it cannot express, for example, simultaneous satisfaction of several requirements as input. Additivity assumes that the insufficient presence of a specific attribute (in an input) can always be compensated for by the sufficient presence of any other attribute. Furthermore, additive models cannot model mandatory requirements; that is, a necessary attribute's or subcharacteristic's total absence cannot be compensated for by another's presence.

A nonlinear multicriteria scoring model lets us deal with simultaneity, neutrality, replaceability, and other input relationships using aggregation operators based on the weighted-power-means mathematical model. This model, called Logic Scoring of Preference (LSP) (Dujmovic, 1996), is a generalization of the additive scoring model and can be expressed as follows:

$$P/GI(r) = (W_1\,EI^r_1 + W_2\,EI^r_2 + ... + W_m\,EI^r_m)^{1/r}, \tag{13.2}$$

where

$$-\infty \leq r \leq +\infty \; ; \; \text{P/GI}\,(-\infty) = \min{(\text{EI}_1\,,\,\text{EI}_2\,,\,...\,,\,\text{EI}_m)},$$
$$\text{P/GI}\,(+\infty) = \max{(\text{EI}_1\,,\,\text{EI}_2\,,\,...\,,\,\text{EI}_m)}.$$

The power r is a parameter selected to achieve the desired logical relationship and polarization intensity of the aggregation function. If $\text{P/GI}(r)$ is closer to the minimum, such a criterion specifies the requirement for input simultaneity. If it is closer to the maximum, it specifies the requirement for input replaceability. Equation (13.2) is additive when $r = 1$, which models the neutrality relationship; that is, the formula remains the same as in the first additive model. Equation (13.2) is supra-additive for $r > 1$, which models input disjunction or replaceability, and it's sub-additive for $r < 1$ (with $r! = 0$), which models input conjunction or simultaneity.

For our case study (as in previous ones), we selected this last model and used a 17-level approach of conjunction–disjunction operators, as defined by Dujmovic. Each operator in the model corresponds to a particular value of the r parameter. When $r = 1$, the operator is tagged with A (or the + sign). The C conjunctive operators range from weak (C–) to strong (C+) quasi-conjunction functions, i.e., from decreasing r values, starting from $r < 1$.

In general, the conjunctive operators imply that low-quality input indicators can never be well compensated for by a high quality of some other input to output a high-quality indicator (in other words, a chain is as strong as its weakest link). Conversely, disjunctive operators (D operators) imply that low-quality input indicators can always be compensated for by the high quality of some other input.

Designing the LSP aggregation schema requires answering the following key basic questions (which are part of the *Global Indicator Definition* task in Figure 13.5):

- What is the relationship among this group of related attributes and subconcepts: conjunctive, disjunctive, or neutral [for instance, when modeling the attributes' relationship for the *Function Suitability* (2.1) subcharacteristic, we can agree they are neutral or independent of each other]?
- What is the level of intensity of the logic operator, from a weak to strong conjunctive or disjunctive polarization?
- What is the relative importance or weight of each element in the aggregation block or group?

Figure 13.15 shows some details of the enacted requirements tree for amazon.com as generated by our tool. Particularly, in the top part of Figure 13.15 we can see LSP operators, weights, and final values for elementary, partial, and global indicators; the bottom part shows only the indicator values and the respective colored bars in a percentage scale.

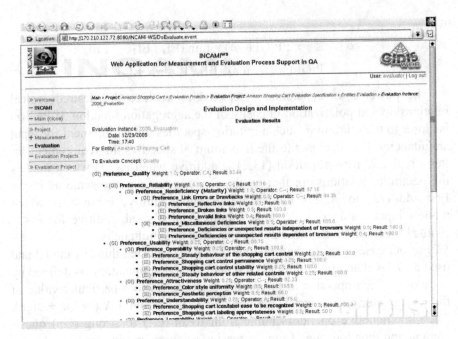

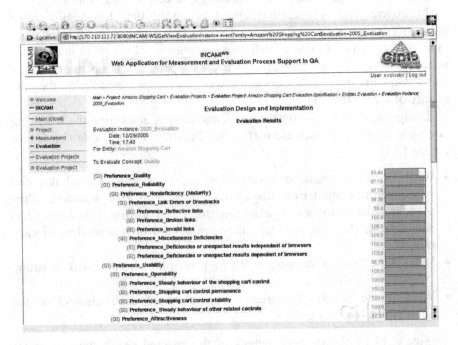

Figure 13.15. Once the weights and operators (in this case for the LSP aggregation model) were agreed on, the INCAMI_Tool yields elementary partial and global indicators in the execution phase, as highlighted in the figures. The top figure shows details of weights and operators, while the bottom figure shows just indicator values and the respective colored bars in the percentage scale.

13.4.4 Analyzing and Recommending

Once we have performed the final execution of the evaluation, decision makers can analyze the results and draw conclusions and recommendations. As stated in Section 13.4.1, we established (for illustration reasons) that the purpose in this study is to understand the external quality of the shopping cart component of a typical e-store, for a general visitor viewpoint in order to incorporate the best features in a new e-bookstore development project. The underlying hypothesis is that at the level of calculable concepts (characteristics in the ISO 9126 vocabulary) they accomplish at least the satisfactory acceptability range.

Table 13.1 shows the final results for the *Usability*, *Functionality*, *Content*, and *Reliability* characteristics and subcharacteristics, as well as partial and global indicator values for the amazon.com shopping cart.

Table 13.1. Summary of Partial and Global Indicators' Values for the Amazon.com Shopping Cart

Code	Concept/Subconcept Name	Indicator Value
	External Quality	*83.44*
1	Usability	88.75
1.1	Understandability	75.00
1.2	Learnability	100.00
1.3	Operability	100.00
1.4	Attractiveness	82.33
2	Functionality	87.61
2.1	Function Suitability	76.40
2.2	Function Accuracy	100.00
3	Content	71.40
3.1	Information Suitability	81.21
3.1.1	Shopping Cart Basic Information	81.70
3.1.2	Shopping Cart Contextual Information	80.47
3.1.2.1	Purchase Policies related Information	77.89
3.2	Content Accessibility	56.79
3.2.1	Readability by Deactivating the Browser Image Feature	67.75
4	Reliability	97.16
4.1	Nondeficiency (Maturity)	97.16
4.1.1	Link Errors or Drawbacks	94.35
4.1.2	Miscellaneous Deficiencies	100

The colored quality bars in the bottom part of Figure 13.15 indicate the acceptability ranges and clearly show the quality level each shopping cart feature has reached. In fact, the final indicator value to the external quality of the Amazon shopping cart was satisfactory getting a rank of 83.44 [that is a similar global indicator value for the study made in late 2004 (Olsina et al., 2006), using the same requirements and criteria, which ranked 84.32%]. Notice that a score within a yellow bar (marginal) indicates a need for improvement actions. An unsatisfactory rating (red bar) means change actions must take high priority. A score within a green bar indicates satisfactory quality of the analyzed feature.

Looking at the *Usability, Functionality, Content,* and *Reliability* characteristics, we can see that the scores fall in the satisfactory level, so that we can emulate these features in a new development project. However, none of them is 100%. For instance, if we look at the *Functionality* characteristic and particularly at the *Function Suitability* subconcept, which ranked 76.40, we can observe that the reason for this score is in part due to the *Capability to Delete Items* (2.1.2) attribute, which is not totally suitable (the indicator value was 66%).

In order to make a thorough causal analysis, we must look at the elementary indicator and metric specification. Regarding the INCAMI_Tool, the following elementary indicator model specification (see Definition 13.26) was edited: CDI _PL = (0.33 * CDI) * 100, where CDI is the direct metric for the *Capability to Delete Items* attribute.

In the example of Definition 13.10, the scale of the direct metric was specified in this way:

1. Does not delete items at all.
2. Delete just all at once.
3. Delete one by one.
4. Delete one by one or delete the selected group at once.

Thus, the resulting indicator value in the execution phase was 66% because the Amazon shopping cart allows users to delete only one item at once, but does not allow the selected group to be deleted at once.

Ultimately, we observe that the state-of-the-art of the shopping cart quality of this typical site is rather high, but the wish list is not empty, because of some weak-designed attributes. Notice that elementary, partial, and global indicators reflect results of these specific requirements for this specific audience and should not be regarded as generalized rankings. Moreover, results themselves from a case study are seldom intended to be interpreted as generalizations (in the sense of external validity).

13.5 DISCUSSION AND FINAL REMARKS

Our experience suggests that it is necessary to select metrics for purpose-oriented attributes as well as to identify contextual indicators in order to start and guide a successful measurement and evaluation program. In fact, organizations must have sound specifications of metric and indicator meta-data associated consistently to data sets, as well as a clear establishment of frameworks and programs in order to make measurement and analyses and quality assurance useful support processes to software and Web development and maintenance projects. Ultimately, the underlying hypothesis is that without appropriate recorded meta-data of information needs, attributes, metrics, and indicators, it is difficult to ensure that measure and indicator values are repeatable and comparable among an organization's projects; consequently, analyses and comparisons can be carried out in an inconsistent way as well.

Throughout this chapter we have stated that in order to build a robust and flexible measurement and evaluation program, at least three pillars are necessary: (1) a process for measurement and evaluation (outlined in Section 13.2); (2) a measurement and evaluation framework based on an ontological base (analyzed in Section 13.3); and (3) specific model-based methods and techniques for the realization of measurement and evaluation activities (a particular inspection method was illustrated in Section 13.4).

As a matter of fact, in the present chapter we have emphasized the importance of counting with a measurement and evaluation conceptual framework. The discussed INCAMI framework is based on the assumption that for an organization to measure and evaluate in a purpose-oriented way, it must first specify nonfunctional requirements starting from information needs, then it must design and select the specific set of metrics for measurement purposes, and last it must interpret the metric values by means of contextual indicators with the aim of evaluating or estimating the degree to which the stated information need has been met. Thus, consistent and traceable analyses, conclusions, and recommendations can be drawn.

Regarding other initiatives, the GQM (*Goal-Question-Metrics*) paradigm (Basili and Rombach, 1989) is a useful, simple, purpose-oriented measurement approach that has been used in different measurement projects and organizations. However, as Kitchenham et al. pointed out (2001), GQM is not intended to define metrics at a level of detail suitable to ensure that they are trustworthy, in particular, whether or not they are repeatable. Contrary to our approach, which is based on an ontological conceptualization of metrics and indicators, GQM lacks this conceptual base, and so it cannot assure that measurement values (and the associated meta-data like scale, unit, measurement method, and so forth) are trustworthy and consistent for ulterior analysis among projects.

On the other hand, GQM is a weak framework for evaluation purposes, i.e. GQM lacks specific concepts for evaluation in order to interpret attributes' measures. For instance, elementary and global indicators and related terms are essential for evaluation as shown in the previous sections. Conversely, GQM is more flexible than INCAMI in the sense that it is not always necessary to have a concept model specification in order to perform a measurement project.

In our humble opinion, an interesting improvement to the GQM approach that considers indicators has recently been issued as a technical note (Goethert and Fisher, 2003). This approach uses both the *Balance Scorecard* technique (Kaplan and Norton, 2001) and the *Goal-Question-Indicator-Measurement* method in order to purposely derive the required enterprise goal-oriented indicators and metrics. It is a robust framework for specifying enterprise-wide information needs and deriving goals and subgoals and then operationalizing questions with associated indicators and metrics. It says, "The questions provide concrete examples that can lead to statements that identify the type of information needed. From these questions, displays or indicators are postulated that provide answers and help link the measurement data that will be collected to the measurement goals" (Goethert and Fisher, 2003). However, this approach is not based on a sound ontological conceptualization of metrics and indicators as ours; furthermore, the terms "measure" and "indicator" are sometimes used ambiguously, which can result in data sets and meta-data being recorded inconsistently.

On the other hand, there exist other close initiatives to our research, such as the Kitchenham et al. (2001) conceptual framework as well as the cited ISO standards related to software measurement and evaluation processes. In summary, we tried to strengthen these contributions not only from the conceptual modeling point of view, but also from the ontological point of view, including a broader set of concepts.

Lastly, we argue that the INCAMI framework can be a useful conceptual base and approach for different qualitative and quantitative evaluation methods and techniques with regard to the requirement, measurement, and evaluation concepts and definitions analyzed in Section 13.3. Apart from inspection or *feature analyses* methods (like WebQEM), this framework can be employed for some other methods, such as neural networks and fuzzy logic, when they are intended to measure and evaluate quality, quality in use, and cost, among other calculable concepts.

Finally, due to the importance of managing the acquired enterprise-wide contextual knowledge during measurement and evaluation and during quality assurance projects, a semantic infrastructure that embraces contextual information and organizational memory management is currently being considered in the INCAMI framework. This will be integrated to the

INCAMI_Tool and framework, also making sure that ontologies and the Semantic Web are enabling technologies for our previous (Molina et al., 2004) and current research aims as well.

ACKNOWLEDGEMENTS

This research is supported by Argentina's UNLPam-09/F037 project, as well as the PICTO 11-30300 and PAV 127-5 research projects.

REFERENCES

Basili, V., and Rombach, H.D., 1989, The TAME project: Towards improvement-oriented software environments. *IEEE Transactions on Software Engineering*, **14**(6): 758–773.

Briand, L., Morasca, S., and Basili, V., 2002, An operational process for goal-driven definition of measures. *IEEE Transactions on Software Engineering*, **28**(12): 1106–1125.

CMMI, 2002, Capability Maturity Model Integration, Version 1.1, CMMI[SM] for Software Engineering (CMMI-SW, V. 1.1) Staged Representation CMU/SEI-2002-TR-029, CMMI Product Team, SEI Carnegie Mellon University (available online).

Dujmovic, J., 1996, A method for evaluation and selection of complex hardware and software systems. *Proceedings 22nd International Conference for the Resource Management and Performance Evaluation of Enterprise CS* (CMG 96), Vol. 1, pp. 368–378.

Goethert, W., and Fisher, M., 2003, Deriving enterprise-based measures using the balanced scorecard and goal-driven measurement techniques. Software Engineering Measurement and Analysis Initiative, CMU/SEI-2003-TN-024 (available online).

ISO/IEC 14598-5, 1998, Information technology—Software product evaluation—Part 5: Process for evaluators.

ISO/IEC 14598-1, 1999, International standard, information technology—Software product evaluation—Part 1: General overview.

ISO/IEC 9126-1, 2001, International standard, software engineering—Product quality—Part 1: Quality model.

ISO/IEC 15939, 2002, Software engineering—Software measurement process.

Kaplan, R., and Norton, D., 2001, *The Strategy-Focused Organization, How Balanced Scorecard Companies Thrive in the New Business Environment.* Harvard Business School Press, Boston.

Kitchenham, B.A., Hughes, R.T., and Linkman, S.G., 2001. Modeling software measurement data. *IEEE Transactions on Software Engineering*, **27**(9): 788–804.

Lee, Y.W., Strong, D.M., Kahn, B.K., and Wang, R.Y., 2002, AIMQ: A methodology for information quality assessment. *Information & Management*, **40**(2): 133–146.

Molina, H., Papa, F., Martín, M., and Olsina, L., 2004, Semantic capabilities for the metrics and indicators cataloging Web system. In *Engineering Advanced Web Applications*, M. Matera and S. Comai, eds., Rinton Press Inc., Princeton, NJ, pp. 97–109, ISBN 1-58949-046-0.

Nielsen, J., Molich, R., Snyder, C., and Farrell, S., 2001, E-Commerce User Experience, NN Group.

Olsina, L., Godoy, D., Lafuente, G., and Rossi, G., 1999, Assessing the quality of academic Websites: A case study. *New Review of Hypermedia and Multimedia (NRHM) Journal*, **5**: 81–103.

Olsina, L., Lafuente, G., and Rossi, G., 2000, E-commerce site evaluation: A case study. *Proceedings 1st International Conference on Electronic Commerce and Web Technologies* (EC-Web 2000), London, Springer LNCS 1875, pp. 239–252.

Olsina, L., Papa, M.F., Souto, M.E., and Rossi, G., 2001, Providing automated support for the Web quality evaluation methodology. *Proceedings 4th Workshop on Web Engineering, at the 10th International WWW Conference*, Hong Kong, pp. 1–11.

Olsina, L., and Rossi, G., 2002, Measuring Web application quality with WebQEM. *IEEE Multimedia*, **9**(4): 20–29.

Olsina, L., and Martin, M., 2004, Ontology for software metrics and indicators. *Journal of Web Engineering*, **2**(4): 262–281, ISSN 1540-9589.

Olsina, L., Papa, F., and Molina, H., 2005, Organization-oriented measurement and evaluation framework for software and Web Engineering projects. *Proceedings International Congress on Web Engineering* (ICWE05), Sydney, Australia, Springer, LNCS 3579, pp. 42–52.

Olsina, L., Covella, G., and Rossi, G., 2006, Web quality. Chapter 4 in *Web Engineering*, E. Mendes and N. Mosley, eds., Springer, New York, ISBN 3-540-28196-7.

Olsina, L., Papa, F., and Molina, H., 2008, Ontological support for a measurement and evaluation framework. To appear in the *Journal of Intelligent Systems*.

Zuse, H., 1998, *A Framework of Software Measurement*, Walter de Gruyter, Berlín.

Chapter 14

THE NEED FOR EMPIRICAL WEB ENGINEERING: AN INTRODUCTION

Emilia Mendes

WETA Research Group, Computer Science Department, The University of Auckland, Private Bag 92019, Auckland, New Zealand

14.1 INTRODUCTION

The World Wide Web (Web) was originally conceived in 1989 as an environment to allow for the sharing of information (e.g., research reports, databases, user manuals) among geographically dispersed individuals. The information itself was stored on different servers and was retrieved by means of a single user interface (a Web browser). The information consisted primarily of text documents interlinked using a hypertext metaphor[1] (Offutt, 2002).

Since its original inception, the Web has changed into an environment employed for the delivery of many different types of applications. Such applications range from small-scale information-dissemination-like applications, typically developed by writers and artists, to large-scale commercial,[2] enterprise-planning and scheduling, collaborative-work applications. The latter are developed by multidisciplinary teams of people with diverse skills and backgrounds using cutting-edge, diverse technologies (Gellersen and Gaedke, 1997; Ginige and Murugesan, 2001; Offutt, 2002).

---

[1] http://www.zeltser.com/web-history/.

[2] The increase in the use of the Web to provide commercial applications has been motivated by several factors, such as the possible increase of an organization's competitive position, and the opportunity for small organizations to project their corporate presence in the same way as that of larger organizations.

Numerous current Web applications are fully functional systems that provide business-to-customer and business-to-business e-commerce, and numerous services to numerous users (Offutt, 2002).

Industries such as travel and hospitality, manufacturing, banking, education, and government have utilized Web-based applications to improve and increase their operations (Ginige and Murugesan, 2001). In addition, the Web allows for the development of corporate intranet Web applications, for use within the boundaries of their organizations (Houghton, 2000). The remarkable spread of Web applications into areas of communication and commerce makes it one of the leading and most important branches of the software industry (Offutt, 2002).

To date the development of industrial Web applications has been in general ad hoc, resulting in poor-quality applications that are difficult to maintain (Murugesan and Deshpande, 2001). The main reasons for such problems are unawareness of suitable design and development processes, and poor project management practices (Ginige, 2002). A survey on Web-based projects, published by the Cutter Consortium in 2000, revealed a number of problems with outsourced, large Web-based projects (Ginige, 2002):

- Eighty-four percent of surveyed delivered projects did not meet business needs.
- Fifty-three percent of surveyed delivered projects did not provide the required functionality.
- Seventy-nine percent of surveyed projects presented schedule delays.
- Sixty-three percent of surveyed projects exceeded their budget.

As the reliance on larger and more complex Web applications increases, so does the need for using methodologies/standards/best practice guidelines to develop applications that are delivered on time and within budget, have a high level of quality, and are easy to maintain (Lee and Shirani, 2004; Ricca and Tonella, 2001; Taylor et al., 2002). To develop such applications, Web development teams need to use sound methodologies, systematic techniques, quality assurance, rigorous, disciplined, and repeatable processes, better tools, and baselines. Web Engineering[3] aims to meet such needs (Ginige and Murugesan, 2001).

Web Engineering is described as (Murugesan and Deshpande, 2001) "the use of scientific, **engineering**, and management principles and systematic

---

[3] The term "Web Engineering" was first published in 1996 in a conference paper by Gellersen et al. (1997). Since then this term has been cited in numerous publications, and numerous activities devoted to discussing Web Engineering have taken place (e.g., workshops, conference tracks, entire conferences).

approaches with the aim of successfully developing, deploying and maintaining high quality Web-based systems and applications."

Engineering is widely taken as a disciplined application of scientific knowledge for the solution of practical problems. A few definitions taken from dictionaries support that:

Engineering is the application of science to the needs of humanity. This is accomplished through knowledge, mathematics, and practical experience applied to the design of useful objects or processes. (Wikipedia, 2004)

Engineering is the application of scientific principles to practical ends, as the design, manufacture, and operation of structures and machines. (Houghton, 1994)

The profession of applying scientific principles to the design, construction, and maintenance of engines, cars, machines, etc. (mechanical engineering), buildings, bridges, roads, etc. (civil engineering), electrical machines and communication systems (electrical engineering), chemical plant and machinery (chemical engineering), or aircraft (aeronautical engineering). (Harper, 2000)

In all of the above definitions, the need for "the application of scientific principles" has been stressed, where scientific principles are the result of applying a scientific process (Goldstein and Goldstein, 1978). A process in this context means that our current understanding, i.e., our theory (hypothesis) of how best to develop, deploy, and maintain high-quality Web-based systems and applications, may be modified or replaced as new evidence is found through the accumulation of data and knowledge. This process is illustrated in Figure 14.1 and described below (Goldstein and Goldstein, 1978):

- *Observation*: To observe or read about a phenomenon or set of facts. In most cases the motivation for such observation is to identify cause-and-effect relationships between observed items, since these entail predictable results. For example, we can observe that an increase in the development of new Web pages seems also to increase the corresponding development effort.

- *Hypothesis*: To formulate a hypothesis represents an attempt to explain an *observation*. It is a tentative theory or assumption that is believed to explain the behavior under investigation (Fenton and Pfleeger, 1997). The items that participate in the *observation* are represented by variables (e.g., number of new Web pages, development effort), and the hypothesis indicates what is expected to happen to these variables (e.g., there is a linear relationship between the number of Web pages and the development effort, showing that as the number of new Web pages increases, so does the effort to develop these pages). These variables first need to be measured; to do so, we need an underlying measurement theory.

- *Prediction*: To predict means to predict results that should be found if the rationale used in the hypothesis formulation is correct (e.g., Web applications with a larger number of new Web pages will use a larger development effort).
- *Validation*: To validate requires experimentation to provide evidence to either support or refute the initial hypothesis. If the evidence refutes the hypothesis, then the hypothesis should be revised or replaced. If the evidence is in support of the hypothesis, then many more replications of the experiment need to be carried out in order to build a better understanding of how variables relate to each other and their cause-and-effect relationships.

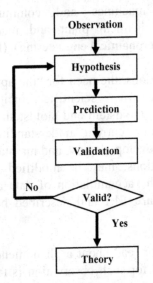

Figure 14.1. WSDM overview.

The scientific process supports knowledge building, which in turn involves the use of empirical studies to test hypotheses previously proposed and to assess if current understanding of the discipline is correct. Experimentation in Web Engineering is therefore essential (Basili, 1996; Basili et al., 1999).

The extent to which scientific principles are applied to developing and maintaining Web applications varies among organizations. More mature organizations generally apply these principles to a larger extent than less mature organizations, where maturity reflects an organization's use of sound development processes and practices (Fenton and Pfleeger, 1997). Some organizations have clearly defined processes that remain unchanged regardless of the people who work on the projects. For such organizations, success is dictated by following a well-defined process, where feedback is constantly obtained using product, process, and resource measures. Other organizations have processes that are not so clearly defined (ad hoc), and therefore the success of a project is often determined by the expertise of the development team. In such a scenario, product, process, and resource measures are rarely used, and each project represents a potential risk that may lead an organization, if it gets it wrong, to bankruptcy (Pressman, 1998).

The variables used in the formulation of hypotheses represent the attributes of real-world entities that we observe. An entity represents a process, product, or resource. A process is defined as a software-related activity. Examples of processes are Web development, Web maintenance, Web design, Web testing, and Web project. A product is defined as an artifact, deliverable, or document that results from a process activity. Examples of products are Web application, design document, testing scripts, and fault reports. Finally, a resource represents an entity required by a process activity. Examples of resources are Web developers, development tools, and programming languages (Fenton and Pfleeger, 1997).

In addition, for each entity's attribute that is to be measured, it is also useful to identify if the attribute is *internal* or *external*. Internal attributes can be measured by examining the product, process, or resource on its own, separate from its behavior. External attributes can only be measured with respect to how the product, process, or resource relates to its environment (Fenton and Pfleeger, 1997). For example, usability is in general an external attribute since its measurement often depends upon the interaction between user and application. An example of classification of entities is presented in Table 14.1.

The measurement of an entity's attributes generates quantitative descriptions of key processes, products, and resources, enabling us to understand behavior and results. This understanding lets us select better techniques and tools to control and improve our processes, products, and resources (Pfleeger et al., 1997).

The measurement theory that has been adopted in this chapter is the representational theory of measurement (Fenton and Pfleeger, 1997). It drives the definition of measurement scales, presented in Section 14.2, and the measures presented in Chapter 13.

Table 14.1. Classification of Process, Product, and Resources for Tukutuku[4] Data Set

Entity	Attribute	Description
PROCESS ENTITIES		
PROJECT		
	TYPEPROJ	Type of project (new or enhancement)
	LANGS	Implementation languages used
	DOCPROC	If project followed defined and documented process
	PROIMPR	If project team is involved in a process improvement program
	METRICS	If project team is part of a software metrics program
	DEVTEAM	Size of project's development team
WEB DEVELOPMENT		
	TOTEFF	Actual total effort used to develop the Web application
	ESTEFF	Estimated total effort necessary to develop the Web application
	ACCURACY	Procedure used to record effort data
PRODUCT ENTITY		
WEB APPLICATION		
	TYPEAPP	Type of Web application developed
	TOTWP	Total number of Web pages (new and reused)
	NEWWP	Total number of new Web pages
	TOTIMG	Total number of images (new and reused)
	NEWIMG	Total number of new images your company created
	HEFFDEV	Minimum number of hours to develop a single function/feature by one experienced developer that is considered high (above average)
	HEFFADPT	Minimum number of hours to adapt a single function/feature by one experienced developer that is considered high (above average)
	HFOTS	Number of reused high-effort features/functions without adaptation
	HFOTSA	Number of adapted high-effort features/functions
	HNEW	Number of new high-effort features/functions
	FOTS	Number of low-effort features off the shelf
	FOTSA	Number of low-effort features off the shelf adapted
	NEW	Number of new low-effort features/functions
RESOURCE ENTITY		
DEVELOPMENT TEAM		
	TEAMEXP	Average team experience with the development language(s) employed

14.2 MEASUREMENT SCALES

When we gather data associated with the attributes of entities we wish to measure, they can be collected using different scales of measurement. The characteristics of each scale type determine the choice of methods and

---

[4] The Tukutuku project collects data on industrial Web projects, for the development of effort estimation models and to benchmark productivity across and within Web companies. (See http://www.cs.auckland.ac.nz/tukutuku.)

statistics that can be used to analyze the data and how to interpret their corresponding measures. In this section we describe the five main scale types (Fenton and Pfleeger, 1997):

- Nominal
- Ordinal
- Interval
- Ratio
- Absolute

14.2.1 The Nominal Scale Type

The Nominal scale type represents the most primitive form of measurement. It identifies classes or categories where each category groups a set of entities based on their attribute's value. Here entities can only be organized into classes or categories, and there is no notion of ranking between classes. Classes can be represented as symbols or numbers; however, if we use numbers, they do not have any numerical meaning. Examples using a Nominal scale are given in Table 14.2.

Table 14.2. Examples of Nominal Scale Measures

Entity	Attribute	Categories
Web application	Type	e-Commerce, academic, corporate, entertainment
Programming language	Type	ASP (VBScript, .Net), Coldfusion, J2EE (JSP, Servlet, EJB), PHP
Web project	Type	New, enhancement, redevelopment
Web company	Type of service	1, 4, 5, 7, 9, 34, 502, 8

14.2.2 The Ordinal Scale Type

The Ordinal scale supplements the Nominal scale with information about the ranking of classes or categories. As with the Nominal scale, it also identifies classes or categories, where each category groups a set of entities based on their attribute's value. The difference between an Ordinal scale and a Nominal scale is that here there is the notion of ranking between classes. Classes can be represented as symbols or numbers; however, if we use numbers, they do not have any numerical meaning and represent ranking only. Therefore addition, subtraction, and other arithmetic operations cannot be applied to classes. Examples using an Ordinal scale are given in Table 14.3.

Table 14.3. Examples of Ordinal Scale Measures

Entity	Attribute	Categories
Web application	Complexity	Very low, low, average, high, very high
Web page	Design quality	Very poor, poor, average, good, very good
Web project	Priority	1,2,3,4,5,6,7

14.2.3 The Interval Scale Type

The Interval scale supplements the Ordinal scale with information about the size of the intervals that separate the classes or categories. As with the Nominal and Ordinal scales, it also identifies classes or categories, where each category groups a set of entities based on their attribute's value. As with the Ordinal scale, there are ranks between classes or categories. The difference between an Interval scale and an Ordinal scale is that here there is the notion that the size of intervals between classes or categories remains constant. Although the Interval scale is a numerical scale and numbers have a numerical meaning, the class zero does not mean the complete absence of the attribute we measured. To illustrate that, let's look at temperatures measured using the Celsius scale. The difference between 1 °C and 2 °C is the same as the difference between 6 °C and 7 °C: exactly 1°. There is a ranking between two classes; thus, 1 °C has a lower rank than 2 °C, and so on. Finally, the temperature 0 °C does not represent the complete absence of temperature, where molecular motion stops. In this example, 0 °C was arbitrarily chosen to represent the freezing point of water. This means that operations such as addition and subtraction between two categories are permitted (e.g., 50 °C − 20 °C = 70 °C − 40 °C; 5 °C + 25 °C = 20 °C + 10 °C); however, calculating the ratio of two categories (e.g., 40 °C/20 °C) is not meaningful (40 °C is not twice as hot as 20 °C), so multiplication and division cannot be calculated directly from categories. If ratios are to be calculated, they need to be based on the differences between categories. Examples using an Interval scale are given in Table 14.4.

Table 14.4. Examples of Interval Scale Measures

Entity	Attribute	Categories
Web project	Number of days relative to start of project	0,1,2,3,4,5,...
Human body	Temperature (Celsius or Fahrenheit)	Decimal numbers

14.2.4 The Ratio Scale Type

The Ratio scale supplements the Interval scale with the existence of a zero element, representing the total absence of the attribute measured. As with the Interval scale, it also provides information about the size of the intervals that separate the classes or categories. As with the Interval and Ordinal scales, there are ranks between classes or categories. As with the Interval, Ordinal, and Nominal scales, it also identifies classes or categories, where each category groups a set of entities based on their attribute's value. The difference between a Ratio scale and an Interval scale is the existence of an absolute zero. The Ratio scale is also a numerical scale, and numbers have a numerical meaning. This means that any arithmetic operations between two categories are permitted. Examples using a Ratio scale are given in Table 14.5.

Table 14.5. Examples of Ratio Scale Measures

Entity	Attribute	Categories
Web project	Effort	Decimal numbers
Web application	Size	Integer numbers
Human body	Temperature in Kelvin	Decimal numbers

14.2.5 The Absolute Scale Type

The Absolute scale supplements the Ratio scale with restricting the classes or categories to a specific unit of measurement. As with the Ratio scale, it also has a zero element, representing the total absence of the attribute measured. As with the Ratio and Interval scales, it also provides information about the size of the intervals that separate the classes or categories. As with the Interval and Ordinal scales, there are ranks between classes or categories. As with the Ratio, Interval, Ordinal, and Nominal scales, it also identifies classes or categories, where each category groups a set of entities based on their attribute's value.

The difference between an Absolute scale and the Ratio scale is the existence of a *fixed unit of measurement* associated with the attribute being measured. For example, using a Ratio scale, if we were to measure the attribute *effort* of a *Web project,* we could obtain an effort value that could represent effort in number of hours, or effort in number of days, and so on. In case we want all effort measures to be kept using number of hours, we can convert effort in number of days to effort in number of hours, or effort in number of weeks to effort in number of hours. Thus, an attribute measured using a given unit of measurement (e.g., number of weeks) can have its class converted into another using a different unit of measurement, but keeping the meaning of the obtained data unchanged. Therefore, assuming a single developer, a Web project's effort of 40 hours is equivalent to a Web project effort's of a week. Thus, the unit of measurement changes, but the data that have been gathered remain unaffected. If we were to measure the attribute *effort* of a *Web project* using an *Absolute scale,* we would need to determine in advance the unit of measurement to be used. Therefore, once the unit of measurement is determined, it is the one used when effort data are being gathered. Using our example on *Web project's effort,* if the unit of measurement associated with the *attribute effort* had been *number of hours,* then all the effort data gathered would have represented effort in number of hours only. Finally, as with the Ratio scale, operations between two categories, such as addition, subtraction, multiplication, and division, are also permitted. Examples using an Absolute scale are given in Table 14.6.

Table 14.6. Examples of Absolute Scale Measures

Entity	Attribute	Categories
Web project	Effort, in number of hours	Decimal numbers
Web application	Size, in number of HTML files	Integer numbers
Web developer	Experience developing Web applications, in number of years	Integer numbers

14.2.6 Summary of Scale Types

Table 14.7 presents one of the summaries we are providing regarding Scale types. It has been adapted from Maxwell (2005). It is also important to note that the Nominal and Ordinal scales do not provide classes or categories that have numerical meaning, and for this reason their attributes are called Categorical or Qualitative. Conversely, given that the Interval, Ratio, and Absolute scales provide classes or categories that have numerical meaning, their attributes are called Numerical or Quantitative (Maxwell, 2005).

Table 14.7. Summary of Scale Type Definitions

Scale Type	Is Ranking Meaningful?	Are Distances Between Classes the Same?	Does the Class Include an Absolute Zero?
Nominal	No	No	No
Ordinal	Yes	No	No
Interval	Yes	Yes	No
Ratio	Yes	Yes	Yes
Absolute	Yes	Yes	Yes

In relation to the statistics relevant to each measurement scale type, Table 14.8 presents a summary adapted from Fenton and Pfleeger (1997).

Table 14.8. Summary of Scale Type Definitions

Scale Type	Examples of Suitable Statistics	Suitable Statistical Tests
Nominal	Mode, frequency	Nonparametric
Ordinal	Median, percentile	Nonparametric
Interval	Mean, standard deviation	Nonparametric and parametric
Ratio	Mean, geometric mean, standard deviation	Nonparametric and parametric
Absolute	Mean, geometric mean, standard deviation	Nonparametric and parametric

14.3 OVERVIEW OF EMPIRICAL ASSESSMENTS

Validating a hypothesis or research question encompasses experimentation, which is carried out using an empirical investigation. This section details the three different types of empirical investigation that can be carried out, which are survey, case study, or formal experiment (Fenton and Pfleeger, 1997):

- *Survey*: a retrospective investigation of an activity in order to confirm relationships and outcomes (Fenton and Pfleeger, 1997). It is also known as "research-in-the-large", as it often samples over large groups of projects. A survey should always be carried out after the activity under focus has occurred (Kitchenham et al., 1995). When performing a survey, a researcher has no control over the situation at hand, i.e., the situation can be documented, compared to other similar situations, but none of the variables being investigated can be manipulated (Fenton and Pfleeger, 1997). Within the scope of software and Web Engineering, surveys are often used to validate the response of organizations and developers to a new development method, tool, or technique, or to reveal trends or relationships between relevant variables (Fenton and Pfleeger, 1997). For example, a survey can be used to measure the success of changing from Sun's J2EE to Microsoft's ASP.NET throughout an organization, because it can gather data from numerous projects. The downside of surveys is time. Gathering data can take many months or even years, and the outcome may only be available after several projects have been completed (Kitchenham et al., 1995).
- *Case study*: an investigation that examines the trends and relationships using as its basis a typical project within an organization. It is also known as "research-in-the-typical" (Kitchenham et al., 1995). A case study can investigate a retrospective event, but this is not the usual trend. A case study is the type of investigation of choice when wishing to examine an event that has not yet occurred and for which there is little or no control over the variables. For example, if an organization wants to investigate the effect of a programming framework on the quality of the resulting Web application but cannot develop the same project using numerous frameworks simultaneously, then the investigative choice is to use a case study. If the quality of the resulting Web application is higher than the organization's quality baseline, it may be due to many different reasons (e.g., chance, or perhaps bias from enthusiastic developers). Even if the programming framework had a legitimate effect on quality, no conclusions outside the boundaries of the case study can be drawn, i.e., the results of a case study cannot be generalized to every possible situation. Had the same application been developed several times, each

time using a different programming framework[5] (as in a formal experiment), then it would have been possible to have had a better understanding of the relationship between framework and quality, given that these variables were controlled. A case study samples *from the variables*, rather than over them. This means that, in relation to the variable programming framework, a value that represents the framework usually used on most projects will be the one chosen (e.g., J2EE). A case study is easier to plan than a formal experiment, but its results are harder to explain and, as previously mentioned, cannot be generalized outside the scope of the study (Kitchenham et al., 1995).

- *Formal experiment*: rigorous and controlled investigation of an event where important variables are identified and manipulated such that their effect on the outcome can be validated (Fenton and Pfleeger, 1997). It is also known as "research-in-the-small" since it is very difficult to carry out formal experiments in software and Web Engineering using numerous projects and resources. A formal experiment samples *over the variable that is being manipulated*, such that all possible variable values are validated, i.e., there is a single case representing each possible situation. If we apply the same example used when explaining case studies above, this means that several projects would be developed, each using a different object-oriented programming language. If one aims to obtain results that are largely applicable across various types of projects and processes, then the choice of investigation is a formal experiment. This type of investigation is most suited to the Web Engineering research community. However, despite the control that needs to be exerted when planning and running a formal experiment, its results cannot be generalized outside the experimental conditions. For example, if an experiment demonstrates that J2EE improves the quality of e-commerce Web applications, one cannot guarantee that J2EE will also improve the quality of educational Web applications (Kitchenham et al., 1995).

Other concrete issues related to using a formal experiment or a case study may impact the choice of study. It may be feasible to control the variables, but at the expense of a very high cost or a high degree of risk. If replication *is* possible, but at a prohibitive cost, then a case study should be used (Fenton and Pfleeger, 1997). A summary of the characteristics of each type of empirical investigation is given in Table 14.9.

---

[5] The values for all other attributes should remain the same (e.g., developers, programming experience, development tools, computing power, and type of application).

Table 14.9. Summary Characteristics of the Three Types of Empirical Investigations

Characteristic	Survey	Case Study	Formal Experiment
Scale	Research-in-the-large	Research-in-the-typical	Research-in-the-small
Control	No control	Low level of control	High level of control
Replication	No	Low	High
Generalization	Results representative of sampled population	Only applicable to other projects of similar type and size	Can be generalized within the experimental conditions

A set of steps broadly common to all three types of investigations is described below.

Define the goal(s) of your investigation and its context. Goals are crucial for the success of all activities in an investigation. Thus, it is important to allow enough time to fully understand and set the goals so that each is clear and measurable. Goals represent the research questions, which may also be presented by a number of hypotheses. By setting the research questions or hypotheses, it becomes easier to identify the dependent and independent variables for the investigation (Fenton and Pfleeger, 1997). A dependent variable is a variable whose behavior we want to predict or explain. An independent variable is believed to have a causal relationship with, or have influence upon, the dependent variable (Wild and Seber, 2000). Goals also help determine what the investigation will do, and what data are to be collected. Finally, by understanding the goals we can also confirm if the type of investigation chosen is the most suitable type to use (Fenton and Pfleeger, 1997).

Each hypothesis of an investigation will later be either supported or rejected. An example of hypotheses is given below (Wild and Seber, 2000):

H_0 *Using J2EE produces the same quality of Web applications as using ASP.NET.*

H_1 *Using J2EE produces a different quality of Web applications than using ASP.NET.*

H_0 is called the null hypothesis and assumes the quality of Web applications developed using J2EE is similar to that of Web applications developed using ASP.NET. In other words, it assumes that data samples for both groups of applications come from the same population. In this instance, we have two samples, one representing quality values for Web applications developed using J2EE, and the other, quality values for Web applications developed using ASP.NET. Here, quality is our dependent variable, and the choice of programming framework (e.g., J2EE or ASP.NET) is the independent variable.

H_1 is called the alternative or research hypothesis and represents what is believed to be true if the null hypothesis is false. The alternative hypothesis assumes that samples do not come from the same sample population. Sometimes the direction of the relationship between dependent and independent variables is also presented as part of an alternative hypothesis. If H_1 also suggested a direction for the relationship, it could be described as

H_1 Using J2EE produces a better quality of Web applications than using ASP.NET.

To confirm H_1 it is first necessary to reject the null hypothesis and, second, to show that quality values for Web applications developed using J2EE are significantly higher than quality values for Web applications developed using ASP.NET.

We have presented both null and alternative hypotheses since they are both equally important when presenting the results of an investigation, and, as such, both should be documented.

To see if the data justify rejecting H_0 we need to perform a statistical analysis. Before carrying out a statistical analysis it is important to decide the level of confidence we have that the data sample we gathered truly represents our population of interest. If we have 95% confidence that the data sample we are using truly represents the general population, there still remains a 5% chance that H_0 will be rejected when, in fact, it truly represents the current situation. Rejecting H_0 incorrectly is called the *Type I error*, and the probability of this occurring is called the *Significance level* (α). Every statistical analysis test uses α when testing whether or not H_0 should be rejected.

14.4 ISSUES TO CONSIDER WITH EMPIRICAL ASSESSMENTS

In addition to defining the goals of an investigation, it is also important to document the context of the investigation (Kitchenham et al., 2002). One suggested way to achieve this is to provide a table, similar to Table 14.1, describing the entities, attributes, and measures that are the focus of the investigation.

14.4.1 Prepare the Investigation

It is important to prepare an investigation carefully to obtain results from which one can draw valid conclusions, even if these conclusions cannot be scaled up. For case studies and formal experiments, it is important to define the variables that can influence the results and, once these are defined, decide how much control one can have over them (Fenton and Pfleeger, 1997).

Consider the following case study, which would represent a *poorly prepared investigation*.

The case study aims to investigate, within a given organization, the effect of using the programming framework J2EE on the quality of the resulting Web application. Most Web projects in this organization are developed using ASP.NET, and consequently all members of the development team have experience with this language. The type of application representative of the majority of applications this organization undertakes is in electronic commerce (e-commerce), and a typical development team has two developers. Therefore, as part of the case study, an e-commerce application is to be developed by two developers using J2EE. Because we have stated that this is a poorly executed case study, we will assume that no other variables have been considered or measured (e.g., developers' experience, development environment).

The e-commerce application is developed, and the results of the case study show that the quality of the delivered application, measured as the number of faults per Web page, is worse than that for the other similar Web applications developed using ASP.NET. When questioned as to why these were the results obtained, the investigator seemed puzzled, and without a clear explanation.

What is missing?

The investigator should have anticipated that other variables can also affect the results of an investigation and should therefore also be taken into account. One such variable is the developers' programming experience. Without measuring experience prior to the case study, it is impossible to discern if the lower quality is due to J2EE or to the effects of learning J2EE as the investigation proceeds. It is possible that one or both developers did not have experience with J2EE and that lack of experience interfered with the benefits of its use.

Variables such as developers' experience should have been anticipated and, if possible, controlled, or risk obtaining results that will be incorrect.

To control a variable is to determine a subset of values for use within the context of the investigation from the complete set of possible values for that variable. For example, using the same case study presented above, if the investigator had measured developers' experience with J2EE (e.g., low, medium, high) and was able to control this variable, then he could have determined that two developers experienced with J2EE should have participated in the case study. If there were no developers with experience in J2EE, two would have been selected and trained.

When conducting a case study, if it is not possible to control certain variables, they should still be measured, and the results documented. If, however, all variables are controllable, then the type of investigation to use is a formal experiment.

Another important issue is to identify the population being studied and the sampling technique used. For example, if a survey was designed to investigate the extent to which project managers use automatic project management tools, then a data sample of software programmers is not going to be representative of the population that has been initially specified.

With formal experiments, it is important to describe the process by which experimental subjects and objects are selected and assigned to treatments (Kitchenham et al., 2002), where a treatment represents the new tool, programming language, or methodology you want to evaluate. The experimental object, also known as experimental unit, represents the object to which the treatment is to be applied (e.g., development project, Web application, code). The control object does not use or is not affected by the treatment (Fenton and Pfleeger, 1997). In software and Web Engineering it is difficult to have a control in the same way as in, say, formal medical experiments. For example, if you are investigating the effect of a programming framework on quality, and your treatment is J2EE, you cannot have a control that is "no programming framework" (Kitchenham et al., 2002). Therefore, many formal experiments use as their control a baseline representing what is typical in an organization. Using the example given previously, our control would be ASP.NET, since it represents the typical programming framework used in the organization. The experimental subject is the "who" applying the treatment (Fenton and Pfleeger, 1997).

As part of the preparation of an investigation we also include the preparation and validation of data collection instruments. Examples are questionnaires, automatic measurement tools, timing sheets, etc. Each has to be prepared carefully such that it clearly and unambiguously identifies what is to be measured. For each variable it is also important to identify its measurement scale and measurement unit. So, if you are measuring effort, then you should also document its measurement unit (e.g., person hours, person months) or else obtain incorrect and conflicting data. It is also important to document at which stage during the investigation the data collection takes place. If an investigation gathers data on developers' programming experience (before they develop a Web application), size and effort used to design the application, and size and effort used to implement the application, then a diagram, such as the one in Figure 14.2, may be provided to all participants to help clarify what instruments to use and when to use them.

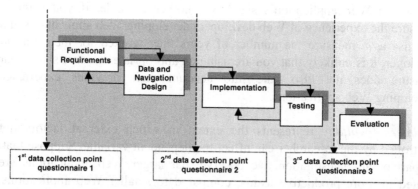

Figure 14.2. Plan detailing when to apply each project.

It is usual for instruments to be validated using pilot studies. A pilot study uses similar conditions to those planned for the real investigation, such that any possible problems can be anticipated. It is highly recommended that those conducting any empirical investigations use pilot studies, as they can provide very useful feedback and reduce or remove any problems not previously anticipated.

Finally, it is also important to document the methods used to reduce any bias.

14.4.2 Analyzing the Data and Reporting the Results

The main aspect of this final step is to understand the data collected and to apply statistical techniques that are suitable for the research questions or hypotheses of the investigation. For example, if the data were measured using a nominal or ordinal scale, then statistical techniques that use the mean cannot be applied, as this would violate the principles of the representational theory of measurement. If the data are not normally distributed, then it is possible to use nonparametric or robust techniques, or transform the data to conform to the normal distribution (Fenton and Pfleeger, 1997). Further details on data analysis are presented later in this chapter.

When interpreting and reporting the results of an empirical investigation, it is also important to consider and discuss the validity of the results obtained. There are three types of threats to the validity of empirical investigations (Kitchenham et al., 1995; Porter et al., 1997): *construct validity, internal validity,* and *external validity.* Each is described below.

Construct validity represents the extent to which the measures you are using in your investigation really measure the attributes of entities being investigated. For example, if you are measuring the size of a Web application using IFPUG function points, can you say that the use of IFPUG function points is really measuring the size of a Web application? How valid will the results of your investigation be if you use IFPUG function points to measure a Web application's size? As another example, if you want to measure the experience of Web developers developing Web applications and you use as a measure the number of years they worked for their current employer, it is unlikely that you are using an appropriate measure since your measure does not also take into account their previous experience developing Web applications.

Internal validity represents the extent to which external factors not controlled by the researcher can affect the dependent variable. Suppose that, as part of an investigation, we observe that larger Web applications are related to more productive teams, compared to smaller Web applications. We must make sure that team productivity is not being affected by using, for example, highly experienced developers to develop larger applications and less experienced developers to develop smaller applications. If the researcher is unaware of developers' experience, it is impossible to discern whether the results are due to developers' experience or due to legitimate economies of scale. Typical factors that can affect the internal validity of investigations are variations in human performance, learning effects where participants' skills improve as the investigation progresses, and differences in treatments, data collection forms used, or other experimental materials.

External validity represents the extent to which we can generalize the results of our investigation to our population of interest. In most empirical investigations in Web Engineering the population of interest often represents industrial practice. Suppose you carried out a formal experiment with postgraduate students to compare J2EE to ASP.NET, using as experimental object a small Web application. If this application is not representative of industrial practice, you cannot generalize the results of your investigation beyond the context in which it took place. Another possible problem with this investigation might be the use of students as subject population. If you have not used Web development professionals, it will also be difficult to generalize the results to industrial practice. Within the context of this example, even if you had used Web development professionals in your investigation, if they did not represent a random sample of your population of interest, you would also be unable to generalize the results to your entire population of interest.

14.5 DETAILING FORMAL EXPERIMENTS

A formal experiment is considered the most difficult type of investigation to carry out since it has to be planned very carefully such that all the important factors are controlled and documented, enabling its further replication. Due to the amount of control that formal experiments use, they can be further replicated and, when replicated under identical conditions, if results are repeatable, they provide a better basis for building theories that explain our current understanding of a phenomenon of interest. Another important point related to formal experiments is that the effects of uncontrolled variables upon the results must be minimized. The way to minimize such effects is to use randomization. Randomization represents the random assignment of treatments and experimental objects to experimental subjects.

In this section we are going to discuss the typical experimental designs used with formal experiments (Wohlin et al., 2005); for each typical design, we will discuss the types of statistical analysis tests that can be used to examine the data gathered from such experiments.

14.5.1 Typical Design 1

There is one independent variable (factor) with two values and one dependent variable. Suppose you are comparing the productivity between Web applications developed using J2EE (treatment) and Web applications developed using ASP.NET (control). Fifty subjects are participating in the experiment, and the experimental object is the same for both groups. Assuming other variables are constant, subjects are randomly assigned to J2EE or ASP.NET (see Figure 14.3).

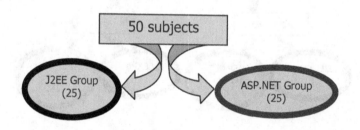

Figure 14.3. Example of one-factor design.

Once productivity data are gathered for both groups the next step is to compare the productivity data to check if productivity values for both development frameworks come from the same population (H_0) or from different populations (H_1). If the subjects in this experiment represent a large random sample or the productivity data for each group are normally distributed, you can use the independent samples t-test statistical technique to compare the productivity between both groups. This is a parametric test; as such, it assumed that the data are normally distributed or that the sample is large and random. Otherwise, the statistical technique to use would be the independent samples Mann–Whitney test, a nonparametric equivalent to the t test. Nonparametric tests make no assumptions related to the distribution of the data, and that is why they are used if you cannot guarantee that your data are normally distributed or represent a large random sample.

14.5.2 Typical Design 1: One Factor and One Confounding Factor

There is one independent variable (factor) with two values and one dependent variable. Suppose you are comparing the productivity between Web applications developed using J2EE (treatment) and Web applications developed using ASP.NET (control). Fifty subjects are participating in the experiment, and the experimental object is the same for both groups. A second factor (confounding factor)—gender—is believed to have an effect on productivity; however, you are only interested in comparing different development frameworks and their effect on productivity, not the interaction between gender and framework type on productivity. The solution is to create two blocks (see Figure 14.4), one with all the female subjects, and another with all the male subjects, and then, within each block, randomly assign a similar number of subjects to J2EE or ASP.NET (balancing).

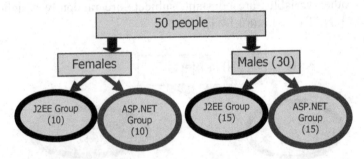

Figure 14.4. Example of blocking and balancing with one-factor design.

Once productivity data have been gathered for both groups, the next step is to compare the productivity data to check if productivity values for both groups come from the same population (H_0) or from different populations (H_1). The mechanism used to analyze the data would be the same one presented previously. Two sets of productivity values are compared, one containing productivity values for the 10 females and the 15 males who used J2EE, and the other containing productivity values for the 10 females and the 15 males who used ASP.NET. If the subjects in this experiment represent a large random sample or the productivity data for each group are normally distributed, you can use the independent samples t-test statistical technique to compare the productivity between both groups. Otherwise, the statistical technique to use would be the independent samples Mann–Whitney test, a nonparametric equivalent to the t test.

14.5.3 Typical Design 2

There is one independent variable (factor) with two values and one dependent variable. Suppose you are comparing the productivity between Web applications developed using J2EE (treatment) and Web applications developed using ASP.NET (control). Fifty subjects are participating in the experiment using the experimental object. You also want every subject to be assigned to both the control and the treatment. Assuming other variables are constant, subjects are randomly assigned to the control or the treatment and then swapped around (see Figure 14.5).

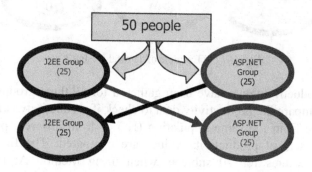

Figure 14.5. Example of Typical Design 2.

   Once productivity data have been gathered for both groups, the next step is to compare the productivity data to check if productivity values for both groups come from the same population (H_0) or from different populations (H_1). Two sets of productivity values are compared: The first contains productivity values for 50 subjects when using J2EE; the second contains productivity values for the same 50 subjects when using ASP.NET. Given that each subject was exposed to both control and treatment, you need to use a paired test. If the subjects in this experiment represent a large random sample or the productivity data for each group are normally distributed, you can use the paired samples t-test statistical technique to compare the productivity between both groups. Otherwise, the statistical technique to use would be the two related samples Wilcoxon test, a nonparametric equivalent to the paired samples t test.

14.5.4 Typical Design 3

There is one independent variable (factor) with more than two values and one dependent variable. Suppose you are comparing the productivity among Web applications designed using Methods A, B, and C. Sixty subjects are participating in the experiment, and the experimental object is the same for all groups. Assuming other variables are constant, subjects are randomly assigned to one of the three groups (see Figure 14.6).

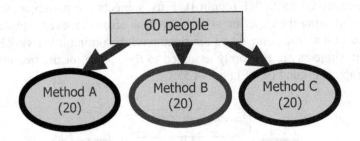

Figure 14.6. Example of Typical Design 3.

Once productivity data have been gathered for all three groups, the next step is to compare the productivity data to check if productivity values for all groups come from the same population (H_0) or from different populations (H_1). Three sets of productivity values are compared: The first contains productivity values for 20 subjects when using Method A; the second contains productivity values for another 20 subjects when using Method B; the third contains productivity values for another 20 subjects when using Method C. Given that each subject was exposed to only a single method, you need to use an independent samples test. If the subjects in this experiment represent a large random sample or the productivity data for each group are normally distributed, you can use the one-way ANOVA statistical technique to compare the productivity among groups. Otherwise, the statistical technique to use would be the Kruskal–Wallis H test, a nonparametric equivalent to the one-way ANOVA technique.

14.5.5 Typical Design 4

There are at least two independent variables (factors) and one dependent variable. Suppose you are comparing the productivity between Web applications developed using J2EE (treatment) and Web applications developed using ASP.NET (control). Sixty subjects are participating in the experiment, and the experimental object is the same for both groups. A second factor—gender—is believed to have an effect on productivity, and you are interested in assessing the interaction between gender and framework type on productivity. The solution is to create four blocks (see Table 14.10) representing the total number of possible combinations. In this example each factor has two values; therefore, the total number of combinations would be given by multiplying the number of values in the first factor by the number of values in the second factor (2 multiplied by 2, which is equal to 4). Then, assuming that all subjects have similar experience using both frameworks, within each gender block, subjects are randomly assigned to J2EE or ASP.NET (balancing). In this scenario each block will provide 15 productivity values.

Table 14.10. Example of Typical Design 4

| | | Gender | |
		Female	Male
Framework	**J2EE**	Female, J2EE (15) *Block 1*	Male, J2EE (15) *Block 2*
	ASP.NET	Female, ASP.NET (15) *Block 3*	Male, ASP.NET (15) *Block 4*

Once productivity data have been gathered for all four blocks, the next step is to compare the productivity data to check if productivity values for males come from the same population (H_0) or from different populations (H_1), and the same has to be done for females. Here productivity values for blocks 2 and 4 are compared; and productivity values for blocks 1 and 3 are compared. If the subjects in this experiment represent a large random sample or the productivity data for each group are normally distributed, you can use the independent samples t-test statistical technique to compare the productivity between groups. Otherwise, the statistical technique to use would be the Mann–Whitney test, a nonparametric equivalent to the independent samples t test.

14.5.6 Summary of Typical Designs

Table 14.11 summarizes the statistical tests to be used with each of the typical designs previously introduced. Each of these tests is explained in detail in statistical books, such as Wild and Seber (2000).

Table 14.11. Examples of Statistical Tests for Typical Designs

Typical Design	Parametric Test	Nonparametric Test
Design 1: no explicit confounding factor	Independent samples t test	Independent samples Mann–Whitney test
Design 1: explicit confounding factor	Independent samples t test	Independent samples Mann–Whitney test
Design 2	Paired samples t test	Two-related samples Wilcoxon test
Design 3	One-way ANOVA	Kruskal–Wallis H test
Design 4	Independent samples t test	Mann–Whitney test

14.6 DETAILING CASE STUDIES

It is often the case that case studies are used in industrial settings to compare two different technologies, tools, or development methodologies. One of the technologies, tools, or development methodologies represents what is currently used by the company, and the other represents what is compared to the company's current situation. Three mechanisms are suggested to organize such comparisons to reduce bias and enforce internal validity (Wohlin et al., 2005):

- To compare the results of using the new technology, tool, or development methodology to a company's baseline. A baseline generally represents an average over a set of finished projects. For example, a company may have established a productivity baseline against which to compare projects. This means that productivity data have been gathered from past finished projects and used to obtain an average productivity (productivity baseline). If this is the case, then the productivity related to the project that used the new technology, tool, or development methodology is compared against the existing productivity baseline, to assess if there was productivity improvement or decline. In addition to productivity, other baselines may also be used by a company, e.g., usability baseline or defect rate baseline.
- To compare the results of using the new technology, tool, or development methodology to a company's sister project, which is used as a baseline. This means that two similar and comparable projects will be carried out, one using the company's current technology, tool, or development methodology, and the other using the new technology, tool, or development methodology. Once both projects are finished, measures such as productivity, usability, and actual effort can be used to compare the results.

- Whenever the technology, tool, or development methodology applies to individual application components, it is possible to apply at random the new technology, tool, or development methodology to some components and not to others. Later measures such as productivity and actual effort can be used to compare the results.

14.7 DETAILING SURVEYS

There are three important points to stress here. The first is that, similarly to formal experiments and case studies, it is very important to define beforehand what is it that we wish to investigate (hypotheses) and what is the population of interest. For example, if you plan to conduct a survey to understand how Web applications are currently developed, the best population to use would be the one of Web project managers, as they have the complete understanding of the development process used. Interviewing Web developers may lead to misleading results, as it is often the case that they do not see the forest for the trees.

The second point is related to piloting the survey. It is important to ask different users, preferably representative of the population of interest, to read the instrument(s) to be used for data collection to make sure questions are clear and no important questions are missing. It is also important to ask these users to actually answer the questions in order to have a feel for how long it will take them to provide the data being asked for. This should be a similar procedure if you are using interviews.

Finally, the third point relates to the preparation of survey instruments. It is generally the case that instruments will be either questionnaires or interviews. In both cases instruments should be prepared with care and avoid misleading questions that can bias the results. If you use ordinary mail to post questionnaires to users, make sure you also include a self-addressed prepaid envelope to be used to return the questionnaire. You can also alternatively have the same questionnaire available on the Web. Unfortunately, the use of email as a means to broadcast a request to participate in a survey has been impaired by the advent of spam emails. Many of us today use filters to stop the receipt of unsolicited junk emails; therefore, many survey invitation requests may end up being filtered and deleted.

14.8 CONCLUSIONS

This chapter discussed the need for empirical investigations in Web Engineering and introduced the three main types of empirical investigation—surveys, case studies, and formal experiments. Each type of investigation was described, although greater detail was given to formal experiments as they are the most difficult type of investigation to conduct.

REFERENCES

Basili, V.R., 1996, The role of experimentation in software engineering: Past, current, and future. *Proceedings 18th International Conference on Software Engineering*, March 25–30, pp. 442–449.

Basili, V.R., Shull, F., and Lanubile, F., 1999, Building knowledge through families of experiments. *IEEE Transactions on Software Engineering*, July–Aug., **25**(4): 456–473.

Fenton, N.E., and Pfleeger, S.L., 1997, *Software metrics: A rigorous and practical approach*, 2nd ed., PWS Publishing Company, Boston.

Gellersen, H., Wicke, R., and Gaedke, M., 1997, WebComposition: An object-oriented support system for the Web engineering lifecycle. *Journal of Computer Networks and ISDN Systems*, September, *29*(8–13): 865–1553. Also (1996) in *Proceedings Sixth International World Wide Web Conference*, pp. 1429–1437.

Gellersen, H.-W., and Gaedke, M., 1999, Object-oriented Web application development. *IEEE Internet Computing*, Jan.–Feb., **3**(1): 60–68.

Ginige, A., 2002, Workshop on Web Engineering: Web Engineering: Managing the complexity of Web systems development. *Proceedings 14th International Conference on Software Engineering and Knowledge Engineering*, July, pp. 72–729.

Ginige, A., and Murugesan, S., 2001, Web Engineering: An introduction. *IEEE Multimedia*, Jan.–Mar., **8**(1):. 14–18.

Goldstein, M., and Goldstein, I.F., 1978, *How We Know: An Exploration of the Scientific Process*, Plenum Press, New York.

Harper Collins Publishers, 2000, *Collins English Dictionary*.

Houghton Mifflin Company, 1994, *The American Heritage Concise Dictionary*, 3rd ed.

Kitchenham, B., Pickard, L., and Pfleeger, S.L., 1995, Case studies for method and tool evaluation. *IEEE Software*, **12**(4): 52–62.

Kitchenham, B.A., Pfleeger, S.L., Pickard, L.M., Jones, P.W., Hoaglin, D.C., El Emam, K., and Rosenberg, J., 2002, Preliminary guidelines for empirical research in software engineering. *IEEE Transactions on Software Engineering*, August, **28**(8): 721–734.

Lee, S.C., and Shirani, A.I., 2004, A component based methodology for Web application development. *Journal of Systems and Software*, **71**(1–2): 177–187.

Maxwell, K., 2005, What you need to know about statistics. In *Web Engineering*, E. Mendes and N. Mosley, eds., Springer, New York, pp. 365–407.

Murugesan, S., and Deshpande, Y., 2001, *Web Engineering, Managing Diversity and Complexity of Web Application Development*, Lecture Notes in Computer Science 2016, Springer-Verlag, Heidelberg.

Murugesan, S., and Deshpande, Y., 2002, Meeting the challenges of Web application development: The Web Engineering approach. In *Proceedings 24th International Conference on Software Engineering*, May, pp. 687–688.

Offutt, J., 2002, Quality attributes of Web software applications. *IEEE Software*, Mar.–Apr., **19**(2): 25–32.

Pfleeger, S.L., Jeffery, R., Curtis, B., and Kitchenham, B., 1997, Status report on software measurement. *IEEE Software*, Mar.–Apr., **14**(2): 33–43.

Porter, A.A., Siy, H.P., Toman, C.A., and Votta, L.G., 1997, An experiment to assess the cost-benefits of code inspections in large-scale software development, *TSE*, **23**(6): 329–346.

Pressman, R.S., 1998, Can Internet-based applications be engineered? *IEEE Software*, Sept.–Oct., **15**(5): 104–110.

Ricca, F., and Tonella, P., 2001, Analysis and testing of Web applications. In *Proceedings 23rd International Conference on Software Engineering*, pp. 25–34.

Taylor, M.J., McWilliam, J., Forsyth, H., and Wade, S., 2002, Methodologies and Website development: A survey of practice. *Information and Software Technology*, **44**(6): 381–391.

Wikipedia, http://en.wikipedia.org/wiki/Main_Page (accessed on 25 October 2004).

Wild, C., and Seber, G., 2000, *Chance Encounters: A First Course in Data Analysis and Inference*, John Wiley & Sons, New York.

Wohlin, C., Host, M., and Henningsson, K., 2005, Empirical research methods in Web and software Engineering. In *Web Engineering*, E. Mendes and N. Mosley, eds., Springer, New York, pp. 409–430.

Chapter 15

CONCLUSIONS

Oscar Pastor,[4] Gustavo Rossi,[1] Luis Olsina,[3] Daniel Schwabe[2]

[1]*LIFIA, Facultad de Informatica,Universidad Nacional de La Plata, (also at CONICET) Argentina,* gustavo@lifia.info.unlp.edu.ar

[2]*Departamento de Informática, PUC-Rio, Rio de Janeiro, Brazil,* dschwabe@inf. puc-rio.br

[3]*GIDIS_Web, Engineering School, Universidad Nacional de La Pampa, Calle 9 y 110, (6360) General Pico, LP, Argentina,* olsinal@ing.unlpam.edu.ar

[4]*DSIC, Valencia University of Technology, Valencia, Spain,* opastor@dsic.upv.es

Historically, software engineering's main challenge has been to provide those processes, methods, and supporting tools capable of producing quality software. Given that the Web is, nowadays, the major delivery platform, and an important development support platform, it is only natural that it should evolve toward Web Engineering.

In the chapter written by San Murugesan (Chapter 2), we have covered different issues of the Web Engineering discipline. In this introductory chapter, San outlines the evolution of the Web and the unique aspects of Web applications and discusses some of the key challenges present in Web application development. It also examines what differentiates development of Web applications from other types of software or computer application development. It then reviews the problems and limitations of current Web development practices and their implications. Finally, it outlines key elements of a Web Engineering process and discusses the role of Web Engineering in successful Web application development.

These ideas are properly complemented with Chapter 3 by Martin Gaedke and Johannes Meinecke, which extends the view of the Web as the right platform to build distributed applications, with all the particular problems of these environments.

In this context, our perception is that well-known problems that have been identified in the so-called conventional software engineering community are translated in a natural and evolutionary way into a Web Engineering context. In particular, model-based software production processes, methods, and tools are strongly required by the Web Engineering community, to make true the MDA basic statement of producing Web applications through an adequate model transformation process, from requirements to the final software product.

Several evolutionary technologies related with Web Engineering are being proposed based on the Model-based Web Application Development Process. Another strong need is to properly fit all the pieces of this apparent Web Engineering puzzle, where we can find issues related with Web services, the Semantic Web, ontologies definition and management, adaptivity, conceptual modeling of Web applications, electronic commerce, and so on. Too often, these technologies are developed and evolve independently, while a sound Web Engineering process will require all of them to be properly aligned and connected.

In this context, it is true that many approaches have already been proposed, providing answers to some of the problems related with all these issues. But more than ever, we think that we need a place where all those approaches that share common roots are presented, their particularities analyzed, and their solutions presented in the context of a common example. Such material will let readers understand commonalities and their differences between the approaches, allowing them to make informed choices that best fit their own needs and situation. This is the spirit of this book.

The Web Engineering discipline is in constant evolution, and over the last few years a set of methods to model, design, and implement Web applications has been proposed. The central core of this book is the presentation of some of these relevant approaches. Clearly, not all such approaches have been presented, but we attempted to present the ones that have been discussed the most in the literature. The methods selected cover a very relevant and big spectrum of what Web application development methods currently mean, addressing the main issues and concepts that are critical in producing good Web applications.

The list of selected methods includes UWE, IDM, WebML, Hera, WSDM, OOWS/OO-Method, and OOHDM. Each one is presented in its own chapter, covering the main aspects of the method, the models used, the expressiveness provided, and the relevant parts of their software process. This is done with the support of a common example: a popular online repository of information related to the movie industry. We have selected an example that is both well-known and easy to interpret in terms of how every method manages it. The proposed requirements included both information recovery (such as, for instance, queries on films or actors) and service execution (such as, for instance, buying tickets to see a particular film). We did that to cover contents and functionality, to make it possible to analyze how the methods deal with these aspects.

Furthermore, this Web application was designed to be used by different types of users (anonymous, registered, system administrators, etc.), each one with a particular behavior and accessing some information and functionality; adaptivity must therefore be properly faced. Thus, a distinguishing feature of this book is precisely the exercise of applying each method to the same problem.

It is our feeling that the ultimate evaluation of each method will be made by the readers. Nevertheless, a preliminary side-by-side comparison shows some noticeable points that raise interesting questions. First, all the methods use different notations to deal with similar concepts. Could a common, standard notation be used? This is an interesting open question for the audience. All the methods share some relevant points of view:

- A clear separation of concerns with respect to conceptual modeling for Web applications, focusing basically on contents, functionality, navigation, and presentation. An interesting task for any reader is to compare how each method represents and manages these different modeling perspectives.
- The modeling and code generation tools developed to support the methods (such as WebRatio, ONME, ArgoUWE, HyperDE) emphasize the use of Model-Driven Software Development strategies as the right approach. It seems that, logically, model transformation technologies are also strongly present in the Web Engineering community.

As stated before, working on the same example, the readers can understand the basic models and primitives provided by the methods and can even personally evaluate the different solutions provided by them. As a matter of fact, it has been interesting for us to verify that all of them share some common conceptual constructs, but at the same time each one orders them in different ways, emphasizing some particular aspects considered more or less relevant. A strong value of this book is in providing adequate material to allow you—our reader—to reach your own conclusions about each method and how they compare.

It has also been remarkable to see how all these approaches are in constant evolution. They are extending their expressive capabilities, to give support to the most advanced characteristics required by modern Web applications. New aspects encompass, among other things, supporting business process execution, the development of adaptive Web applications, the proper use of Semantic Web representations in the Web application construction process, the use of Web services, the multidevice-oriented development of Web applications, etc. This simply emphasizes the fact that research continues, constantly extending the material already presented here.

Model transformation is present throughout the book, and it is behind all the presented methods for Web application design and implementation. To delve further into this, the chapter written by Antonio Vallecillo et al. provides a precise view on the current status of what we call Model-Driven Web Engineering (MDWE) in the context of MDA. Apart from introducing the main concepts and mechanisms related to MDWE and MDA, it also discusses the strengths and benefits of the use of MDA for MDWE, as well as its major limitations and the challenges it currently faces for wider adoption. We think that this is the right point to anchor the ideas introduced in this book addressing the applicability of model transformation to obtain a sound Web development process.

We would like to close these conclusions by commenting on interesting aspects that we have learned during the editing process. First, it should be realized that the development of private notations to model Web applications can make the wider adoption and acceptance of these methods by the industry more difficult. Representing the same concepts in the same way would improve the understanding of the models used by the different approaches, which would help their use in practice

Standards are being continuously updated, especially in the context of Web services definition languages and Semantic Web-oriented languages. It could be argued that we should have sound solutions before having their associated standards. But looking at the methods presented, we can easily conclude that they already provide solutions that are sound enough to be incorporated in appropriate standards for Web application development methods. This is probably a task to be accomplished in the near future, not unlike the context where UML was initially proposed, as an attempt to unify the diverse set of notations for object-oriented analysis and design that were present in the mid-1990s. For instance, if the required conceptual primitives for specifying Web navigation were fixed, a proper notation to represent them in a clear way could be proposed with major agreement.

Furthermore, as we are talking about engineering, we cannot forget those aspects related to quality evaluation and with empirical Web Engineering. Luis Olsina et al. analyzed in their chapter the rationale to measure and evaluate software and Web applications or products, from different perspectives. To complement this view, there is a strong need to evaluate the software artifacts obtained with the methods presented in the book together with their associated tools. Empirical studies and techniques such as those presented in the chapter written by Emilia Mendes are very relevant when the objective is to demonstrate the quality and precision of the generated software product. We feel that this provides the proper tone to end our book.

Readers interested in such aspects will find basic information and pointers to further reading in these two final chapters.

So, this is all folks... . If you have reached this point, which could mean that you have read the whole book, first of all, congratulations!, and second and more important, we really hope we have been able to provide interesting and fruitful material that will help anyone better understand what modern Web Engineering means, and how all the ideas involved can be successfully put into practice, from both an academic and an industrial point of view.

INDEX